The
B O N H A M S
Directory 1993

The BONHAMS Directory 1993

A county-by-county guide
to repairers and restorers
of art and antiques

COMPILED BY
TIM FORREST AND JOHN KIRKWOOD

WITH AN INTRODUCTION BY
ERIC KNOWLES

KYLE CATHIE LIMITED

First published in Great Britain in 1992 by
Kyle Cathie Limited
3 Vincent Square London SW1P 2LX

Introduction copyright © 1992 by Eric Knowles
'Seeking Professional Advice' copyright © 1992 by Annabelle Ruston
This compilation copyright © Bonhams 1992

Tim Forrest and John Kirkwood are hereby identified as compilers of this work in accordance with
Section 77 of the Copyright, Designs and Patents Act 1988.

ISBN 1 85626 073 9

A CIP catalogue record for this book is available from the British Library.

Filmset by Selwood Systems, Midsomer Norton
Printed by Butler & Tanner, Frome and London

CONTENTS

IMPORTANT NOTICE TO READERS

Entries in *The Bonhams Directory* are intended only as a means of identifying and locating specialist goods and services, and inclusion does not imply recommendation by Bonhams. Prospective customers must satisfy themselves as to the appropriateness, quality and cost of the goods or services offered.

Customers should also ask about the security of the premises and establish whether the restorer provides insurance cover or if it is necessary for the customer to arrange appropriate cover under existing policies, including transit to and from the workshop. If your property is not covered the risk is yours.

Neither Bonhams nor the Publishers will enter into correspondence concerning entries in *The Directory* but recommendations and/or complaints (which should be sent to Tim Forrest, c/o Bonhams, Montpelier Street, London SW7 1HH) will be followed up and taken into account in any future editions.

ACKNOWLEDGEMENTS

Many thanks to the staff of Bonhams for their encouragement and support, especially:

Helen Grantham
Odile Jackson
Heather Mann

HOW THE DIRECTORY WORKS

Each section of the book contains alphabetical lists of restorers and services in the following order:

England – by county (London is treated as a county and the postal districts follow each other alphabetically; West Midlands comes under M, East and West Sussex under S and North, South and West Yorkshire under Y)
Northern Ireland – by county
Southern Ireland – by county
Scotland – by region
Wales – by county

Double rules divide the entries for each county or region.

The *Collectors' Items* section is divided alphabetically by subject (Cameras, Dolls and Dolls' Houses, etc), with lists within each subject arranged as above. *Musical Instruments* follow *Collectors' Items*.

Arms and Armour are followed by *Sporting Equipment*, again divided alphabetically into subjects.

Specialist Booksellers are followed by *Specialist Photographers*.

If a restorer provides services that fall into more than one section, these are cross-referenced at the end of each entry.

INTRODUCTION

I have always considered myself fortunate to have grown up in an era that allowed a childhood to persist beyond the age of ten. In these rose-coloured days school holidays seemed never-ending and, regrettably, so too did the summer rain storms that homed in on my part of North-East Lancashire. Keeping myself entertained during these often prolonged dripping sojourns stretched my imagination to the full.

My passion at that time was the collection of fossils, a passion which culminated in the base of my wardrobe giving way under excessive pressure, much to my bewilderment and the consternation of my parents. The fossils were just one of several collecting manias that I contracted during these formative years. I was without doubt the bane of our local greengrocer, who could never get to his shop door quickly enough on Saturday mornings to switch his open sign to closed before I lunged through those portals in search of exotic fruit wrappers. When I was a child, large quantities of citrus fruits arrived on these shores individually wrapped in highly decorative and colourful tissue wrapping, which I found totally irresistible and could acquire completely *gratis*.

My magpie instincts resulted in many other diverse acquisitions, including ancient arrowheads; a musket ball from the English Civil War, found on the site of a local skirmish; several music boxes, made by the skilled hand of my grandfather; a Gurkha's kukri knife and various oddments of Victorian pottery.

One activity that proved absorbing necessitated combining forces with equally frustrated chums who lived nearby. Many of these boys were ardent participants in that now banished pursuit, the collecting of birds' eggs. One lad's collection amounted to several hundred specimens, all carefully labelled and housed in small cabinets, with each egg individually nestling in cotton wool removed with stealth and bravado from his mother's dressing table.

During one of our many retreats from the rain-soaked streets we hit upon the idea of putting all our collections on show to make what together might be considered our own museum. With hindsight, it is now clear that this motley bunch of young Lancastrians were well ahead of their time, since we discovered it was possible to combine capitalism with our venture and consequently levied an admission charge of one penny per person. Our few days as museum curators showed a substantial profit, allowing some of us to purchase a previously prohibitively expensive model aeroplane kit, together with a tube of that horrendously sticky and stringy glue.

The collecting mania of those distant days has mushroomed into many unforeseen areas, but the fact remains that whether today your preference is for Fabergé eggs or crested china, every collector is his or her own curator. The art of collecting is at all times a personal matter: some collectors choose to collect only perfect examples, while others are happy to have a larger collection that might include damaged or repaired pieces.

For the curators or custodians of collections great or small, the question of display takes into account secure shelving or cabinets. The display of pottery, glass and metalwork often requires little more than cool lighting. The collector of furniture, paintings and textiles must pay heed to several other factors in order to maintain the fabric of these various media. Positioning furniture, textiles and watercolours well away from strong sunlight is absolutely essential, for example, and failure to do so is akin to the type of gross irresponsibility that could cost the professional curator his or her job.

However, there are sure to be occasions when, despite all proper precautions having being observed, an item will develop a problem that needs attention and subsequent treatment. My personal heart-felt plea to all DIY enthusiasts is to restrict your efforts to the built-in wardrobes or fitted kitchens and to allow an expert loose on the cleaning of your oil painting or the repair of your Chippendale chairs. There are tips at the start of each section of this book which tell you what you can safely have a go at yourself and what you should on no account attempt. In my many years in the employ of Messrs Bonhams, and almost as many years working on the team of the BBC TV *Antiques Roadshow*, I have had occasion to witness some pretty awful repairs. In fact, the word repair is probably too kind – 'botch up' is nearer the mark.

Even worse than 'botch ups' are the range of objects that qualify for my personal technical term of having been 'murdered' – such as the bronze horse by the mid-19th century French *animalier*, P-J Mêne, which the owner had decided was in need of a good clean and had duly polished to oblivion courtesy of Brasso.

I will also never forget a pair of superb Georgian needlework samplers that fell foul of biological washing powder with the result that both are now pale pastiches of their former selves. How can people do it?

My commitments to both Bonhams and the BBC have resulted in extensive travels through the length and breadth of the United Kingdom. Meeting many people as I do on such travels, I am often asked for advice on matters of repair and restoration. Until recent years, I have tended to recommend a few known, qualified restorers working in or near London. Regrettably, such recommendations often prove impractical for people living in North Yorkshire or Norfolk.

The 1993 edition of *The Bonhams Directory* contains a unique and relatively comprehensive listing of this country's most respected repair and restoration specialists. I can only hope that the proper use of their services will prove significant in the preservation of objects from the past for the enjoyment of the collectors of today and the generations to follow. Failure to follow this advice just might result in your being found guilty of 'botching up' or, worse still, the crime of 'murder'!

ERIC KNOWLES

SEEKING PROFESSIONAL ADVICE

A brown stain appears on your Victorian watercolour or the writing surface on your antique desk needs re-leathering – who do you ask for advice? Should you restore the work to resemble its original state, or conserve it from further deterioration leaving its appearance imperfect? Your local antique shop may offer conservation services, but how can you be sure that they will do a professional job? Works of art can be irreparably damaged by incompetent conservators and the use of inappropriate materials and techniques. Both the financial value and the physical appearance of the work can be severely diminished. However, there exist several professional associations who would be happy to discuss your requirements and to give you unbiased advice as to your choice of conservator. (See the Glossary at the back of this book for addresses and telephone numbers.)

The Conservation Unit (part of the Museums and Galleries Commission) holds a computerised list of 550 conservation workshops. For a fee of five pounds they will send you a detailed report on the appropriate conservators. The list includes experts in such diverse areas as taxidermy, mother-of-pearl, rocking horses and musical boxes. Recommended workshops must have been established for seven years and references and other documentation are requested. The Unit also holds details of over 300 societies and organisations relevant to conservation in the UK. The organisations listed include special-interest groups such as the Society of Gilders, the Federation of Master Organ Builders and the Guild of Toy Makers. Many of these bodies would be happy to discuss the care of your work of art with you.

The United Kingdom Institute for Conservation (UKIC) has 2,000 conservator members worldwide, specialising in furniture, porcelain, glass, textiles, paintings, metals, books and objects. They publish a wide range of informative material and hold conferences. If you send them an SAE stating your geographical location and area of interest they will send you a list of appropriate conservators.

The British Antique Furniture Restorers Association (BAFRA) has eighty-four members who have all been closely vetted by the Association. Members must have been working as restorers for a minimum of six years; their work is inspected by Committee members and references are followed up. So if you select a BAFRA-recommended restorer you can be sure of the highest standards of workmanship.

The Fine Art Trade Guild is the trade association representing those involved in the picture business. It was established in 1910 to regulate the trade and improve standards of practice. Guild staff are happy to help you to find a framer with expertise in conservation framing methods. Guild-recommended framers work to a strict code of practice and are answerable to the Framers' & Retailers' Committee. You can contact the Guild with queries ranging from the framing of tapestries and fabric art to frame restoration and re-gilding. They can also put you in touch with stockists of fine art products, such as picture-hanging systems and acid-free packing materials. If you are looking for a dealer who specialises in a particular artist or type of art, the Guild can also help you.

There are two bodies representing picture restorers. The Institute of Paper Conservation (IPC) is concerned with works on paper such as watercolours, prints and maps, and the Association of British Picture Restorers (ABPR) is concerned with oil paintings. The IPC holds a register of over 100 conservators and will recommend one local to you. The ABPR has sixty full members who have all been closely vetted by the Committee. Vetting procedures are so strict that over half of the applicants fail to be admitted, so you can rest assured that your painting will receive the best possible treatment from an ABPR member.

The Scottish Society for Conservation and Restoration (SSCR) publishes informative leaflets and promotes interest in conservation. However, it does not refer people to specific conservators. You should contact the Scottish Conservation Bureau, part of Historic Scotland, if you need a conservator for your work of art. They publish a list of 180 conservators working in fourteen different fields, and will advise you and help you to find a conservator. The Irish Professional Conservators and Restorers Association (IPCRA) also publishes a directory of its members.

If someone recommends a conservator to you, you can always ring up the appropriate association and enquire whether that person or workshop is known to them. There are several other points you should check with a conservator before entrusting him/her with your work of art. Ask for details of previous clients and work undertaken, and follow up these references. If the conservator has repeatedly worked for a specialist organisation such as the National Trust or your local museum, this should be taken as a good sign. Many conservators keep a summary of their work experience and training on file for potential clients, otherwise you should ask if they attended an established course or served an apprenticeship in a reputable workshop. It is also import-ant to check that the workshop is secure and that your work of art will be properly insured. Be sure to discuss the work to be carried out in detail, so that you know exactly what is being done to your work of art and why. Explain how you want the object to look and discuss whether or not this is possible or advisable.

You must also remember that conservation is an on-going process. Your conservator should advise you as to the safest conditions in which to keep your work of art and how best to maintain it. For example, works of art displayed in rooms with high central heating may require a humidifying device to keep the atmosphere moist. Your conservator should also explain any signs to look for which mean that further deterioration is beginning.

The main point to remember is that it is better to do nothing than to rush in and do the wrong thing without due care and attention. Do not hesitate to contact any of the above organisations for advice and information, as they would be only too glad to help you.

ANNABELLE RUSTON
Framing and Gallery Manager
Fine Art Trade Guild

OIL PAINTINGS,
WATERCOLOURS,
PRINTS
AND PHOTOGRAPHS

DO

Always carry pictures with the surface facing you
Transport pictures upright in a car or van
Stack pictures face to face in twos to avoid frame and canvas damage
Ensure that holly does not fall down behind a picture
Remember that sunlight is the enemy of any work on paper

DON'T

Hang paintings over a radiator
Hang watercolours in a bathroom or other damp place
Hang pictures in any room subject to extremes of temperature
Try to clean your own pictures
Dust glass over pastels too vigorously: static electricity can cause the pastel to
transfer
Allow glass to be in contact with any picture surface

1

ADAM GALLERY
13 John Street, Bath, **Avon BA1 2JL**
TEL   0225 480406
OPEN   9.30–5.30 Mon–Sat.

Specialise in consolidation, restoration and cleaning of oil paintings and cleaning, defoxing and conservation of watercolours and drawings.

PROVIDE Home Inspections. Free Estimates. Collection/Delivery Service by arrangement.
SPEAK TO Paul or Philip Dye.

SEE Picture Frames.

DAVID A. CROSS GALLERY
7 Boyce's Avenue, Clifton, Bristol, **Avon BS8 4AA**
TEL   0272 732614
OPEN   9.30–6 Mon–Fri; 9.30–5.30 Sat.

Specialise in restoring oil paintings, watercolours and prints of all periods.

PROVIDE Home Inspections. Free Estimates. Chargeable Collection/Delivery Service.
SPEAK TO Jo David.

THE FRAME STUDIO
2nd Floor, 14 Waterloo Street, Clifton, Bristol, **Avon BS8 4BT**
TEL   0272 238279
OPEN   10–6 Tues–Sat.

Specialise in restoring oil paintings and watercolours.

PROVIDE Home Inspections. Free Estimates. Chargeable Collection/Delivery Service.
SPEAK TO Graeme Dowling

Member of the Guild of Master Craftsmen.

GEORGE GREGORY
Manvers Street, Bath, **Avon BA1 1JW**
TEL   0225 466055
FAX   0225 482122
OPEN   9–1, 2–5.30 Mon–Fri; 9.30–1 Sat By Appointment.

Specialise in cleaning and restoring old prints.

PROVIDE Home Inspections. Free Estimates.
SPEAK TO Mr H. H. Bayntun-Coward.

INTERNATIONAL FINE ART CONSERVATION STUDIOS
43–45 Park Street, Bristol, **Avon BS1 5NL**
TEL   0272 293480
FAX   0272 225511
OPEN   10–5.30 Mon–Fri.

Specialise in the conservation and restoration of oil paintings from both traditional and modern periods with sizes ranging from small easel paintings to very large wall murals. Recent examples include works by Van Dyck, Hondecoeter, Luca Giordano, Monet, Whistler and Sargent.

PROVIDE Free Estimates.
SPEAK TO A. J. Bush, S. R. Sands or R. J. Pelter.

ANTHONY REED
94–96 Walcot Street, Bath, **Avon BA1 5BG**
TEL   0225 461969 or 0272 333595
OPEN   9–6 Mon–Sat.

Specialise in cleaning and restoring oils, watercolours and prints.

PROVIDE Home Inspections. Chargeable Estimates. Chargeable Local Collection/Delivery Service.

SPEAK TO Anthony Reed.
Member of the IIC.
SEE Furniture, Picture Frames.

SIMON WELLBY AND NICHOLAS WRIGHT
Epstein Building, Mivart Street, Easton,
Bristol, **Avon BS5 6JF**
TEL   0272 354478
OPEN   9–6 Mon–Fri.

Specialise in restoring oil paintings,
lining, transfer and panel work.

PROVIDE Home Inspections.
Free/Chargeable Estimates.
Free/Chargeable Collection/Delivery
Service.
SPEAK TO Simon Wellby and Nicholas
Wright.
Member of ABPR.

K. A. WHEELER
4 Bayswater Avenue, Westbury Park,
Bristol, **Avon BS6 7NS**
TEL   0272 423003
OPEN   9.30–1, 2–5.30 Mon–Fri.

Specialise in conserving and restoring
fine prints, watercolours and drawings.

PROVIDE Free Estimates.
SPEAK TO Keith Wheeler.

Member of the Institute of Paper
Conservation and the UKIC. This studio
is included on the register maintained by
the Conservation Unit of the Museums
and Galleries Commission.

LIEUT. COL. R. L. V. ffrench BLAKE DSO.
Loddon Lower Farm, Spencers Wood,
Reading, **Berkshire RG7 1JE**
TEL   0734 883212
OPEN   By Appointment.

Specialise in restoring oil paintings,
church hatchments, as well as repairing
gesso frames, calligraphy picture labelling
and high class copying of Dutch flower

paintings, marine pictures and winter
landscapes.

PROVIDE Home Inspections. Free
Estimates. Chargeable
Collection/Delivery Service.
SPEAK TO Lieut. Col. ffrench Blake.

THE COLLECTORS' GALLERY
8 Bridge Street, Caversham Bridge,
Reading, **Berkshire RG4 8AA**
TEL   0734 483663
OPEN   10–5 Mon–Fri; 10–4 Sat.

Specialise in conserving and restoring
18th and 19th century oils and
watercolours.

PROVIDE Home Inspections. Free
Estimates. Collection/Delivery Service
by arrangement.
SPEAK TO Helen Snook.

GRAHAM GALLERY
Highwoods, Burghfield Common,
Reading, **Berkshire RG7 3BG**
TEL   0734 832320
FAX   071 930 4261
OPEN   By Appointment.

Specialise in restoring 19th and early
20th century watercolours and prints.

PROVIDE Home Inspections. Free
Estimates. Free Collection/Delivery
Service.
SPEAK TO John Steeds.

HERON PICTURES
High Street, Whitchurch-on-Thames,
Reading, **Berkshire RG8 7EX**
TEL   0734 843286
OPEN   10–7 Tues–Sat.

Specialise in cleaning and restoring oil
paintings.

PROVIDE Home Inspections. Free
Estimates. Free Local
Collection/Delivery Service.
SPEAK TO George Duckett.
SEE Picture Frames.

CHESS ANTIQUES
85 Broad Street, Chesham,
Buckinghamshire HP5 3EF
TEL   0494 783043
FAX   0494 791302
OPEN   8–5 Mon–Sat.

Specialise in restoring oil paintings.

PROVIDE Home Inspections. Chargeable
Estimates. Chargeable
Collection/Delivery Service.
SPEAK TO M. Wilder.
SEE Furniture.

ARTHUR CLARK trading as CLARK GALLERIES
Daneswood, Church Lane,
Deanshanger, Milton Keynes,
Buckinghamshire MK19 6HG
TEL   0908 563369
OPEN   9–5.30 or By Appointment.

Specialise in restoring oil paintings and
also relining.

PROVIDE Home Inspections. Chargeable
Estimates. Chargeable
Collection/Delivery Service.
SPEAK TO Arthur Clark.
Established 1963 and Member of ABPR.
This workshop is included on the register
of conservators maintained by the
Conservation Unit of the Museums and
Galleries Commission.

BRIAN NEWSON
9 Slade Road, Stokenchurch,
Buckinghamshire HP14 3QQ
TEL   0494 482123
OPEN   9–6 Mon–Fri.

Specialise in all aspects of oil painting
conservation.

PROVIDE Home Inspections. Free Local
Estimates. Free Collection/Delivery
Service.
SPEAK TO Brian Newson.

Member of ABPR and UKIC.

H. S. WELLBY LTD
The Malt House, Church End,
Haddenham, **Buckinghamshire
HP17 8AB**
TEL   0844 290036
OPEN   9–5 Mon–Sat.

Specialise in the lining, cleaning and
restoration of oil paintings.

PROVIDE Home Inspections. Free
Estimates. Free Collection/Delivery
Service.
SPEAK TO Christopher Wellby.

CAMBRIDGE FINE ART LTD
Priesthouse, 33 Church Street, Little
Shelford, Cambridge, **Cambridgeshire
CB2 5HG**
TEL   0223 842866 or 843537
OPEN   10–6 Mon–Sat.

Specialise in restoring oil paintings and
watercolours (1780–1950).

PROVIDE Free/Chargeable Estimates.
Chargeable Collection/Delivery
Service.
SPEAK TO Ralph Lury.

ALAN CANDY
Old Manor House, 4 Cambridge Street,
Godmanchester, Huntingdon,
Cambridgeshire PE18 8AT
TEL   0480 453198
OPEN   By Appointment.

Specialise in restoring oils, watercolours
and prints.

PROVIDE Free Estimates.
SPEAK TO Alan Candy.

WENDY A. CRAIG
Cambridge Conservation Studio,
Balsham Road, Linton, Cambridge,
Cambridgeshire CB2 6LE
TEL   0223 881295
FAX   0223 894056
OPEN   9–6 Mon–Sat.

Specialise in conserving and restoring works of art on paper. Collection surveys and advice on storage and environment.

PROVIDE Home Inspections. Free Estimates. Free/Chargeable Collection/Delivery Service.
SPEAK TO Wendy Ann Craig.

This workshop is included on the register of conservators maintained by the Conservation Unit of the Museums and Galleries Commission.
SEE Picture Frames.

HARPER FINE PAINTINGS
Overdale, Woodford Road, Poynton, **Cheshire SK12 1ED**
TEL   0625 879105
OPEN   By Appointment.

Specialise in restoring 18th, 19th and early 20th century British and European oils and watercolours.

PROVIDE Home Inspections. Chargeable Estimates. Free Collection/Delivery Service.
SPEAK TO Peter Harper.

DEBBIE COLEMAN
Watchtower Studio, Church End, East Looe, **Cornwall PL13 1BX**
TEL   0503 263232 or 263344
OPEN   10.30–5 Mon–Sat or By Appointment.

Specialise in restoring oil paintings, watercolours, prints and drawings.

PROVIDE Home Inspections. Free Estimates. Collection/Delivery Service.
SPEAK TO Debbie Coleman.

Associate Member of ABPR. This workshop is included on the register of conservators maintained by the Conservation Unit of the Museums and Galleries Commission.
SEE Picture Frames.

TAMAR GALLERY (ANTIQUES & FINE ART)
5 Church Street, Launceston, **Cornwall PL15 8AW**
TEL   0566 774233 or 82444
OPEN   10–1, 2.30–5 Tues–Sat; Early Closing Thur.

Specialise in restoring and cleaning watercolours of all periods.

PROVIDE Free Estimates.
SPEAK TO N. O. Preston.

TIMES PAST ANTIQUES
13 Chatsworth Road, Chesterfield, **Derbyshire**
TEL   0246 234578
OPEN   9.30–5 Mon–Sat; closed Wed.

Specialise in restoring oil paintings.

PROVIDE Home Inspections. Refundable Estimates. Chargeable Collection/Delivery Service.
SPEAK TO L. Lewis.

RITA BUTLER
Stour Gallery, 28 East Street, Blandford, **Dorset DT11 7DR**
TEL   0258 456293
OPEN   10–1, 2–4 Tues, Thur–Sat; 10–1 Wed.

Specialise in cleaning and restoring oil paintings, watercolours and prints.

PROVIDE Home Inspections. Free Estimates. Chargeable Collection/Delivery Service.
SPEAK TO Rita Butler.
SEE Books.

GALERIE LAFRANCE
647 Wimborne Road, Winton, Bournemouth, **Dorset BH9 2AR**
TEL   0202 522313
OPEN   8.30–1, 2–5.30 Mon–Fri; 9–1 Sat.

Specialise in cleaning and restoring oils, watercolours and prints.

PROVIDE Home Inspections. Free Estimates. Free/Chargeable Collection/Delivery Service.
SPEAK TO Pierre Lafrance.
SEE Picture Frames.

THE SWAN GALLERY
57 Cheap Street, Sherborne, **Dorset DT9 3AX**
TEL   0935 814465
FAX   0308 68195
OPEN   9.30–5 Mon–Sat; 9.30–1 Wed.

Specialise in cleaning works of art on paper.

PROVIDE Free Estimates.
SPEAK TO Simon Lamb.

WESSEX PICTURE RESTORERS
Northwood, Monkton Wylde, Bridport, **Dorset DT6 6DE**
TEL   03005 456
OPEN   By Appointment Only.

Specialise in restoring oil paintings, wax/resin relining with vacuum hot table.

PROVIDE Chargeable Home Inspections. Free Estimates. Chargeable Collection/Delivery Service.
SPEAK TO Iain Geffers or Elizabeth Hopley.
Member of ABPR. This workshop is included on the register of conservators maintained by the Conservation Unit of the Museums and Galleries Commission.

STEPHEN AND PAMELA ALLEN
3 West Terrace, Western Hill, Durham, **Durham DH1 4RN**
TEL   091 386 4601
OPEN   8.30–6 Mon–Fri or By Appointment.

Specialise in restoring works of art on paper, watercolours, prints, drawings, posters.

PROVIDE Home Inspections. Free Estimates. Chargeable Collection/Delivery Service.
SPEAK TO Stephen Allen or Pamela Allen.
Member of IPC.
SEE Art Researchers, Books.

ALLYSON McDERMOTT (INTERNATIONAL CONSERVATION CONSULTANTS)
Lintz Green Conservation Centre, Lintz Green House, Lintz Green, Rowlands Gill, **Durham NE39 1NL**
TEL   0207 71547 or 0831 104145 or 0831 257584
FAX   0207 71547
OPEN   9–5.30 Mon–Fri.

Specialise in conservation of easel paintings, pastels, chalks, prints, drawings, photographs, watercolours and historic wallpapers.

PROVIDE Home Inspections. Free Estimates. Chargeable Collection/Delivery Service.
SPEAK TO Allyson McDermott or Gillian Lee.

They have a Southern Regional Office at 45 London Road, Cheltenham, **Gloucestershire**.
SEE Art Researchers, Carpets, Lighting, Picture Frames, Specialist Photographers.

S. BOND & SON
14/15 North Hill, Colchester, **Essex CO1 1DZ**
TEL   0206 572925
OPEN   9–5 Mon–Sat.

Specialise in restoring oil paintings.

PROVIDE Home Inspections. Free Estimates. Free Local Collection/Delivery Service.
SPEAK TO Robert Bond.

This family firm has been established 140 years and is run by the fifth generation. SEE Furniture.

RICHARD ILES GALLERY
10 Northgate Street, Colchester, **Essex CO1 1HA**
TEL   0206 577877
OPEN   9.30–4.30 Mon–Sat.

Specialise in restoring 19th and early 20th century watercolours.

PROVIDE Free Estimates.
SPEAK TO Richard Iles.
SEE Picture Frames.

MEYERS' GALLERY
66 High Street, Ingatestone, **Essex CM4 0BA**
TEL   0277 355335
OPEN   10–5 Mon–Sat, closed Wed.

Specialise in restoring oil paintings and watercolours.

PROVIDE Home Inspections. Free Estimates. Free Local Collection/Delivery Service.
SPEAK TO Mrs Meyers.

Member of LAPADA.

MILLSIDE ANTIQUE RESTORATION
Parndon Mill, Parndon Mill Lane, Harlow, **Essex CM20 2HP**
TEL   0279 428148
FAX   0279 415075
OPEN   10–5 Mon–Fri.

Specialise in cleaning and restoring watercolours, prints and oil paintings. Also do watercolour tinting of sepia and black and white prints.

PROVIDE Home Inspections. Free/Chargeable Estimates. Chargeable Collection/Delivery Service.
SPEAK TO David Sparks or Angela Wickliffe-Philp.
SEE Picture Frames, Porcelain, Silver.

PEARLITA FRAMES LTD
30 North Street, Romford, **Essex RM11 2LB**
TEL   0708 760342
OPEN   9–5.30 Mon–Sat.

Specialise in restoring oil paintings, watercolours and engravings.

PROVIDE Home Inspections. Free Estimates. Free Collection/Delivery Service.
SPEAK TO Trevor Woodward.
SEE Picture Frames.

ELIZABETH POWELL
5 Royal Square, Dedham, Colchester, **Essex CO7 6AA**
TEL   0206 322279
OPEN   9–5.30 Mon–Sat.

Specialise in conserving and restoring oil paintings, watercolours, pastels and prints.

PROVIDE Home Inspections, Free Estimates, Free Local Collection/Delivery Service.
SPEAK TO Elizabeth Powell.
Member of IIC.

CHRISTINE SNELL PICTURE CONSERVATION
Painter's Farm, Butlers Lane, Ashdon, Saffron Walden, **Essex CB10 2ND**
TEL   0799 523332
OPEN   10.30–5 Mon, Tues, Thur, Fri.

Specialise in restoring oil paintings.

PROVIDE Home Inspections. Free Estimates.
SPEAK TO Christine Snell.
Associate Member of ABPR and UKIC.

MRS JACQUELINE TABER

Jaggers, Fingringhoe, Colchester, **Essex CO5 7DN**

TEL   0206 729334
OPEN   9–6 Mon–Fri or By
            Appointment.

Specialise in conserving and restoring oil paintings.

PROVIDE Home Inspections. Free Estimates. Collection/Delivery Service by arrangement.
SPEAK TO Jacqueline Taber.
Associate Member of APBR.

ASTLEY HOUSE FINE ART

Astley House, High Street, Moreton-in-Marsh, **Gloucestershire GL56 0LL**

TEL   0608 50601
FAX   0608 51777
OPEN   9–5.30 Mon–Sat.

Specialise in cleaning and restoring oil paintings, watercolours.

PROVIDE Free Estimates. Chargeable Collection/Delivery Service.
SPEAK TO David or Nanette Glaisyer.
SEE Picture Frames.

DAVID BANNISTER

26 Kings Road, Cheltenham, **Gloucestershire GL52 6BG**

TEL   0242 514287
FAX   0242 513890
OPEN   By Appointment.

Specialise in restoring, colouring and cataloguing topographic prints.

PROVIDE Free Estimates. Chargeable Collection/Delivery Service.
SPEAK TO David Bannister.

SEE Books.

KEITH BAWDEN

Mews Workshop, Montpellier Retreat, Cheltenham, **Gloucestershire GL50 2XS**

TEL   0242 230320
OPEN   7–4.30 Mon–Fri.

Specialise in conserving and restoring all aspects of paintings.

PROVIDE Free Estimates. Home Inspections. Local Collection/Delivery Service.
SPEAK TO Keith Bawden.

SEE Clocks, Furniture, Silver, Porcelain.

CLEEVE PICTURE FRAMING

Coach House Workshops, Stoke Road, Bishops Cleeve, Cheltenham, **Gloucestershire GL52 4RP**

TEL   0242 672785
FAX   0242 676827
OPEN   9–1 Mon–Sat.

Specialise in restoring and conserving oil paintings, watercolours, papers and prints.

PROVIDE Home Inspections. Free Estimates. Free Collection/Delivery Service.
SPEAK TO James Gardner.
SEE Picture Frames.

JOHN DAVIES

Church Street Gallery, Stow-on-the-Wold, **Gloucestershire GL54 1BB**

TEL   0451 31698
FAX   0451 32477
OPEN   9.30–1, 2–5.30 Mon–Sat.

Specialise in restoring pictures in all mediums, including oil, watercolour, tempera and pastel.

PROVIDE Home Inspections. Free Estimates. Chargeable Collection/Delivery Service.
SPEAK TO John Davies.

G. M. S. RESTORATIONS
The Workshops (rear of Bell Passage Antiques), High Street, Wickwar, **Gloucestershire GL12 8NP**
TEL   0454 294251
FAX   0454 294251
OPEN   8–5 Mon–Fri.

Specialise in restoring oil paintings and watercolours.

PROVIDE Home Inspections. Refundable Estimates. Chargeable Collection/Delivery Service.
SPEAK TO Mr G. M. St George-Stacey. Member of LAPADA, Upholsterers Guild, Guild of Master Craftsmen, Guild of Woodcarvers, Guild of Antique Dealers and Restorers.
SEE Furniture.

PIPPA JEFFRIES
1 St James Terrace, Suffolk Parade, Cheltenham, **Gloucestershire GL50 2AA**
TEL   0242 239895
OPEN   9–6 Mon–Fri or By Appointment.

Specialise in relining and all aspects of restoration of oil paintings on canvas and panel.
PROVIDE Home Inspections. Free Estimates. Chargeable Collection/Delivery Service.
SPEAK TO Pippa Jeffries.

Associate Member of ABPR. This workshop is included on the register of conservators maintained by the Conservation Unit of the Museums and Galleries Commission.

KENULF FINE ART LTD
5 North Street, Winchcombe, Nr. Cheltenham, **Gloucestershire GL54 5LH**
TEL   0242 603204
FAX   0242 604042
OPEN   9.30–1, 2–5.30 Mon–Sat.

Specialise in restoration of oils and watercolours.

PROVIDE Home Inspections. Free Estimates. Collection/Delivery Service.
SPEAK TO Eric Ford.
SEE Picture Frames.

A. J. PONSFORD ANTIQUES
51–53 Dollar Street, Cirencester, **Gloucestershire GL7 2AS**
TEL   0285 652355
OPEN   8.30–5.30 Mon–Fri.

Specialise in restoring oil paintings.

PROVIDE Home Inspections. Free Estimates. Free Collection/Delivery Service.
SPEAK TO A. J. Ponsford.
SEE Furniture, Picture Frames.

PETER WARD GALLERY
11 Gosditch Street, Cirencester, **Gloucestershire GL7 2AG**
TEL   0285 658499
OPEN   9.30–5.30 Mon–Sat.

Specialise in restoring oils and watercolours.

PROVIDE Home Inspections. Free Collection/Delivery Service.
SPEAK TO Peter Ward.
SEE Picture Frames.

CORFIELD RESTORATIONS LTD
120 High Street, Lymington, **Hampshire SO41 9AQ**
TEL   0590 673532
OPEN   9.15–5.30 Mon–Sat.

Specialise in picture restoration.

PROVIDE Home Inspections. Free Estimates. Local Free Collection/Delivery Service.
SPEAK TO Alan Bloomfield or Michael Corfield.

Also at Setters Farm, Lymington. 0590
671977.
SEE Furniture, Picture Frames.

JAMES FLAVELL BOOKBINDER AND RESTORER
26 Foreland Road, Bembridge, Isle of
Wight, **Hampshire PO35 5XW**
TEL   0983 872856
OPEN   9–5.30 Mon–Fri, 9–12.30 Sat.

Specialise in restoring prints.

PROVIDE Home Inspections. Free
Estimates. Free Collection/Delivery
Service.
SPEAK TO James Flavell.
Mr Flavell is City and Guilds qualified,
Member of Society of Bookbinders,
Associate Member of Designer
Bookbinders. This workshop is included
on the register of conservators
maintained by the Conservation Unit of
the Museums and Galleries Commission.
SEE Books, Furniture.

R. & L. LANCEFIELD
'Toad Hall', Burnetts Lane, Horton
Heath, Eastleigh, **Hampshire SO5 7DJ**
TEL   0703 692032
OPEN   9–5.30 Mon–Fri or By
        Appointment.

Specialise in restoring prints.

PROVIDE Home Inspections. Free
Estimates. Free/Chargeable
Collection/Delivery Service.
SPEAK TO Rex Lancefield.

Member of IPC. This workshop is
included on the register of conservators
maintained by the Conservation Unit of
the Museums and Galleries Commission.
SEE Books.

JOAN A. LEWRY
'Wychelms', 66 Gorran Avenue, Rowner,
Gosport, **Hampshire PO13 0NF**
TEL   0329 286901
OPEN   By Appointment.

Specialise in cleaning, conserving and
restoring pictures.

PROVIDE Home Inspections. Refundable
Estimates. Free Local
Collection/Delivery Service.
SPEAK TO Joan Lewry.

THE PETERSFIELD BOOKSHOP
16a Chapel Street, Petersfield,
Hampshire GU32 3DS
TEL   0730 263438
FAX   0730 269426
OPEN   9–5.30 Mon–Sat.

Specialise in restoring and cleaning oil
paintings, watercolours.

PROVIDE Home Inspections. Free
Estimates. Collection/Delivery Service
available.
SPEAK TO Frank Westwood.
SEE Books, Picture Frames.

PRINTED PAGE
2–3 Bridge Street, Winchester,
Hampshire SO23 9BH
TEL   0962 854072
FAX   0962 862995
OPEN   9.30–5.30 Tues–Sat.

Specialise in cleaning, colouring and
repairing old prints and restoring oil
paintings and watercolours.

PROVIDE Home Inspections. Refundable
Estimates. Chargeable
Collection/Delivery Service.
SPEAK TO Jean or Christopher Wright.
Member of the FATG and IPC.

DR IAN SCOTT

Coach Hill House, Burley Street, Nr.
Ringwood, **Hampshire BH24 4HN**
TEL   04253 3361
OPEN   By Appointment.

Specialise in restoring, mounting and
framing Oriental paintings on paper or
silk.

PROVIDE Free Local Home Inspections.
Free Estimates. Chargeable
Collection/Delivery Service.
SPEAK TO Ian Scott.

A. SCOTT-MONCRIEFF

6 Newcombe Road, Southampton,
Hampshire SO1 2FL
TEL   0703 635706
OPEN   By Appointment.

Specialise in restoring oil paintings. Will
also carry out condition surveys of
collections.

PROVIDE Home Inspections. Free
Estimates. Chargeable
Collection/Delivery Service.
SPEAK TO A. Scott-Moncrieff.
Associate Member of UKIC, Associate
Member of ABPR. This workshop is
included on the register of conservators
maintained by the Conservation Unit of
the Museums and Galleries Commission.

J. T. BURNS

Fairview Cottage, Shucknall Hill,
Hereford, **Hereford & Worcester
HR1 3SW**
TEL   0432 850213
OPEN   10–5 Mon–Sat.

Specialise in restoring and conserving
oil paintings only, including cleaning,
varnishing, relining and damage repair.

PROVIDE Home Inspections. Free
Estimates. Chargeable
Collection/Delivery Service.
SPEAK TO Mr or Mrs Burns

Member of UKIC, Associate Member of
ABPR. This workshop is included on the

register of conservators maintained by
the Conservation Unit of the Museums
and Galleries Commission.

EDWIN COLLINS

Coltsfoot Gallery, Hatfield, Leominster,
Hereford & Worcester HR6 0SF
TEL   056 882 277
OPEN   By Appointment.

Specialise in restoring and conserving all
works of art on paper.

PROVIDE Home Inspections. Free
Estimates.
SPEAK TO Edwin Collins.
Member of IPC.
SEE Picture Frames.

JAMES GRINDLEY

2 Fownhope Court, Fownhope,
Hereford, **Hereford & Worcester
HR1 4PB**
TEL   0432 860396
OPEN   By Appointment.

Specialise in restoring and conserving
works of art on paper, particularly
watercolours and prints.

PROVIDE Free Estimates.
Collection/Delivery Service by
arrangement.
SPEAK TO James Grindley.

HAY LOFT GALLERY

Berry Wormington, Broadway,
Hereford & Worcester WR12 7NH
TEL   0242 621202
OPEN   10–5.30 Mon–Fri or By
         Appointment.

Specialise in restoring paintings,
particularly 19th century.

PROVIDE Home Inspections. Free
Estimates. Chargeable
Collection/Delivery Service.
SPEAK TO Jane or Sally Pitt.

T. M. HUGUENIN
20 Albany Terrace, Worcester,
Hereford & Worcester WR1 3DU
TEL   0905 28133
OPEN   Mon–Sat By Appointment.

Specialise in restoring works of art on paper, prints, drawings, watercolours.
PROVIDE Home Inspections. Free Estimates. Chargeable Collection/Delivery Service.
SPEAK TO T. M. Huguenin.
Member of UKIC and IPC. This workshop is included on the register of conservators maintained by the Conservation Unit of the Museums and Galleries Commission.

GEORGE JACK & CO.
Notre Val, Laverton, Broadway,
Hereford & Worcester WR12 7NA
TEL   038673 691
FAX   038673 691
OPEN   By Appointment.

Specialise in restoring oil paintings from 15th century to present day but particularly Victorian period.
PROVIDE Home Inspections. Negotiable Estimates. Free Collection/Delivery Service.
SPEAK TO Mr George Jack.
Mr Jack has forty-three years' experience. Associate Member IIC and ABPR. This workshop is included on the register of conservators maintained by the Conservation Unit of the Museums and Galleries Commission.

EUGENE B. OKARMA
Brobury House Gallery, Brobury,
Hereford & Worcester HR3 6BS
TEL   09817 229
OPEN   9–4 Mon–Sat.
Specialise in restoring old prints, watercolours and oil paintings.
PROVIDE Local Home Inspections.
SPEAK TO Mr Okarma.

LEONORA WEAVER
6 Aylestone Drive, Hereford,
Hereford & Worcester HR1 1HT
TEL   0432 267816
OPEN   By Appointment.

Specialise in restoring and hand-colouring prints.
PROVIDE Free Estimates. Collection/Delivery Service sometimes available.
SPEAK TO Leonora Weaver.
SEE Books.

WOODLAND FINE ART
16 The Square, Alvechurch, **Hereford & Worcester B48 7LA**
TEL   021 445 5886
OPEN   10–6 Mon–Sat.

Specialise in restoring oil paintings and watercolours.

PROVIDE Home Inspections, Free Estimates, Free Collection/Delivery Service.
SPEAK TO C. J. Haynes.
SEE Furniture.

JOHN ESSEX
The Studio, Chapel Street, Berkhamsted,
Hertfordshire HP4 3EA
TEL   0442 864821
OPEN   9.30–5 Mon–Fri By Appointment only.

Specialise in wax impregnating and glue lining up to nine by fifteen feet. Their speciality is panel work from rejoins and blister laying to semi and total transfers on to conservation panels.

PROVIDE Home Inspections. Free Estimates. Chargeable Collection/Delivery Service.
SPEAK TO John Essex.
Member of ABPR.

12

HERTFORDSHIRE CONSERVATION SERVICE
Seed Warehouse, Maidenhead Yard,
The Wash, Hertford, **Hertfordshire
SG14 1PX**
TEL   0992 588966
FAX   0992 588971
OPEN   9–6 Mon–Fri By Appointment.

Specialise in restoring works of art on
paper, including prints, drawings,
wallpaper and photographs.

PROVIDE Home Inspections.
Free/Chargeable Estimates. Chargeable
Collection/Delivery Service.
SPEAK TO J. M. MacQueen.
This workshop is included on the register
of conservators maintained by the
Conservation Unit of the Museums and
Galleries Commission.
SEE Collectors (Dolls), Lighting,
Porcelain, Furniture, Picture Frames,
Carpets.

SUSAN LAMBERT
108 Harmer Green Lane, Welwyn,
Hertfordshire AL6 0ET
TEL   043 879 234
FAX   043 879 628
OPEN   9–5 Mon–Fri By Appointment.

Specialise in conserving and restoring
works of art on paper, paintings, prints,
drawings.

PROVIDE Home Inspections. Free
Estimates. Chargeable
Collection/Delivery Service.
SPEAK TO Susan Lambert.
Member of IPC, IIC and Museums'
Association.
SEE Picture Frames.

ST OUEN ANTIQUES LTD
Vintage Corner, Old Cambridge Road,
Puckeridge, **Hertfordshire SG11 1SA**
TEL   0920 821336
FAX   0920 822877
OPEN   10–5 Mon–Sat.

Specialise in restoring 19th century
paintings.

PROVIDE Home Inspections. Refundable
Estimates. Chargeable
Collection/Delivery Service.
SPEAK TO Tim or John Blake.
SEE Furniture.

VICTORIA FRAMING SERVICES
Long Spring, Porters Wood, St Albans,
Hertfordshire AL3 6NQ
TEL   0727 59044
FAX   0727 861660
OPEN   8.30–5.30 Mon–Fri.

Specialise in restoring oil paintings.

PROVIDE Local Home Inspections.
Chargeable Estimates. Chargeable
Collection/Delivery Service.
SPEAK TO David Prior.
SEE Picture Frames.

CASTLE FINE ART STUDIO
26 Castle Street, Dover, **Kent
CT16 1PW**
TEL   0304 206360
OPEN   10–1, 2–5.30 Mon–Fri; 10–1
          Sat.

Specialise in restoring works of art on
paper, prints, drawings, watercolours.

PROVIDE Home Inspections. Free
Estimates. Free Local
Collection/Delivery Service.
SPEAK TO Ms Deborah Colam.
Member of IPC. This workshop is
included on the register of conservators
maintained by the Conservation Unit of
the Museums and Galleries Commission.
SEE Books, Picture Frames.

CLARE GALLERY
21 High Street, Royal Tunbridge Wells, **Kent TN1 1UT**
TEL 0892 538717
FAX 0323 29588
OPEN 8.15–5.30 Mon–Sat.

Specialise in restoring 19th and 20th century oil paintings and watercolours.
PROVIDE Home Inspections. Free Estimates. Chargeable Collection/Delivery Service.
SPEAK TO M. Ettinger.
SEE Picture Frames.

ROGER GREEN FINE ART
Hales Place Studio, High Halden, Nr. Ashford, **Kent TN26 3JQ**
TEL 0233 850716
FAX 0233 850219
OPEN 9–5 Mon–Sat.

Specialise in conservation and restoration of oils and paper works of art. Intaglio platemaking and editioning and the restoration and printing of antique copperplates. Also have an in-house photographic studio.
PROVIDE Local Home Inspections. Free Estimates.
SPEAK TO Roger Green or Ellen Green.
SEE Picture Frames.

FRANCES ILES FINE PAINTINGS
Rutland House, 103 High Street, Rochester, **Kent ME1 1LX**
TEL 0634 843081
FAX 0474 822403
OPEN 9–5.30 Mon–Sat.

Specialise in conserving and restoring oil paintings and works on paper.
PROVIDE Home Inspections. Free Estimates. Free Collection/Delivery Service.
SPEAK TO Jeanette or Lucy Iles.
SEE Picture Frames.

GILLIAN M. KINLOCH
Adams Well, Gover Hill, Maidstone, **Kent ME18 5JP**
TEL 0732 850845
OPEN 9–6 Mon–Sat or By Appointment.

Specialise in restoring oil paintings and providing advice on all aspects of restoration and conservation.
PROVIDE Home Inspections. Free Estimates. Chargeable Collection/Delivery Service.
SPEAK TO Gillian Kinloch. Member of ABPR and IIC. This workshop is included on the register of conservators maintained by the Conservation Unit of the Museums and Galleries Commission.

G. & D. I. MARRIN & SONS
149 Sandgate Road, Folkestone, **Kent CT20 2DA**
TEL 0303 53016
FAX 0303 850956
OPEN 9.30–5.30 Mon–Sat.

Specialise in restoring prints.
PROVIDE Home Inspections. Chargeable Estimates. Chargeable Collection/Delivery Service.
SPEAK TO John or Patrick Marrin.
SEE Books.

W. J. MORRILL LTD
437 Folkestone Road, Dover, **Kent CT17 9JX**
TEL 0304 201989
OPEN 8–5 Mon–Fri.

Specialise in relining and restoring oil paintings of all periods.
PROVIDE Home Inspections. Free Collection/Delivery Service.
SPEAK TO Mr Barnes.
SEE Picture Frames.

Paintings, Prints & Photographs

DYSONS ARTS LTD
87 Scotland Road, Nelson, **Lancashire BB9 7UY**
TEL   0282 65468
OPEN   9.30–5.30 Mon–Sat, closed
       Tues.

Specialise in cleaning, repairing and restoring oil paintings.

PROVIDE Free Estimates.
SPEAK TO O. A. Davies.
SEE Picture Frames.

BARBARA WILDMAN
9 Woodside Terrace, Nelson, **Lancashire BB9 7TB**
TEL   0282 699679
OPEN   By Appointment.

Specialise in restoring oil paintings of all periods, including relining.

PROVIDE Home Inspections. Free Estimates. Chargeable Collection/Delivery Service.
SPEAK TO Barbara Wildman.
SEE Picture Frames.

RICHARD ZAHLER
Lane House, Fowgill, Bentham, Lancaster, **Lancashire LA2 7AH**
TEL   05242 61988
OPEN   9–6 Mon–Fri or By
       Appointment.

Specialise in restoring easel paintings, icons, ceiling and some mural types, frames, watercolours, prints, drawings, maps, sketches, Oriental works of art. Will cosmetically clean whole collections in situ for customers who wish to rejuvenate their collections harmoniously. Also provide an emergency first aid service when unforeseen damage has occurred.
SPEAK TO Richard Zahler.
Member of UKIC and the Guild of Master Craftsmen. This workshop is

included on the register maintained by the Conservation Unit of the Museums and Galleries Commission.
SEE Books, Picture Frames.

JOHN GARNER
51–53 High Street East, Uppingham, **Leicestershire LE15 9PY**
TEL   0572 823607
FAX   0572 821654
OPEN   9–5.30 Mon–Sat; Sun By
       Appointment.

Specialise in restoring 18th and 19th century pictures.

PROVIDE Home Inspections. Free Collection/Delivery Service.
SPEAK TO John or Wendy Garner.
SEE Furniture.

JULIET HAWKER
Ford House Studio, 7 Queen Street, Uppingham, Rutland, **Leicestershire LE15 9QR**
TEL   0572 821733
OPEN   10–4 Mon–Thur or By
       Appointment. It is advisable to
       phone for directions.

Specialise in restoring and cleaning paintings in oil and acrylic on canvas, panel or metal. Large works can be treated on location.

PROVIDE Home Inspections. Free Estimates. Free Local Collection/Delivery Service.
SPEAK TO Juliet Hawker.
Member of ABPR and UKIC. This workshop is included on the register of conservators maintained by the Conservation Unit of the Museums and Galleries Commission.

THE OLD HOUSE GALLERY
13–15 Market Place, Oakham, **Leicestershire LE15 6DT**
TEL   0572 755538
OPEN   10–5 Mon–Fri; 10–4 Sat; closed Thur p.m.

Specialise in restoring Victorian and Modern British oils, watercolours and antiquarian prints.

PROVIDE Home Inspections. Free Local Collection/Delivery Service.
SPEAK TO Richard Clarke.
SEE Books, Picture Frames.

SUE RAWLINGS
17 Nithsdale Crescent, Market Harborough, **Leicestershire LE16 9HA**
TEL   0858 464605
OPEN   9–5.30 Mon–Fri.

Specialise in restoring works of art on paper.

PROVIDE Home Inspections. Free Estimates. Free Local Collection/Delivery Service.
SPEAK TO Sue Rawlings.
Member of IPC. This workshop is included on the register of conservators maintained by the Conservation Unit of the Museums and Galleries Commission.
SEE Books.

BURGHLEY FINE ART CONSERVATION
Burghley House, Stamford, **Lincolnshire PE9 3JY**
TEL   0780 62155
OPEN   By Appointment.

Specialise in conserving and restoring easel paintings, wall paintings (oil on plaster).

PROVIDE Home Inspections. Free Estimates. Chargeable Collection/Delivery Service.
SPEAK TO Michael Cowell.

Any work undertaken is fully documented.
SEE Furniture, Picture Frames.

SARAH COVE: CONSERVATION OF PAINTINGS
Tower Farm, Grimsthorpe, Nr. Bourne, **Lincolnshire PE10 0NF**
TEL   077 832239 or 081 801 9039 (answerphone)
OPEN   9.30–6 Mon–Fri By Appointment Only.

Specialise in conservation and restoration of easel paintings, particularly English portraiture and 18th and 19th century landscape. Also modern mixed media works. Will carry out collection surveys and give advice on treatment, future planning, transportation, framing etc.

PROVIDE Chargeable Home Inspections. Refundable Estimates. Chargeable Collection/Delivery Service.
SPEAK TO Sarah Cove or Alan Cummings.
Associate Member of IIC, UKIC and ABPR. This workshop is included on the register of conservators maintained by the Conservation Unit of the Museums and Galleries Commission.

PAOLA CAMUSSO
46 Pennybank Chambers, 33–35 St John's Square, **London EC1M 4DS**
TEL   071 250 3278
FAX   071 250 0297
OPEN   10–6 Mon–Fri.

Specialise in restoring oil paintings on canvas, panel and metal.

PROVIDE Home Inspections. Free Estimates. Free Collection/Delivery Service.
SPEAK TO Ms Paola Camusso.

Associate of ABPR. This workshop is
included on the register of conservators
maintained by the Conservation Unit of
the Museums and Galleries Commission.
SEE Porcelain.

HOWARD & STONE CONSERVATORS
27 Pennybank Chambers, 33–35 St
John's Square, **London EC1M 4DS**
TEL   071 490 0813
OPEN   9.30–6 Mon–Fri.

Specialise in conserving prints, drawings
and watercolours.

PROVIDE Home Inspections. Free
Estimates. Chargeable
Collection/Delivery Service.
SPEAK TO Deryn Howard or Rosemary
Stone.

MARIA KELLER CONSERVATION AND RESTORATION
Unit 46, Pennybank Chambers, St John's
Square, **London EC1M 4DS**
TEL   071 386 8723 or 081 250 3278
OPEN   10–7 Mon–Fri or By
         Appointment.

Specialise in restoring paintings on
canvas, panel and copper in oil and
tempera from local repairs of canvas as
well as full restoration.

PROVIDE Home Inspections. Free
Estimates. Chargeable
Collection/Delivery Service.
SPEAK TO Maria Keller.

Member of ABPR and UKIC. This
workshop is included on the register of
conservators maintained by the
Conservation Unit of the Museums and
Galleries Commission.
SEE Porcelain.

PRUDENCE SEWARD
30 Sekforde Street, **London**
EC1R 0HH
TEL   071 251 8152
OPEN   By Appointment.

Specialise in conserving works of art on
paper.

PROVIDE Home Inspections. Free
Estimates. Chargeable
Collection/Delivery Service.
SPEAK TO Prudence Seward.
Ms Seward is ARCA, Dip. Conservation,
Camberwell and a Member of UKIC.
This workshop is included on the register
of conservators maintained by the
Conservation Unit of the Museums and
Galleries Commission.
SEE Picture Frames.

JENNIFER ARCHBOLD
54 Northchurch Road, **London N1 4EJ**
TEL   071 254 1562
OPEN   By Appointment.

Specialise in restoring easel paintings,
oil, acrylic, tempera, mixed media on
canvas or panel.

PROVIDE Home Inspections. Free Local
Estimates.
SPEAK TO Jennifer Archbold.

Member of IIC, UKIC and ABPR. This
workshop is included on the register of
conservators maintained by the
Conservation Unit of the Museums and
Galleries Commission.

GRAHAM BIGNELL PAPER CONSERVATION
27–29 New North Road, **London**
N1 6JB
TEL   071 251 2791
OPEN   9–6 Mon–Sat By Appointment.

Specialise in restoring prints, drawings,
watercolours and posters. Also do
collection surveys.

PROVIDE Home Inspections. Free

17

Estimates. Chargeable
Collection/Delivery Service.
SPEAK TO Graham Bignell.

Member of AIC, UKIC and IPC. This
workshop is included on the register of
conservators maintained by the
Conservation Unit of the Museums and
Galleries Commission.
SEE Books.

PETER CHAPMAN ANTIQUES
Incorporating **CHAPMAN RESTORATIONS**
10 Theberton Street, **London N1 0QX**
TEL   071 226 5565
FAX   081 348 4846
OPEN   9.30–6 Mon–Sat.

Specialise in cleaning, relining and
restoring oil paintings.

PROVIDE Home Inspections. Refundable
Estimates. Chargeable
Collection/Delivery Service.
SPEAK TO Peter Chapman or Tony
Holohan.

SEE Furniture, Picture Frames, Porcelain,
Silver.

WARWICK MacCALLUM
Unit N3, Metropolitan Workshops,
Enfield Road, **London N1 5AZ**
TEL   071 359 6737
OPEN   By Appointment Only.

Specialise in all aspects of the
conservation and restoration of easel
paintings; oil, tempera or acrylic on
canvas, wood or card. Also specialise in
the restoration of very large paintings and
all restoration is to museum standards.
Reports and photo documentation
supplied if required.

PROVIDE Home Inspections.
Free/Chargeable Estimates. Chargeable
Collection/Delivery Service.
SPEAK TO Warwick MacCallum.
Member of ABPR and UKIC.

JOHN JONES FRAMES LTD
Unit 4, Finsbury Park Trading Estate,
Morris Place, **London N4 3JG**
TEL   071 281 5439
FAX   071 281 5956
OPEN   8–6 Mon–Fri, 9–2 Sat, 12–4 Sun.

Specialise in restoring prints,
watercolours and paintings.

PROVIDE Free Estimates. Chargeable
Collection/Delivery Service.
SPEAK TO John Jones or John Dawson or
Nick Hawker.

SEE Picture Frames, Specialist
Photographers.

WILLIAM JONES
7 Winchester Road, **London N6 5HW**
TEL   081 341 9804
OPEN   By Appointment.

Specialise in picture hanging at
exhibitions and private homes.

PROVIDE Free Estimates. Chargeable
Collection/Delivery Service.
SPEAK TO Bill Jones.

WILLIAM CHARLES MACKINNON
176 Park Road, **London N8 8JT**
TEL   081 340 6172
OPEN   9–6 Mon–Fri.

Specialise in conserving and restoring
both traditional and modern oil
paintings.

PROVIDE Free/Chargeable Estimates.
SPEAK TO Bill Mackinnon.

HARRIS FINE ART LTD
712 High Road, North Finchley,
London N12 9QD
TEL   081 445 2804 or 081 446 5579
FAX   081 445 0708
OPEN   9–6 Mon–Sat.

Specialise in restoring Victorian
paintings.

PROVIDE Home Inspections. Free Estimates. Free Local Collection/Delivery Service.
SPEAK TO Clive Harris.
SEE Picture Frames.

SUDBURY-JONES LTD
44–48 Birkbeck Road, **London N12 8DZ**
TEL   081 446 3164
OPEN   9–6 Mon–Fri.

Specialise in a comprehensive picture restoration service. Oil paintings re-lined, cleaned and varnished. Watercolours and prints de-acidified, cleaned and restored.

PROVIDE Home Inspections. Free Estimates. Collection/Delivery Service.
SPEAK TO Tom Jones or Chris Frost.
SEE Picture Frames.

THE PAINTING CONSERVATION STUDIO
Address withheld by request.
TEL   071 281 9997
OPEN   10–5 By Appointment.

Specialise in restoring easel paintings. Collection surveys.

PROVIDE Home Inspections. Free/Chargeable Estimates. Chargeable Collection/Delivery Service.
SPEAK TO Carol Willoughby, Isabel Horovitz, Andrea Gall, Helen White, Amanda Paulley.

This workshop is included on the register of conservators maintained by the Conservation Unit of the Museums and Galleries Commission.
SEE Picture Frames.

DEANSBROOK GALLERY
134 Myddleton Road, **London N22 4NQ**
TEL   081 889 8389
OPEN   10–5 Mon–Sat.

Specialise in restoring oil paintings and prints.

PROVIDE Home Inspections. Free Estimates. Chargeable Collection/Delivery Service.
SPEAK TO Anthony Edmunds.

SEE Picture Frames.

CATHERINE RICKMAN ART CONSERVATION
11 Berkley Road, **London NW1 8XX**
TEL   071 586 0384
OPEN   9–6 Mon–Fri By Appointment.

Specialise in restoring works of art on paper, prints, drawings, watercolours, wallpapers.

PROVIDE Home Inspections. Free Verbal Estimates.
SPEAK TO Catherine Rickman.

Member of IPC, UKIC, IIC and AIC. This workshop is included on the register of conservators maintained by the Conservation Unit of the Museums and Galleries Commission.
SEE Books.

COLLERAN and CIANTAR LTD
17 Frognal, **London NW3 6AR**
TEL   071 435 4652 or 0895 256410
FAX   071 435 4652 or 0895 256410
OPEN   9–5 Mon–Fri or By Appointment.

Specialise in conserving and restoring watercolours, drawings, prints and other items on paper.

PROVIDE Chargeable Home Inspections. Free/Chargeable Estimates. Collection/Delivery Service by arrangement.
SPEAK TO Kate Colleran or Marcel Ciantar.

JUDITH MacCOLUM
143 King Henry's Road, **London NW3 3RD**
TEL   071 922 6208
OPEN   By Appointment.

Specialise in restoring prints and drawings.

PROVIDE Home Inspections. Free Estimates. Collection/Delivery Service.
SPEAK TO Mrs Judith MacColum.

Member of IPC. This workshop is included on the register of conservators maintained by the Conservation Unit of the Museums and Galleries Commission.

JOHN DENHAM GALLERY
50 Mill Lane, **London NW6 1NJ**
TEL   071 794 2635
OPEN   11–5 Sun, Tues–Fri.

Specialise in restoring oil paintings and works of art on paper.

PROVIDE Home Inspections. Free Estimates. Free Collection/Delivery Service.
SPEAK TO John Denham.

SEE Picture Frames.

JOHN JACOBS
240 Webheath, Netherwood Street, **London NW6 2JX**
TEL   071 328 6354
OPEN   10–6 Mon–Fri or By Appointment.

Specialise in restoring oil paintings on canvas, paper or board, specialising in structural work.

PROVIDE Home Inspections. Free Estimates. Chargeable Collection/Delivery Service.
SPEAK TO John Jacobs.

Member of ABPR.

JANE AND PAUL ZAGEL
31 Pandora Road, **London NW6 1TS**
TEL   071 794 1663
OPEN   9–6 Mon–Fri.

Specialise in restoring watercolours, prints and gouache drawings. Fine art photography undertaken as part of the restoration record.

PROVIDE Home Inspections. Refundable Estimates. Chargeable Collection/Delivery Service.
SPEAK TO Jane Zagel.
This workshop is included on the register of conservators maintained by the Conservation Unit of the Museums and Galleries Commission.

SEE Books, Specialist Photographers.

FRANCES BUTLIN
73 Loudoun Road, **London NW8 0DQ**
TEL   071 328 1395
OPEN   10–6 Mon–Fri.

Specialise in restoring easel paintings, canvas and panel paintings.

PROVIDE Home Inspections. Free Estimates. Chargeable Collection/Delivery Service.
SPEAK TO Frances Butlin.
Member of IIC, UKIC and ABPR. This workshop is included on the register of conservators maintained by the Conservation Unit of the Museums and Galleries Commission.

DROWN AND COMPANY LTD
117 Boundary Road, **London NW8 0RG**
TEL   071 624 6100
OPEN   9–6 Mon–Fri or By Appointment.

Specialise in restoring oil paintings of all periods with specialisation in Impressionist and Modern fields.

PROVIDE Home Inspections. Free Estimates. Free Collection/Delivery Service.
SPEAK TO David or Duncan Drown.

Member of ABPR. Duncan Drown is a Fellow of the IIC and David Drown is a Member of UKIC.

WELLINGTON GALLERY
1 St John's Wood High Street, **London NW8 7NG**
TEL   071 586 2620
OPEN   10–5.30 Mon–Sat.

Specialise in restoring oil paintings.

PROVIDE Home Inspections. Free Estimates. Chargeable Collection/Delivery Service.
SPEAK TO Mrs Maureen Barclay or Mr K. J. Barclay.
Member of LAPADA.
SEE Furniture, Porcelain, Silver.

TRADE PICTURE SERVICES LIMITED
Neckinger Mills, Abbet Street, **London SE1 2AN**
TEL   071 237 4388
FAX   071 237 4388
OPEN   9–5.30 Mon–Fri.

Specialise in lining, conservation and restoration of oil paintings. Also ceiling and wall paintings.

PROVIDE Home Inspections. Free/Refundable Estimates. Free Collection/Delivery Service.
SPEAK TO Matthew Goldsmith.

VOITEK
Conservation of Works of Art, 9 Whitehorse Mews, Westminster Bridge Road, **London SE1 7QD**
TEL   071 928 6094
FAX   071 928 6094
OPEN   10.30–5 Mon–Fri.

Specialise in conserving and restoring Old Master drawings, prints, watercolours and works of art on paper.

PROVIDE Home Inspections. Delivery Service.
SPEAK TO Elizabeth Sobczynski.
SEE Porcelain.

ALEXANDRA WALKER
4 Whitehorse Mews, 37–39 Westminster Bridge Road, **London SE1 7QD**
TEL   071 261 1419
OPEN   10–6 Mon–Fri.

Specialise in restoring easel paintings of all periods.

PROVIDE Home Inspections. Free/Chargeable Estimates.
SPEAK TO Alexandra Walker.

VALENTINE WALSH
3 Whitehorse Mews, **London SE1 7QD**
TEL   071 261 1691
FAX   071 401 9049
OPEN   By Appointment.

Specialise in restoring easel paintings from 1400 to 1950 particularly paintings on panel and can also accommodate very large paintings.

PROVIDE Home Inspections. Free/Chargeable Estimates. Free/Chargeable Collection/Delivery Service.
SPEAK TO Valentine Walsh.
Member of UKIC. This workshop is included on the register of conservators maintained by the Conservation Unit of the Museums and Galleries Commission.
SEE **Borders.**

CLAIRE GASKELL
32 St John's Park, **London SE3 7JH**
TEL   081 858 2756
OPEN   10–5 Mon–Fri.

Specialise in restoring prints, drawings, watercolours, Japanese prints and Indian paintings.

PROVIDE Home Inspections. Free Estimates. Free Collection/Delivery Service.
SPEAK TO Claire Gaskell.

SARAH JENNINGS CONSERVATION OF FINE ART
Linnell Road, **London SE5 8NJ**
TEL　　071 701 0866
OPEN　By Appointment.

Specialise in conserving and restoring paintings in oil, tempera, fresco, on copper, wood, plaster, board and canvas.

PROVIDE Home Inspections. Refundable Estimates. Chargeable Collection/Delivery Service.
SPEAK TO Sarah Jennings.

GREENWICH CONSERVATION WORKSHOPS
Spread Eagle Antiques of Greenwich, 8–9 Nevada Street, **London SE10 9JL**
TEL　　081 305 1666
OPEN　10–5.30 Mon–Sat.

Specialise in restoring oil paintings, watercolours and prints.

PROVIDE Home Inspections. Refundable Estimates. Free/Chargeable Collection/Delivery Service.
SPEAK TO Richard Moy.
SEE Furniture.

RELCY ANTIQUES
9 Nelson Road, **London SE10 9JB**
TEL　　081 858 2812
FAX　　081 293 4135
OPEN　10–6 Mon–Sat.

Specialise in restoring oil paintings and prints.

PROVIDE Home Inspections. Free/Chargeable Estimates. Collection/Delivery Service by arrangement.
SPEAK TO Robin Challis.

SEE Collectors (Scientific Instruments), Furniture, Silver.

KIM ELIZABETH LEYSHON PICTURE RESTORER
2 Walerand Road, **London SE13 7PG**
TEL　　081 318 1277
OPEN　By Appointment.

Specialise in restoring works of art on paper, Old Master and modern prints, drawings, watercolours, Indian miniatures.

PROVIDE Home Inspections. Free Estimates. Free Collection/Delivery Service.
SPEAK TO Kim Leyshon.

Member of IPC, IIC and UKIC. This workshop is included on the register of conservators maintained by the Conservation Unit of the Museums and Galleries Commission.
SEE Books.

ORDE SOLOMONS
50 Amersham Road, **London SE14 6QE**
TEL　　081 692 2016
OPEN　By Appointment.

Specialise in restoring historic wallpaper schemes and any decorative wall coverings, including paper, lincrusta, Tynecastle, Chinese, William Morris, papier mâché and artificial leather.

PROVIDE Home Inspections. Free/Chargeable Estimates. Chargeable Collection/Delivery Service.
SPEAK TO Orde Solomons.

Member of Wallpaper History Society and wallpaper conservator to the National Trust and English Heritage. Longest established and most experienced conservator of European wallpaper in the UK.
This workshop is included on the register of conservators maintained by the Conservation Unit of the Museums and Galleries Commission.

PETER ROBERT MALLOCH
75C London Road, **London** SE23 3TY
TEL   081 699 8754
OPEN   By Appointment.

Specialise in restoring oil paintings and pastels.

PROVIDE Free Estimates.
SPEAK TO Peter Malloch.

CLARE REYNOLDS
20 Gubyon Avenue, **London** **SE24 ODX**
TEL   071 326 0458
OPEN   9–5 Mon–Fri.

Specialise in restoring works of art on paper.

PROVIDE Home Inspections. Free Estimates. Chargeable Collection/Delivery Service.
SPEAK TO Clare Reynolds.

SEE Books.

JANE McNAMARA CONSERVATOR
14 Chelsfield Gardens, **London** **SE26 4DJ**
TEL   081 699 7173
OPEN   9–5 Mon–Fri By Appointment.

Specialise in conservation of art on paper, prints, drawings, watercolours, paper-based photographs.

PROVIDE Home Inspections. Free Estimates. Free Local Collection/Delivery Service.
SPEAK TO Jane McNamara.

Member of IPC. This workshop is included on the register of conservators maintained by the Conservation Unit of the Museums and Galleries Commission.
SEE Collectors (Paper).

DAVID KER GALLERY
85 Bourne Street, **London** SW1W 8HF
TEL   071 730 8365
FAX   071 730 3352
OPEN   9.30–5.30 Mon–Fri or By Appointment.

Specialise in restoring decorative oil paintings 1750–1950, particularly Scottish colourists.

PROVIDE Home Inspections. Free Estimates. Chargeable Collection/Delivery Service.
SPEAK TO David Ker or Miles Cato.

SEE Picture Frames.

KING STREET GALLERIES
17 King Street, **London** SW1Y 6QU
TEL   071 930 9392 or 930 3993
OPEN   9.30–5.30 Mon–Fri; 10–1 Sat.

Specialise in restoring oils and watercolours.

PROVIDE Home Inspections. Free Estimates. Chargeable Collection/Delivery Service.
SPEAK TO Hal O'Nians.

AMANDA MEHIGAN
11 Charlwood Place, **London** **SW1V 2LX**
TEL   071 834 3477 or 071 821 5453
OPEN   By Appointment Only.

Specialise in conservation and restoration of art on paper, especially in Old Master prints and drawings.

PROVIDE Free Estimates.
SPEAK TO Amanda Mehigan.

Member of IPC. This workshop is included on the register of conservators maintained by the Conservation Unit of the Museums and Galleries Commission.

CLAUDIO MOSCATELLI
46 Cambridge Street, **London**
SW1V 4QH
TEL   071 828 8475
OPEN   9–5 Mon–Fri or By
Appointment.

Specialise in restoring oil paintings, relining, retouching, varnishing.

PROVIDE Home Inspections. Free Estimates. Chargeable Collection/Delivery Service.
SPEAK TO Claudio Moscatelli.

SHEPHERD'S BOOKBINDERS LTD
76B Rochester Row, **London**
SW1P 1JU
TEL   071 630 1184
FAX   071 931 0541
OPEN   9–5.30 Mon–Fri; 10–1 Sat.

Specialise in restoring works of art on paper, including prints and watercolours.

PROVIDE Free Estimates.
SPEAK TO Rob Shepherd.
SEE Books.

ALWAY FINE ART CONSERVATION
238 Brompton Road, **London**
SW3 2BB
TEL   071 225 3389
FAX   0753 541163
OPEN   10.30–6.30 Mon–Fri, 10.30–
4.30 Sat.

Specialise in restoring oil paintings, relining, conservation and restoration to ground, medium and varnish layers. Conservation of drawings, watercolours and all works of art on paper.

PROVIDE Home Inspections. Free Estimates. Free Collection/Delivery Service.
SPEAK TO Stephen Alway.
Member of IPC.

MARIA ANDIPA ICON GALLERY
162 Walton Street, **London SW3 2JL**
TEL   071 589 2371
FAX   071 589 2371
OPEN   11–6 Mon–Fri; 11–2 Sat.

Specialise in restoring icons from all Eastern European countries, Syria, Egypt, Ethiopia. Also give lectures on restoration.

PROVIDE Home Inspections. Free/Chargeable Estimates. Chargeable Collection/Delivery Service.
SPEAK TO Maria Andipa.

JOHN CAMPBELL PICTURE FRAMES LTD
164 Walton Street, **London SW3 2JL**
TEL   071 584 9268
FAX   071 581 3499
OPEN   9.30–5.30 Mon–Fri; 1–5 Sat.

Specialise in restoring oil paintings and watercolours.

PROVIDE Home Inspections. Free Estimates. Free Collection/Delivery Service.
SPEAK TO Roy Hogben.
Member of the Guild of Master Craftsmen.

PATRICK CORBETT
1 Beaufort Street, **London SW3 5AQ**
TEL   071 352 7883
FAX   071 352 1033
OPEN   9.30–6 Mon–Fri.

Specialise in restoring oil paintings, especially 17th century Dutch and Flemish, 18th century English and in particular the works of George Stubbs.

PROVIDE Home Inspections. Free Estimates. Free Collection/Delivery Service.
SPEAK TO Patrick Corbett.

Member of ABPR, Associate Member IIC and UKIC. This workshop is included on the register of conservators maintained by the Conservation Unit of the Museums and Galleries Commission.

P. DOWLING
Chenil Galleries, 181–183 Kings Road, **London SW3 5EB**
TEL   071 376 5056
FAX   071 493 9344
OPEN   10–6 Mon–Sat.

Specialise in restoring antique pictures.

PROVIDE Free Estimates.
SPEAK TO P. Dowling.
SEE Picture Frames.

GREEN AND STONE
259 Kings Road, **London SW3 5EL**
TEL   071 352 6521
FAX   071 351 1098
OPEN   9–5.30 Mon–Fri; 9.30–6 Sat.

Specialise in restoring oil paintings, watercolours and prints.

PROVIDE Local Home Inspections. Free Estimates. Free Local Collection/Delivery Service.
SPEAK TO Mrs Hiscott or Miss Moore.
SEE Lighting, Picture Frames.

MALCOLM INNES GALLERY
172 Walton Street, **London SW3 2JL**
TEL   071 584 0575
OPEN   9.30–6 Mon–Fri; Sat 10–1.

Specialise in restoring oil paintings.

PROVIDE Free Estimates. Chargeable Collection/Delivery Service.
SPEAK TO Malcolm Innes.
SEE **Lothian.**
SEE Picture Frames.

STAVROS P. MIHALARIAS
2A Avenue Studios, Sydney Close, **London SW3 6HN**
TEL   071 589 6114
FAX   071 581 2962
OPEN   10–4 Mon–Fri.

Specialise in restoring icons.

PROVIDE Free Estimates.
SPEAK TO Miss Hilary Pinder.

FELIX ROSENSTIEL'S WIDOW & SON
33–35 Markham Street, **London SW3 3NR**
TEL   071 352 3551
FAX   071 351 5300
OPEN   8.30–5 Mon–Fri.

Specialise in hand-colouring prints.

PROVIDE Chargeable Collection/Delivery Service.
SPEAK TO David Roe or Sylvie Schnabel.

COOPER FINE ARTS LTD
768 Fulham Road, **London SW6 5SJ**
TEL   071 731 3421
OPEN   10–7 Mon–Fri; 10–4 Sat.

Specialise in restoring oil paintings and watercolours.

PROVIDE Free Estimates.
SPEAK TO Jonathan Hill-Reid.
SEE Picture Frames.

BRIGID RICHARDSON
91 Langthorne Street, **London SW6 6JS**
TEL   071 381 0198
OPEN   Mon–Sat By Appointment.

Specialise in conservation of works of art on paper, prints, drawings, watercolours, wallpaper.

PROVIDE Home Inspections. Free/Chargeable Estimates. Chargeable Collection/Delivery Service.
SPEAK TO Brigid Richardson.

Member of IPC. This workshop is included on the register of conservators maintained by the Conservation Unit of the Museums and Galleries Commission.
SEE Books.

20th CENTURY GALLERY
821 Fulham Road, **London SW6 5HG**
TEL 071 731 5888
OPEN 10–6 Mon–Fri; 10–1 Sat.

Specialise in restoring oil paintings.

PROVIDE Free Estimates.
SPEAK TO Erika Brandl.

SEE Picture Frames.

CLARE FINN & CO. LTD
38 Cornwall Gardens, **London
SW7 4AA**
TEL 071 937 1895
FAX 071 937 4198
OPEN By Appointment.

Specialise in restoring oil, tempera and easel paintings and oil mural paintings.

PROVIDE Home Inspections. Free Estimates. Chargeable Collection/Delivery Service.
SPEAK TO Clare Finn or Deborah Bichner.

Member of IIC, UKIC and IPC. This workshop is included on the register of conservators maintained by the Conservation Unit of the Museums and Galleries Commission.

SIMON FOLKES
Studio 6, 5 Thurloe Square, **London
SW7 2TA**
TEL 071 589 1649
OPEN By Appointment.

Specialise in restoring 15th–early 20th century oil paintings.

PROVIDE Home Inspections. Free/Chargeable Estimates. Free Local Collection/Delivery Service.
SPEAK TO Simon Folkes.
This workshop is included on the register of conservators maintained by the Conservation Unit of the Museums and Galleries Commission.

DEREK AND ROGER HULME FINE ART RESTORERS
31 Palfrey Place, **London SW8 1PE**
TEL 071 735 1218
FAX 071 582 9975
OPEN 8–6 Mon–Fri.

Specialise in conserving and restoring European Old Master and modern oil paintings. They also do in-house lining of paintings, transferring and panel work.

PROVIDE Home Inspections. Chargeable Estimates. Collection/Delivery Service by arrangement.
SPEAK TO Derek or Roger Hulme.
This is a third-generation firm.

LOWE AND BUTCHER
Unit 23, Abbey Business Centre, Ingate Place, **London SW8 3NS**
TEL 071 498 6981
OPEN 9.03–5 Mon–Fri.

Specialise in restoring Old Master, 19th century and Impressionist oil paintings.

PROVIDE Home Inspections. Free/Refundable Estimates. Free Collection/Delivery Service.
SPEAK TO D. C. Butcher.

SUSANNAH WATTS-RUSSELL
44 Lamont Road, **London SW10 0JA**
TEL 071 352 4508
OPEN By Appointment.

Specialise in restoring oil paintings.

PROVIDE Home Inspections. Free Estimates. Free Collection/Delivery Service.
SPEAK TO Susannah Watts-Russell.

SOPHIE WYSOCKA
2 Knights Studios, Hortensia Road, **London SW10 0QX**
TEL   071 352 0547
OPEN   By Appointment.

Specialise in restoring large paintings for private collections, schools and churches.

PROVIDE Home Inspections. Free Estimates.
SPEAK TO Mrs S. Wysocka.

Member of ABPR, UKIC and CAS.

BATES AND BASKCOMB
191 St John's Hill, **London SW11 1TH**
TEL   071 223 1629
OPEN   9.30–5.30 Mon–Fri and By Appointment.

Specialise in restoring works of art on paper, including prints, drawings, watercolours, gouaches, pastels, and photographs.

PROVIDE Local Home Inspections. Free/Chargeable Collection/Delivery Service.
SPEAK TO Debbie Bates or Camilla Baskcomb.

SEE Books.

HELEN DE BORCHGRAVE
Fine Art Restorer, 103 Albert Bridge Road, **London SW11 4PF**
TEL   071 738 1951
OPEN   By Appointment.

Specialise in cleaning, relining and restoring oil paintings on canvas, panel or board. Large or awkward paintings can be cleaned and restored on site.

PROVIDE Home Inspections. Free Local Estimates. Collection/Delivery Service.
SPEAK TO Helen de Borchgrave.

Member of UKIC, IIC and ABPR. This workshop is included on the register of conservators maintained by the

Conservation Unit of the Museums and Galleries Commission.
SEE Picture Frames.

REGENCY RESTORATIONS
Studio 21, Thames House, 140 Battersea Park Road, **London SW11**
TEL   071 622 5275
OPEN   9–6 Mon–Fri or By Appointment.

Specialise in restoring pictures.

PROVIDE Home Inspections. Free Estimates. Chargeable Collection/Delivery Service.
SPEAK TO Peter Curry or Elizabeth Ball.

SEE Picture Frames.

TREVOR CUMINE
133 Putney Bridge Road, **London SW15 2PA**
TEL   081 870 1525
OPEN   By Appointment.

Specialise in picture lining.
SPEAK TO Trevor Cumine.

SEE Picture Frames.

SHEILA FAIRBRASS
27 Dalebury Road, **London SW17 7HQ**
TEL   081 672 4606
OPEN   9–7 By Appointment Only.

Specialise in restoring works of art on paper; particularly 20th century art.

PROVIDE Free/Chargeable Estimates.
SPEAK TO Sheila Fairbrass.

Fellow of IIC. This workshop is included on the register of conservators maintained by the Conservation Unit of the Museums and Galleries Commission.

KEITH HOLMES
27 Dalebury Road, **London**
SW17 7HQ
TEL   081 672 4606
OPEN   8–8 Daily.

Specialise in restoring prints, drawings, watercolours, watercolours on silk.

PROVIDE Home Inspections. Free Estimates. Chargeable Local Collection/Delivery Service.
SPEAK TO Keith Holmes.

Member of IIC. This workshop is included on the register of conservators maintained by the Conservation Unit of the Museums and Galleries Commission.
SEE Books.

MAURICE E. KEEVIL
60 East Hill, **London SW18 2HQ**
TEL   081 874 5236
OPEN   By Appointment.

Specialise in restoring oil paintings, murals and ceiling paintings.

PROVIDE Home Inspections. Free Estimates.
Fellow of the IIC.

PH7 PAPER CONSERVATORS
Unit 210, The Business Village, 3–9 Broomhill Road, **London SW18 4JQ**
TEL   081 871 5075
FAX   081 877 1940
OPEN   9–5.30 Mon–Fri or By Appointment.

Specialise in restoring works of art on paper, including watercolours, prints, drawings.

PROVIDE Home Inspections. Free Estimates. Free Collection/Delivery Service.
SPEAK TO Victoria Pease.
Member of IPC, UKIC and IIC. This workshop is included on the register of conservators maintained by the

Conservation Unit of the Museums and Galleries Commission.
SEE Books.

PLOWDEN AND SMITH LTD
190 St Ann's Hill, **London SW18 2RT**
TEL   081 874 4005
FAX   081 874 7248
OPEN   9–5.30 Mon–Fri.

Specialise in conserving and restoring paintings.

PROVIDE Home Inspections. Free Estimates. Chargeable Collection/Delivery Service.
SPEAK TO Bob Butler.

They also advise on conservation strategy, environmental control and microclimates for collections as well as installing, mounting and displaying temporary and permanent exhibitions.
SEE Furniture, Porcelain, Silver.

R. M. S. SHEPHERD ASSOCIATES LTD
11 Berkley Place, **London SW19 4NN**
TEL   081 946 5293
FAX   081 946 5293
OPEN   9–6 Mon–Fri.

Specialise in restoring easel paintings.

PROVIDE Home Inspections. Free Estimates. Chargeable Collection/Delivery Service.
SPEAK TO Mr R. Shepherd.
Member of ABPR and a Fellow of the IIC.

HAMISH DEWAR
1st Floor, 9 Old Bond Street, **London W1X 3TA**
TEL   071 629 0317
FAX   071 493 6390
OPEN   9–6 Mon–Fri.

Specialise in conserving and restoring oil paintings.

PROVIDE Home Inspections.

Free/Refundable Estimates. Chargeable Collection/Delivery Service.
SPEAK TO Hamish Dewar.

HAHN AND SON LTD
47 Albemarle Street, **London W1X 3FE**
TEL   071 493 9196
OPEN   9.30–5.30 Mon–Fri.

Specialise in conserving and restoring oil paintings.

PROVIDE Home Inspections. Free Estimates. Free Collection/Delivery Service.
SPEAK TO Paul Hahn.

Established 1870.

CHRISTOPHER HARRAP
1st Floor, 26–27 Conduit Street, **London W1R 9TA**
TEL   071 499 1488
OPEN   9–5 Wed only.

Specialise in restoring and conserving watercolours, prints and drawings.

PROVIDE Free Estimates.
SPEAK TO Christopher Harrap.

Member of IPC.
SEE Picture Frames.

DAVID MESSUM
34 St George Street, Hanover Square, **London W1R 9FA**
TEL   071 408 0243
OPEN   9.30–5.30 Mon–Fri.

Specialise in restoring 18th century–modern day British paintings, particularly Impressionists.

PROVIDE Home Inspections. Chargeable Collection/Delivery Service.
SPEAK TO Carol Tee.

SEE Picture Frames.

PAUL MITCHELL LTD
99 New Bond Street, **London W1Y 9LF**
TEL   071 493 8732
FAX   071 409 7136
OPEN   9.30–5.30 Mon–Fri.

Specialise in the conservation and restoration of paintings.

PROVIDE Home Inspections. Free Estimates. Chargeable Collection/Delivery Service.
Member of BADA, the Guild of Master Craftsmen, ABPR and the IIC.
SPEAK TO Paul Mitchell.
SEE Picture Frames.

BOURLET
32 Connaught Street, **London W2 2AY**
TEL   071 724 4837
OPEN   11–5.30 Mon–Fri and most Sats.

Specialise in restoring oil paintings and watercolours.

PROVIDE Home Inspections. Free Estimates. Collection/Delivery Service.
SPEAK TO Gabrielle Rendell.
SEE Furniture, Picture Frames.

FENELLA HOWARD
14 Shaa Road, **London W3 7LN**
TEL   081 749 5656
OPEN   By Appointment.

Specialise in conserving and restoring 18th–20th century British and European oil paintings.

PROVIDE Home Inspections. Free Estimates. Chargeable Collection/Delivery Service.
SPEAK TO Fenella Howard.

R. A. BUCHANAN
3 Arlington Cottages, Sutton Lane, **London W4 4HB**
TEL   081 995 9780
OPEN   By Appointment.

Specialise in restoring works of art on

paper, prints, drawings, watercolours, pastels.

PROVIDE Home Inspections. Free Estimates. Chargeable Collection/Delivery Service. SPEAK TO R. A. Buchanan. Member of IPC.

THE CONSERVATION STUDIO

The Studio, 107 Shepherds Bush Road, **London W6 7LP**
TEL   071 602 0757 and 081 871 5075
OPEN   9–5 Mon–Fri.

Specialise in restoring items made from paper, including Old Master drawings, 18th–20th century British and European watercolours and prints as well as Oriental prints and watercolours. Posters, wallpaper screens and 19th and 20th century photographs are also repaired.

PROVIDE Home Inspections. Free Estimates. Chargeable Collection/Delivery Service. SPEAK TO Norma McCaw.

DR POPPY COOKSEY

Aston House, 8 Lower Mall, **London W6 9DJ**
TEL   081 846 9279
OPEN   By Appointment.

Specialise in cleaning and restoring oil paintings watercolours.

PROVIDE Home Inspections. Free Estimates in London. Chargeable Collection/Delivery Service. SPEAK TO Dr Poppy Cooksey. SEE Picture Frames.

CLAUDIO ASTROLOGO

59–61 Kensington High Street, **London W8 5ED**
TEL   071 937 7820
OPEN   By Appointment.

Specialise in restoring easel paintings, paintings on panels and icons.

PROVIDE Chargeable Estimates. SPEAK TO Claudio Astrologo. Member of IIC and UKIC. SEE Porcelain.

ANTHONY BELTON

14 Holland Street, **London W8 4LT**
TEL   071 937 1012
OPEN   10–1 Mon–Fri; 10–4.30 Sat.

Specialise in restoring paintings.

PROVIDE Home Inspections. SPEAK TO Anthony Belton. SEE Porcelain.

DAGGETT GALLERY

1st Floor, 153 Portobello Road, **London W11 2DY**
TEL   071 229 2248
FAX   071 584 2950
OPEN   10–4 Mon–Fri, please ring first, 9–4 Sat.

Specialise in restoring oil paintings, lining etc.

PROVIDE Home Inspections. Free/Chargeable Estimates. Chargeable Collection/Delivery Service. SPEAK TO Charles or Caroline Daggett. Member of LAPADA. SEE Picture Frames.

ROBERT O'RORKE

17 Lonsdale Road, **London W11 2BY**
TEL   071 229 2892
OPEN   10–5.30 Mon–Fri or By Appointment.

Specialise in restoring oil paintings and can also copy paintings.

PROVIDE Local Home Inspections. Free Estimates in studio. Free Local Collection/Delivery Service. SPEAK TO Robert O'Rorke. Associate of ABPR.

NICOLE RYDER
Studio 3, George And Dragon Hall, Mary Place, **London W11 4PL**
TEL 071 229 5855
OPEN 9–5.30 By Appointment.

Specialise in restoring easel paintings.

PROVIDE Home Inspections. Free Estimates. Free/Chargeable Collection/Delivery Service.
SPEAK TO Nicole Ryder.
Member of ABPR and UKIC. This workshop is included on the register of conservators maintained by the Conservation Unit of the Museums and Galleries Commission.

COUTTS GALLERIES
75 Blythe Road, **London W14 0HD**
TEL 071 602 3980
OPEN 10–5 Mon–Fri.

Specialise in restoration of pictures.

PROVIDE Home Inspections, Free Estimates, Free Collection/Delivery Service.
SPEAK TO Seabury Burdett-Coutts.
SEE Furniture, Picture Frames.

RICHARD JOSLIN
150 Addison Gardens, **London W14 0ER**
TEL 071 603 6435
OPEN By Appointment.

Specialise in restoration of oil paintings and watercolours.

PROVIDE Home Inspections, Chargeable Estimates, Chargeable Collection/Delivery Service.
SPEAK TO Richard Joslin.

DIANA REEVES
24 Applegarth Road, **London W14 0HY**
TEL 071 603 8603
OPEN 9–6 Mon–Fri and By Appointment.

Specialise in restoring oil paintings of all ages on canvas or panel.

PROVIDE Chargeable Home Inspections. Free/Chargeable Estimates. Chargeable Local Collection/Delivery Service.
SPEAK TO Diana Reeves.
Member of ABPR and Fellow of IIC. This workshop is included on the register of conservators maintained by the Conservation Unit of the Museums and Galleries Commission.

MS LIBBY SHELDON
UCL Painting Analysis Ltd, History of Art Department, University College London, 43 Gordon Square, **London WC1**
TEL 071 383 2090
OPEN 9.30–5.30 Mon–Fri By Appointment Only.

Specialise in restoring a limited number of small easel paintings. Their main business is the analysis of painting materials on paintings for dating or conservation purposes including pigment, cross-section analysis, x-ray, infra-red and u.v. photography.

PROVIDE Home Inspections. Free Estimates.
SPEAK TO Libby Sheldon or Catherine Hassall.
This workshop is included on the register of conservators maintained by the Conservation Unit of the Museums and Galleries Commission.

BLACKMAN HARVEY LTD
36 Great Queen Street, **London WC2B 5AA**
TEL 071 836 1904
FAX 071 404 5896
OPEN 9.30–6 Mon–Fri; 10–4 Sat.

Specialise in restoring works of art on paper and oil paintings on canvas and board.

PROVIDE Home Inspections. Free Estimates. Chargeable Collection/Delivery Service.

SPEAK TO R. M. Wooton Wooley
SEE Picture Frames.

HENRY DONN GALLERY
138–142 Bury New Road, Whitefield,
Greater Manchester M25 6AD
TEL　061 766 8819
OPEN　9.30–1, 2–5.15 Mon–Sat.

Specialise in restoring modern British oils.

PROVIDE Home Inspections. Chargeable Estimates. Chargeable Collection/Delivery Service.
SPEAK TO H. or N. Donn.

Mr Donn is Past Master of the FATG.

J. G. TREVOR-OWEN
181–193 Oldham Rd, Rochdale,
Greater Manchester OL16 5QZ
TEL　0706 48138
OPEN　1.30–7 Mon–Fri or By Appointment.

Specialise in restoring paintings.

PROVIDE Home Inspections. Refundable Estimates.
SPEAK TO J. G. Trevor-Owen.
SEE Clocks, Collectors (Musical Instruments), Furniture.

HARRIET OWEN HUGHES
41 Bluecoat Chambers, School Lane,
Liverpool, **Merseyside L1 3BX**
TEL　051 708 6808
OPEN　9.30–5 By Appointment Only.

Specialise in restoring easel paintings (16th–20th century) as well as contemporary paintings.

PROVIDE Home Inspections. Free Estimates. Chargeable Collection/Delivery Service.
SPEAK TO Harriet Owen Hughes.
Member of ABPR.

LYVER & BOYDELL GALLERIES
15 Castle Street, Liverpool, **Merseyside L2 4SX**
TEL　051 236 3256
OPEN　10.30–5.30 Mon–Fri; Sat By Appointment.

Specialise in restoring watercolours and prints.

PROVIDE Home Inspections. Free Estimates.
SPEAK TO Paul or Gill Breen.
SEE Books, Picture Frames.

PATRICIA GARNER PICTURE RESTORERS
55 Arragon Road, Twickenham,
Middlesex TW1 3NG
TEL　081 892 1819
FAX　081 891 0115
OPEN　8.30–5.30 Mon–Fri or By Appointment.

Specialise in restoring panel, modern or easel paintings. Work also includes technical examination of paintings.

PROVIDE Home Inspections. Chargeable Estimates. Free Collection/Delivery Service.
SPEAK TO Patricia Garner.

THE HAMPTON HILL GALLERY
203 & 205 High Street, Hampton Hill,
Middlesex TW12 1NP
TEL　081 977 5273
OPEN　9–5 Tues–Sat.

Specialise in restoring 18th–20th century watercolours, drawings and prints. Oil painting restoration is also undertaken.

PROVIDE Home Inspections. Free Estimates.
SPEAK TO Tony Wilson.

ANNE HORNE PAPER CONSERVATOR
36 Lebanon Park, Twickenham,
Middlesex TW1 3DG
TEL   081 892 0688
FAX   081 744 2177
OPEN   By Appointment Only.

Specialise in restoring prints, drawings and watercolours.

PROVIDE Local Home Inspections. Free Estimates. Free Local Collection/Delivery Service.
SPEAK TO Anne Horne.
SEE Books.

MARIA J. LESIAK
Leliwa, 71 St Anne's Avenue, Stanwell, Staines, **Middlesex TW19 7RL**
TEL   0784 257401
FAX   0784 257401
OPEN   By Appointment.

Specialise in restoring oil paintings on canvas, panel and metal plate.

PROVIDE Home Inspections. Free Estimates. Free Local Collection/Delivery Service.
SPEAK TO Maria J. Lesiak.
Member of UKIC and an Associate Member of ABPR. This workshop is included on the register of conservators maintained by the Conservation Unit of the Museums and Galleries Commission.
SEE Picture Frames, Furniture.

JOHN MALCOLM FINE ART RESTORATION
62 Linden Avenue, Ruislip, **Middlesex HA4 8UA**
TEL   0895 621616
OPEN   8.30–5 Mon–Fri or By Appointment.

Specialise in restoring oil paintings, works of art on paper and murals.

PROVIDE Home Inspections. Free Estimates. Free Collection/Delivery Service.

SPEAK TO John Malcolm.
SEE Picture Frames.

COLMORE GALLERIES
52 High Street, Henley–in–Arden, Solihull, **West Midlands B95 5AN**
TEL   0564 792938
OPEN   11–5.30 Mon–Fri; 11–4.30 Sat.

Specialise in restoring 19th and 20th century oils and watercolours.

PROVIDE Home Inspections. Refundable Estimates. Collection/Delivery Service available.
SPEAK TO B. D. Jones.
SEE Picture Frames.

BARBARA CONWAY
155 Whoberley Avenue, Chapelfields, Coventry, **West Midlands CV5 8FB**
TEL   0203 678986
OPEN   By Appointment.

Specialise in restoring and conserving prints, drawings and watercolours.

PROVIDE Home Inspections. Free Estimates. Free Collection/Delivery Service.
SPEAK TO Mrs Barbara Conway.
Member of IPC.

MOIRA TWIST
5 Percival Road, Edgbaston, Birmingham, **West Midlands B16 9SX**
TEL   021 429 8310
OPEN   By Appointment.

Specialise in conservation and restoration of oil paintings, mainly British 18th and 19th century, major European schools and modern contemporary work, including cleaning, varnish removal, restoration of paint loss. Work can be undertaken on site when necessary. Advice given on condition of paintings and long-term care of collections, detailed post-inspection reports on work and treatment recommended and full reports on work carried out.

PROVIDE Home Inspections. Free Estimates. Free Local Collection/Delivery Service.
SPEAK TO Moira Twist.
Member of IIC, UKIC and Associate Member of ABPR. This workshop is included on the register of conservators maintained by the Conservation Unit of the Museums and Galleries Commission.

THE BANK HOUSE GALLERY

71 Newmarket Road, Norwich, **Norfolk NR2 2HN**
TEL   0603 633380
FAX   0603 633387
OPEN   By Appointment.

Specialise in restoration of 18th and 19th century oil paintings and watercolours with emphasis on the Norfolk and Suffolk schools.

PROVIDE Home Inspections, Free Estimates, Free Collection/Delivery Service.
SPEAK TO Robert Mitchell.

Member of LAPADA.

PENNY LAWRENCE

Fairhurst Gallery, Bedford Street, Norwich, **Norfolk NR2 1AS**
TEL   0603 632064
OPEN   9–5 Mon–Fri.

Specialise in restoring and conserving oil paintings, watercolours and prints.

PROVIDE Home Inspections. Free Estimates. Free/Chargeable Collection/Delivery Service.
SPEAK TO Penny Lawrence.

This workshop is included on the register of conservators maintained by the Conservation Unit of the Museums and Galleries Commission.
SEE Furniture, Picture Frames, Silver.

LEON LIDDAMENT

St Seraphim's, Station Road, Little Walsingham, **Norfolk NR22 6DG**
TEL   0328 820610
OPEN   By Appointment.

Specialise in restoring icons.

PROVIDE Home Inspections. Free/Chargeable Estimates. Collection/Delivery Service by arrangement.
SPEAK TO Leon Liddament.

FRANK WASS

Cambridge Studio Workshop, Seafront, Cromer, **Norfolk NR27 9HD**
TEL   0263 512085
OPEN   By Appointment.

Specialise in restoring easel paintings (oil), panel or canvas. Comprehensive lining service.

PROVIDE Home Inspections. Free Estimates. Free Local Collection/Delivery Service.
SPEAK TO Frank or Michael Wass.
Member of ABPR.

WESTCLIFFE GALLERY AND ART FRAMES

2–8 Augusta Street, Sheringham, **Norfolk NR26 8LA**
TEL   0263 824320
OPEN   9.30–5.30 Mon–Sat. Closed Wed.

Specialise in oil, watercolour and print restoration.

PROVIDE Home Inspections. Free Estimates. Free/Chargeable Collection/Delivery Service.
SPEAK TO Richard Parks.
SEE Picture Frames.

BROADWAY FINE ART

61 Park Avenue South, Abington, Northampton, **Northamptonshire NN3 3AB**
TEL   0604 32011
OPEN   By Appointment.

Specialise in restoring oil paintings.

PROVIDE Home Inspections. Estimates. Collection/Delivery Service. All by arrangement.
SPEAK TO Michael Robinson.

SAVAGE FINE ART
Alfred Street, Northampton, **Northamptonshire NN1 5EY**
TEL   0604 20327
FAX   0604 27417
OPEN   9–5.15 Mon–Fri; 9–12.30 Sat.

Specialise in restoring oil paintings and 19th–20th century watercolours and prints.

PROVIDE Home Inspections. Free Estimates. Free Collection/Delivery Service.
SPEAK TO Michael Savage.

SEE Picture Frames.

FLORENCE CONSERVATION & RESTORATION
102 Nottingham Road, Long Eaton, Nottingham, **Nottinghamshire NG10 2BZ**
TEL   0602 733625
OPEN   8–5 Mon–Fri; 9–12 Sat.

Specialise in cleaning and restoring oil paintings, watercolours, pastels, drawings, prints and photographs.

PROVIDE Home Inspections. Refundable Estimates. Chargeable Collection/Delivery Service.
SPEAK TO Ron Florence.

SEE Furniture, Porcelain.

DIAN HALL
The Church House, Thrumpton, **Nottinghamshire NG11 0AX**
TEL   0602 830446
OPEN   9–6 Mon–Fri or By Appointment.

Specialise in restoring easel paintings, drawings and watercolours, pastels and miniatures, wall and ceiling paintings.

PROVIDE Home Inspections. Free Estimates. Free Collection/Delivery Service.
SPEAK TO Dian Hall.

Member of UKIC. This workshop is included on the register of conservators maintained by the Conservation Unit of the Museums and Galleries Commission.

BART LUCKHURST
The Gallery, 9 Union Street, Bingham, **Nottinghamshire NG13 8AD**
TEL   0949 837668
OPEN   9–5 Thur; 9–1 Sat or By Appointment.

Specialise in restoring oils and watercolours, relining and handmade stretcher bars. Also restore old photographs.

PROVIDE Home Inspections. Free Estimates. Collection/Delivery Service by arrangement.
SPEAK TO Bart Luckhurst.

Member of FATG.
SEE Picture Frames.

MARK ROBERTS
1 West Workshops, Tan Gallop, Welbeck, Nr. Worksop, **Nottinghamshire S80 3LW**
TEL   0909 484270
OPEN   By Appointment.

Specialise in conserving and restoring European easel paintings.

PROVIDE Home Inspections. Refundable Estimates. Chargeable Collection/Delivery Service.
SPEAK TO Mark or Diana Roberts.

SEE Picture Frames.

ARTHUR AND ANN RODGERS
7 Church Street, Ruddington,
Nottingham, **Nottinghamshire
NG11 6HA**
TEL   0602 216214
OPEN   9–5 Tues, Wed; 9–1 Thur, Fri;
        9–5 Sat.

Specialise in hand-colouring, cleaning, restoring and repairing prints and paintings.

PROVIDE Home Inspections. Chargeable Estimates. Free Collection/Delivery Service.
SPEAK TO Arthur Rodgers.
SEE Books.

BARBARA BIBB
149 Kingston Road, Oxford,
Oxfordshire OX2 6RP
TEL   0865 56444
OPEN   9–5 Mon–Sat.

Specialise in restoring oil and easel paintings.

PROVIDE Home Inspections. Free Estimates. Free Local Collection/Delivery Service.
SPEAK TO Barbara Bibb.

Member of ABPR. This workshop is included on the register of conservators maintained by the Conservation Unit of the Museums and Galleries Commission.
SEE Furniture.

RUTH E. BUBB, CONSERVATION OF PAINTINGS
Poplars Farmhouse, 63 Main Road,
Banbury, **Oxfordshire OX17 2LU**
TEL   0295 710213
OPEN   By Appointment Only.

Specialise in restoring easel paintings on canvas and solid supports of all periods. Also offer surveys of collections and condition reports. All work is fully documented.

PROVIDE Home Inspections. Free Estimates. Chargeable Collection/Delivery Service.
SPEAK TO Ruth Bubb.

Associate Member of UKIC and ABPR. This workshop is included on the register of conservators maintained by the Conservation Unit of the Museums and Galleries Commission.

ANNA HULBERT
1 The Green, Childrey, Wantage,
Oxfordshire OX12 9UG
TEL   023559 602
OPEN   By Appointment. It is best to
        write first of all.

Specialise in restoring Mediaeval panel paintings, wall paintings, architectural polychromy, including painted stone. Also 17th century wall paintings. Will work on site if required.

PROVIDE Home Inspections. Chargeable Estimates.
SPEAK TO Anna Hulbert.

Member of ABPR. This workshop is included on the register of conservators maintained by the Conservation Unit of the Museums and Galleries Commission.

OXFORD CONSERVATIONS
Underwood, Jack Straw's Lane, Oxford,
Oxfordshire OX3 0DN
TEL   0865 62614
FAX   0865 750311
OPEN   By Appointment Only.

Specialise in restoring paintings and can provide technical analysis, surveys, condition reports and other documentation and advice on exhibition, transport and storage.

PROVIDE Home Inspections. Free Estimates. Chargeable Collection/Delivery Service.
SPEAK TO Candy Kuhl, Chief Conservator.

Member of UKIC and IIC, Associate Member of ABPR. This workshop is included on the register of conservators maintained by the Conservation Unit of the Museums and Galleries Commission. SEE Picture Frames, Porcelain.

DIANNE BRITTON AND GRAEME STOREY

The Grange, Maesbrook, Oswestry, **Shropshire SY10 8QP**
TEL   069185 260
OPEN   By Appointment.

Specialise in restoring works on paper, oil paintings. Specialists in on-site work.

PROVIDE Home Inspections. Chargeable Estimates. Chargeable Collection/Delivery Service.
SPEAK TO Dianne Britton or Graeme Storey.
Member of IIC, IPC and UKIC. This workshop is included on the register of conservators maintained by the Conservation Unit of the Museums and Galleries Commission.

MAUREEN A. BURD

Station House, Church Stretton, **Shropshire SY6 6AX**
TEL   0694 722057
OPEN   By Appointment.

Specialise in restoring and conserving prints, drawings, watercolours, easel paintings, pastels.

PROVIDE Home Inspections. Free/Chargeable Estimates. Collection/Delivery Service by arrangement.
SPEAK TO Mrs Maureen Burd.
Member of IPC and IIC.

JULIET MARGUERITE CELIA GIBBS

The Old Vicarage, Stanton-Upon-Hine Heath, Shrewsbury, **Shropshire SY4 4LR**
TEL   0939 250881
OPEN   9–5 Mon–Fri or By Appointment.

Specialise in restoring easel paintings, lining, blister laying, transfers, cleaning.

PROVIDE Home Inspections. Free Estimates. Collection/Delivery Service.
SPEAK TO Juliet Gibbs.

Established sixteen years. This workshop is included on the register of conservators maintained by the Conservation Unit of the Museums and Galleries Commission.

OLIVIA RUMENS

30 Corve Street, Ludlow, **Shropshire SY8 1DN**
TEL   0584 87 3952
OPEN   10–5 Mon–Sat; closed Thur.

Specialise in conserving and restoring oil paintings.

PROVIDE Home Inspections. Free Estimates.
SPEAK TO Olivia Rumens.
Member of IIC.

NICK COTTON FINE ART

Beachstone House, 46/47 Swain Street, Watchet, **Somerset TA23 0AG**
TEL   0984 31814
OPEN   10–6 Mon–Sat.

Specialise in restoring and conserving paintings, watercolours and drawings from the period 1850–1991.

PROVIDE Home Inspections. Refundable Estimates. Chargeable Collection/Delivery Service.
SPEAK TO Nick Cotton.

TIM EVERETT

Pitminster Studio, Taunton, **Somerset TA3 7AZ**
TEL   0823 42710
OPEN   By Appointment.

Specialise in conservation and restoration of oil paintings on canvas and panel. Also paper restoration.

PROVIDE Home Inspections. Free
Estimates. Free Collection/Delivery
Service.
SPEAK TO Tim Everett.
This workshop is included on the register
of conservators maintained by the
Conservation Unit of the Museums and
Galleries Commission.
SEE Picture Frames.

THE ANTIQUE RESTORATION STUDIO

The Old Post Office, Haughton,
Staffordshire ST18 9JH
TEL   0785 780424
FAX   0785 780157
OPEN   9–5 Mon–Fri.

Specialise in restoring antique and
modern paintings.

PROVIDE Home Inspections. Free
Estimates. Free Collection/Delivery
Service.
SPEAK TO D. P. Albright.
SEE Carpets, Furniture, Porcelain.

VICTORIA DES BEAUX ARTS LTD

11 Newcastle Street, Burslem, Stoke-on-
Trent, **Staffordshire ST6 3QB**
TEL   0782 836490
OPEN   9–5.30 Mon–Sat.

Specialise in cleaning and restoring
17th–19th century oil paintings.

PROVIDE Home Inspections.
Free/Chargeable Estimates. Free
Collection/Delivery Service.
SPEAK TO Mrs Bryden.
SEE Picture Frames.

ROGER & SYLVIA ALLAN

The Old Red Lion, Bedingfield, Eye,
Suffolk IP23 7LQ
TEL   0728 76 491
OPEN   By Appointment.

Specialise in restoring oil paintings on
panel or canvas and miniatures.

PROVIDE Home Inspections. Free
Estimates.
SPEAK TO Roger Allan.
SEE Furniture, Silver.

MICHAEL BRIAN BECKHAM

Chilton Mount, Newton Road, Sudbury,
Suffolk CO10 6RN
TEL   0787 73683 or 73610
OPEN   By Appointment.

Specialise in restoration and
conservation of drawings, watercolours
and prints.

PROVIDE Home Inspections.
Free/Chargeable Estimates. Chargeable
Collection/Delivery Service.
SPEAK TO Michael Beckham.
Member of IPC, SSCR and UKIC.
SEE Books.

PHILIPPA ELLISON

Fords Farm, Winston, Nr. Stowmarket,
Suffolk IP14 6BD
TEL   0728 860572
OPEN   9–5 Mon–Fri.

Specialise in restoring works of art on
paper. Advice on general care available.

PROVIDE Home Inspections. Free
Estimates. Collection/Delivery Service.
SPEAK TO Philippa Ellison.
Member of IPC. This workshop is
included on the register of conservators
maintained by the Conservation Unit of
the Museums and Galleries Commission.
SEE Books, Picture Frames.

JOHN GAZELEY ASSOCIATES FINE ART

17 Fonnereau Road, Ipswich, **Suffolk
IP1 3JR**
TEL   0473 252420
OPEN   By Appointment.

Specialise in cleaning, relining and
restoring oil paintings, particularly 17th
and 18th century English portraits.

PROVIDE Free Estimates.
SPEAK TO Dr John Gazeley.

SEE Furniture, Picture Frames.

CHARLES W. P. KEYES
6 Moores Close, Debenham,
Stowmarket, **Suffolk IP14 6RU**
TEL   0728 860624
OPEN   By Appointment.

Specialise in restoration of watercolours
and prints.

PROVIDE Home Inspections. Free
Estimates. Chargeable
Collection/Delivery Service.
SPEAK TO Charles Keyes.
Member of IPC.
SEE Books.

JANE McAUSLAND
Nether Hall Barn, Old Newton,
Stowmarket, **Suffolk IP14 4PP**
TEL   0449 673571
FAX   0449 770689
OPEN   9–6 Mon–Fri.

Specialise in restoring and conserving all
items considered to be art on paper. This
includes prints, drawings, watercolours,
pastels and artist photographs. All work
is carried out in a fully equipped, secure
studio. They also give advice on
preventative conservation for collections
and have a consultancy service one day a
week at 41 Lexington Street, London
W1R 3LG.
TEL   071 437 1070.

PROVIDE Home Inspections. Free
Estimates. Free Local
Collection/Delivery Service.
SPEAK TO Jane McAusland.

Fellow of the IIC, Founder Member of
IPC, member of UKIC and the AIC.
This workshop is included on the register
of conservators maintained by the
Conservation Unit of the Museums and
Galleries Commission.

NORTHWOLD GALLERY
206 High Street, Newmarket, **Suffolk
CB8 9AP**
TEL   0638 668758
OPEN   10–5 Mon–Sat; closed Wed.

Specialise in restoring watercolours and
prints.

PROVIDE Home Inspections. Free
Estimates. Free Collection/Delivery
Service.
SPEAK TO C. G. Troman.

SEE Picture Frames.

PEASENHALL ART &
ANTIQUES GALLERY
Peasenhall, Nr. Saxmundham, **Suffolk
IP17 2HJ**
TEL   072 879 224
OPEN   9–6 Daily.

Specialise in cleaning and restoring oils,
watercolours and prints.

PROVIDE Local Home Inspections. Free
Estimates. Free Local
Collection/Delivery Service.
SPEAK TO Mike Wickins.
SEE Furniture.

BOURNE GALLERY
LIMITED
31–33 Lesbourne Street, Reigate,
Surrey RH2 7JS
TEL   0737 241614
OPEN   10–1, 2–5.30 Mon–Sat; 10–1
          Wed.

Specialise in restoring 19th and 20th
century oil paintings.

PROVIDE Home Inspections. Free
Estimates. Collection/Delivery Service
by arrangement.
SPEAK TO John Robertson.

J. H. COOK AND SON LTD
Station Avenue, Kew, **Surrey TW9 3QA**
TEL   081 948 5644
OPEN   9.30–5.30 Mon–Fri.

Specialise in restoring oil paintings.

PROVIDE Home Inspections. Free
Estimates. Free Collection/Delivery
Service.
SPEAK TO Mr Robinson.
Member of ABPR.

S. A. ESDAILE
69 Farley Road, Selsdon, South
Croydon, **Surrey CR2 7NG**
TEL   081 657 6708
OPEN   By Appointment.

Specialise in restoring works of art on
paper, European and Oriental prints,
drawings in different media,
watercolours, ephemera on paper,
posters. Surveys of collections
undertaken.

PROVIDE Home Inspections. Free
Estimates. Free Local
Collection/Delivery Service.
SPEAK TO Sally Esdaile.
Member of IIC, UKIC, IPC. This
workshop is included on the register of
conservators maintained by the
Conservation Unit of the Museums and
Galleries Commission.

KING'S COURT GALLERIES
54 West Street, Dorking, **Surrey
RH4 1BS**
TEL   0306 881757
FAX   0306 75305
OPEN   9.30–5.30 Mon–Sat.

Specialise in paper conservation and
restoration, including engravings,
decorative and sporting prints.

PROVIDE Home Inspections. Free
Estimates.
SPEAK TO Mrs J. Joel.
SEE Books.

LIMPSFIELD WATERCOLOURS
High Street, Limpsfield, **Surrey**
TEL   0883 717010 and 722205
OPEN   11–3 Tues; 9.30–2 Thur–Sat.

Specialise in conserving, cleaning and
restoring prints and watercolours.

PROVIDE Local Home Inspections,
Refundable Estimates.
SPEAK TO Christine Reason.

SEE Picture Frames.

JACK MAY
'Beukenhof', Hogs Back, Guildford,
Surrey GU3 1DD
TEL   0483 570615
OPEN   All hours except Sunday.

Specialise in restoring watercolours and
prints. Also advise on presentation.

PROVIDE Home Inspections by
arrangement. Free Estimates. Free Local
Collection/Delivery Service.
SPEAK TO Jack May.

SEE Picture Frames.

PETER NEWMAN RESTORER LTD
The Studio, Newmans Lane, Surbiton,
Surrey KT6 4QQ
TEL   081 390 8672
OPEN   9.30–6 Mon–Fri.

Specialise in restoring Old Masters and
contemporary oil paintings. Specialist in
lining and panel work.

PROVIDE Home Inspections. Free
Estimates. Chargeable
Collection/Delivery Service.
SPEAK TO Peter Newman.

Member of ABPR.

HILARY PINDER
1st Floor, St Kilda, The Hermitage, Richmond, **Surrey TW10 6SH**
TEL   081 948 4426
OPEN   10–7 Daily.

Specialise in restoring icons and paintings.

PROVIDE Home Inspections. Free Estimates. Free Collection/Delivery Service.
SPEAK TO Hilary Pinder.
Member of IIC and ABPR. This workshop is included on the register of conservators maintained by the Conservation Unit of the Museums and Galleries Commission.

CHARLES RAKE
7 Avonmore Avenue, Guildford, **Surrey GU1 1TW**
TEL   0483 37211
OPEN   8.30–6.30 Mon–Sat.

Specialise in complete cleaning and restoration of oil paintings on canvas and panel.

PROVIDE Home Inspections. Free Estimates. Free Collection/Delivery Service.
SPEAK TO Charles Rake.
This workshop is included on the register of conservators maintained by the Conservation Unit of the Museums and Galleries Commission.

SAGE ANTIQUES & INTERIORS
High Street, Ripley, **Surrey GU23 6BB**
TEL   0483 224396
FAX   0483 211996
OPEN   9.30–5.30 Mon–Sat.

Specialise in restoring oil paintings and watercolours.

PROVIDE Free Estimates. Free Collection/Delivery Service.
SPEAK TO Howard or Chrissie Sage.

Member of LAPADA and the Guild of Master Craftsmen.
SEE Porcelain, Furniture.

S. & S. PICTURE RESTORATION STUDIOS
The Rookery, Frensham, Farnham, **Surrey GU10 3DU**
TEL   025 125 3673
OPEN   10–6 Mon–Fri.

Specialise in restoring oil paintings, watercolours and prints of all periods.

PROVIDE Home Inspections. Free/Chargeable Estimates. Collection/Delivery Service by arrangement.
SPEAK TO Roy Skelton.

R. SAUNDERS
71 Queens Road, Weybridge, **Surrey KT13 9UQ**
TEL   0932 842601
OPEN   9.15–5 Mon–Sat; closed Wed.

Specialise in cleaning and restoring oil paintings and watercolours.

PROVIDE Home Inspections. Free Estimates. Free Collection/Delivery Service.
SPEAK TO J. B. Tonkinson.
SEE Furniture, Porcelain, Silver.

JULIAN SPENCER-SMITH
The Studio, 30A College Road, Woking, **Surrey GU22 8BU**
TEL   0483 726070
OPEN   9–1, 2–5 Mon–Fri.

Specialise in all aspects of conservation work to oil paintings such as their own lining and panel work etc.

PROVIDE Home Inspections. Free Estimates. Free Collection/Delivery Service.
SPEAK TO Julian Spencer–Smith.
Member of ABPR.

THE CONSERVATION WORKSHOP
6 Green Man Yard, Boreham Street,
Nr. Herstmonceaux, **East Sussex
BN27 4SF**
TEL   0323 833842
OPEN   9.30–6 Mon–Fri or By
Appointment.

Specialise in conserving works of art on
paper, photographs, modern media.
They run workshops on paper and
photographic conservation.

PROVIDE Home Inspections. Free
Estimates. Free Local
Collection/Delivery Service.
SPEAK TO Ian Maver or Corinne Hillman.
Member of IPC, UKIC, Royal
Photographic Society, Society of
Archivists and Wallpaper History Society.
This workshop is included on the register
of conservators maintained by the
Conservation Unit of the Museums and
Galleries Commission.
SEE Books.

JOHN DAY OF EASTBOURNE FINE ART
9 Meads Street, Eastbourne, **East Sussex
BN20 7QY**
TEL   0323 25634
OPEN   10–5 Mon, Tues, Thur, Fri.

Specialise in cleaning, restoring and
relining oil paintings, particularly East
Anglian and Victorian Schools.

PROVIDE Home Inspections. Free
Estimates. Chargeable
Collection/Delivery Service.
SPEAK TO John Day.

FIRELEAD LTD
Banff Farm, Upper Clayhill, Uckfield
Road, Ringmer, Lewes, **East Sussex
BN8 5RR**
TEL   0273 890918
FAX   0273 890691
OPEN   8–5.30 Mon–Fri By
Appointment.

Specialise in restoring oil paintings and
watercolours.

PROVIDE Local Home Inspections. Local
Free Estimates. Chargeable
Collection/Delivery Service.
SPEAK TO David Gilbert.

SEE Furniture.

E. R. KINANE
R & K Enterprises, Old Brewery Centre,
Old Brewery Yard, High Street, Hastings,
East Sussex TN34 3ER
TEL   0424 446431 or 439261
OPEN   9–4 Mon–Fri, 10–1 Sat or By
Appointment.

Specialise in restoring easel paintings
and murals.

PROVIDE Home Inspections. Free
Estimates. Free Collection/Delivery
Service.
SPEAK TO E. R. Kinane.

Associate Member of IIC, UKIC and
ABPR. This workshop is included on the
register of conservators maintained by
the Conservation Unit of the Museums
and Galleries Commission.

MICHAEL LESLIE FINE ARTS
The Garden Studio, Denniker Cottage,
Fletching, Nr. Uckfield, **East Sussex
TN22 3SH**
TEL   0825 724176
FAX   0825 768410
OPEN   By Appointment.

Specialise in restoring all easel paintings
from mediaeval to 20th century. Also
large-scale paintings, if necessary on
location. They also specialise in fire and
water damaged pictures.

PROVIDE Home Inspections. Free
Estimates. Free Local
Collection/Delivery Service.
SPEAK TO Michael Leslie.

G. MURRAY-BROWN PICTURE SERVICES
Silverbeach House, Norman Road,
Pevensey Bay, **East Sussex BN24 6JR**
TEL   0323 764298
OPEN   By Appointment.

Specialise in restoring oil and
watercolour paintings and old prints.

PROVIDE Home Inspections. Free
Estimates. Collection/Delivery Service.
SPEAK TO Geoffrey Murray-Brown.
SEE Furniture, Picture Frames.

SOUTH EAST CONSERVATION CENTRE
5 North Street, St Leonards-on-Sea, **East
Sussex TN38 0EY**
TEL   0424 431157
FAX   0424 431807
OPEN   9–5 Mon–Fri or By
        Appointment.

Specialise in restoring fine oil paintings
on canvas or panel, gilding.

PROVIDE Home Inspections. Free
Estimates. Chargeable
Collection/Delivery Service.
SPEAK TO Rupert Smith.

This workshop is included on the register
of conservators maintained by the
Conservation Unit of the Museums and
Galleries Commission.

STEWART GALLERY
48 Devonshire Road, Bexhill-on-Sea,
East Sussex TN40 1AX
TEL   0424 223410
FAX   0323 29588
OPEN   9–5.30 Mon–Sat.

Specialise in restoring 19th and 20th
century oil paintings and watercolours.

PROVIDE Home Inspections. Free
Estimates. Free Collection/Delivery
Service.
SPEAK TO Mrs L. Knight.

STEWART GALLERY
25 Grove Road, Eastbourne, **East
Sussex BN20 4TT**
TEL   0323 29588
FAX   0323 29588
OPEN   9–5.30 Mon–Fri; 11–4 Sat.

Specialise in restoring 19th and 20th
century oil paintings and watercolours.

PROVIDE Home Inspections. Free
Estimates. Free Collection/Delivery
Service.
SPEAK TO S. A. Ettinger.

ANNETTS (HORSHAM) LTD
7B Carfax, Horsham, **West Sussex
RH12 1DW**
TEL   0403 65878
OPEN   9–5.30 Mon–Sat.

Specialise in restoring oil paintings.

PROVIDE Free Estimates.
SPEAK TO M. W. Annetts.
SEE Picture Frames.

NATALIE COPELAND
39 Fairlea Close, Burgess Hill, **West
Sussex RH15 8NW**
TEL   0444 248976
OPEN   9.30–5.30 Mon–Fri or By
        Appointment.

Specialise in conserving and restoring
works of art on paper. Also do surveys of
collections, give advice on storage
mounting and framing and will give free
written estimates detailing condition and
work to be carried out backed up by
photographic documentation.

PROVIDE Home Inspections. Free
Estimates. Free Local
Collection/Delivery Service.
SPEAK TO Mrs Natalie Copeland.

Member of IPC, ABPR and the American
Institute of Conservation, Mrs
Copeland is a Visiting Lecturer at
Camberwell College of Art.
This workshop is included on the register

of conservators maintained by the Conservation Unit of the Museums and Galleries Commission.

JENNIFER RIDD
White Cat Cottage, Birch Grove, Horsted Keynes, **West Sussex RH17 7BU**
TEL   0825 740559
OPEN   9–6.30 Mon–Sat, By
         Appointment.

Specialise in restoring fine oil or tempera paintings on a variety of supports, usually of canvas, wood or copper.

PROVIDE Home Inspections. Free Estimates. Free/Chargeable Collection/Delivery Service.
SPEAK TO Mrs Ridd.
Member of ABPR.

RPM RESTORATIONS
7 Hurst Close, Amberley, **West Sussex BN18 9NX**
TEL   0798 831845
OPEN   By Appointment.

Specialise in paper conservation and restoring watercolours, drawings and prints.

PROVIDE Home Inspections. Free Estimates. Free Collection/Delivery Service.
SPEAK TO James Jacob.

SURREY PRINT WATERCOLOUR CLEANING COMPANY
Mockingbird, Spy Lane, Loxwood, **West Sussex RH14 0SS**
TEL   0403 752097
OPEN   By Appointment.

Specialise in cleaning and restoring of works of art on paper, particularly watercolours and prints.

PROVIDE Free Estimates. Chargeable Collection/Delivery Service.
SPEAK TO Ken Downs.

SUSSEX CONSERVATION STUDIO
'Hill Bank', Broad Street, Cuckfield, **West Sussex RH17 5DX**
TEL   0444 451964
OPEN   8.30–5.30 Mon–Fri or By
         Appointment.

Specialise in restoring all types of works of art on paper, including prints, drawings, pastels, watercolours, etc. Cleaning, relining, repair work and retouching are all carried out to conservation standards using up-to-date techniques.

PROVIDE Free Estimates. Home Inspections by arrangement. Free Local Collection/Delivery Service.
SPEAK TO Reginald or Bernadette Selous.
Member of IPC. This workshop is included on the register of conservators maintained by the Conservation Unit of the Museums and Galleries Commission.
SEE Books.

JUTTA DIXON
St Thomas Street Workshops, St Thomas Street, Newcastle-upon-Tyne, **Tyne & Wear NE1 4LE**
TEL   091 232 4895 ext. 212
OPEN   9–5 Mon–Fri or By
         Appointment.

Specialise in restoration and conservation of watercolours, prints and drawings.

PROVIDE Home Inspections. Free Estimates.
SPEAK TO Jutta Dixon.
Member of IPC. This workshop is included on the register of conservators maintained by the Conservation Unit of the Museums and Galleries Commission.
SEE Picture Frames.

MACDONALD FINE ART
2 Ashburton Road, Gosforth, **Tyne & Wear NE3 4XN**
TEL   091 285 6188 or 284 4214
OPEN   10–1, 2.30–5.30 Mon–Sat;
            closed Wed.

Specialise in framing and restoring Victorian watercolours and oil paintings.

PROVIDE Free Estimates. Free Collection/Delivery Service.
SPEAK TO Tom MacDonald.

OSBORNE ART & ANTIQUES
18C Osborne Road, Jesmond, Newcastle-upon-Tyne, **Tyne & Wear NE2 2AD**
TEL   091 281 6380

Specialise in restoring oil paintings, watercolours and conserving paper.

PROVIDE Home Inspections. Free Collection/Delivery Service.
SPEAK TO S. Jackman.
Member of FATG.

D. M. BEACH
52 High Street, Salisbury, **Wiltshire SP1 2PG**
TEL   0722 333801
OPEN   9–5.30 Mon–Sat.

Specialise in restoring oils, watercolours and prints.

PROVIDE Home Inspections. Free Estimates. Free Local Collection/Delivery Service.
SPEAK TO Anthony Beach.
SEE Books.

CHARLES BOOTH-JONES
Fox Conservation Studio, Hill Barn, Monkton Deverill, Warminster, **Wiltshire BA12 7EY**
TEL   0985 844479
OPEN   By Appointment.

Specialise in restoring fine oil paintings of all periods.

PROVIDE Home Inspections. Free Estimates. Chargeable Collection/Delivery Service.
SPEAK TO Charles Booth–Jones.
This workshop is included on the register of conservators maintained by the Conservation Unit of the Museums and Galleries Commission.

BOOTH'S ANTIQUE MAPS AND PRINTS
30 Edenvale Road, Westbury, **Wiltshire BA13 3NY**
TEL   0373 823271
FAX   0373 858185
OPEN   By Appointment.

Specialise in restoring antique prints.

PROVIDE Home Inspections. Chargeable Collection/Delivery Service.
SPEAK TO John Booth.

Mr Booth is FRSA.
SEE Books.

ANDREW FANE
Thistle Cottage, Great Bedwyn, Nr. Marlborough, **Wiltshire SN8 3LH**
TEL   0672 870549
OPEN   8.30–5.30 Mon–Fri or By
            Appointment.

Specialise in restoring watercolours, pastels, prints, drawings, posters.

PROVIDE Home Inspections. Free Estimates. Free/Chargeable Collection/Delivery Service.
SPEAK TO Andrew Fane.

Member of IPC.
This workshop is included on the register of conservators maintained by the Conservation Unit of the Museums and Galleries Commission.
SEE Books.

LANTERN GALLERY
Hazeland House, Kington St Michael,
Chippenham, **Wiltshire SN14 6JJ**
TEL   0249 750306
FAX   0249 758896
OPEN   9–4 Mon–Fri or By
        Appointment.

Specialise in restoring prints,
watercolours and oil paintings.

PROVIDE Home Inspections. Free
Estimates. Free Collection/Delivery
Service.
SPEAK TO Anne Campbell Macinnes.
Member of BADA.
SEE Picture Frames, Porcelain.

RESTORATIONS UNLIMITED
Pinkney Park, Malmesbury, **Wiltshire
SN16 0NX**
TEL   0666 840888
OPEN   9–12.30, 1.30–5 Mon–Fri;
        9.30–12 Sat.

Specialise in restoring oil paintings and
watercolours.

PROVIDE Home Inspections. Free
Estimates. Free Collection/Delivery
Service.
SPEAK TO David Ellis.

SEE Furniture, Porcelain, Clocks.

WINSTANLEY SALISBURY BOOKBINDERS
213 Devizes Road, Salisbury, **Wiltshire
SP2 9LT**
TEL   0722 334998
OPEN   8.30–5.30 Mon–Fri.

Specialise in restoring prints and paper
conservation.

PROVIDE Free Estimates.
Collection/Delivery Service
SPEAK TO Alan Winstanley.

SEE Books.

SARAH WITHERLOW
Pinhills Farm, Bowood Estate, Calne,
Wiltshire SN11 0LY
TEL   0249 816848
FAX   0249 821174
OPEN   9–6 Mon–Sat.

Specialise in restoring Old Master
paintings and panels, oil on paper.

PROVIDE Home Inspections. Free
Estimates. Free/Chargeable
Collection/Delivery Service.
SPEAK TO Sarah Witherlow.

Member of ABPR.

AMELIA RAMPTON
29 Portland Street, York, **North
Yorkshire YO3 7EH**
TEL   0904 628048
OPEN   9–5 Mon–Fri.

Specialise in restoring prints, drawings
and watercolours.

PROVIDE Home Inspections. Free
Estimates. Free Collection/Delivery
Service.
SPEAK TO Amelia Rampton.

This workshop is included on the register
of conservators maintained by the
Conservation Unit of the Museums and
Galleries Commission.
SEE Books.

FRANCIS W. DOWNING
Winlayton Cottage, 203 Wetherby Road,
Harrogate, **North Yorkshire
HG2 7AE**
TEL   0423 886962
OPEN   10–5 Mon–Fri or By
        Appointment.

Specialise in conserving and restoring
oil and tempera paintings. Also
authenticity investigations.

PROVIDE Home Inspections. Free
Estimates. Free Collection/Delivery
Service.
SPEAK TO Francis Downing.

This workshop is included on the register of conservators maintained by the Conservation Unit of the Museums and Galleries Commission.

KIRKGATE PICTURE GALLERY
18 Kirkgate, Thirsk, **North Yorkshire YO7 1PQ**
TEL   0845 524085
OPEN   10–1, 2–5 Mon, Thur, Sat or By Appointment.

Specialise in restoring and conserving oil paintings.

PROVIDE Chargeable Estimates. Collection/Delivery Service by arrangement.
SPEAK TO Richard Bennett.

Member of ABPR.
SEE Picture Frames.

THE DAVIE GALLERY
8 Castlegate, Tickhill, Doncaster, **South Yorkshire DN11 9QU**
TEL   0302 751199
OPEN   9.30–5 Mon–Sat; closed Wed.

Specialise in conserving and restoring works of art on canvas and paper.

PROVIDE Home Inspections. Free Estimates. Free Collection/Delivery Service.
SPEAK TO Ian Davie.

Member of FATG.
SEE Picture Frames, Carpets.

GERRY TOMLINSON MEMORABILIA
Booth's Yard, Pudsey, **West Yorkshire**
TEL   0532 563653
OPEN   9.30–5 Mon–Sat.

Specialise in restoring sepia photographs.

PROVIDE Home Inspections. Free Collection/Delivery Service.
SPEAK TO Gerry Tomlinson.

PHYLLIS ARNOLD GALLERY ANTIQUES
Hoops Courtyard, Greyabbey, **Co. Down BT22 2NE**
TEL   024774 8199 or 0247 853322 (answerphone)
OPEN   11–5 Wed–Sat.

Specialise in restoring watercolours and portrait miniatures.

PROVIDE Free Estimates. Collection/Delivery Service by arrangement.
SPEAK TO Phyllis Arnold.
Member of the Royal Society of Miniature Painters.
SEE Picture Frames.

BARBARA BEST
9 Acton Road, Poyntzpass, Newry, **Co. Down BT35 6TB**
TEL   0762 86727
OPEN   By Appointment.

Specialise in conserving oil paintings.

PROVIDE Home Inspections. Free Estimates. Chargeable Collection/Delivery Service.
SPEAK TO Barbara Best. Member of IPCRA.
SEE Picture Frames.

KIERAN CULLIVAN
25 Cathedral Road, Cavan, **Co. Cavan**
TEL   049 31254
OPEN   By Appointment.

Specialise in restoring oil paintings on canvas.

PROVIDE Home Inspections. Free Estimates. Collection/Delivery Service by arrangement.
SPEAK TO Kieran Cullivan

Member of IPCRA.

SERGIO BENEDETTI
National Gallery of Ireland, Merrion Square West, Dublin 2, **Co. Dublin**
TEL　　01 615133
OPEN　By Appointment.

Specialise in restoring and conserving oil paintings.

PROVIDE Free/Chargeable Estimates.
SPEAK TO Sergio Benedetti.

SUSAN CORR
Paper Conservation Studio, 48 Woodley Park, Dundrum, Dublin 14, **Co. Dublin**
TEL　　01 2987661
OPEN　By Appointment.

Specialise in conservation of watercolours, prints, drawings and pastels.

PROVIDE Home Inspections. Free Estimates. Collection/Delivery Service by arrangement.
SPEAK TO Susan Corr.

Member of IPCRA and IPC.
SEE Books.

JAMES A. GORRY
20 Molesworth Street, Dublin 2, **Co. Dublin**
TEL　　01 6795319
OPEN　10–6 Mon–Fri.

Specialise in restoring oil paintings.

PROVIDE Home Inspections.
SPEAK TO James Gorry.
SEE Picture Frames.

STELLA HARTE
94 Martin's Row, Chapelizod, Dublin 20, **Co. Dublin**
TEL　　01 6266127
OPEN　By Appointment.

Specialise in restoring oil paintings on canvas.

PROVIDE Home Inspections. Free Estimates. Free Collection/Delivery Service.
SPEAK TO Stella Harte.
Member of IPCRA.

ROLAND HULME-BEAMAN
30 Leeson Park Avenue, Dublin 6, **Co. Dublin**
TEL　　01 604850
OPEN　By Appointment.

Specialise in restoring easel paintings, mainly Irish, European and American 18th to 20th century.

PROVIDE Chargeable Home Inspections. Free/Chargeable Estimates.
SPEAK TO Roland Hulme-Beaman.
Member of IPCRA.

LARKIN STUDIO
2 Stoneview Place, Dun Laoghaire, Dublin, **Co. Dublin**
TEL　　01 2805030
OPEN　By Appointment.

Specialise in restoring 19th and 20th century easel paintings, wax relining.

PROVIDE Home Inspections. Free Estimates.
SPEAK TO Elizabeth Larkin.
Member of IPCRA.

PATRICK McBRIDE
Paper Conservation Studio, IDA Tower Complex, Pearse Street, Dublin 2, **Co. Dublin**
TEL　　01 775656
FAX　　01 775487
OPEN　By Appointment.

Specialise in restoring works of art on paper, watercolours, prints and drawings.

PROVIDE Home Inspections. Chargeable Estimates. Free Collection/Delivery Service.

SPEAK TO Patrick McBride.
Member of IPCRA, IPC and ICOM.
SEE Books.

ANDREW O'CONNOR
National Gallery of Ireland, Merrion
Square West, Dublin 2, **Co. Dublin**
TEL   01 615133
OPEN   By Appointment.

Specialise in restoring and conserving
oil paintings.

PROVIDE Free/Chargeable Estimates.
SPEAK TO Andrew O'Connor.
Member of IPCRA.

KAREN REIHILL
Conservation Dept., National Gallery of
Ireland, Merrion Square West, Dublin 2,
Co. Dublin
TEL   01 615133
OPEN   By Appointment.

Specialise in restoring and conserving
works of art on paper, including
watercolours, pastels, prints and
drawings.

PROVIDE Free/Chargeable Estimates.
SPEAK TO Karen Reihill.
Member of IPCRA.
SEE Books.

THOMAS IRISH
Newcastle Upper, Crossabeg, Wexford,
Co. Wexford
TEL   053 28232
OPEN   By Appointment.

Specialise in restoring oil paintings.

PROVIDE Home Inspections. Free
Estimates. Free Collection/Delivery
Service.
SPEAK TO Thomas Irish.
Member of IPCRA and the Guild of
Glass Engravers.

SIMON BLACKWOOD FINE ARTS LTD
10–11 Bourtree Terrace, Roxburgh,
Borders TD9 9HN
TEL   0450 78547
FAX   0450 77780
OPEN   9.30–5.30 Mon–Fri; 10–2 Sat.

Specialise in restoring art works on
canvas, panel, paper, in oil, tempera,
watercolour, gouache, pastel, charcoal,
pencil.

PROVIDE Home Inspections. Free
Estimates. Chargeable
Collection/Delivery Service.
SPEAK TO Carol Sutherland.
Member of SSCR. This workshop is in
the Scottish Conservation Directory.
SEE Picture Frames.

VALENTINE WALSH
Caldra, Fogo, Duns, Berwickshire,
Borders
TEL   071 261 1691
FAX   071 401 9049
OPEN   By Appointment.

Specialise in restoring easel paintings
from 1400 to 1950, particularly
paintings on panel and can also
accommodate very large paintings.

PROVIDE Home Inspections.
Free/Chargeable Estimates.
Free/Chargeable Collection/Delivery
Service.
SPEAK TO Valentine Walsh.
Member of UKIC. This workshop is
included on the register of conservators
maintained by the Conservation Unit of
the Museums and Galleries Commission.
SEE **London SE1**

JOSEPH SCHERRER
30 Harbour Street, Creetown,
Wigtownshire, **Dumfries & Galloway
DG8 7JJ**
TEL   067182 268
OPEN   10–5 Mon–Sat or By
Appointment.

Specialise in restoring paintings on canvas, panel and paper.

PROVIDE Home Inspections. Free Estimates.
SPEAK TO Joseph Scherrer.
This workshop is in the Scottish Conservation Directory.
SEE Picture Frames.

JAMES ANDERSON RITCHIE
Art Restoration Service, 6 Woodhill Place, Aberdeen, **Grampian AB2 4LF**
TEL   0224 310491
OPEN   9–5.30 or By Appointment.

Specialise in restoring oil paintings, watercolours and prints.

PROVIDE Local Home Inspections. Free Estimates. Chargeable Collection/Delivery Service.
SPEAK TO J. Anderson Ritchie.
This workshop is in the Scottish Conservation Directory.
SEE Carpets, Picture Frames.

ALDER ARTS
57 Church Street, Inverness, **Highland IV1 1DR**
TEL   0463 243575
OPEN   9–5.30 Mon–Sat.

Specialise in cleaning and restoring 17th–19th century oil paintings.

PROVIDE Home Inspections. Free/Chargeable Estimates. Free Collection/Delivery Service.
SPEAK TO Ken Hardiman.
SEE Picture Frames.

ORBOST GALLERY
Bolvean, Isle of Skye, **Highland IV55 8ZB**
TEL   047 022 207
OPEN   By Appointment.

Specialise in repairing and restoring oil paintings as well as wood and marble

finishes for interior restoration, presentation calligraphy and illumination.

PROVIDE Home Inspections. Free/Chargeable Collection/Delivery Service.
SPEAK TO Dr David L. Roberts MA FSA (Scotland).

This workshop is in the Scottish Conservation Directory.
SEE Picture Frames.

THURSO ANTIQUES
Drill Hall, 21 Sinclair Street, Thurso, **Highland**
TEL   0847 63291 or 05934 276
FAX   0847 62824
OPEN   10–5 Mon–Fri; 10–1 Sat.

Specialise in cleaning and restoring oil paintings and watercolours.

PROVIDE Free Estimates. Collection/Delivery Service by arrangement.
SPEAK TO G. Atkinson.

SEE Silver.

CELIA BLAIR
The Studio, Cramond Brig Farm, Edinburgh, **Lothian EH4 6DY**
TEL   031 339 6502
OPEN   By Appointment.

Specialise in restoring easel paintings and carrying out conservation surveys.

PROVIDE Home Inspections. Free/Chargeable Estimates. Free/Chargeable Collection/Delivery Service.
SPEAK TO Celia Blair.

This workshop is in the Scottish Conservation Directory.

BOURNE FRAMES AND RESTORATION LTD
4 Dundas Street, Edinburgh, **Lothian EH3 6HZ**
TEL   031 557 4874
FAX   031 557 8382
OPEN   10–6 Mon–Fri; 10–1 Sat.

Specialise in restoring paintings.

PROVIDE Home Inspections. Free Estimates. Free/Chargeable Collection/Delivery Service.
SPEAK TO Susan Heys.

This workshop is in the Scottish Conservation Directory.
SEE Picture Frames.

CHRISTINE BULLICK
5 Belford Terrace, Edinburgh, **Lothian EH4 3DQ**
TEL   031 332 6948
OPEN   By Appointment.

Specialise in restoring early panel painting, Elizabethan and Jacobean and also contemporary painting.

PROVIDE Home Inspections. Free/Chargeable Estimates.
SPEAK TO Christine Bullick.
Member of IIC, UKIC and SSCR. This workshop is in the Scottish Conservation Directory.

MALCOLM INNES GALLERY
67 George Street, Edinburgh, **Lothian EH2 2JG**
TEL   031 226 4151
FAX   031 226 4151
OPEN   9.30–6 Mon–Fri.

Specialise in restoring oils, watercolours and prints especially natural history, Scottish and sporting subjects.

PROVIDE Home Inspections. Free Estimates. Free/Chargeable Collection/Delivery Service.

SPEAK TO Anthony Woodd.
SEE **London SW3.**
SEE Picture Frames.

CLARE MEREDITH
Conservation Studio, Hopetoun House, South Queensferry, **West Lothian EH30 9SL**
TEL   031 331 2003
OPEN   By Appointment Only.

Specialise in the conservation and restoration of easel paintings and condition surveys of collections.

PROVIDE Inspections on site. Chargeable Estimates.
SPEAK TO Clare Meredith.
Clare Meredith is Chair of SSCR, a Member of ABPR and UKIC and an Associate Member of IIC and the Museums Association. This workshop is in the Scottish Conservation Directory.

PARKES & BORDONE
Unit 01, St Mary's Workshops, Henderson Street, Leith, Edinburgh **Lothian EH6 6DD**
TEL   031 553 5111
FAX   031 555 1211
OPEN   9–5 Mon–Fri or By Appointment.

Specialise in conserving, cleaning, lining and restoring oil paintings, as well as some frame repairs. They also do surveys of collections.

PROVIDE Home Inspections. Free Estimates. Collection/Delivery Service by arrangement.
SPEAK TO Jane Hutchison.
This workshop is in the Scottish Conservation Directory.

FIONA BUTTERFIELD
Overhall, Kirkfield Bank, Lanark, **Strathclyde ML11 9TZ**
TEL   0555 66291
OPEN   By Appointment.

Specialise in conserving paper, prints, watercolours, drawings and screens.

PROVIDE Home Inspections. Free/Chargeable Estimates. SPEAK TO Fiona Butterfield.

Member of SSCR. This workshop is in the Scottish Conservation Directory.

DAPHNE FRASER
Glenbarry, 58 Victoria Road, Lenzie, Glasgow, **Strathclyde G66 5AP**
TEL   041 776 1281
OPEN   By Appointment.

Specialise in restoring antique oil paintings.

PROVIDE Free Estimates. SPEAK TO Daphne Fraser. This workshop is in the Scottish Conservation Directory. SEE Collectors (Dolls; Toys), Furniture, Picture Frames.

McIAN GALLERY
10 Argyll Square, Oban, **Strathclyde PA34 4AZ**
TEL   0631 66755
OPEN   9–5.30 Mon–Sat.

Specialise in fine art restoration.

PROVIDE Chargeable Collection/Delivery Service. SPEAK TO Rory Campbell-Gibson. SEE Picture Frames.

KENNETH McKENZIE
91 Hyndland Street, Glasgow, **Strathclyde G11 5PU**
TEL   041 339 6408
OPEN   Mon–Fri By Appointment.

Specialise in restoring oil paintings.

PROVIDE Home Inspections. Free Estimates. Free Collection/Delivery Service. SPEAK TO Kenny McKenzie.

Member of SSCR. This workshop is in the Scottish Conservation Directory.

JOHN MELROSE
74 Manse Road, Motherwell, **Strathclyde ML1 2PT**
TEL   0698 64249
OPEN   By Appointment.

Specialise in restoring easel paintings.

PROVIDE Home Inspections. Free/Chargeable Estimates. Chargeable Collection/Delivery Service. SPEAK TO John Melrose. Associate Member of the ABPR and the IIC. This workshop is included on the register of conservators maintained by the Conservation Unit of the Museums and Galleries Commission. This workshop is in the Scottish Conservation Directory.

NEIL LIVINGSTONE
3 Old Hawkhill, Dundee, **Tayside DD1 5EU**
TEL   0382 21751
OPEN   9–5 Mon–Fri.

Specialise in cleaning oil paintings and framing.

PROVIDE Free Estimates. Chargeable Collection/Delivery Service. SPEAK TO Neil Livingstone. SEE Arms, Furniture, Picture Frames, Silver.

CARL UTTERIDGE
Capel Bethel, Dinas Mawddwy, Machynlleth, **Powys SY20 9JA**
TEL   0650 531432
OPEN   9–6 Mon–Sat.

Specialise in restoring oil paintings on canvas, board and panels, prints and watercolours.

PROVIDE Home Inspections. Free Estimates. Free Local Collection/Delivery Service. SPEAK TO Carl Utteridge or Jennifer A'Brook. Member of UKIC. This workshop is included on the register of conservators

Specialise in gilding and carving picture frames.

PROVIDE Home Inspections. Free/Chargeable Estimates. Chargeable Collection/Delivery Service.
SPEAK TO Jock Hopson.
Member of UKIC. This workshop is included on the register of conservators maintained by the Conservation Unit of the Museums and Galleries Commission.
SEE Furniture, Arms.

WENDY A. CRAIG
Cambridge Conservation Studio, Balsham Road, Linton, Cambridge, **Cambridgeshire CB2 6LE**
TEL 0223 881295
FAX 0223 894056
OPEN 9–6 Mon–Sat.

Specialise in mounting and framing.

PROVIDE Home Inspections. Free Estimates. Free/Chargeable Collection/Delivery Service.
SPEAK TO Wendy Ann Craig.
This workshop is included on the register of conservators maintained by the Conservation Unit of the Museums and Galleries Commission.
SEE Oil Paintings.

FRANK GOODINGHAM
Studio 3, Hope Street Yard, Hope Street, Cambridge, **Cambridgeshire CB1 3NA**
TEL 0223 410702
OPEN 10–6 Mon–Fri.

Specialise in restoring 18th and 19th century gilded work, including composition or carved frames.

PROVIDE Home Inspections. Refundable Estimates. Collection/Delivery by arrangement.
SPEAK TO Frank Goodingham.
SEE Furniture.

A. ALL[
RESTO[
Buxton Rd
Stockport,
TEL 066
OPEN 8–5

Specialise i
gilding.

PROVIDE H[
Free/Char[
Collection,
SPEAK TO T[
SEE Clocks.

DEBBI[
Watchtowe
Looe, **Cor**
TEL 05[
OPEN 10
Ap

Specialise

PROVIDE H
Estimates.
SPEAK TO I
Associate
workshop
of conserv
Conservat
Galleries (
SEE Oil Pa

ACOR[
Ghylwooc
CA20 1A
TEL 09
OPEN B

Specialise
especially

PROVIDE I
Estimates
SPEAK TO
Member
IPC.

---

maintained by the Conservation Unit of the Museums and Galleries Commission.
SEE Books.

MANOR HOUSE FINE ARTS
73 Pontcanna Street, Cardiff, **South Glamorgan CF1 9HS**
TEL 0222 227787
OPEN 10.30–5.30 Tues, Thur, Fri, Sat or By Appointment.

Specialise in restoring and conserving oil paintings, watercolours and prints.

PROVIDE Home Inspections. Free Estimates at the gallery. Chargeable Collection/Delivery Service.
SPEAK TO Steven Denley–Hill.
SEE Picture Frames.

PICTURE I

ADAM GALLERY
13 John Street, Bath, **Avon BA1 2JL**
TEL　0225 480406
OPEN　9.30–5.30 Mon–Sat.

Specialise in framing of oil paintings, watercolours and drawings.

PROVIDE Home Inspections. Free Estimates. Collection/Delivery Service by arrangement.
SPEAK TO Paul or Philip Dye.

SEE Oil Paintings.

ANTHONY REED
94–96 Walcot Street, Bath, **Avon BA1 5BG**
TEL　0225 461969 or 0272 333595
OPEN　9–6 Mon–Sat.

Specialise in restoring picture frames, including gilding.

PROVIDE Home Inspections. Chargeable Estimates. Chargeable Local Collection/Delivery Service.
SPEAK TO Anthony Reed.

GALERIE LAFRANCE
647 Wimborne Road, Winton, Bournemouth, **Dorset BH9 2AR**
TEL　0202 522313
OPEN　8.30–1, 2–5.30 Mon–Fri; 9–1 Sat.

Specialise in cleaning and restoring picture frames. Gesso and composition replaced, gilding as necessary.

PROVIDE Home Inspections. Free Estimates. Free/Chargeable Collection/Delivery Service.
SPEAK TO Pierre Lafrance.
SEE Oil Paintings.

MRS CATHERINE MATHEW
Kiwi Cottage, Maperton Road, Charlton Horethorne, Sherborne, **Dorset DT9 4NT**
TEL　096 322 595
OPEN　9–6 Mon–Fri or By Appointment.

Specialise in cleaning picture frames to leave the original gold, regilding where new moulding has been applied or where necessary.

PROVIDE Home Inspections. Free Estimates. Free Collection/Delivery Service.
SPEAK TO Catherine Mathew.
SEE Porcelain, Furniture.

ALLYSON McDERMOTT (INTERNATIONAL CONSERVATION CONSULTANTS)
Lintz Green Conservation Centre, Lintz Green House, Lintz Green, Rowlands Gill, **Durham NE39 1NL**
TEL　0207 71547 or 0831 104145 or 0831 257584
FAX　0207 71547
OPEN　9–5.30 Mon–Fri.

Specialise in conservation mounting and

framing to museum standards, including gilding.

PROVIDE Home Inspections. Free Estimates. Chargeable Collection/Delivery Service.
SPEAK TO Allyson Mc Dermott or Gillian Lee.
They have a Southern Regional Office at 45 London Road, Cheltenham, **Gloucestershire**.
SEE Art Researchers, Carpets, Lighting, Oil Paintings, Specialist Photographers.

BECKERMAN'S
521 London Road, Westcliff-on-Sea, **Essex SS0 9LJ**
TEL　0702 346123
OPEN　9–12.30, 2–6, Mon–Sat, 9–12.30 Wed.

Specialise in picture framing service.

PROVIDE Home Inspections. Free Estimates.

TERRY HILLIARD
The Barn, Master Johns, Thoby Lane, Mountnessing, Brentwood, **Essex CM15 0JY**
TEL　0277 354717
OPEN　By Appointment.

Specialise in restoring gilded picture frames and carving and gilding, including making reproduction frames.

PROVIDE Home Inspections. Free Estimates. Free Collection/Delivery Service.
SPEAK TO Terry Hilliard.
Member of the Guild of Master Craftsmen.
SEE Furniture.

RICHARD ILES GALLERY
10 Northgate Street, Colchester, **Essex CO1 1HA**
TEL　0206 577877
OPEN　9.30–4.30 Mon–Sat.

Specialise in picture framing.

Specialise in gilding and carving picture frames.

PROVIDE Home Inspections. Free/Chargeable Estimates. Chargeable Collection/Delivery Service.
SPEAK TO Jock Hopson.
Member of UKIC. This workshop is included on the register of conservators maintained by the Conservation Unit of the Museums and Galleries Commission.
SEE Furniture, Arms.

WENDY A. CRAIG
Cambridge Conservation Studio, Balsham Road, Linton, Cambridge, **Cambridgeshire CB2 6LE**
TEL   0223 881295
FAX   0223 894056
OPEN   9–6 Mon–Sat.

Specialise in mounting and framing.

PROVIDE Home Inspections. Free Estimates. Free/Chargeable Collection/Delivery Service.
SPEAK TO Wendy Ann Craig.
This workshop is included on the register of conservators maintained by the Conservation Unit of the Museums and Galleries Commission.
SEE Oil Paintings.

FRANK GOODINGHAM
Studio 3, Hope Street Yard, Hope Street, Cambridge, **Cambridgeshire CB1 3NA**
TEL   0223 410702
OPEN   10–6 Mon–Fri.

Specialise in restoring 18th and 19th century gilded work, including composition or carved frames.

PROVIDE Home Inspections. Refundable Estimates. Collection/Delivery by arrangement.
SPEAK TO Frank Goodingham.
SEE Furniture.

A. ALLEN ANTIQUE RESTORERS
Buxton Rd, Newtown, Newmills, Via Stockport, **Cheshire SK12 3JS**
TEL   0663 745274
OPEN   8–5 Mon–Fri; 9–12 Sat.

Specialise in restoring picture frames and gilding.

PROVIDE Home Inspections. Free/Chargeable Estimates. Free Collection/Delivery Service.
SPEAK TO Tony Allen.
SEE Clocks, Furniture, Silver.

DEBBIE COLEMAN
Watchtower Studio, Church End, East Looe, **Cornwall PL13 1BX**
TEL   0503 263232 or 263344
OPEN   10.30–5 Mon–Sat or By Appointment.

Specialise in restoring gilt frames.

PROVIDE Home Inspections. Free Estimates. Collection/Delivery Service.
SPEAK TO Debbie Coleman.
Associate Member of ABPR. This workshop is included on the register of conservators maintained by the Conservation Unit of the Museums and Galleries Commission.
SEE Oil Paintings.

ACORN STUDIO
Ghylwood House, Gosforth, **Cumbria CA20 1AH**
TEL   09467 25516
OPEN   By Appointment.

Specialise in conservation framing especially of needlework.

PROVIDE Home Inspections. Free Estimates.
SPEAK TO Rodney Mostyn.
Member of the Fine Art Trade Guild and IPC.

GALERIE LAFRANCE
647 Wimborne Road, Winton,
Bournemouth, **Dorset BH9 2AR**
TEL   0202 522313
OPEN   8.30–1, 2–5.30 Mon–Fri; 9–1
       Sat.

Specialise in cleaning and restoring
picture frames. Gesso and composition
replaced, gilding as necessary.

PROVIDE Home Inspections. Free
Estimates. Free/Chargeable
Collection/Delivery Service.
SPEAK TO Pierre Lafrance.
SEE Oil Paintings.

MRS CATHERINE MATHEW
Kiwi Cottage, Maperton Road, Charlton
Horethorne, Sherborne, **Dorset
DT9 4NT**
TEL   096 322 595
OPEN   9–6 Mon–Fri or By
       Appointment.

Specialise in cleaning picture frames to
leave the original gold, regilding where
new moulding has been applied or where
necessary.

PROVIDE Home Inspections. Free
Estimates. Free Collection/Delivery
Service.
SPEAK TO Catherine Mathew.
SEE Porcelain, Furniture.

ALLYSON McDERMOTT (INTERNATIONAL CONSERVATION CONSULTANTS)
Lintz Green Conservation Centre, Lintz
Green House, Lintz Green, Rowlands
Gill, **Durham NE39 1NL**
TEL   0207 71547 or 0831 104145 or
       0831 257584
FAX   0207 71547
OPEN   9–5.30 Mon–Fri.

Specialise in conservation mounting and
framing to museum standards, including
gilding.

PROVIDE Home Inspections. Free
Estimates. Chargeable
Collection/Delivery Service.
SPEAK TO Allyson Mc Dermott or Gillian
Lee.
They have a Southern Regional Office at
45 London Road, Cheltenham,
Gloucestershire.
SEE Art Researchers, Carpets, Lighting,
Oil Paintings, Specialist Photographers.

BECKERMAN'S
521 London Road, Westcliff-on-Sea,
Essex SS0 9LJ
TEL   0702 346123
OPEN   9–12.30, 2–6, Mon–Sat, 9–
       12.30 Wed.

Specialise in picture framing service.

PROVIDE Home Inspections. Free
Estimates.

TERRY HILLIARD
The Barn, Master Johns, Thoby Lane,
Mountnessing, Brentwood, **Essex
CM15 0JY**
TEL   0277 354717
OPEN   By Appointment.

Specialise in restoring gilded picture
frames and carving and gilding,
including making reproduction frames.

PROVIDE Home Inspections. Free
Estimates. Free Collection/Delivery
Service.
SPEAK TO Terry Hilliard.
Member of the Guild of Master
Craftsmen.
SEE Furniture.

RICHARD ILES GALLERY
10 Northgate Street, Colchester, **Essex
CO1 1HA**
TEL   0206 577877
OPEN   9.30–4.30 Mon–Sat.

Specialise in picture framing.

PROVIDE Free Estimates.
SPEAK TO Richard Iles.
SEE Oil Paintings.

MILLSIDE ANTIQUE RESTORATION
Parndon Mill, Parndon Mill Lane, Harlow, **Essex CM20 2HP**
TEL 0279 428148
FAX 0279 415075
OPEN 10–5 Mon–Fri.
Specialise in restoring picture frames.

PROVIDE Home Inspections. Free/Chargeable Estimates. Chargeable Collection/Delivery Service.
SPEAK TO David Sparks or Angela Wickliffe-Philp.
SEE Oil Paintings, Porcelain, Silver.

PEARLITA FRAMES LTD
30 North Street, Romford, **Essex RM11 2LB**
TEL 0708 760342
OPEN 9–5.30 Mon–Sat.

Specialise in picture framing.

PROVIDE Home Inspections. Free Estimates. Free Collection/Delivery Service.
SPEAK TO Trevor Woodward.
SEE Oil Paintings.

ASTLEY HOUSE FINE ART
Astley House, High Street, Moreton-in-Marsh, **Gloucestershire GL56 0LL**
TEL 0608 50601
FAX 0608 51777
OPEN 9–5.30 Mon–Sat.

Specialise in framing.

PROVIDE Free Estimates. Chargeable Collection/Delivery Service.
SPEAK TO David or Nanette Glaisyer.
SEE Oil Paintings.

CLEEVE PICTURE FRAMING
Coach House Workshops, Stoke Road, Bishops Cleeve, Cheltenham, **Gloucestershire GL52 4RP**
TEL 0242 672785
FAX 0242 676827
OPEN 9–1, 2–5.30 Mon–Fri; 9–1 Sat.

Specialise in restoring and conserving picture frames as well as bespoke framing and decorative mounts.

PROVIDE Home Inspections. Free Estimates. Free Collection/Delivery Service.
SPEAK TO James Gardner.
SEE Oil Paintings.

CRISPIN ART SERVICES
68 Crispin Road, Winchcombe, Cheltenham, **Gloucestershire GL54 5JX**
TEL 0242 602947
FAX 0242 603723
OPEN 9–5 Mon–Sat or By Appointment.

Specialise in restoring gilt frames, repairing and refinishing. Missing decoration can be cast and replaced. They also carry out bronze powder and gold gilding, gesso and polychrome work. All types of decorated and washline mounts for watercolours supplied.

PROVIDE Home Inspections. Free Estimates. Chargeable Collection/Delivery Service.
SPEAK TO Mr R. E. Holness.

KENULF FINE ART LTD
5 North Street, Winchcombe, Nr. Cheltenham, **Gloucestershire GL54 5LH**
TEL 0242 603204
FAX 0242 604042
OPEN 9.30–1, 2–5.30 Mon–Sat.

Specialise in restoration of frames.

PROVIDE Home Inspections. Free

Estimates. Collection/Delivery Service.
SPEAK TO Eric Ford.
SEE Oil Paintings.

A. J. PONSFORD ANTIQUES
51–53 Dollar Street, Cirencester,
Gloucestershire GL7 2AS
TEL   0285 652355
OPEN   8.30–5.30 Mon–Fri.

Specialise in restoring picture frames.

PROVIDE Home Inspections. Free
Estimates. Free Collection/Delivery
Service.
SPEAK TO A. J. Ponsford.
SEE Furniture, Oil Paintings.

PETER WARD GALLERY
11 Gosditch Street, Cirencester,
Gloucestershire GL7 2AG
TEL   0285 658499
OPEN   9.30–5.30 Mon–Sat

Specialise in framing and mounting.

PROVIDE Home Inspections. Free
Collection/Delivery Service.
SPEAK TO Peter Ward.
SEE Oil Paintings.

CORFIELD RESTORATIONS LTD
120 High Street, Lymington,
Hampshire SO41 9AQ
TEL   0590 673532
OPEN   9.15–5.30 Mon–Sat.

Specialise in picture mounting and
framing.

PROVIDE Home Inspections. Free
Estimates. Local Free
Collection/Delivery Service.
SPEAK TO Alan Bloomfield or Michael
Corfield.

Also at Setters Farm, Lymington. 0590
671977.
SEE Furniture, Oil Paintings.

THE PETERSFIELD BOOKSHOP
16a Chapel Street, Petersfield,
Hampshire GU32 3DS
TEL   0730 263438
FAX   0730 269426
OPEN   9–5.30 Mon–Sat.

Specialise in restoring frames and
framing.

PROVIDE Home Inspections. Free
Estimates. Collection/Delivery Service
available.
SPEAK TO Frank Westwood.
SEE Books, Oil Paintings.

EDWIN COLLINS
Coltsfoot Gallery, Hatfield, Leominster,
Hereford & Worcester HR6 0SF
TEL   056 882 277
OPEN   By Appointment.

Specialise in a mounting and framing
service.

PROVIDE Free Estimates.
SPEAK TO Edwin Collins.
Member of IPC.
SEE Oil Paintings.

JENNINGS & JENNINGS
30 Bridge Street, Leominster,
Hereford & Worcester HR6 9JQ
TEL   05448 586
OPEN   By Appointment.

Specialise in conserving and restoring
gilded picture frames.

PROVIDE Home Inspections. Free
Estimates. Free/Chargeable
Collection/Delivery Service.
SPEAK TO Sabina Jennings.
SEE Furniture.

EUGENE B. OKARMA
Brobury House Gallery, Brobury,
Hereford & Worcester HR3 6BS
TEL   09817 229
OPEN   9–4 Mon–Sat.

Specialise in restoring frames.

PROVIDE Local Home Inspections.
SPEAK TO Mr Okarma.
SEE Oil Paintings.

HERTFORDSHIRE CONSERVATION SERVICE
Seed Warehouse, Maidenhead Yard,
The Wash, Hertford, **Hertfordshire
SG14 1PX**
TEL   0992 588966
FAX   0992 588971
OPEN   9–6 Mon–Fri By Appointment.

Specialise in repair, restoration or
replacement of picture frames.

PROVIDE Home Inspections.
Free/Chargeable Estimates. Chargeable
Collection/Delivery Service.
SPEAK TO J. M. MacQueen.

This workshop is included on the
register of conservators maintained by
the Conservation Unit of the Museums
and Galleries Commission.
SEE Collectors (Dolls), Furniture,
Lighting, Porcelain, Oil Paintings,
Carpets.

SUSAN LAMBERT
108 Harmer Green Lane, Welwyn,
Hertfordshire AL6 0ET
TEL   043 879 234
FAX   043 879 628
OPEN   9–5 Mon–Fri By Appointment.

Specialise in conservation mounting and
framing.

PROVIDE Home Inspections. Free
Estimates. Chargeable
Collection/Delivery Service.
SPEAK TO Susan Lambert.

Member of IPC, IIC and Museums'
Association.
SEE Oil Paintings.

VICTORIA FRAMING SERVICES
Long Spring, Porters Wood, St Albans,
Hertfordshire AL3 6NQ
TEL   0727 59044
FAX   0727 861660
OPEN   8.30–5.30 Mon–Fri.

Specialise in restoring picture frames.
Also manufacture reproduction frames.

PROVIDE Local Home Inspections.
Chargeable Estimates. Chargeable
Collection/Delivery Service.
SPEAK TO David Prior.
SEE Furniture.

CASTLE FINE ART STUDIO
26 Castle Street, Dover, **Kent
CT16 1PW**
TEL   0304 206360
OPEN   10–1, 2–5.30 Mon–Fri; 10–1
       Sat.

Specialise in a bespoke and trade framing
service to museum conservation quality
standards.

PROVIDE Home Inspections. Free
Estimates. Free Local
Collection/Delivery Service.
SPEAK TO Ms Deborah Colam.
Member of IPC. This workshop is
included on the register of conservators
maintained by the Conservation Unit of
the Museums and Galleries Commission.
SEE Books, Oil Paintings.

CLARE GALLERY
21 High Street, Royal Tunbridge Wells,
Kent TN1 1UT
TEL   0892 538717
FAX   0323 29588
OPEN   8.15–5.30 Mon–Sat

Specialise in a framing service.

PROVIDE Home Inspections. Free
Estimates. Chargeable
Collection/Delivery Service.
SPEAK TO M. Ettinger.
SEE Oil Paintings.

ROGER GREEN FINE ART
Hales Place Studio, High Halden, Nr.
Ashford, **Kent TN26 3JQ**
TEL　　0233 850716
FAX　　0233 850219
OPEN　　9–5 Mon–Sat.

Specialise in conservation, quality
mounting and framing, and gilding and
hand-finishing of frames.

PROVIDE Local Home Inspections. Free
Estimates.
SPEAK TO Roger Green or Ellen Green.
SEE Oil Paintings.

FRANCES ILES FINE PAINTINGS
Rutland House, 103 High Street,
Rochester, **Kent ME1 1LX**
TEL　　0634 843081
FAX　　0474 822403
OPEN　　9–5.30 Mon–Sat.

Specialise in a framing service for all
mediums, including early samplers and
needlepoint.

PROVIDE Home Inspections. Free
Estimates. Free Collection/Delivery
Service.
SPEAK TO Jeanette or Lucy Iles.

SEE Oil Paintings.

W. J. MORRILL LTD
437 Folkestone Road, Dover, **Kent
CT17 9JX**
TEL　　0304 201989
OPEN　　8–5 Mon–Fri.

Specialise in making both wood and
composition period frames.

PROVIDE Home Inspections. Free
Collection/Delivery Service.
SPEAK TO Mr Barnes.
SEE Oil Paintings.

DYSONS ARTS LTD
87 Scotland Road, Nelson, **Lancashire
BB9 7UY**
TEL　　0282 65468
OPEN　　9.30–5.30 Mon–Sat, closed
　　　　Tues.

Specialise in mounting and framing
pictures.

PROVIDE Free Estimates.
SPEAK TO O. A. Davies.
SEE Oil Paintings.

BARBARA WILDMAN
9 Woodside Terrace, Nelson, **Lancashire
BB9 7TB**
TEL　　0282 699679
OPEN　　By Appointment.

Specialise in restoring gilt frames, gesso
work and gold leaf.

PROVIDE Home Inspections. Free
Estimates. Chargeable
Collection/Delivery Service.
SPEAK TO Barbara Wildman.

SEE Oil Paintings.

RICHARD ZAHLER
Lane House, Fowgill, Bentham,
Lancaster, **Lancashire LA2 7AH**
TEL　　05242 61988
OPEN　　9–6 Mon–Fri or By
　　　　Appointment.

Specialise in restoring frames.
SPEAK TO Richard Zahler.

Member of UKIC and the Guild of
Master Craftsmen. This workshop is
included on the register maintained by
the Conservation Unit of the Museums
and Galleries Commission.
SEE Books, Oil Paintings.

GREEN AND STONE
259 Kings Road, **London SW3 5EL**
TEL   071 352 6521
FAX   071 351 1098
OPEN   9–5.30 Mon–Fri; 9.30–6 Sat.

Specialise in restoring antique frames, including gilding and veneer work. They also offer a picture framing service.

PROVIDE Local Home Inspections. Free Estimates. Free Local Collection/Delivery Service.
SPEAK TO Mrs Hiscott or Miss Moore.
SEE Oil Paintings, Lighting.

MALCOLM INNES GALLERY
172 Walton Street, **London SW3 2JL**
TEL   071 584 0575
OPEN   9.30–6 Mon–Fri; Sat 10–1.

Specialise in framing oil paintings.

PROVIDE Free Estimates. Chargeable Collection/Delivery Service.
SPEAK TO Malcolm Innes.
SEE **Lothian.**
SEE Oil Paintings.

COOPER FINE ARTS LTD
768 Fulham Road, **London SW6 5SJ**
TEL   071 731 3421
OPEN   10–7 Mon–Fri; 10–4 Sat.

Specialise in framing oil paintings and watercolours.

PROVIDE Free Estimates.
SPEAK TO Jonathan Hill-Reid.
SEE Oil Paintings.

PIERS FEETHAM GALLERY
475 Fulham Road, **London SW6 1HL**
TEL   071 381 5958
OPEN   10–1, 2–6 Mon–Fri; 2–6 Sat.

Specialise in framing works on paper to conservation standard and general framing.

PROVIDE Home Inspections. Free Estimates.
SPEAK TO Piers Feetham.

ROY FRANDSEN
7 Lillie Yard, **London SW6 1HB**
TEL   071 385 9930
OPEN   8–5 Mon–Fri.

Specialise in restoring antique picture frames and manufacturing period and modern frames.

PROVIDE Home Inspections. Free Local Estimates. Free Local Collection/Delivery Service.
SPEAK TO Derek Tanous or Jimmy Greenland.

GILT EDGE
275 Wandsworth Bridge Road, **London SW6 2TX**
TEL   071 731 7703
OPEN   10–6 Mon–Fri; 10–1 Sat.

Specialise in picture framing.

PROVIDE Free Estimates.
SPEAK TO Richard Pitt.

Member of the Guild of Master Craftsmen.

PETER L. JAMES
681 Fulham Road, **London SW6 5PZ**
TEL   071 736 0183
OPEN   7.30–5.30 Mon–Fri.

Specialise in restoring lacquer, painted and gilded frames.

PROVIDE Home Inspections. Refundable Estimates. Chargeable Collection/Delivery Service.
SPEAK TO Peter L. James.
SEE Furniture.

MICHAEL MARRIOTT LTD
588 Fulham Road, **London SW6 5NT**
TEL   071 736 3110
FAX   071 731 2632
OPEN   9.30–5.30 Mon–Fri.

Specialise in mounting and framing of prints.

PROVIDE Home Inspections. Free Estimates. Collection/Delivery Service.
SPEAK TO Jean Marriott.
SEE Furniture.

JOHN TANOUS LTD
115 Harwood Road, Fulham, **London SW6 4QL**
TEL   071 736 7999
FAX   071 371 5237
OPEN   9–1, 2–5 Mon–Fri.

Specialise in making and restoring picture frames and gilding.

PROVIDE Free Estimates.
SPEAK TO Peter Copcutt.

This firm was established in 1913.

20th CENTURY GALLERY
821 Fulham Road, **London SW6 5HG**
TEL   071 731 5888
OPEN   10–6 Mon–Fri; 10–1 Sat.

Specialise in bespoke framing.

PROVIDE Free Estimates.
SPEAK TO Erika Brandl.
SEE Oil Paintings.

CALLANAN LTD
Unit 7, Parkfields Industrial Estate, Culvert Place, Culvert Road, **London SW11 5BA**
TEL   071 828 7577
OPEN   9–6.30 Mon–Fri.

Specialise in restoring picture frames. They have a large stock of period frames of all types: washline, eglomisé, sanded mounts. They will also copy period frames.

PROVIDE Home Inspections. Free Estimates. Chargeable Collection/Delivery Service.
SPEAK TO David Callanan.
SEE Furniture.

HELEN DE BORCHGRAVE
Fine Art Restorer, 103 Albert Bridge Road, **London SW11 4PF**
TEL   071 738 1951
OPEN   By Appointment.

Specialise in restoring picture frames.

PROVIDE Home Inspections. Free Local Estimates. Collection/Delivery Service.
SPEAK TO Helen de Borchgrave.

Member of UKIC, IIC and ABPR. This workshop is included on the register of conservators maintained by the Conservation Unit of the Museums and Galleries Commission.
SEE Oil Paintings.

REGENCY RESTORATIONS
Studio 21, Thames House, 140 Battersea Park Road, **London SW11**
TEL   071 622 5275
OPEN   9–6 Mon–Fri or By Appointment.

Specialise in restoring frames, including carving and gilding.

PROVIDE Home Inspections. Free Estimates. Chargeable Collection/Delivery Service.
SPEAK TO Peter Curry or Elizabeth Ball.
SEE Oil Paintings.

RUPERT BEVAN
75 Lower Richmond Road, **London SW15 1ET**
TEL   081 780 1190
OPEN   9–6 Mon–Fri.

Specialise in restoring gilded picture frames.

PROVIDE Home Inspections. Free
Estimates. Chargeable
Collection/Delivery Service.
SPEAK TO Rupert Bevan.

SEE Furniture.

TREVOR CUMINE
133 Putney Bridge Road, **London
SW15 2PA**
TEL   081 870 1525
OPEN   By Appointment.

Specialise in antique frames and making
gilt frames for 20th century pictures.
SPEAK TO Trevor Cumine.

SEE Oil Paintings.

SERENA CHAPLIN
32 Elsynge Road, **London SW18 2HN**
TEL   081 870 9455
OPEN   By Appointment.

Specialise in restoring gilded picture
frames.

PROVIDE Free Estimates within the
London area.
SPEAK TO Serena Chaplin.

Ms Chaplin also runs gilding courses.
SEE Furniture.

COURT PICTURE FRAMERS
8 Bourdon Street, **London W1Y 9AD**
TEL   071 493 3265
OPEN   9.30–5 Mon–Fri.

Specialise in carrying out all kinds of
framing, including hand-gilded, limed,
stained and painted mouldings, and
conservation mounting and mount
decoration.

PROVIDE Free Estimates. Free
Collection/Delivery Service (for orders
over £100 in London area).
SPEAK TO Andrew Butwright.

Member of the Fine Art Trade Guild.

RICCARDO GIACHERRINI FINE FRAMES
39 Newman Street, **London W1P 3PG**
TEL   071 580 1783
FAX   071 637 5221
OPEN   9.30–6 Mon–Fri or By
Appointment.

Specialise in providing fine quality
carved and gilded antique frames (not
composition).

PROVIDE Local Home Inspections. Free
Estimates. Chargeable
Collection/Delivery Service.
SPEAK TO Riccardo Giacherrini.

CHRISTOPHER HARRAP
1st Floor, 26–27 Conduit Street,
London W1R 9TA
TEL   071 499 1488
OPEN   9–5 Wed only.

Specialise in mounting and framing
watercolours, prints and drawings.

PROVIDE Free Estimates.
SPEAK TO Christopher Harrap.

Member of IPC.
SEE Oil Paintings.

DAVID MESSUM
34 St George Street, Hanover Square,
London W1R 9FA
TEL   071 408 0243
OPEN   9.30–5.30 Mon–Fri.

Specialise in framing 18th century to
modern day British paintings,
particularly Impressionists.

PROVIDE Home Inspections. Chargeable
Collection/Delivery Service.
SPEAK TO Carol Tee.

SEE Oil Paintings.

PAUL MITCHELL LTD
99 New Bond Street, **London W1Y 9LF**
TEL   071 493 8732
FAX   071 409 7136
OPEN   9.30–5.30 Mon–Fri.

Specialise in supplying hand-carved replica frames and the conservation and restoration of antique picture frames.

PROVIDE Home Inspections. Free Estimates. Chargeable Collection/Delivery Service.
SPEAK TO Paul Mitchell.
Member of BADA, the Guild of Master Craftsmen, ABPR and the IIC.
SEE Oil Paintings.

MATTEI RADEV
10 Ogle Street, **London W1P 7LQ**
TEL   071 580 4704
OPEN   8–5 Mon–Fri.

Specialise in restoring antique picture frames.

PROVIDE Home Inspections. Free Estimates. Collection/Delivery Service by arrangement.
SPEAK TO Mattei Radev or Charles Rhodes.
SEE Furniture.

STEPHEN WELLS
1A Silver Place, **London W1R 3LL**
TEL   071 734 4660
OPEN   8.30–5.30 Mon–Fri.

Specialise in restoring picture frames.

PROVIDE Home Inspections. Free Estimates. Chargeable Collection/Delivery Service.
SPEAK TO Stephen Wells.
Member of the Guild of Master Craftsmen and Conservation Mount Makers. This workshop is included on the register of conservators maintained by the Conservation Unit of the Museums and Galleries Commission.

BOURLET
32 Connaught Street, **London W2 2AY**
TEL   071 724 4837
OPEN   11–5.30 Mon–Fri and most Sats.

Specialise in restoring picture frames.

PROVIDE Home Inspections. Free Estimates. Collection/Delivery Service.
SPEAK TO Gabrielle Rendell.
SEE Oil Paintings, Furniture.

C. J. G. GILDERS & CARVERS
Unit 10, Sandringham Mews, **London W5 5DF**
TEL   081 579 2341
FAX   081 571 9022
OPEN   10–5 Mon–Sat.

Specialise in restoring antique picture frames.

PROVIDE Home Inspections. Free Estimates. Free Local Collection/Delivery Service.
SPEAK TO Chris Gostonski or Richard Kosmala.
SEE Furniture.

DR POPPY COOKSEY
Aston House, 8 Lower Mall, **London W6 9DJ**
TEL   081 846 9279
OPEN   By Appointment.

Specialise in picture frame repairs.

PROVIDE Home Inspections. Free Estimates in London. Chargeable Collection/Delivery Service.
SPEAK TO Dr Poppy Cooksey.
SEE Oil Paintings.

PORCELAIN AND PICTURES LTD
The Studio, 1B Gastein Road, **London W6 8LT**
TEL   071 385 7512
OPEN   9–5.30 Mon–Sat.

Specialise in framing pictures of any medium to full conservation standard, lining, colour washing plus a wide selection of moulding from antique to modern.

PROVIDE Home Inspections. Free Estimates. Free Local Collection/Delivery Service.
SPEAK TO David or Edward Toms.

Member of the Fine Art Trade Guild.
SEE Porcelain.

THE ROWLEY GALLERY LTD

115 Kensington Church Street, **London W8 7LN**
TEL   071 727 6495
OPEN   9–5 Mon–Fri; 9–7 Thur.

Specialise in restoring antique picture frames, bespoke framing, gilding and veneering.

PROVIDE Home Inspections. Free Estimates. Free Collection/Delivery
SPEAK TO A. J. Savill.

This firm was founded in 1898.

DAGGETT GALLERY

1st Floor, 153 Portobello Road, **London W11 2DY**
TEL   071 229 2248
FAX   071 584 2950
OPEN   10–4 Mon–Fri, please ring first, 9–4 Sat.

Specialise in restoring frames, gilding and cutting down.

PROVIDE Home Inspections. Free/Chargeable Estimates. Chargeable Collection/Delivery Service.
SPEAK TO Charles or Caroline Daggett.

Member of LAPADA.
SEE Oil Paintings.

THE CORK STREET FRAMING COMPANY LTD

8 Bramber Road, **London W14 9PB**
TEL   071 381 9211
FAX   071 381 9034
OPEN   10–6 Mon–Fri; By Appointment Sat.

Specialise in supplying hand-finished frames, including gilding, metal leaf and decorative paint effects and restoration of frames.

PROVIDE Home Inspections. Free Estimates. Free Collection/Delivery Service.
SPEAK TO Gabrielle Coles.

COUTTS GALLERIES

75 Blythe Road, **London W14 OHD**
TEL   071 602 3980
OPEN   10–5 Mon–Fri.

Specialise in restoration of antique frames.

PROVIDE Home Inspections, Free Estimates, Free Collection/Delivery Service.
SPEAK TO Seabury Burdett-Coutts.
SEE Furniture, Oil Paintings.

FELLOWES AND SAUNDERSON

116 Blythe Road, **London W14 0UH**
TEL   071 603 7475
OPEN   9.30–5.30 Tues–Fri, 10–4 Sat.

Specialise in restoration of antique frames and all aspects of framing and conservation mounting. They have their own range of gilded and hand-finished frames.

PROVIDE Home Inspections. Free Estimates. Free Collection/Delivery Service.
SPEAK TO Joan Burdett-Coutts.
SEE Furniture.

PAUL FERGUSON
Unit 20, 21 Wren Street, **London**
WC1X 0HF
TEL　　071 278 8759
FAX　　071 278 8759
OPEN　9–5.30 Mon–Fri.

Specialise in restoring carved and gilded picture frames.

PROVIDE Home Inspections by arrangement. Free Estimates. Collection/Delivery Service by arrangement.
SPEAK TO Paul Ferguson.

SEE Furniture.

BLACKMAN HARVEY LTD
36 Great Queen Street, **London**
WC2B 5AA
TEL　　071 836 1904
FAX　　071 404 5896
OPEN　9.30–6 Mon–Fri; 10–4 Sat.

Specialise in repairing picture frames, including replacement of lost details, gilding and restoration.

PROVIDE Home Inspections. Free Estimates. Chargeable Collection/Delivery Service.
SPEAK TO R. M. Wooton Wooley
SEE Oil Paintings.

LYVER & BOYDELL GALLERIES
15 Castle Street, Liverpool, **Merseyside**
L2 4SX
TEL　　051 236 3256
OPEN　10.30–5.30 Mon–Fri; Sat By Appointment.

Specialise in framing watercolours and prints.

PROVIDE Home Inspections. Free Estimates.
SPEAK TO Paul or Gill Breen.

SEE Books, Oil Paintings.

WELLINGTON CRAFTS (1980)
121A/123A St John's Road, Waterloo, Liverpool, **Merseyside L22 9QE**
TEL　　051 920 5511
OPEN　9.30–5 Mon–Sat.

Specialise in a full picture-framing service.

PROVIDE Home Inspections. Refundable Estimates. Chargeable Collection/Delivery Service.
SPEAK TO Neville Hymus.
SEE Furniture.

MARIA J. LESIAK
Leliwa, 71 St Anne's Avenue, Stanwell, Staines, **Middlesex TW19 7RL**
TEL　　0784 257401
FAX　　0784 257401
OPEN　By Appointment.

Specialise in restoring antique gilt picture frames.

PROVIDE Home Inspections. Free Estimates. Free Local Collection/Delivery Service.
SPEAK TO Maria J. Lesiak.
Ms Lesiak is a Full Member of UKIC and an Associate Member of ABPR. This workshop is included on the register of conservators maintained by the Conservation Unit of the Museums and Galleries Commission.
SEE Oil Paintings, Furniture.

JOHN MALCOLM FINE ART RESTORATION
62 Linden Avenue, Ruislip, **Middlesex**
HA4 8UA
TEL　　0895 621616
OPEN　8.30–5 Mon–Fri or By Appointment.

Specialise in framing oil paintings and works of art on paper.

PROVIDE Home Inspections. Free Estimates. Free Collection/Delivery Service.

SPEAK TO John Malcolm.
SEE Oil Paintings.

COLMORE GALLERIES
52 High Street, Henley-in-Arden,
Solihull, **West Midlands B95 5AN**
TEL   0564 792938
OPEN   11–5.30 Mon–Fri; 11–4.30 Sat.

Specialise in picture framing, gilding.

PROVIDE Home Inspections. Refundable
Estimates. Collection/Delivery Service
Available.
SPEAK TO B. D. Jones.

SEE Oil Paintings.

W. F. GADSBY LTD
9 Bradford Street, Walsall, **West
Midlands WS1 1TB**
TEL   0922 23104
OPEN   9–5 Mon–Sat.

Specialise in framing oils, watercolours
etc.

PROVIDE Free Estimates. Free Local
Collection/Delivery Service.
SPEAK TO Mr S. Roberts.

HAMPTON UTILITIES (B'HAM) LTD
15 Pitsford Street, Hockley,
Birmingham, **West Midlands B18 6LJ**
TEL   021 554 1766
OPEN   9–5 Mon–Thur; 9–4 Fri.

Specialise in restoring and repairing
picture frames, including gilding.

PROVIDE Free Estimates. Chargeable
Collection/Delivery Service.
SPEAK TO B. Levine.

SEE Furniture, Silver.

CATHERINE MEADS
37 Cadbury Road, Moseley,
Birmingham, **West Midlands B13 9BH**
TEL   021 449 4840
OPEN   9–7 Mon–Fri.

Specialise in picture frame restoration,
including gilding.

PROVIDE Home Inspections. Free
Estimates. Free Local
Collection/Delivery Service.
SPEAK TO Catherine Meads.

Member of UKIC. This workshop is
included on the register of conservators
maintained by the Conservation Unit of
the Museums and Galleries Commission.

PENNY LAWRENCE
Fairhurst Gallery, Bedford Street,
Norwich, **Norfolk NR2 1AS**
TEL   0603 632064
OPEN   9–5 Mon–Fri.

Specialise in restoring and conserving
picture frames.

PROVIDE Home Inspections. Free
Estimates. Free/Chargeable
Collection/Delivery Service.
SPEAK TO Penny Lawrence.

This workshop is included on the register
of conservators maintained by the
Conservation Unit of the Museums and
Galleries Commission.
SEE Furniture, Oil Paintings, Silver.

WESTCLIFFE GALLERY AND ART FRAMES
2–8 Augusta Street, Sheringham,
Norfolk NR26 8LA
TEL   0263 824320
OPEN   9.30–5.30 Mon–Sat. Closed
        Wed.

Specialise in conservation mounting,
gilding, period frame restoration.

PROVIDE Home Inspections. Free
Estimates. Free/Chargeable
Collection/Delivery Service.

SPEAK TO Richard Parks.

SEE Oil Paintings.

SAVAGE FINE ART
Alfred Street, Northampton,
Northamptonshire NN1 5EY
TEL   0604 20327
FAX   0604 27417
OPEN   9–5.15 Mon–Fri; 9–12.30 Sat.

Specialise in restoring picture frames.

PROVIDE Home Inspections. Free
Estimates. Free Collection/Delivery
Service.
SPEAK TO Michael Savage.
SEE Oil Paintings.

J. A. & T. HEDLEY
3 St Mary's Chare, Hexham,
Northumberlandshire NE46 1NQ
TEL   0434 602317
OPEN   9–5 Mon–Sat; 9–12 Thur.

Specialise in picture framing.

PROVIDE Free Estimates. Chargeable
Collection/Delivery Service.
SPEAK TO D. Hall or W. H. Jewitt.
SEE Furniture.

BART LUCKHURST
The Gallery, 9 Union Street, Bingham,
Nottinghamshire NG13 8AD
TEL   0949 837668
OPEN   9–5 Thur; 9–1 Sat or By
          Appointment.

Specialise in restoring period frames.

PROVIDE Home Inspections. Free
Estimates. Collection/Delivery Service
by arrangement.
SPEAK TO Bart Luckhurst.

Member of FATG.
SEE Oil Paintings.

MARK ROBERTS
1 West Workshops, Tan Gallop, Welbeck,
Nr. Worksop, **Nottinghamshire**
S80 3LW
TEL   0909 484270
OPEN   By Appointment.

Specialise in conserving and restoring
gilded frames.

PROVIDE Home Inspections. Refundable
Estimates. Chargeable
Collection/Delivery Service.
SPEAK TO Mark or Diana Roberts.
SEE Oil Paintings.

BARBARA BIBB
149 Kingston Road, Oxford,
Oxfordshire OX2 6RP
TEL   0865 56444
OPEN   9–5 Mon–Sat.

Specialise in restoring gilded frames.

PROVIDE Home Inspections. Free
Estimates. Free Local
Collection/Delivery Service.
SPEAK TO Barbara Bibb.

Member of ABPR. This workshop is
included on the register of conservators
maintained by the Conservation Unit of
the Museums and Galleries Commission.
SEE Furniture, Oil Paintings.

OXFORD CONSERVATIONS
Underwood, Jack Straw's Lane, Oxford,
Oxfordshire OX3 0DN
TEL   0865 62614
FAX   0865 750311
OPEN   By Appointment Only.

Specialise in restoring picture frames.

PROVIDE Home Inspections. Free
Estimates. Chargeable
Collection/Delivery Service.
SPEAK TO Candy Kuhl, Chief Conservator.

Member of UKIC and IIC, Associate
Member of ABPR. This workshop is
included on the register of conservators

maintained by the Conservation Unit of the Museums and Galleries Commission. SEE Oil Paintings, Porcelain.

SWALLOWS
16 Main Road, East Hagbourne, **Oxfordshire OX11 9LN**
TEL   0235 818273
OPEN   9–5.30 Mon–Fri or By Appointment.

Specialise in all mediums of framing with particular attention to conservation framing and preservation of artworks. Also specialise in mount decoration, including washline and applied decoration of all kinds.

PROVIDE Home Inspections. Free Estimates. Chargeable Collection/Delivery Service.
SPEAK TO Jennie Kuga.

TIM EVERETT
Pitminster Studio, Taunton, **Somerset TA3 7AZ**
TEL   0823 42710
OPEN   By Appointment.

Specialise in conservation and restoration of picture frames.

PROVIDE Home Inspections. Free Estimates. Free Collection/Delivery Service.
SPEAK TO Tim Everett.
This workshop is included on the register of conservators maintained by the Conservation Unit of the Museums and Galleries Commission.
SEE Oil Paintings.

CLARE HUTCHISON
1A West Street, Ilminster, **Somerset TA19 9AA**
TEL   0460 53369
OPEN   10–3 Mon–Fri; 10–1 Sat; closed Thur.

Specialise in restoring antique picture frames.

PROVIDE Free Estimates.
SPEAK TO Clare Hutchison.
SEE Furniture.

VICTORIA DES BEAUX ARTS LTD
11 Newcastle Street, Burslem, Stoke-on-Trent, **Staffordshire ST6 3QB**
TEL   0782 836490
OPEN   9–5.30 Mon–Sat.

Specialise in framing paintings.

PROVIDE Home Inspections. Free/Chargeable Estimates. Free Collection/Delivery Service.
SPEAK TO Mrs Bryden.
SEE Oil Paintings.

PHILIPPA ELLISON
Fords Farm, Winston, Nr. Stowmarket, **Suffolk IP14 6BD**
TEL   0728 860572
OPEN   9–5 Mon–Fri.

Specialise in advice on framing works of art on paper.

PROVIDE Home Inspections. Free Estimates. Collection/Delivery Service.
SPEAK TO Philippa Ellison.
Member of IPC. This workshop is included on the register of conservators maintained by the Conservation Unit of the Museums and Galleries Commission.
SEE Oil Paintings, Books.

JOHN GAZELEY ASSOCIATES FINE ART
17 Fonnereau Road, Ipswich, **Suffolk IP1 3JR**
TEL   0473 252420
OPEN   By Appointment.

Specialise in gilding and repairing of picture frames as well as making reproduction frames.

PROVIDE Free Estimates.
SPEAK TO Dr John Gazeley.
SEE Furniture, Oil Paintings.

NORTHWOLD GALLERY
206 High Street, Newmarket, **Suffolk CB8 9AP**
TEL   0638 668758
OPEN   10–5 Mon–Sat; closed Wed.

Specialise in framing watercolours and prints.

PROVIDE Home Inspections. Free Estimates. Free Collection/Delivery Service.
SPEAK TO C. G. Troman.
SEE Oil Paintings.

DAVID EMBLING
45 Fairfield, Farnham, **Surrey GU9 8AG**
TEL   0252 712660
OPEN   8–1, 2–5 Mon–Fri.

Specialise in restoring lacquered and gilded picture frames.

PROVIDE Home Inspections. Free Estimates. Chargeable Collection/Delivery Service.
SPEAK TO David Embling.
SEE Furniture.

LIMPSFIELD WATERCOLOURS
High Street, Limpsfield, **Surrey**
TEL   0883 717010 and 722205
OPEN   11–3 Tues; 9.30–2 Thur–Sat.

Specialise in framing prints and watercolours.

PROVIDE Local Home Inspections, Refundable Estimates.
SPEAK TO Christine Reason.
SEE Oil Paintings.

MANOR ANTIQUES AND RESTORATIONS
2 New Shops, High Street, Old Woking, **Surrey GU22 9JW**
TEL   0483 724666
OPEN   10–5 Mon–Fri; 10–4.30 Sat.

Specialise in picture framing.

PROVIDE Home Inspections. Free Estimates. Collection/Delivery Service.
SPEAK TO Alan Wellstead or Paul Thomson.

Member of the Guild of Master Craftsmen.
SEE Clocks, Furniture.

JACK MAY
'Beukenhof', Hogs Back, Guildford, **Surrey GU3 1DD**
TEL   0483 570615
OPEN   By Appointment.

Specialise in mounting and framing paintings. Also advise on presentation.

PROVIDE Home Inspections by arrangement. Free Estimates. Free Local Collection/Delivery Service.
SPEAK TO Jack May.
Established 1970.
SEE Oil Paintings.

CHARLES OWEN RESTORATIONS (GILDER)
The Studio, 1 Hillrise, Shere Road, West Horsley, **Surrey KT24 6EF**
TEL   04865 5271
OPEN   By Appointment.

Specialise in restoring picture frames.

PROVIDE Home Inspections. Free Estimates.
SPEAK TO Charles Owen.
SEE Furniture.

DAVID SAMUELS
Carters Framing Service, The Old Forge, 35 High Street, Godstone, **Surrey RH9 8LS**
TEL   0883 742457
OPEN   9–5 Mon–Fri.

Specialise in picture framing to the trade and public.

PROVIDE Free Estimates.
Collection/Delivery Service.
SPEAK TO David Samuels.

JUDITH WETHERALL
trading as **J.B. SYMES**
28 Silverlea Gardens, Horley, **Surrey
RH6 9BB**
TEL   0293 775024
OPEN   8.30–5.30 daily By Appointment
Only.

Specialise in restoring gilded picture
frames.

PROVIDE Free Local Home Inspections.
Free Estimates. Chargeable
Collection/Delivery Service.
SPEAK TO Judith Wetherall.
Member of UKIC and IIC. This
workshop is included on the register of
conservators maintained by the
Conservation Unit of the Museums and
Galleries Commission.
SEE Clocks, Furniture, Porcelain.

GOLDEN FISH
GILDING &
RESTORATION
94 Gloucester Road, Brighton, **East
Sussex BN1 4AP**
TEL   0273 691164
FAX   0273 691164
OPEN   9–5 Mon–Fri.

Specialise in gilding and restoring
picture frames, including carving.
PROVIDE Home Inspections. Free
Estimates. Free Collection/Delivery
Service.
SPEAK TO Marianne Hatchwell.
Ms Hatchwell will also teach gilding
techniques.
SEE Furniture, Porcelain.

G. MURRAY-BROWN
PICTURE SERVICES
Silverbeach House, Norman Road,
Pevensey Bay, **East Sussex BN24 6JR**
TEL   0323 764298
OPEN   By Appointment.

Specialise in restoring old frames.

PROVIDE Home Inspections. Free
Estimates. Collection/Delivery Service.
SPEAK TO Geoffrey Murray-Brown.
SEE Furniture.

SOUTH DOWN FINE ART
LTD
28 Western Road, Hove, **East Sussex
BN3 1HF**
TEL   0273 723760
OPEN   9.30–5 Mon–Fri; 9–5.30 Sat;
closed Wed p.m.

Specialise in framing in both traditional
swepts and modern metal, customised
mounting, washlines, marble mounts.

PROVIDE Home Inspections. Free
Estimates. Free Collection/Delivery
Service.
SPEAK TO John Forester.
Member of the Fine Art Trade Guild and
the Guild of Master Craftsmen.

STEWART GALLERY
48 Devonshire Road, Bexhill-on-Sea,
East Sussex TN40 1AX
TEL   0424 223410
FAX   0323 29588
OPEN   9–5.30 Mon–Sat.

Specialise in a framing service.

PROVIDE Home Inspections. Free
Estimates. Free Collection/Delivery
Service.
SPEAK TO Mrs L. Knight.
SEE Oil Paintings.

STEWART GALLERY
25 Grove Road, Eastbourne, **East
Sussex BN20 4TT**
TEL   0323 29588
FAX   0323 29588
OPEN   9–5.30 Mon–Fri; 11–4 Sat.

Specialise in a framing service.

PROVIDE Home Inspections. Free

Estimates. Free Collection/Delivery
Service.
SPEAK TO S. A. Ettinger.
SEE Oil Paintings.

ANNETTS (HORSHAM) LTD

7B Carfax, Horsham, **West Sussex
RH12 1DW**
TEL   0403 65878
OPEN   9–5.30 Mon–Sat.

Specialise in a full framing service.

PROVIDE Free Estimates.
SPEAK TO M. W. Annetts.
SEE Oil Paintings.

CAROL BANKS AND SON

September Cottage, 88 Victoria Road,
Shoreham-by-Sea, **West Sussex
BN4 5WS**
TEL   0273 461647.
OPEN   By Appointment
Specialise in conservation and
restoration of carved and gilded finished
picture frames.

PROVIDE Local Home Inspections. Free
Estimates.
SPEAK TO Carol Banks.
SEE Furniture, Porcelain.

DAVID WESTON

East Lodge, Woldringfold, Lower
Beeding, Horsham, **West Sussex
RH13 6NJ**
TEL   0403 891617
OPEN   By Appointment.

Specialise in restoring composition
frames and gilding and make
reproduction composition frames.

PROVIDE Free Estimates.
SPEAK TO David Weston.

SEE Furniture.

JUTTA DIXON

St Thomas Street Workshops, St Thomas
Street, Newcastle-Upon-Tyne, **Tyne &
Wear NE1 4LE**
TEL   091 232 4895 ext. 212
OPEN   9–5 Mon–Fri or By
       Appointment.

Specialise in framing and mounting of
watercolours, prints and drawings.

PROVIDE Home Inspections. Free
Estimates.
SPEAK TO Jutta Dixon.

Member of IPC. This workshop is
included on the register of conservators
maintained by the Conservation Unit of
the Museums and Galleries Commission.
SEE Oil Paintings.

LANTERN GALLERY

Hazeland House, Kington St Michael,
Chippenham, **Wiltshire SN14 6JJ**
TEL   0249 750306
FAX   0249 758896
OPEN   9–4 Mon–Fri or By
       Appointment.

Specialise in restoring period frames.

PROVIDE Home Inspections. Free
Estimates. Free Collection/Delivery
Service.
SPEAK TO Anne Campbell Macinnes.
Member of BADA.
SEE Oil Paintings, Porcelain.

ROOTHS OF BRADFORD-ON-AVON

18 Market Street, Bradford-on-Avon,
Wiltshire BA15 1LL
TEL   02216 4191
OPEN   9.30–1.00, 2.15–6 Mon–Sat.

Specialise in restoring picture frames.

PROVIDE Home Inspections. Free
Estimates. Collection/Delivery Service.
SPEAK TO Edward Rooth or Julia Rooth.

SEE Furniture.

W. C. GREENWOOD FINE ART
The Gallery, Oakdene Burneston, Nr. Bedale, **North Yorkshire DL8 2JE**
TEL 0677 424830 and 423217
OPEN By Appointment.

Specialise in restoring old frames.

PROVIDE Home Inspections. Chargeable Collection/Delivery Service.
SPEAK TO William Greenwood.

KIRKGATE PICTURE GALLERY
18 Kirkgate, Thirsk, **North Yorkshire YO7 1PQ**
TEL 0845 524085
OPEN 10–1, 2–5 Mon, Thur, Sat or By Appointment.

Specialise in framing oil paintings.

PROVIDE Chargeable Estimates. Collection/Delivery Service by arrangement.
SPEAK TO Richard Bennett.
Member of ABPR.
SEE Oil Paintings.

THE DAVIE GALLERY
8 Castlegate, Tickhill, Doncaster, **South Yorkshire DN11 9QU**
TEL 0302 751199
OPEN 9.30–5 Mon–Sat; closed Wed.

Specialise in picture framing.

PROVIDE Home Inspections. Free Estimates. Free Collection/Delivery Service.
SPEAK TO Ian Davie.
Member of the Fine Art Trade Guild.
SEE Oil Paintings, Carpets.

W. F. GADSBY LTD
33 New Briggate. Leeds, **West Yorkshire LS3 8JD**
TEL 0532 455326
OPEN 9–5 Mon–Sat.

Specialise in framing oils, watercolours etc.

PROVIDE Free Estimates. Free Local Collection/Delivery Service.
SPEAK TO Mr K. Crossland.

PHYLLIS ARNOLD GALLERY ANTIQUES
Hoops Courtyard, Greyabbey, **Co. Down BT22 2NE**
TEL 024774 8199 or 0247 853322 (answerphone)
OPEN 11–5 Wed–Sat.

Specialise in conservation framing.

PROVIDE Free Estimates. Collection/Delivery Service by arrangement.
SPEAK TO Phyllis Arnold.
Member of the Royal Society of Miniature Painters.
SEE Oil Paintings.

BARBARA BEST
9 Acton Road, Poyntzpass, Newry, **Co. Down BT35 6TB**
TEL 0762 86727
OPEN By Appointment.

Specialise in restoring picture frames, including gilding.

PROVIDE Home Inspections. Free Estimates. Chargeable Collection/Delivery Service.
SPEAK TO Barbara Best.
Member of IPCRA.
SEE Furniture.

MARION CAFFERKEY-BYRNE
Deerfield, Paulville, Tullow, **Co. Carlow**
TEL 0503 51750
OPEN By Appointment.

Specialise in restoring gilding on picture frames.

PROVIDE Home Inspections. Free

Estimates. Chargeable
Collection/Delivery Service.
SPEAK TO Marion Cafferkey.
Member of IPCRA and IGS.
SEE Furniture.

JAMES A. GORRY
20 Molesworth Street, Dublin 2,
Co. Dublin
TEL   01 6795319
OPEN   10–6 Mon–Fri.

Specialise in restoring frames.

PROVIDE Home Inspections.
SPEAK TO James Gorry.
SEE Oil Paintings.

JENNY SLEVIN
China Restoration Studio, Monkstown,
Co. Dublin
TEL   01 280 3429
OPEN   By Appointment.

Specialise in cleaning and repairing
picture frames.

PROVIDE Home Inspections.
Free/Chargeable Estimates.
Collection/Delivery Service by
arrangement.
SPEAK TO Jenny Slevin.

Member of IPCRA.
SEE Carpets, Furniture, Porcelain,
Collectors (Wax).

GLEBE STUDIO
Straffan, **Co. Kildare**
TEL   01 6271129
OPEN   10–4 Mon–Fri.

Specialise in restoring water and oil
gilded picture frames.

PROVIDE Chargeable Home Inspections.
Free Estimates. Collection/Delivery at
Automobile Club, Dublin.
SPEAK TO Phillipa Hynde, Dominique
Synott or Esen Philcox.

Member of IPCRA and UKIC.
SEE Furniture, Porcelain.

SUSAN MULHALL
Blackwood, Robertstown, Naas,
Co. Kildare
TEL   01 045 60336
OPEN   By Appointment.

Specialise in restoring picture frames,
including gilding and gessowork.

PROVIDE Home Inspections.
Free/Chargeable Estimates.
Collection/Delivery Service by
arrangement.
SPEAK TO Susan Mulhall.
Member of IPCRA.
SEE Furniture.

WLODEK SZUSTKIEWICZ
Stacumny House, Celbridge,
Co. Kildare
TEL   01 628 8345 ex. 10
OPEN   By Appointment.

Specialise in restoring picture frames,
including carving and gilding, gesso
work.

PROVIDE Home Inspections. Free
Estimates. Free Collection/Delivery
Service.
SPEAK TO Wlodek Szustkiewicz.

Member of IPCRA.
SEE Furniture.

EMILY NAPER
Loughcrew, Oldcastle, **Co. Meath**
TEL   049 41356
FAX   049 41722
OPEN   By Appointment.

Specialise in restoring water and oil
gilded picture frames.

PROVIDE Home Inspections. Free
Estimates. Chargeable Local
Collection/Delivery Service.
SPEAK TO Emily Naper.

Member of IPCRA.
SEE Furniture.

ANNE HYLAND
Beechmount, Roscrea, **Co. Tipperary**
TEL   0503 22310
OPEN   By Appointment.

Specialise in conserving picture frames, including water and oil gilded, eglomisé, gessowork.

PROVIDE Home Inspections. Free Estimates. Chargeable Collection/Delivery Service.
SPEAK TO Anne Hyland.
Member of IPCRA.
SEE Furniture.

VALERIE McCOY
Fan-na-Greine, Glendalough, **Co. Wicklow**
TEL   0404 45125
OPEN   By Appointment.

Specialise in restoring and gilding picture frames.

PROVIDE Home Inspections. Free/Chargeable Estimates. Free Collection/Delivery Service.
SPEAK TO Valerie McCoy.
Member of IPCRA.
SEE Furniture, Porcelain.

SIMON BLACKWOOD FINE ARTS LTD
10–11 Bourtree Terrace, Roxburgh, **Borders TD9 9HN**
TEL   0450 78547
FAX   0450 77780
OPEN   9.30–5.30 Mon–Fri; 10–2 Sat.

Specialise in framing and mounting and restoring gilt frames, including gilding and carving.

PROVIDE Home Inspections. Free Estimates. Chargeable Collection/Delivery Service.
SPEAK TO Carol Sutherland.
Member of SSCR. This workshop is in the Scottish Conservation Directory.
SEE Oil Paintings.

LYNWOOD REPRODUCTIONS
Lynwood, Eskdalemuir, Langholm, Dumfriesshire, **Dumfries & Galloway DG13 0QH**
TEL   03873 73211
OPEN   9–6 Mon–Fri.

Specialise in restoring carved and gilded wood frames. They also have the facility to make copies of most woodcarvings and can undertake gilding of any sort.

PROVIDE Home Inspections. Free Estimates. Chargeable Collection/Delivery Service.
SPEAK TO John or Nancy Chinnery.
Member of SSCR and the Guild of Master Craftsmen.
SEE Furniture.

JOSEPH SCHERRER
30 Harbour Street, Creetown, Wigtownshire, **Dumfries & Galloway DG8 7JJ**
TEL   067182 268
OPEN   10–5 Mon–Sat or By Appointment.

Specialise in restoring and reproducing picture frames, including mouldings of all dimensions and periods. They also make up their own frames and water gild, carve and polish.

PROVIDE Home Inspections. Free Estimates.
SPEAK TO Joseph Scherrer.
This workshop is in the Scottish Conservation Directory.
SEE Oil Paintings.

JAMES ANDERSON RITCHIE
Art Restoration Service, 6 Woodhill Place, Aberdeen, **Grampian AB2 4LF**
TEL   0224 310491
OPEN   9–5.30 or By Appointment.

Specialise in restoring picture frames and also provide a framing service.

PROVIDE Local Home Inspections. Free Estimates. Chargeable Collection/Delivery Service.
SPEAK TO J. Anderson Ritchie.

This workshop is in the Scottish Conservation Directory.
SEE Carpets, Oil Paintings.

ALDER ARTS
57 Church Street, Inverness, **Highland IV1 1DR**
TEL   0463 243575
OPEN   9–5.30 Mon–Sat.

Specialise in framing 17th–19th century oil paintings.

PROVIDE Home Inspections. Free/Chargeable Estimates. Free Collection/Delivery Service.
SPEAK TO Ken Hardiman.
SEE Oil Paintings.

ORBOST GALLERY
Bolvean, Isle of Skye, **Highland IV55 8ZB**
TEL   047 022 207
OPEN   By Appointment.

Specialise in repairing and restoring ornate Victorian frames, also framed presentation calligraphy and illumination.

PROVIDE Home Inspections. Free/Chargeable Collection/Delivery Service.
SPEAK TO Dr David L. Roberts MA FSA (Scotland).

This workshop is in the Scottish Conservation Directory.
SEE Oil Paintings.

BOURNE FRAMES AND RESTORATION LTD
4 Dundas Street, Edinburgh, **Lothian EH3 6HZ**
TEL   031 557 4874
FAX   031 557 8382
OPEN   10–6 Mon–Fri; 10–1 Sat.

Specialise in restoring and gilding antique frames. They also keep a large stock of antique frames.

PROVIDE Home Inspections. Free Estimates. Free/Chargeable Collection/Delivery Service.
SPEAK TO Susan Heys.

This workshop is in the Scottish Conservation Directory.
SEE Oil Paintings.

MALCOLM INNES GALLERY
67 George Street, Edinburgh, **Lothian EH2 2JG**
TEL   031 226 4151
FAX   031 226 4151
OPEN   9.30–6 Mon–Fri.

Specialise in framing pictures.

PROVIDE Home Inspections. Free Estimates. Free/Chargeable Collection/Delivery Service.
SPEAK TO Anthony Woodd.
SEE **London SW3.**
SEE Oil Paintings.

DAPHNE FRASER
Glenbarry, 58 Victoria Road, Lenzie, Glasgow, **Strathclyde G66 5AP**
TEL   041 776 1281
OPEN   By Appointment.

Specialise in restoring ornate picture frames.

PROVIDE Free Estimates.
SPEAK TO Daphne Fraser.
SEE Collectors (Dolls, Toys), Furniture, Oil Paintings.

McIAN GALLERY
10 Argyll Square, Oban, **Strathclyde PA34 4AZ**
TEL   0631 66755
OPEN   9–5.30 Mon–Sat.

Specialise in picture framing.

PROVIDE Chargeable
Collection/Delivery Service.
SPEAK TO Rory Campbell-Gibson.
SEE Oil Paintings.

NEIL LIVINGSTONE
3 Old Hawkhill, Dundee, **Tayside
DD1 5EU**
TEL   0382 21751
OPEN   9–5 Mon–Fri.

Specialise in framing paintings.

PROVIDE Free Estimates. Chargeable
Collection/Delivery Service.
SPEAK TO Neil Livingstone.
SEE Arms, Furniture, Oil Paintings, Silver.

MANOR HOUSE FINE ARTS
73 Pontcanna Street, Cardiff, **South
Glamorgan CF1 9HS**
TEL   0222 227787
OPEN   10.30–5.30 Tues, Thur, Fri, Sat
       or By Appointment.

Specialise in a bespoke framing service.

PROVIDE Home Inspections. Free
Estimates at the gallery. Chargeable
Collection/Delivery Service.
SPEAK TO Steven Denley-Hill.
SEE Oil Paintings.

PORCELAIN, GLASS AND SCULPTURE

DO

Always use both hands when lifting – never lift by handles
Remove lids before lifting
Interleave stacked plates with clean paper, and never stack them more than six deep
Avoid using force to release jammed decanter stoppers: try immersing in warm water, and gradually adding hot water to increase the temperature
Avoid displaying ceramics at floor level

DON'T

Hang plates by spring-clip wallhangers which are not plastic covered
Stack plates flat when transporting them
Stack cups or glasses inside one another
Leave tea or coffee in cups for long periods
Use adhesive tape or sticky labels, especially on gilding
Put anything old in a microwave
Put flowerpots or containers directly on to plates or dishes
Keep wine for long in decanters
Store wineglasses with rims touching
Use more than a drop of detergent when washing
Warm old plates in the oven
Wear loose-sleeved clothes when arranging on shelves

IAN AND DIANNE McCARTHY
Arcadian Cottage, 112 Station Road, Clutton, **Avon BS18 4RA**
TEL   0761 53188
OPEN   By Appointment.

Specialise in restoring bronze and spelter figures and table lamps.

PROVIDE Home Inspections. Free Estimates. Chargeable Collection/Delivery Service.
SPEAK TO Ian or Dianne McCarthy.
SEE Furniture, Silver.

JANE WAY RESTORATIONS LTD
(Ceramic Restorer), 26 Foxcombe Road, Weston, Bath, **Avon BA1 3ED**
TEL   0225 446770
OPEN   10–5 Mon–Fri By Appointment.

Specialise in restoring all types of ceramics, especially Meissen, 18th and 19th century Chinese and English porcelain.

PROVIDE Free/Chargeable Estimates.
SPEAK TO Jane Way.
Member of UKIC. This workshop is included on the register of conservators maintained by the Conservation Unit of the Museums and Galleries Commission.

HERITAGE RESTORATIONS
36B High Street, Great Missenden, **Buckinghamshire HP16 OAU**
TEL   02406 5710
OPEN   10–5 Mon–Sat.

Specialise in restoring porcelain.

PROVIDE Free Estimates. Home Inspections.
SPEAK TO John Wilshire.
SEE Clocks, Furniture.

SAFAVID CERAMIC RESTORATIONS
29 Blacksmiths Lane, Prestwood, Great Missenden, **Buckinghamshire HP16 0AP**
TEL   02406 5231
OPEN   By Appointment.

Specialise in restoring ceramics, particularly English blue and white transfer wares.

PROVIDE Home Inspections. Free Estimates.
SPEAK TO Bridget Syms.

WILLIAM DAWSON
The Gatehouse, Buckden Towers, Buckden, **Cambridgeshire PE18 9TA**
TEL   0480 811868
OPEN   By Appointment.

Specialise in repairing and restoring ceramics, particularly Oriental and English porcelain, as well as 19th and 20th century decorative pottery and figures.

PROVIDES Home Inspections. Free Estimates. Chargeable Collection/Delivery Service.
SPEAK TO William Dawson.

DIANA FRANCES DRYSDALE
4 Collipriest House, Tiverton, **Devon EX16 4PT**
TEL   0884 258145
OPEN   10–6 Mon–Fri.

Specialise in restoring fine porcelain.

PROVIDE Home Inspections. Free Estimates. Chargeable Collection/Delivery Service.
SPEAK TO Diana Frances.

This workshop is included on the register of conservators maintained by the Conservation Unit of the Museums and Galleries Commission.

THE LANTERN SHOP
4 New Street, Sidmouth, **Devon**
EX10 8AP
TEL   0395 516320
OPEN   9.45–12.45, 2.15–4.45 Mon–
        Sat; closed Mon & Sat p.m.

Specialise in restoring antique items of lighting and conversion to electricity. Silk shade-making undertaken.

PROVIDE Home Inspections. Free Estimates. Chargeable Collection/Delivery Service.
SPEAK TO Julia Creeke.

MRS CATHERINE MATHEW
Kiwi Cottage, Maperton Road, Charlton Horethorne, Sherborne, **Dorset DT9 4NT**
TEL   096 322 595
OPEN   9–6 Mon–Fri or By Appointment.

Specialise in repairing ceramics and glass.

PROVIDE Home Inspections. Free Estimates. Free Collection/Delivery Service.
SPEAK TO Catherine Mathew.
SEE Furniture, Picture Frames.

QUARTER JACK ANTIQUES
Bridge Street, Sturminster Newton, **Dorset DT10 1BZ**
TEL   0258 72558
OPEN   9–5.30 Mon–Sat.

Specialise in restoring glass, including grinding.

PROVIDE Home Inspections. Chargeable Estimates. Chargeable Collection/Delivery Service.
SPEAK TO Mr A. J. Nelson.

CHANDELIER CLEANING AND RESTORATION SERVICES LTD
Gypsy Mead, Fyfield, **Essex CM5 0RB**
TEL   0277 899444
FAX   0277 899642
OPEN   8–5 Mon–Fri.

Specialise in restoration of fine period chandeliers employing their own skilled glass blowers, glass cutters, gilders and metal finishers.

PROVIDE Home Inspections. Free/Refundable Estimates. Free Collection/Delivery Service.
SPEAK TO Mr Stewart L. Nardi.

Members of the Lighting Association and the British Glass Manufacturers Association. This workshop is included on the register of conservators maintained by the Conservation Unit of the Museums and Galleries Commission.

CHARMAINE
P.O.BOX 255, Brentwood, **Essex CM15 9AP**
TEL   0277 224224
OPEN   9–5 Mon–Fri.

Specialise in mechanically polishing the inside of hollow glass vessels (decanters, vases, glassware) to remove the etched surface which causes the glass to look white.

PROVIDE Free Estimates.
SPEAK TO Charmaine Cox.

MILLSIDE ANTIQUE RESTORATION
Parndon Mill, Parndon Mill Lane, Harlow, **Essex CM20 2HP**
TEL   0279 428148
FAX   0279 415075
OPEN   10–5 Mon–Fri.

Specialise in restoring Oriental and European porcelain and coloured glass.

PROVIDE Home Inspections.

Free/Chargeable Estimates. Chargeable Collection/Delivery Service.
SPEAK TO David Sparks or Angela Wickliffe-Philp.
Also provide tuition courses in china and porcelain restoration. Member of the Guild of Master Craftsmen.
SEE Oil Paintings, Picture Frames, Silver.

FRANCIS STEPHENS
Bush House, Church Road, Corringham, Stanford-le-Hope, **Essex SS17 9AP**
TEL   0375 673463
OPEN   By Appointment.

Specialise in restoring Staffordshire figures 1775–1900 and will advise on their display.

PROVIDE Home Inspections. Free Estimates. Free Collection/Delivery Service.
SPEAK TO Francis Stephens.

KEITH BAWDEN
Mews Workshop, Montpellier Retreat, Cheltenham, **Gloucestershire GL50 2XS**
TEL   0242 230320
OPEN   7–4.30 Mon–Fri.

Specialise in conserving and restoring all aspects of porcelain.

PROVIDE Free Estimates. Home Inspections. Local Collection/Delivery Service.
SPEAK TO Keith Bawden.
SEE Clocks, Silver, Furniture, Oil Paintings.

ATELIER FINE ART CASTINGS LTD
Hulfords Lane, Nr. Hartley Wintney, **Hampshire RG27 8AG**
TEL   0252 844388
OPEN   8.30–5 Mon–Fri.

Specialise in restoring bronze art work and bronze casting.

Restoration of most other metalwork undertaken.

PROVIDE Free Estimates. Chargeable Collection/Delivery Service.
SPEAK TO Mrs A. Wills.
SEE Silver.

JUST THE THING
High Street, Hartley Wintney, Basingstoke, **Hampshire RG27 8NS**
TEL   025126 3393 and 2916
OPEN   9–5 Mon–Sat.

Specialise in china restoration.
SPEAK TO Sue Carpenter.
Members of LAPADA.

PHILIPPA M. NELSON
China Fix, 4 Setters Workshops, Mount Pleasant Lane, Lymington, **Hampshire SO41 8LS**
TEL   0590 679869
OPEN   9.30–3.30 Mon–Fri; By
        Appointment Sat & Sun.

Specialise in restoration of all types of ceramics, china, porcelain and pottery. The modelling of missing pieces is a speciality as well as colour matching and detail in finishing to highest standards.

PROVIDE Free Estimates.
SPEAK TO Philippa Nelson.

KATHARINE SILCOCK ANTIQUE CHINA RESTORATION
Mercury Yacht Harbour, Satchell Lane, Hamble, Southampton, **Hampshire SO3 5HQ**
TEL   0703 455056
OPEN   9–6.30 Mon–Thur.

Specialise in restoring and repairing all forms of china, including Meissen, Bow, Chelsea, Oriental, Belleek, Doulton and Parian ware.

PROVIDE Estimates.
SPEAK TO Katharine Silcock
Also run china restoration courses.

MARY ROSE WRANGHAM
Studio 304, Victory Business Centre,
Somers Road North, Portsmouth,
Hampshire PO1 1PJ
TEL   0705 829863
OPEN   10–5 Daily.

Specialise in restoring ceramics,
including Oriental and Chinese style
decorative repairs in gold leaf.

PROVIDE Chargeable Home Inspections.
Chargeable Estimates. Chargeable
Collection/Delivery Service.
SPEAK TO Mary Rose Wrangham.
Also provide studio ceramic repair
courses and have a ninety-minute
training video.

PIPE ELM PORCELAIN
Pipe Elm, Leigh Sinton, Malvern,
Hereford & Worcester WR13 5EA
TEL   0886 832492
OPEN   By Appointment.

Specialise in restoring European and
Oriental pottery and porcelain,
including antiquities.

PROVIDE Home Inspections. Free
Estimates. Free Collection/Delivery
Service every two months at the IAC
Fair, Newark.
SPEAK TO Fred or Maggie Covins.

HERTFORDSHIRE CONSERVATION SERVICE
Seed Warehouse, Maidenhead Yard,
The Wash, Hertford, **Hertfordshire
SG14 1PX**
TEL   0992 588966
FAX   0992 588971
OPEN   9–6 Mon–Fri By Appointment.

Specialise in restoring ceramic, glass and
stone vessels and ornaments.

PROVIDE Home Inspections.
Free/Chargeable Estimates. Chargeable
Collection/Delivery Service.

SPEAK TO J. M. MacQueen.
This workshop is included on the
register of conservators maintained by
the Conservation Unit of the Museums
and Galleries Commission.
SEE Carpets, Collectors (Dolls), Lighting,
Furniture, Oil Paintings, Picture Frames.

WILLIAM H. STEVENS
8 Eton Avenue, East Barnet,
Hertfordshire EN4 8TU
TEL   081 449 7956
OPEN   9–5.30 Mon–Fri

Specialise in restoring Japanese and
Chinese pottery.

PROVIDES Home Inspections. Free
Estimates. Free Collection/Delivery
Service.
SPEAK TO John Robin or Daniel Stevens.
The fifth generation of a family firm
founded in 1836.
SEE Silver.

A. & S. ALLEN
40 Clarendon Way, Chislehurst, **Kent
BR7 6RF**
TEL   0689 826345
OPEN   9–5 Mon–Fri.

Specialise in restoring ceramics,
European and Oriental porcelain and
pottery, enamels.

PROVIDE Free Estimates.
Collection/Delivery Service by
arrangement.
SPEAK TO Adrian Allen.
SEE Clocks.

AUDREY BURFORD
North West Kent. (full address withheld
by request)
TEL   081 467 9757
OPEN   9–5 Mon–Fri.

Specialise in restoring European
ceramics, principally earthenware, tin-
glaze and ironstone pieces.

PROVIDE Free Estimates.
Collection/Delivery Service by
arrangement.
SPEAK TO Audrey Burford.

HENWOOD DECORATIVE METAL STUDIOS
The Bayle, Folkestone, **Kent CT20 1SQ**
TEL 0303 50911
FAX 0303 850224
OPEN 8.30–5 Mon–Fri.

Specialise in restoring small bronze
statues.

PROVIDE Local Home Inspections. Free
Estimates. Local Free
Collection/Delivery Service.
SPEAK TO Mr P. J. Rose.
Member of UKIC, Federation of Master
Craftsmen and National Church Craft
Association.
SEE Silver.

SARGEANT RESTORATIONS
21 The Green, Westerham, **Kent
TN16 1AX**
TEL 0959 62130
OPEN 8.30–5.30 Mon–Sat.

Specialise in restoration, cleaning and
wiring of chandeliers, lustres, candelabra
and general light fittings.

PROVIDE Home Inspections. Free
Estimates. Chargeable
Collection/Delivery Service.
SPEAK TO Ann, David or Denys Sargeant.
SEE Silver.

BROTHERIDGE CHANDELIERS
3 Maytree Walk, Woodley Park,
Skelmersdale, **Lancashire WN8 6UP**
TEL 0695 26276
FAX 0695 35634
OPEN By Appointment.

Specialise in conserving and restoring
glass chandeliers.

PROVIDE Home Inspections. Free
Estimates. Chargeable
Collection/Delivery Service.
SPEAK TO Terry Brotheridge.

E. & C. ROYALL
10 Waterfall Way, Medbourne, Nr.
Market Harborough, **Leicestershire
LE15 8EE**
TEL 0858 83744
OPEN 8.30–5 Mon–Fri.

Specialise in restoring European
bronzes, as well as Oriental ivories,
bronzes and wood-carvings.

PROVIDE Home Inspections. Free
Estimates. Chargeable
Collection/Delivery Service.
SPEAK TO C. Royall.
SEE Furniture.

LINCOLN CONSERVATION STUDIO
c/o Museum of Lincolnshire Life,
Burton Road, Lincoln, **Lincolnshire
LN1 3LY**
TEL 0522 533207
OPEN 9–5 Mon–Fri.

Specialise in restoring ceramics, wood
and metal statuary to museum
conservation standards.

PROVIDE Home Inspections.
Free/Chargeable Estimates. Chargeable
Collection/Delivery Service.
SPEAK TO John Hurd, Stephanie Margrett
or David Fisher.

Members of UKIC. This workshop is
included on the register of conservators
maintained by the Conservation Unit of
the Museums and Galleries Commission.
SEE Arms, Furniture, Lighting.

COLIN SCHLAPOBERSKY
20 Sandringham Road, **London E8 2LP**
TEL 071 249 4527
OPEN 9–5 Mon–Fri By Appointment.

Specialise in restoring sculpture.

PROVIDE Home Inspections. Free Estimates. Chargeable Collection/Delivery Service.
SPEAK TO Colin Schlapobersky

Member of IIC and UKIC. This workshop is included on the register of conservators maintained by the Conservation Unit of the Museums and

Galleries Commission.

DAVID TURNER
4 Atlas Mews, Ramsgate Street, **London E8 2NA**
TEL   071 249 2379
OPEN   10–6 Mon–Fri.

Specialise in restoring glass light fittings and lamp conversions.

PROVIDE Home Inspections. Free Estimates. Free Collection/Delivery Service.
SPEAK TO David Turner.

SEE Furniture, Silver.

RUPERT HARRIS
Studio 5, 1 Fawe Street, **London E14 6PD**
TEL   071 987 6231 or 515 2020
FAX   071 987 7994
OPEN   9–6 Mon–Fri.

Specialise in restoring fine sculpture.

PROVIDE Home Inspections. Chargeable Estimates. Collection/Delivery Service by arrangement.
SPEAK TO Rupert Harris.

Member of UKIC and IIC. This workshop is included on the register of conservators maintained by the Conservation Unit of the Museums and Galleries Commission.

SEE Silver.

PAOLA CAMUSSO
46 Pennybank Chambers, 33–35 St John's Square, **London EC1M 4DS**
TEL   071 250 3278
FAX   071 250 0297
OPEN   10–6 Mon–Fri.

Specialise in restoring polychrome wood sculptures.

PROVIDE Home Inspections. Free Estimates. Free Collection/Delivery Service.
SPEAK TO Ms Paola Camusso.

Associate of ABPR. This workshop is included on the register of conservators maintained by the Conservation Unit of the Museums and Galleries Commission.
SEE Oil Paintings.

THE CONSERVATION STUDIO
Unit 21, Pennybank Chambers, 33–35 St John's Square, **London EC1M 4DS**
TEL   071 251 6853
OPEN   9.30–5 Mon–Fri.

Specialise in restoring ceramics and glass, including pieces for chandeliers.

PROVIDE Home Inspections (large items only). Refundable Estimates. Chargeable Collection/Delivery Service.
SPEAK TO Sandra Davison.
SEE Clocks, Silver.

MARIA KELLER CONSERVATION AND RESTORATION
Unit 46, Pennybank Chambers, St John's Square, **London EC1M 4DS**
TEL   071 386 8723 or 081 250 3278
OPEN   10–7 Mon–Fri or By Appointment.

Specialise in restoring polychrome wood sculpture.

PROVIDE Home Inspections. Free Estimates. Chargeable Collection/Delivery Service.
SPEAK TO Maria Keller.

Member of ABPR and UKIC. This workshop is included on the register of conservators maintained by the Conservation Unit of the Museums and Galleries Commission.
SEE Oil Paintings.

CERAMIC RESTORATIONS
7 Alwyne Villas, **London N1 2HG**
TEL   071 359 5240
OPEN   By Appointment Only.

Specialise in all types of pottery and porcelain restoration, especially decorative items.

PROVIDE Home Inspections. Free/Chargeable Estimates. Collection/Delivery Service by arrangement.
SPEAK TO John Parker.

Member of UKIC. This workshop is included on the register of conservators maintained by the Conservation Unit of the Museums and Galleries Commission.

PETER CHAPMAN ANTIQUES
Incorporating **CHAPMAN RESTORATIONS**
10 Theberton Street, **London N1 0QX**
TEL   071 226 5565
FAX   081 348 4846
OPEN   9.30–6 Mon–Sat.

Specialise in repairing bronze and other metalwork.

PROVIDE Home Inspections. Refundable Estimates. Chargeable Collection/Delivery Service.
SPEAK TO Peter Chapman or Tony Holohan.

SEE Furniture, Oil Paintings, Picture Frames, Silver.

ROCHEFORT ANTIQUES LTD
32–34 The Green, **London N21 1AX**
TEL   081 886 4779 or 363 0910
OPEN   10–6 Mon, Tues, Thur, Sat.

Specialise in restoring porcelain.

PROVIDE Home Inspections. Free Estimates. Chargeable Collection/Delivery Service.
SPEAK TO L. W. Stevens-Wilson.
SEE Furniture, Silver.

ROSS ANTHONY FULLER
23 Rosecroft Avenue, **London NW3 7QA**
TEL   071 435 4562
OPEN   Mon–Sat By Appointment.

Specialise in restoration and conservation of sculpture and three-dimensional works of art concentrating on wood carving and finishing.

PROVIDE Home Inspections. Free/Chargeable Estimates. Free Local Collection/Delivery Service.
SPEAK TO Ross Anthony Fuller.

This workshop is included on the register of conservators maintained by the Conservation Unit of the Museums and Galleries Commission.
SEE Furniture.

JEFF OLIVER trading as OLIVERS
34A Malden Road, **London NW5 3HH**
TEL   071 284 4529
OPEN   9–5.30 Mon–Fri By Appointment Only.

Specialise in restoring all types of ceramics as well as cloisonné, decorative glass.

PROVIDE Free Estimates.
SPEAK TO Jeff Oliver.

CHINA REPAIRERS
64 Charles Lane, **London** NW8 7SB
TEL　　071 722 8407
OPEN　　9.30–5.30 Mon–Thur; 9.30–
4.30 Fri.

Specialise in conservation and restoration of all antique and modern ceramics. They use invisible and museum techniques with the modelling of missing parts being a speciality. Glass repairs are also undertaken

PROVIDE Free Estimates.
SPEAK TO Virginia Baron.

Provide courses and individual tuition in restoration. Member of the Guild of Master Craftsmen.

WELLINGTON GALLERY
1 St John's Wood High Street, **London**
NW8 7NG
TEL　　071 586 2620
OPEN　　10–5.30 Mon–Sat.

Specialise in restoring glass and European and Oriental porcelain.

PROVIDE Home Inspections. Free Estimates. Chargeable Collection/Delivery Service.
SPEAK TO Mrs Maureen Barclay or Mr K. J. Barclay.

Member of LAPADA.
SEE Silver, Oil Paintings, Furniture.

VOITEK
Conservation of Works of Art,
9 Whitehorse Mews, Westminster Bridge Road, **London** SE1 7QD
TEL　　071 928 6094
FAX　　071 928 6094
OPEN　　10.30–5 Mon–Fri.

Specialise in conservation of sculpture in marble, stone, terracotta.

PROVIDE Home Inspections with advice on condition, display, damage assessments and conservation strategy subject to fee. Chargeable

Collection/Delivery Service.
SPEAK TO Wojtek Sobczynski.
SEE Oil Paintings.

R. WILKINSON & SON
5 Catford Hill, **London** SE6 4NU
TEL　　081 314 1080
FAX　　081 690 1524
OPEN　　9–5 Mon–Fri.

Specialise in restoring glass chandeliers, decanters, glasses and stoppers. Will also make glass shades to match existing ones.

PROVIDE Home Inspections. Free Estimates. Chargeable Collection/Delivery Service.
SPEAK TO Peter Prickett, Jane Milnes or David Wilkinson.

SEE Silver.

ASHTON-BOSTOCK (CHINA REPAIRS)
21 Charlwood Street, **London**
SW1V 2EA
TEL　　071 828 3656
OPEN　　9.30–1, 2–5.30 Tues–Thur.

Specialise in restoring fine porcelain.

PROVIDE Refundable Estimates.
SPEAK TO David Ashton-Bostock.

CLARE HOUSE LIMITED
35 Elizabeth Street, **London**
SW1W 9RP
TEL　　071 730 8480
FAX　　071 259 9752
OPEN　　9.30–5.30 Mon–Fri.

Specialise in restoring lamps, lampshades and porcelain.

PROVIDE Home Inspections. Free Estimates. Chargeable Collection/Delivery Service.
SPEAK TO Elizabeth Hanley.

SEE Silver.

GRANVILLE & BURBIDGE

111 Kingsmead Road, **London** SW2 3HZ

TEL 081 674 1969
OPEN 9–6 Mon–Sat.

Specialise in conserving and restoring sculpture, including polychrome, wood, stone, marble, terracotta, alabaster and plaster.

PROVIDE Home Inspections. Free Estimates in the London area. Chargeable Collection/Delivery Service. SPEAK TO John Burbidge.

Will also do condition surveys, environmental monitoring and historical research and provision and/or recommendations for maintenance, display facilities, packing and transport.

W. G. T. BURNE (ANTIQUE GLASS) LTD

11 Elystan Street, **London** SW3 3NT

TEL 071 589 6074
FAX 081 944 1977
OPEN 9–5 Mon–Sat; closed Thur p.m. & Sat p.m.

Specialise in restoring English and Irish 18th and 19th century glass, including chandeliers, candelabra, lustres, wall-lights, decanters, tableware and collectors' pieces. Also remove chips from glasses and arrange for glass linings.

PROVIDE Home Inspections. Free Estimates.
SPEAK TO Andrew Burne.

JOHN HEAP

No.1 The Polygon, **London** SW4

TEL 071 627 4498
OPEN By Appointment.

Specialise in restoring terracotta figures, remodelling sculpture.

PROVIDE Home Inspections. Free Estimates. Free Collection/Delivery Service.

SPEAK TO John Heap.
SEE Furniture, Silver.

SALLY NICHOLSON AND SHIRLEY PAUL

34 Perrymead Street, **London** SW6 3SP

TEL 071 731 3226
OPEN 9–5 Mon–Fri.

Specialise in all china restoration especially antique porcelain.

PROVIDE Free Estimates.
SPEAK TO Sally Nicholson or Shirley Paul.

This workshop is included on the register of conservators maintained by the Conservation Unit of the Museums and Galleries Commission.

SCULPTURE RESTORATIONS

1 Michael Road, Kings Road, **London** SW6 2ER

TEL 071 736 7292
OPEN 8–4.30 Mon–Fri.

Specialise in restoring, repairing and conserving all works under the general classification of sculpture; bronze, other metals, wood, ivory, stone, marble, also including works which are painted or gilded.

PROVIDE Home Inspections. Free Estimates. Chargeable Collection/Delivery Service.
SPEAK TO John Doubleday or Michael Gaskin.

CHRISTOPHER WRAY'S LIGHTING EMPORIUM

600 Kings Road, **London** SW6 2DX

TEL 071 736 8434
FAX 071 731 3507
OPEN 9.30–6 Mon–Sat.

Specialise in restoring original Victorian and Edwardian light fittings.

PROVIDE Free Estimates. Chargeable
Collection/Delivery Service.
SPEAK TO Christopher Wray.
SEE Silver.

H. W. POULTER & SON
279 Fulham Road, **London SW10 9PZ**
TEL   071 352 7268
FAX   071 351 0984
OPEN   9–5 Mon–Fri; 10–1 Sat.

Specialise in restoring antique marble
and sculpture.

PROVIDE Home Inspections. Refundable
Estimates. Chargeable
Collection/Delivery Service.
SPEAK TO Douglas Poulter.

Have a workshop at 1A Adelaide Grove,
off Uxbridge Road, London W12.
TEL   081 749 4557;
OPEN   7.30–5.30 Mon–Fri.

PETER AND FRANCES BINNINGTON
65 St Johns Hill, **London SW11**
TEL   071 223 9192
FAX   071 924 1668
OPEN   8.30–5.30 Mon–Fri.

Specialise in restoring verre eglomisé
(gilt glass). They also make copies to
commission, including table tops and
wall panels.

PROVIDE Home Inspections. Free
Estimates. Chargeable
Collection/Delivery Service.
SPEAK TO Joanne Neal.
SEE Furniture.

IMOGEN PAINE LIMTED
8 Juer Street, **London SW11 4RF**
TEL   071 223 4648
FAX   071 223 7113
OPEN   9–5 Mon–Fri.

Specialise in restoring sculpture in
bronze, marble, terracotta, plaster,
stone, especially 19th century works.

PROVIDE Home Inspections. Free Local
Estimates. Collection/Delivery Service.
SPEAK TO Imogen Paine.

JUDITH LARNEY
Unit 2, Fovant Mews, 12A Noyna Road,
London SW17 7PH
TEL   081 682 3781
OPEN   9–5.30 Mon–Fri or By
        Appointment.

Specialise in restoring ceramics,
enamels, terracotta and marble.

PROVIDE Free Estimates.
SPEAK TO Judith Larney.
Member of UKIC, IIC and Museums
Association. This workshop is included
on the register of conservators
maintained by the Conservation Unit of
the Museums and Galleries Commission.

PLOWDEN AND SMITH LTD
190 St Ann's Hill, **London SW18 2RT**
TEL   081 874 4005
FAX   081 874 7248
OPEN   9–5.30 Mon–Fri.

Specialise in restoring and conserving
bronze, stone, marble, ceramics, glass,
ivory.

PROVIDE Home Inspections. Free
Estimates. Chargeable
Collection/Delivery Service.
SPEAK TO Bob Butler.

They also advise on conservation
strategy, environmental control and
microclimates for collections, as well as
installing, mounting and displaying
temporary and permanent exhibitions.
SEE Oil Paintings, Furniture, Silver.

BLOOMFIELD CERAMIC RESTORATIONS LTD
4th Floor, 58 Davies Street, **London
W1Y 1LB**
TEL   071 580 5761
FAX   071 636 1625
OPEN   By Appointment.

Specialise in restoring antique European and Oriental ceramics and bronzes.

PROVIDE Free Estimates.
SPEAK TO Steven P. Bloomfield.
SEE Silver.

W. SITCH & CO. LTD
48 Berwick Street, **London W1V 4JD**
TEL   071 437 3776
OPEN   8.30–5.30 Mon–Fri; 9–10 Sat.

Specialise in restoring late 19th century lighting.

PROVIDE Home Inspections. Free Estimates. Free/Chargeable Collection/Delivery Service.
SPEAK TO Ron Sitch.
SEE Silver.

N. DAVIGHI
117 Shepherds Bush Road, **London W6**
TEL   071 603 5357
OPEN   9–5 Mon–Sat.

Specialise in gilding, polishing and repairing lighting, especially crystal and ormolu chandeliers.

PROVIDE Home Inspections. Free Estimates. Chargeable Collection/Delivery Service.
SPEAK TO Mr N. Davighi.

PORCELAIN AND PICTURES LTD
The Studio, 1B Gastein Road, **London W6 8LT**
TEL   071 385 7512
OPEN   9–5.30 Mon–Sat.

Specialise in restoring porcelain.

PROVIDE Home Inspections. Free Estimates.
SPEAK TO June Spinella.

Member of the FATG.
SEE Picture Frames.

CLAUDIO ASTROLOGO
59–61 Kensington High Street, **London W8 5ED**
TEL   071 937 7820
OPEN   By Appointment.

Specialise in restoring polychrome statues.

PROVIDE Chargeable Estimates.
SPEAK TO Claudio Astrologo.

Member of IIC and UKIC.
SEE Oil Paintings.

ANTHONY BELTON
14 Holland Street, **London W8 4LT**
TEL   071 937 1012
OPEN   10–1 Mon–Fri; 10–4.30 Sat.

Specialise in restoring English and Continental pottery.

PROVIDE Home Inspections.
SPEAK TO Anthony Belton.
SEE Oil Paintings.

BRETT MANLEY
Studio 1D, Kensington Church Walk, **London W8 4NB**
TEL   071 937 7583
OPEN   11–5 Mon–Fri.

Specialise in restoring ceramics.

PROVIDE Free Estimates.
SPEAK TO Brett Manley.

Run a two-week beginners' course in ceramic restoration three times a year.

ROSEMARY COOK RESTORATION
78 Stanlake Road, **London W12 7HJ**
TEL   081 749 7977
OPEN   By Appointment.

Specialise in restoring statuary, including polychrome surfaces.

PROVIDE Home Inspections. Free
Estimates. Free Collection/Delivery
Service in London.
SPEAK TO Rosemary Cook.
SEE Furniture, Silver.

THE GLASSHOUSE
65 Long Acre, **London WC2E 9JH**
TEL   071 836 9785
FAX   071 240 7508
OPEN   10–6 Mon–Fri; 11–5 Sat.

Specialise in restoring both antique and
contemporary glass, including making
liners, shades and pieces for chandeliers.

PROVIDE Home Inspections.
SPEAK TO Christopher Williams.

HELEN POTTER
Ivy Cottage, Grove Road, Wallasey,
Wirral, **Merseyside L45 3HF**
TEL   051 639 2826
OPEN   9–5 Mon–Fri.

Specialise in all aspects of restoring
ceramics, including gilding and
modelling missing areas.

PROVIDE Home Inspections. Free
Estimates. Chargeable Delivery Service.
SPEAK TO Helen Potter.
Member of Ceramic and Glass
Conservation Group. This workshop is
included on the register of conservators
maintained by the Conservation Unit of
the Museums and Galleries Commission.

WILLIAM ALLCHIN
22–24 St Benedicts Street, Norwich,
Norfolk NR2 4AQ
TEL   0603 660046
FAX   0603 660046
OPEN   10.30–5 Mon–Sat.

Specialise in restoring period lighting,
including glass chandeliers and wall
brackets.

PROVIDE Home Inspections. Free
Estimates.
SPEAK TO William Allchin.
SEE Silver.

JASPER ANTIQUES
11A Hall Road, Snettisham, King's
Lynn, **Norfolk PE31 7LU**
TEL   0485 541485 (Home 0485
        540604)
OPEN   10.30–1 Mon, Wed, Fri; 10.30–
        1, 2–4 Sat.

Specialise in repairing ceramics.

PROVIDE Home Inspections. Free
Estimates. Free Collection/Delivery
Service.
SPEAK TO Mrs A. Norris.
SEE Clocks, Furniture, Silver.

MARIANNE MORRISH
South Cottage Studio, Union Lane,
Wortham Ling, Diss, **Norfolk IP22 ISP**
TEL   0379 643831
OPEN   10–4 Mon–Fri.

Specialise in restoring 18th century
porcelain and early Staffordshire.

PROVIDE Home Inspections. Free
Estimates. Chargeable
Collection/Delivery Service.
SPEAK TO Marianne Morrish.

Ms Morrish is a member of the Guild of
Master Craftsmen; she gives three-week
tuition courses in ceramic restoration.
SEE Silver.

SUSAN NOEL
The Studio, Roundways, Holt, **Norfolk
NR25 6BN**
TEL   0263 711362
OPEN   10–4 Tues, Wed, Thur, or By
        Appointment.

Specialise in restoring ceramic figures,
bowls and vases, both European and
Oriental.

PROVIDE Free Estimates. Free
Collection/Delivery Service.
SPEAK TO Susan Noel.

RICHARD SCOTT
30 High Street, Holt, **Norfolk**
NR21 0QT
TEL   0263 712479
OPEN   11–5 Mon–Wed; 10–5 Fri–Sat.
Specialise in undertaking some repairs
and restoration of porcelain and pottery.

PROVIDE Free Estimates.
SPEAK TO Richard Scott.

GIUDICI–MARTIN
The Old Chapel, Newtown Street,
Woodford, Kettering,
Northamptonshire NN14 4HW
TEL   0536 743787
FAX   0536 745900
OPEN   By Appointment.

Specialise in conservation, restoration
and reproduction of all types of stone
sculpture.

PROVIDE Home Inspections. Refundable
Estimates. Chargeable
Collection/Delivery Service.
SPEAK TO Paul Giudici.

For conservation purposes they will
provide a detailed condition report with
recommendation, specification and
estimates.

FLORENCE CONSERVATION & RESTORATION
102 Nottingham Road, Long Eaton,
Nottingham, **Nottinghamshire**
NG10 2BZ
TEL   0602 733625
OPEN   8–5 Mon–Fri; 9–12 Sat

Specialise in repairing ceramics, bronzes
and marbles.

PROVIDE Home Inspections. Refundable

Estimates. Chargeable
Collection/Delivery Service.
SPEAK TO Ron Florence.
SEE Oil Paintings, Furniture.

ROGER HAWKINS
Top Hat Antique Centre, 66 Derby
Road, Nottingham, **Nottinghamshire**
NG1 5FD
TEL   0602 507589
OPEN   9.30–5 Mon–Fri.

Specialise in restoring pottery,
porcelain, some glass, alabaster, marble,
spelter.

PROVIDE Home Inspections. Free
Estimates. Chargeable
Collection/Delivery Service.
SPEAK TO Roger Hawkins.

THE CONSERVATION STUDIO
68 East Street, Thame, **Oxfordshire**
OX9 3JS
TEL   0844 214498
OPEN   By Appointment.

Specialise in restoration of all types of
ceramics and glass (except stained glass),
faience and enamels.

PROVIDE Free/Chargeable Estimates.
Free Local Collection/Delivery Service.
SPEAK TO Sandra Davison.
Fellow of IIC. This workshop is included
on the register of conservators
maintained by the Conservation Unit of
the Museums and Galleries Commission.

OXFORD CONSERVATIONS
Underwood, Jack Straw's Lane, Oxford,
Oxfordshire OX3 0DN
TEL   0865 62614
FAX   0865 750311
OPEN   By Appointment Only.

Specialise in restoring polychromed
wood sculpture and can provide
technical analysis, surveys, condition

reports and other documentation and advice on exhibition, transport and storage.

PROVIDE Home Inspections. Free Estimates. Chargeable Collection/Delivery Service.
SPEAK TO Candy Kuhl, Chief Conservator.

Member of UKIC and IIC, Associate Member of ABPR. This workshop is included on the register of conservators maintained by the Conservation Unit of the Museums and Galleries Commission.
SEE Oil Paintings, Picture Frames.

JOANNA SEAWARD
Mulberry House Studio, Mulberry House, The Ridings, Shotover, **Oxfordshire OX3 8TB**
TEL　　0865 61033
FAX　　0865 791772
OPEN　　9–5 Mon–Sat By Appointment.

Specialise in restoring in all types of ceramics.

PROVIDE Free Estimates.
SPEAK TO Joanna Seaward.
Member of UKIC. This workshop is included on the register of conservators maintained by the Conservation Unit of the Museums and Galleries Commission.

F. C. MANSER & SON LTD
53–54 Wyle Cop, Shrewsbury, **Shropshire SY1 1XJ**
TEL　　0743 351120
FAX　　0743 271047
OPEN　　9–5.30 Mon–Wed, Fri; 9–1 Thur; 9–5 Sat.

Specialise in restoration of glass; chipped glass repaired, decanter stoppers, mirrors, light fittings, porcelain repairs, specialists in Tunbridge ware.

PROVIDE Home Inspections. Free Estimates. Chargeable Collection/Delivery Service.
SPEAK TO Paul Manser.

Member of LAPADA and the Guild of Master Craftsmen.
SEE Clocks, Silver.

G. J. DICK-READ
Duxhams, Dulverton, **Somerset TA22 9EJ**
TEL　　0398 23460
OPEN　　By Appointment.

Specialise in a glass and china repair service.

PROVIDE Home Inspections. Free Local Estimates. Chargeable Collection/Delivery Service.
SPEAK TO John Dick-Read.
This workshop is included on the register of conservators maintained by the Conservation Unit of the Museums and Galleries Commission.
SEE Furniture.

THE ANTIQUE RESTORATION STUDIO
The Old Post Office, Haughton, **Staffordshire ST18 9JH**
TEL　　0785 780424
FAX　　0785 780157
OPEN　　9–5 Mon–Fri.

Specialise in restoring antique and modern ceramics.

PROVIDE Home Inspections. Free Estimates Free Collection/Delivery Service.
SPEAK TO D. P. Albright.
SEE Furniture, Oil Paintings, Carpets.

RAVENSDALE STUDIOS
77A Roundwell Street, Tunstall, Stoke-On-Trent, **Staffordshire ST6 5AW**
TEL　　0782 836810
OPEN　　9–5 Mon–Sat.

Specialise in restoring all types of ceramics.

PROVIDE Free Estimates.

SPEAK TO Lingard Simpson or Stuart Nicholls.

Member of the Guild of Master Craftsmen and UKIC. This workshop is included on the register of conservators maintained by the Conservation Unit of the Museums and Galleries Commission.

NORMAN FLYNN RESTORATIONS
37 Lind Road, Sutton, **Surrey SM1 4PP**
TEL   081 661 9505
OPEN   7.45–3.30 Mon–Fri.

Specialise in restoring antique and modern porcelain and pottery.

PROVIDE Home Inspections. Free Estimates. Free Collection/Delivery Service each week to London.
SPEAK TO Norman Flynn.

Member of the Guild of Master Craftsmen.
SEE Silver.

SAGE ANTIQUES & INTERIORS
High Street, Ripley, **Surrey GU23 6BB**
TEL   0483 224396
FAX   0483 211996
OPEN   9.30–5.30 Mon–Sat.

Specialise in restoring English and Oriental ceramics.

PROVIDE Free Estimates. Free Collection/Delivery Service.
SPEAK TO Howard or Chrissie Sage.

Member of LAPADA and the Guild of Master Craftsmen.
SEE Furniture, Oil Paintings.

R. SAUNDERS
71 Queens Road, Weybridge, **Surrey KT13 9UQ**
TEL   0932 842601
OPEN   9.15–5 Mon–Sat; closed Wed.

Specialise in restoring English porcelain.

PROVIDE Home Inspections. Free

Estimates. Free Collection/Delivery Service.
SPEAK TO J. B. Tonkinson.
SEE Silver, Furniture, Oil Paintings.

SIMPSON DAY RESTORATION
Studio 13, Acorn House, Cherry Orchard Road, Croydon, **Surrey CR0 6BA**
TEL   081 681 8339
OPEN   9.30–6 Mon–Fri

Specialise in restoring fine porcelain and pottery.

PROVIDES Free Estimates.
SPEAK TO Sarah Simpson or Sarah Day.
SEE Silver.

JUDITH WETHERALL
trading as **J.B. SYMES**
28 Silverlea Gardens, Horley, **Surrey RH6 9BB**
TEL   0293 775024
OPEN   8.30–5.30 Daily By Appointment Only.

Specialise in restoring polychromed sculpture.

PROVIDE Free Local Home Inspections. Free Estimates. Chargeable Collection/Delivery Service.
SPEAK TO Judith Wetherall.

Member of UKIC and IIC. This workshop is included on the register of conservators maintained by the Conservation Unit of the Museums and Galleries Commission.
SEE Clocks, Furniture, Picture Frames.

DOREEN BROWN
1 Dunstan Terrace, Cockmount Lane, Wadhurst, **East Sussex TN5 6UF**
TEL   089288 3432
OPEN   By Appointment.

Specialise in restoring European and Oriental porcelain and pottery and antique ceramic figures. Missing pieces are replaced, previous outdated repairs removed.

PROVIDE Local Home Inspections. Free Estimates. Free Local Collection/Delivery Service.
SPEAK TO Doreen Brown.

Ms Brown is West Dean trained.

DAVID CRAIG
Toll Cottage, Station Road, Durgates, Wadhurst, **East Sussex TN5 6RS**
TEL   089288 2188
OPEN   9–5.30 Mon–Fri.

Specialise in restoring antique porcelain and pottery.

PROVIDE Chargeable Estimates. Chargeable Collection/Delivery Service.
SPEAK TO David Sutcliffe.

SEE Silver.

GOLDEN FISH GILDING & RESTORATION
94 Gloucester Road, Brighton, **East Sussex BN1 4AP**
TEL   0273 691164
FAX   0273 691164
OPEN   9–5 Mon–Fri.

Specialise in eglomisé panels.

PROVIDE Home Inspections. Free Estimates. Free Collection/Delivery Service.
SPEAK TO Marianne Hatchwell.
Also teach gilding techniques.
SEE Furniture, Oil Paintings.

SUZY SMITH
86 Upper North Street, Brighton, **East Sussex BN1 3FL**
TEL   0273 220460
OPEN   9.30–6.30 Mon–Sat.

Specialise in restoring china and ceramics.

PROVIDE Home Inspections. Free Estimates. Free Local Delivery Service.
SPEAK TO Suzy Smith.

Member of UKIC. Ms Smith trained at West Dean and the Musée de Sèvres. Also teach ceramic restoration at all levels.

HAZEL WELDON
Flat 1, Holland Road, Hove, **East Sussex BN3 1JF**
TEL   0273 726281
OPEN   By Appointment.

Specialise in restoring porcelain and pottery figures, particularly European. Will also restore plaster figures.

PROVIDE Free Estimates.
SPEAK TO Hazel Weldon.

CAROL BANKS AND SON
September Cottage, 88 Victoria Road, Shoreham-by-Sea, **West Sussex BN4 5WS**
TEL   0273 461647.
OPEN   By Appointment.

Specialise in repair and restoration of most types of pottery and porcelain figures and animals, including objects sculptured in wood and metal.

PROVIDE Free Estimates.
SPEAK TO Carol Banks.
SEE Furniture, Picture Frames.

DAVID FILEMAN ANTIQUES
Squirrels, Bayards, Steyning, **West Sussex BN44 3AA**
TEL   0903 813229
OPEN   By Appointment.

Specialise in restoring and repairing 18th and 19th century glass chandeliers and candelabra. This includes cleaning and repinning.

PROVIDE Home Inspections. Free

Estimates. Chargeable Collection/Delivery Service.
SPEAK TO David Fileman.

GARNER & CO.
Stable Cottage, Steyning Road, Westiston, **West Sussex BN44 3DD**
TEL   0903 814565
OPEN   By Appointment (Tel Mon–Fri 9–5.30)

Specialise in the conservation and repair of lead and bronze sculpture and glass chandeliers.

PROVIDE Home Inspections. Estimates.
SPEAK TO Sid Garner.

SEE Clocks, Furniture, Silver.

SHEILA SOUTHWELL
7 West Street, Burgess Hill, **West Sussex RH15 8NN**
TEL   0444 244307
OPEN   10–4 Mon–Fri By Appointment.

Specialise in restoring porcelain and all ceramics, some glass repairs and particularly Oriental vases.

PROVIDE Home Inspections. Free Estimates. Free/Chargeable Collection/Delivery Service.
SPEAK TO Sheila Southwell.

This workshop is included on the register of conservators maintained by the Conservation Unit of the Museums and Galleries Commission.

WEST DEAN COLLEGE
West Dean, Chichester, **West Sussex PO18 0OZ**
TEL   0243 63 301
FAX   0243 63 342
OPEN   9–5 Mon–Fri.

Specialise in training conservators and restorers in the field of antique ceramics and will also undertake restoration.

PROVIDE Local Home Inspections. Free Estimates.
SPEAK TO Peter Sarginson.
SEE Books, Clocks, Furniture, Silver.

ROBERT MILLAR CRAIG
Clockwise Studio, 22A Stoneleigh Road, Gibbet Hill, Coventry, **Warwickshire CV4 7AD**
TEL   0203 410402
OPEN   8.30–5.30 Mon–Fri or By Appointment.

Specialise in restoration and repair of china and glass.

PROVIDE Home Inspections. Free Estimates. Free Local Collection/Delivery Service.
SPEAK TO Robert Millar Craig.

Member of UKIC. This workshop is included on the register of conservators maintained by the Conservation Unit of the Museums and Galleries Commission.

GILLIAN ARENGO-JONES
Glebe House, Church Walk, Ashton Keynes, **Wiltshire SN6 6PB**
TEL   0285 861433
OPEN   By Appointment.

Specialise in restoring pottery and porcelain.

PROVIDE Free Estimates.
SPEAK TO Mr or Mrs Arengo-Jones.
Member of UKIC. This workshop is included on the register of conservators maintained by the Conservation Unit of the Museums and Galleries Commission.

DELOMOSNE & SON LTD
Court Close, North Wraxall, Chippenham, **Wiltshire SN14 7AD**
TEL   0225 891505
FAX   0225 891907
OPEN   9.30–5.30 Mon–Sat.

Specialise in restoring English period glass light fittings.

PROVIDE Home Inspections. Free
Estimates. Collection/Delivery Service
available.
SPEAK TO Martin Mortimer or Timothy
Osborne.

LANTERN GALLERY
Hazeland House, Kington St Michael,
Chippenham, **Wiltshire SN14 6JJ**
TEL　　0249 750306
FAX　　0249 758896
OPEN　9–4 Mon–Fri or By
　　　Appointment.

Specialise in supplying eglomisé glass.

PROVIDE Home Inspections. Free
Estimates. Free Collection/Delivery
service.
SPEAK TO Anne Campbell Macinnes.

SEE Oil Paintings, Picture Frames.

ROD NAYLOR
208 Devizes Road, Hilperton,
Trowbridge, **Wiltshire BA14 7QP**
TEL　　0225 754497
OPEN　By Appointment.

Specialise in supplying hand-blown glass
caddy bowls.

PROVIDE Home Inspections. Free
Estimates. Free Local
Collection/Delivery Service.
SPEAK TO Rod Naylor.
SEE Lighting, Furniture.

RESTORATIONS UNLIMITED
Pinkney Park, Malmesbury, **Wiltshire
SN16 0NX**
TEL　　0666 840888
OPEN　9–12.30, 1.30–5 Mon–Fri;
　　　9.30–12 Sat.

Specialise in restoring European and
Oriental ceramics.

PROVIDE Home Inspections. Free
Estimates. Free Collection/Delivery
Service.
SPEAK TO David Ellis.
SEE Clocks, Furniture, Oil Paintings.

JANE WINCH CHINA REPAIRS
Westport Granary, Malmesbury,
Wiltshire SN16 0AL
TEL　　0666 822119
OPEN　10–5 Mon–Fri.

Specialise in restoring and repairing
decorative ceramics, antique and
modern.

PROVIDE Home Inspections. Free
Estimates.
SPEAK TO Jane Winch or Pat Paterson.

===

NIDD HOUSE ANTIQUES
Nidd House, Bogs Lane, Harrogate,
North Yorkshire HG1 4DY
TEL　　0423 884739
OPEN　9–5 Mon–Fri or By
　　　Appointment.

Specialise in repairing statues up to 24
inches high.

PROVIDE Home Inspections. Free Local
Estimates. Chargeable
Collection/Delivery Service.
SPEAK TO Mr D. Preston.
Member of the Guild of Master
Craftsmen and UKIC. This workshop is
included on the register of conservators
maintained by the Conservation Unit of
the Museums and Galleries Commission.
SEE Collectors (Scientific Instruments),
Furniture, Silver.

===

TERESA RESTORATIONS
Westleigh Coach House, 11 Stubley
Lane, Dronfield, Sheffield, **South
Yorkshire S18 6PE**
TEL　　0246 417037
OPEN　9–5.30 Mon–Fri or By
　　　Appointment.

Specialise in restoring china, stone, alabaster and marble.

PROVIDE Free Estimates.
SPEAK TO Teresa Goodlad.

DUNLUCE ANTIQUES
33 Ballytober Road, Bushmills, **Co. Antrim BT57 8UU**
TEL   02657 31140
OPEN   10–6 Mon–Thur; 2–6 Sat.

Specialise in restoring European and Oriental porcelain.

PROVIDE Home Inspections. Free Estimates. Chargeable Collection/Delivery Service.
SPEAK TO Clare Ross.

DENIS CLANCY
31 Forest Hills, Rathcoole, **Co. Dublin**
TEL   01 580439
OPEN   By Appointment.

Specialise in restoring glass chandeliers.

PROVIDE Home Inspections. Free Estimates. Free Collection/Delivery Service.
SPEAK TO Derek Clancy.

Member of IPCRA.
SEE Silver.

LEINSTER STUDIOS
10 Leinster Square, Dublin 6, **Co. Dublin**
TEL   01 974009
OPEN   10–5 Mon–Fri.

Specialise in restoring ceramics, enamel, glass, alabaster and marble.

PROVIDE Home Inspections by arrangement. Free Estimates. Collection/Delivery Service by arrangement.
SPEAK TO Anne Reeves-Smyth or Eileen O'Leary.
Member of IPCRA.

DESIRÉE SHORTT
38 North Great George Street, Dublin 1, **Co. Dublin**
TEL   01 722285
OPEN   9.30–5 Mon–Fri or By Appointment Sat, Sun.

Specialise in restoring porcelain, jade, stone, plastic, ivory.

PROVIDE Local Home Inspections. Free Estimates.
SPEAK TO Desirée Shortt.

Member of IPCRA.

JENNY SLEVIN
China Restoration Studio, Monkstown, **Co. Dublin**
TEL   01 280 3429
OPEN   By Appointment.

Specialise in restoring ceramics, glass, jade, ivory, marble.

PROVIDE Home Inspections. Free/Chargeable Estimates. Collection/Delivery Service by arrangement.
SPEAK TO Jenny Slevin.

Member of IPCRA.
SEE Carpets, Furniture, Picture Frames, Collectors (Wax).

GLEBE STUDIO
Straffan, **Co. Kildare**
TEL   01 6271129
OPEN   10–4 Mon–Fri.

Specialise in restoring porcelain, bronze, ivory, marble.

PROVIDE Chargeable Home Inspections. Free Estimates. Collection/Delivery at Automobile Club, Dublin.
SPEAK TO Phillipa Hynde, Dominique Synott or Esen Philcox.

Member of IPCRA and UKIC.
SEE Furniture, Picture Frames.

VALERIE McCOY
Fan-na-Greine, Glendalough,
Co. Wicklow
TEL   0404 45125
OPEN   By Appointment.

Specialise in restoring European and Oriental ceramics.

PROVIDE Home Inspections. Free/Chargeable Estimates. Free Collection/Delivery Service.
SPEAK TO Valerie McCoy.
Member of IPCRA.
SEE Furniture, Picture Frames.

ST JAMES'S GALLERY LTD
Smith Street, St Peter Port, **Guernsey, Channel Islands**
TEL   0481 720070
OPEN   9–5.30 Mon–Sat or By Appointment.

Specialise in some porcelain restoration.

PROVIDE Home Inspections. Chargeable Estimates. Collection/Delivery Service by arrangement.
SPEAK TO Mrs Whittam.
SEE Clocks, Furniture.

HELEN WARREN
26 Forbes Road, Rosyth, Dunfermline, **Fife KY11 2AN**
TEL   0383 419564
OPEN   By Appointment.

Specialise in restoring European and Oriental pottery and porcelain.

PROVIDE Free Estimates.
SPEAK TO Helen Warren
Member of UKIC and SSCR.

ANNE AND JAMES DAVIDSON, SCULPTORS
15 Redmoss Park, Aberdeen, **Grampian AB1 4JF**
TEL   0224 871759
OPEN   By Arrangement.

Specialise in restoring plaster statuary.

PROVIDE Home Inspections. Free Estimates. Chargeable Collection/Delivery Service.
SPEAK TO Anne Davidson or James Davidson.
Anne Davidson is a Member of the Royal Society of British Sculptors. This workshop is in the Scottish Conservation Directory.

BENITA MILLER
30 Wester Links, Fortrose, **Highland IV10 8RZ**
TEL   0381 20479
OPEN   By Appointment.

Specialise in restoring European and Oriental ceramics.

PROVIDE Home Inspections. Free/Chargeable Estimates. Chargeable Collection/Delivery Service.
SPEAK TO Benita Miller.

Member of SSCR. This workshop is in the Scottish Conservation Directory.

LUIGI M. VILLANI
Traditional Antique Restoration and Consultancy Service, The Stable, Altyre, Forres, **Highland IV36 0SH**
TEL   0309 672572
OPEN   8–10 Mon–Fri.

Specialise in repair and restoration of wooden sculpture and objets d'art, angels, candlesticks, cupids, crucifixes etc.

PROVIDE Home Inspections. Estimates.
SPEAK TO Luigi M. Villani or Rosalie Stuart.
Run a consultancy and training service on restoration, wood stains and finishes and also give lectures.
SEE Furniture.

BEAVER GLASS RESTORATION
23 Hatton Place, Edinburgh, **Lothian EH9 1UB**
TEL   031 667 8996
FAX   031 667 8996
OPEN 9–5 Mon–Fri.

Specialise in restoring glass, including grinding and polishing. Able to de-cloud non-leaded decanters.

PROVIDE Free Estimates.
SPEAK TO Marilyn or Derek Beaver.
Members of SSCR.

ELLEN BREHENY
Conservation Studio, Hopetoun House, South Queensferry, **Lothian EH30 9SL**
TEL   031 331 2003
OPEN By Appointment.

Specialise in restoring all ceramics and vessel glass.

PROVIDE Home Inspections. Free/Chargeable Estimates. Free/Chargeable Collection/Delivery Service.
SPEAK TO Ellen Breheny.

Member of SSCR and UKIC.

HOUNDWOOD ANTIQUES RESTORATION
7 West Preston Street, Edinburgh **Lothian EH8 9PX**
TEL   031 667 3253
OPEN By Appointment.

Specialise in restoring antique ceramics.

PROVIDE Home Inspections. Free Estimates. Chargeable Collection/Delivery Service.
SPEAK TO Mr A. Gourlay.
SEE Furniture, Silver.

G. & A. MURRAY
Millburn Cottage, Skelmorlie, **Strathclyde PA17 5EZ**
TEL   0475 520251
OPEN 8.30–6 Mon–Sat or By Appointment.

Specialise in restoring porcelain, earthenware, ivory and some glass. They do not do domestic china.

PROVIDE Free Estimates.
SPEAK TO George or Aline Murray.

Established 1979. Member of UKIC, CGCG, SSCR. This workshop is in the Scottish Conservation Directory.

CATHERINE RITCHIE
72 Novar Drive, Glasgow, **Strathclyde G12 9TZ**
TEL   041 339 0331
OPEN By Appointment.

Specialise in restoring European and Oriental ceramics.

PROVIDE Free Estimates.
SPEAK TO Catherine Ritchie.

PETER J. DAVID
(address withheld by request) Barry, **South Glamorgan CF6 8RG**
TEL   0446 748153
OPEN By Appointment.

Specialise in restoring all types of ceramics and porcelain, particularly Welsh and early English.

PROVIDE Free Estimates.
SPEAK TO Peter David.

This workshop is included on the register of conservators maintained by the Conservation Unit of the Museums and Galleries Commission.

IRENA ANTIQUES
111 Broad Street, Barry, **South Glamorgan CF6 8SX**
TEL   0446 747626 or 732517
OPEN   10–4 Mon–Fri.

Specialise in restoring European and Oriental porcelain.

PROVIDE Free Estimates. Free Collection/Delivery Service.
SPEAK TO Irena Halabuda
SEE Furniture.

FURNITURE AND
MIRRORS

DO

Keep (and label) any veneers or mouldings which become detached
Dust marquetry furniture very carefully
Always pull out bearers for bureau lids fully
Lift, rather than drag, when moving large pieces
Check annually for active woodworm
Lift antique chairs by the seat-rail, not the back

DON'T

Place flower vases on polished surfaces
Polish metal mounts with metal polish – use a dry, medium-hard toothbrush to
remove dust
Use spray or silicone polishes
Restore gilding with paint
Put furniture near radiators or under sunny windows
Tilt chests of drawers forwards when moving them
Allow chairs to be tilted on two legs

THE BAROMETER SHOP
2 Lower Park Row, Bristol, **Avon**
BS1 5BJ
TEL 0272 272565
OPEN 9–5.30 Mon, Wed, Fri, 9–1 Sat.

Specialise in restoring furniture, including hand French polishing, hand engraving, metalware. Mirrors re-silvered.

PROVIDE Home Inspections. Free Estimates. Free Collection/Delivery Service.
SPEAK TO Mrs Honey.
SEE Clocks, Collectors (Scientific Instruments).
SEE **Hereford & Worcester**

M. AND S. BRADBURY
The Barn, Hanham Lane, Paulton, **Avon**
BS18 5PF
TEL 0761 418910
OPEN 8–5 Mon–Fri or By Appointment.

Specialise in restoring furniture from all periods.

PROVIDE Home Inspections. Free Estimates. Free Local Collection/Delivery Service.
SPEAK TO M. or S. Bradbury.
Member of BAFRA. This workshop is included on the register of conservators maintained by the Conservation Unit of the Museums and Galleries Commission.

LAWRENCE BRASS AND SON
93–95 Walcot Street, Bath, **Avon**
BA1 5BW
TEL 0225 464051
OPEN 8–5 Mon–Fri. By Appointment Sat.

Specialise in restoring fine furniture, including metalwork, gilding, upholstery. They cast furniture mounts and do firegilt ormolu. They also specialise in 'impossible' commissions.

PROVIDE Home Inspections.

Free/Chargeable Estimates. Free Collection/Delivery Service.
SPEAK TO Mr Brass.

Established twenty–five years. Member of BAFRA and UKIC. This workshop is included on the register of conservators maintained by the Conservation Unit of the Museums and Galleries Commission.
SEE **London W9**

D. J. DAVIS
13 Castle Street, Thornbury, Bristol, **Avon BS12 1HA**
TEL 0454 412430
OPEN By Appointment.

Specialise in restoring smaller items of furniture, occasional tables, chairs, cabinets, trays, mirrors etc. All aspects of cleaning, polishing and finishing covered.

PROVIDE Home Inspections. Free Estimates. Free Local Collection/Delivery Service.
SPEAK TO David Davis.

Mr Davis is a member of the Guild of Master Craftsmen and a director of the local museum.
SEE Clocks.

T. H. DEWEY
The Cottage, Kelston, Bath, **Avon**
BA1 9AF
TEL 0225 447944
OPEN 8–5 Mon–Fri or By Appointment.

Specialise in restoring antique period furniture, including metalwork, but will repair a kitchen chair if requested.

PROVIDE Home Inspections. Free Local Estimates. Free Local Collection/Delivery Service.
SPEAK TO Tim Dewey.

FRANK DUX ANTIQUES
33 Belvedere, Bath, **Avon BA1 5HR**
TEL   0225 312367
OPEN   10–6 Mon–Sat.

Specialise in restoring antique furniture, all cabinet work and polishing.

PROVIDE Home Inspections. Refundable Estimates. Free Collection/Delivery Service on small items.
SPEAK TO Frank Dux.

Member of the UKIC.

IAN AND DIANNE McCARTHY
Arcadian Cottage, 112 Station Road, Clutton, **Avon BS18 4RA**
TEL   0761 53188
OPEN   By Appointment.

Specialise in restoring period upholstery.

PROVIDE Home Inspections. Free Estimates. Chargeable Collection/Delivery Service.
SPEAK TO Ian or Dianne McCarthy.
SEE Silver, Porcelain.

PENNARD HOUSE ANTIQUES
3/4 Piccadilly, London Road, Bath, **Avon BA1 6PL**
TEL   0225 313791
FAX   0225 448196
OPEN   9.30–5.30 Mon–Sat

Specialise in restoring English and French country furniture. Also undertake upholstery work, rushing and caning.

PROVIDE Home Inspections. Free Estimates. Free Collection/Delivery Service.
SPEAK TO Martin Dearden.

ANTHONY REED
94–96 Walcot Street, Bath, **Avon BA1 5BG**
TEL   0225 461969 or 0272 333595
OPEN   9–6 Mon–Sat.

Specialise in cleaning, restoring and gilding mirror frames.

PROVIDE Home Inspections. Chargeable Estimates. Chargeable Local Collection/Delivery Service.
SPEAK TO Anthony Reed.
Member of the IIC.
SEE Oil Paintings, Picture Frames.

ANGELA BURGIN FURNISHING AND DESIGN LTD
6–8 Gordon Street, Luton, **Bedfordshire LU1 2QP**
TEL   0582 22563
FAX   0582 30413
OPEN   8–5 Mon–Thur or By Appointment.

Specialise in offering a highly specialised conservation service on all periods of upholstery.

PROVIDE Home Inspections. Free Estimates. Free Collection/Delivery Service.
SPEAK TO Angela Burgin.
Member of Association of Master Upholsterers.
SEE Carpets.

D. M. E. RESTORATIONS LTD
11 Church Street, Ampthill, **Bedfordshire MK45 2PL**
TEL   0525 405819
OPEN   8–5.30 Mon–Fri; 8–1 Sat or By Appointment.

Specialise in restoring English furniture, including polishing and gilding.

PROVIDE Home Inspections. Free Estimates. Collection/Delivery Service by arrangement.
SPEAK TO Duncan Everitt.

RICHARD HAGEN
The Stables, Wakes End Farm, Eversholt, **Bedfordshire MK17 9EA**
TEL 0525 28505
OPEN By Arrangement.

Specialise in conserving and restoring antique furniture and woodwork sympathetically.

PROVIDE Home Inspections by arrangement. Free Estimates.
SPEAK TO Richard Hagen.

THOMAS HUDSON
The Barn, 117 High Street, Odell, **Bedfordshire MK43 7AS**
TEL 0234 721133
OPEN 8–6 Mon–Fri; 8–12 Sat.

Specialise in restoring antique furniture and old woodwork sympathetically. Can also make chairs to match existing sets.

PROVIDE Home Inspections. Chargeable Estimates.
SPEAK TO Thomas Hudson.

Please ring to discuss your requirements or to make an appointment to visit the workshop.

J. MOORE RESTORATIONS
College Farmhouse Workshops, Chawston, Bedford, **Bedfordshire MK44 3BH**
TEL 0480 214165
OPEN 8.30–5.30 Mon–Fri.

Specialise in restoring antique furniture in all aspects, including carving, gilding, and marquetry. Chairs and other furniture copied and distressed to match existing finishes.

PROVIDE Home Inspections. Free Estimates. Free Collection/Delivery Service locally.
SPEAK TO Mr John Moore.

SIMON PALLISTER
33 Albion Road, Luton, **Bedfordshire LU2 0DS**
TEL 0582 453292
OPEN 8.30–6 Mon–Fri.

Specialise in restoring antique English and Continental furniture.

PROVIDE Home Inspections. Free Estimates. Free Collection/Delivery Service.
SPEAK TO Simon Pallister.

Member of BAFRA.

WATERLOO HOUSE ANTIQUES
Unit 2/3 College Farm, High Street, Pulloxhill, **Bedfordshire MK45 5HP**
TEL 0525 717786
OPEN 10.30–4 Mon–Fri; 10.30–12 Sat. Closed Tues.

Specialise in restoring and re-upholstering Victorian and Edwardian furniture by traditional methods. Recaning service also available.

PROVIDE Home Inspections. Free Local Estimates. Free Collection/Delivery Service.
SPEAK TO Mr R. J. Jennings.

ALPHA (ANTIQUE) RESTORATIONS
High Street, Compton, Nr. Newbury, **Berkshire RG16 0NL**
TEL 0635 578245 and 0860 575203
OPEN 7–4 Mon–Fri.

Specialise in fine furniture restoration, both English and Continental, veneering, inlaying, specialised copy chair making.

PROVIDE Home Inspections. Free/Chargeable Estimates. Chargeable

Collection/Delivery Service.
SPEAK TO Graham Childs.
Member of BAFRA.

ASHLEY ANTIQUES AND FURNITURE
129 High Street, Hungerford, **Berkshire RG17 0DL**
TEL   0488 682771
OPEN   10–1, 2–5 Mon–Fri; 11–1, 2–5 Sat.

Specialise in restoring English and Continental furniture and making furniture to order.

PROVIDE Home Inspections. Free Estimates. Free Local Collection/Delivery Service.
SPEAK TO Robert Duff.
SEE Clocks.

HAMILTON HAVERS
58 Conisboro Avenue, Caversham Heights, Reading, **Berkshire RG4 7JE**
TEL   0734 473379
OPEN   Daily By Appointment.

Specialise in restoring Boulle, marquetry, ivory, tortoiseshell, mother-of-pearl, brass, lapis lazuli and malachite on furniture.

PROVIDE Free/Chargeable Estimates.
SPEAK TO Hamilton Havers.
Mr Havers has worked for the National Trust.
SEE Clocks, Silver.

J. J. ANTIQUE RESTORATION
Braemar, Waltham Road, White Waltham, **Berkshire SL9 3SH**
TEL   0628 823741
OPEN   8–5 Mon–Fri.

Specialise in restoring 17th–19th century furniture.

PROVIDE Home Inspections. Free Estimates. Free Collection/Delivery Service.

SPEAK TO John White.
Member of the Guild of Master Craftsmen.

BEN NORRIS
Knowl Hill Farm, Knowl Hill, Kingsclere, Newbury, **Berkshire RG15 8WY**
TEL   0635 297950
FAX   0635 299851
OPEN   8.30–5.30 Mon–Fri.

Specialise in restoring antique furniture pre-1830, gilding and supplying and restoring brass furniture fittings.

PROVIDE Home Inspections. Free/Refundable Estimates. Free Local Collection/Delivery Service and to London.
SPEAK TO Ben Norris.
Member of BAFRA.

JOHN ARMISTEAD
Malham Cottage, Bellingdon, Nr. Chesham, **Buckinghamshire HP5 2UR**
TEL   0494 758209
OPEN   9–5 Mon–Fri.

Specialise in repairing metalwork, including brass beds.

PROVIDE Home Inspections, Free Estimates. Collection/Delivery Service by arrangement.
SPEAK TO John Armistead.
Member of the Guild of Master Craftsmen and UKIC. This workshop is included on the register of conservators maintained by the Conservation Unit of the Museums and Galleries Commission.
SEE Silver.

BROWNS OF WEST WYCOMBE
Church Lane, West Wycombe, **Buckinghamshire HP14 3AH**
TEL   0494 524537
FAX   0494 439548
OPEN   8–6 Mon–Fri; 8–12 Sat.

Specialise in restoring antique furniture and will make chairs to match existing sets.

PROVIDE Home Inspections. Free/Refundable Estimates. Free Collection/Delivery Service.
SPEAK TO D. A. Hines

CHESS ANTIQUE RESTORATIONS
85 Broad Street, Chesham, **Buckinghamshire HP5 3EF**
TEL   0494 783043
FAX   0494 791302
OPEN   8–5 Mon–Sat.

Specialise in restoration of furniture.

PROVIDE Home Inspections. Chargeable Estimates. Chargeable Collection/Delivery Service.
SPEAK TO T. F. Chapman.
SEE Clocks, Oil Paintings.

CONY CRAFTS
Hale Acre Workshops, Watchet Lane, Nr. Great Missenden, **Buckinghamshire HP16 ODR**
TEL   02406 5668
OPEN   9–5.30 Mon–Fri (answering service after these hours).

Specialise in sympathetically restoring antique and modern furniture, including traditional upholstery work, wood-carving, chair-rushing, chair-caning and French polishing. Pieces can be made to individual commission. Insurance work undertaken.

PROVIDE Home Inspections. Free Estimates. Inclusive Collection/Delivery Service.
SPEAK TO Mr Nowlan.
Member of the Guild of Master Craftsmen.

HERITAGE RESTORATIONS
36B High Street, Great Missenden, **Buckinghamshire HP16 0AU**
TEL   02406 5710
OPEN   10–5 Mon–Sat.

Specialise in restoring furniture, caning and rushing and upholstery.

PROVIDE Free Estimates. Home Inspections.
SPEAK TO John Wilshire.
SEE Clocks, Porcelain.

JOCK HOPSON CONSERVATION SERVICE
Holes Lane, Olney, **Buckinghamshire MK46 4BX**
TEL   0234 712306
FAX   0234 712306
OPEN   By Appointment.

Specialise in gilding and carving furniture and mirror frames. Also Japanese lacquer work.

PROVIDE Home Inspections. Free/Chargeable Estimates. Chargeable Collection/Delivery Service.
SPEAK TO Jock Hopson.

Member of UKIC. This workshop is included on the register of conservators maintained by the Conservation Unit of the Museums and Galleries Commission.
SEE Picture Frames, Arms.

PERIOD FURNITURE SHOWROOMS
49 London End, Beaconsfield, **Buckinghamshire HP9 2HW**
TEL   0494 674112
OPEN   9–5 Mon–Sat.

Specialise in restoring English furniture, including cabinetmaking, chair-making, polishing and upholstery.

PROVIDE Home Inspections. Free

Estimates. Free Collection/Delivery
Service.
SPEAK TO R. E. W. Hearne.

TINGEWICK ANTIQUES CENTRE

Main Street, Tingewick,
Buckinghamshire MK18 4PB
TEL   0280 847922
OPEN   10.30–5 Mon–Sat; 11–5 Sun.

Specialise in restoring metalware on
furniture.

PROVIDE Home Inspections. Free
Estimates. Collection/Delivery Service
by arrangement.
SPEAK TO Rosemarie or Barry Smith.
SEE Clocks.

WYCOMBE CANE AND RUSH WORKS

Victoria Street, High Wycombe,
Buckinghamshire HP11 2LU
TEL   0494 442429
OPEN   9–5 Mon–Fri.

Specialise in all types of canework,
including spider and fan work patterns
and blind or secret cane. Also carry out
rush seating.

PROVIDE Local Home Inspections.
Refundable Estimates.
SPEAK TO Peter Gilbert.

Established in 1880. Visitors are always
welcome to come and see work being
carried out.

GRAHAM BARNES

14 St Mary's Street, Ely,
Cambridgeshire CB7 4ES
TEL   0353 665218
OPEN   By Appointment.

Specialise in restoring pre-1830 fine
furniture, marquetry and brass inlay.

PROVIDE Free Estimates.
SPEAK TO Graham Barnes.
Member of BAFRA.

CLADGILD LTD

Vine House, Reach, Cambridge,
Cambridgeshire CB5 0JD
TEL   0638 741989
FAX   0638 743239
OPEN   By Appointment.

Specialise in restoring wood products,
including antique furniture and
panelling. Also offer an upholstery
service. Replicas can be made to order.

PROVIDE Home Inspections. Free
Collection/Delivery Service.
SPEAK TO Jo Ann Dudley.

Members of the Association of Master
Upholsterers and the Guild of Master
Craftsmen.

DODDINGTON HOUSE ANTIQUES

2 Benwick Road, Doddington, Nr.
March, **Cambridgeshire PE15 0TG**
TEL   0354 740755
OPEN   10–6 Mon–Sat.

Specialise in restoring painted furniture,
lacquer work, cane and rush work.

PROVIDE Refundable Estimates. Free
Collection/Delivery Service.
SPEAK TO Brian or Lynette Frankland.
SEE Clocks.

A. F. DUDLEY trading as 'THE FURNITURE CLINIC'.

Vine House, Reach, **Cambridgeshire
CB5 0JD**
TEL   0638 741989
FAX   0638 743239
OPEN   By Appointment.

Specialise in restoring antique and
modern furniture, including French
polishing, marquetry, carving,
upholstery, re-leathering, gold tooling,
re-silvering, caning and rushing.

PROVIDE Home Inspections. Free
Estimates. Free Collection/Delivery
Service.

SPEAK TO Mr A. Dudley.
Member of the Guild of Master
Craftsmen and the Association of Master
Upholsterers.
SEE Clocks, Collectors (Dolls, Toys,
Mechanical Music).

FRANK GOODINGHAM
Studio 3, Hope Street Yard, Hope Street,
Cambridge, **Cambridgeshire**
CB1 3NA
TEL   0223 410702
OPEN   10–6 Mon–Fri.

Specialise in restoring 18th and 19th
century gilded work, including
composition or carved overmantels and
pier glass frames.

PROVIDE Home Inspections. Refundable
Estimates. Collection/Delivery by
arrangement.
SPEAK TO Frank Goodingham.
SEE Picture Frames.

KENDAL FURNITURE RESTORATIONS
2 Clifton Road, Huntingdon,
Cambridgeshire PE18 7EJ
TEL   0480 411811
FAX   0480 411444
OPEN   8–5 Mon–Fri.

Specialise in repairing, polishing and
upholstering antique furniture as well as
cane and rush seating, desk leather lining,
manufacturing individually hand-made
furniture.

PROVIDE Home Inspections. Free
Collection/Delivery Service.
SPEAK TO Terence Brazier.
Member of LAPADA.

PAUL WALDMANN
41 Norfolk Street, Cambridge,
Cambridgeshire CB1 2LD
TEL   0223 314001
OPEN   By Appointment.

Specialise in all aspects of furniture

restoration plus fine cabinetmaking to
commission.

PROVIDE Home Inspections. Free
Estimates. Free Local
Collection/Delivery Service.
SPEAK TO Paul Waldmann.

Member of BAFRA. This workshop is
included on the register of conservators
maintained by the Conservation Unit of
the Museums and Galleries Commission.

ROBERT WILLIAMS
Osbourn's Farm, 32 Church Street,
Willingham, **Cambridgeshire**
CB4 5HT
TEL   0954 60972
OPEN   9–6 Mon–Fri.

Specialise in all aspects of furniture
restoration, including marquetry,
carving and brass inlay, carefully cleaning
and retaining old patinated surfaces.

PROVIDE Home Inspections. Free
Estimates. Free Local
Collection/Delivery Service.
SPEAK TO Robert Williams.
Member of BAFRA.

A. ALLEN ANTIQUE RESTORERS
Buxton Rd, Newtown, Newmills, Via
Stockport, **Cheshire SK12 3JS**
TEL   0663 745274
OPEN   8–5 Mon–Fri; 9–12 Sat.

Specialise in restoring antique furniture,
including 17th and 18th century oak and
walnut pieces. Also restore Boulle work,
inlay, gilding, upholstery and metalwork.
Furniture can be designed or copied.

PROVIDE Home Inspections.
Free/Chargeable Estimates.
Collection/Delivery Service.
SPEAK TO Tony Allen.

SEE Clocks, Picture Frames, Silver.

ARROWSMITH ANTIQUES AND RESTORATIONS
Unit 1A, Bridge Street Mill, Macclesfield, **Cheshire**
TEL   0625 611880
OPEN   8.30–5.30 Mon–Sat

Specialise in restoring 18th and 19th century furniture.

PROVIDE Home Inspections. Free Estimates. Free Collection/Delivery Service.
SPEAK TO Paul Arrowsmith.

COPPELIA ANTIQUES
Holford Lodge, Plumley Moor Road, Plumley, **Cheshire WA16 9RS**
TEL   0565 722197
OPEN   By Appointment.

Specialise in restoring mahogany, oak and walnut antique furniture.

PROVIDE Home Inspections and Estimates by arrangement. Chargeable Collection/Delivery Service.
SPEAK TO K. R. Clements.

SEE Clocks.

STEWART EVANS
Church View, Church Street, Malpas, **Cheshire SY14 8PD**
TEL   0948 860974 or 860214
OPEN   By Appointment.

Specialise in restoring antique furniture. Mr Evans also makes hand-made fine quality reproduction furniture using old timber.

PROVIDE Home Inspections. Free/Chargeable Estimates. Chargeable Collection/Delivery Service.
SPEAK TO Stewart Evans.
Established in 1953.

JOHN HETHERINGTON FURNITURE
Unit 2, First Floor, Albion Mill, Hollingworth, Via Hyde, **Cheshire SK14 8LS**
TEL   0457 765781
OPEN   8.30–5.30 Mon–Fri.

Specialise in restoring oak and walnut country furniture.

PROVIDE Home Inspections. Free Estimates. Chargeable Collection/Delivery Service.
SPEAK TO John Hetherington.

THE OLD BAKERY
21–23 Lower Fold, Marple Bridge, Via Stockport, **Cheshire SK6 5DU**
TEL   061 427 4699
OPEN   9–6 Mon–Fri.

Specialise in antique furniture restoration and the supply of feet, rockers, mouldings etc. No upholstery work carried out.
SPEAK TO Geoffrey Douglas.

ROGER G. TURNER
Hext Farm, Birch Vale, Stockport, **Cheshire SK12 5DH**
TEL   0663 742491
OPEN   Daily By Appointment Only.

Specialise in restoring good quality period furniture, including all refinishing and structural work, but excluding major upholstery.

PROVIDE Home Inspections. Free Estimates. Free Local Collection/Delivery Service.
SPEAK TO Roger G. Turner.

Member of UKIC. This workshop is included on the register of conservators maintained by the Conservation Unit of the Museums and Galleries Commission.

ANN & DEREK MASON
11 Redmire Road, Grangefield,
Stockton-on-Tees, **Cleveland**
TS18 4JR
TEL   0642 614583
OPEN   9–7 Mon–Fri.

Specialise in restoring antique furniture.

PROVIDE Free estimates.
SPEAK TO Derek Mason.
Will do on-site work within a thirty-mile
radius of Stockton.

MALCOLM JOHNSON
'Dunmere', Tregrehan, St Austell,
Cornwall PL25 3TG
TEL   072681 2537
OPEN   By Appointment.

Specialise in restoring by hand polished
furniture, antique or modern; complete
suites, grand pianos or table tops in situ.
Also colour matching limed oak finishing
if needed to blend with existing items.
All work is hand stripped.

PROVIDE Home Inspections. Free Local
Estimates. Free Local
Collection/Delivery Service.
SPEAK TO Malcolm Johnson.

This is a three-generation family business.
This workshop is included on the register
of conservators maintained by the
Conservation Unit of the Museums and
Galleries Commission.

FELIKS B. SADOWSKI
10 Chapel Street, Penzance, **Cornwall**
TR18 4AJ
TEL   0736 63124
OPEN   10–5 Mon–Sat.

Specialise in restoring antique furniture,
including Boulle work and marquetry.

PROVIDE Home Inspections. Free
Estimates. Chargeable
Collection/Delivery Service.
SPEAK TO Feliks Sadowski.

A family business which spans three
generations back to the beginning of the
century.

ST AUSTELL ANTIQUES CENTRE
(formerly The Furniture Store)
37/39 Truro Road, St Austell, **Cornwall**
PL25 5JE
TEL   0726 63178 or 0288 81548
OPEN   10–5 Mon–Sat or By
          Appointment.

Specialise in furniture restoration.

PROVIDE Home Inspections. Free
Estimates. Free Local
Collection/Delivery Service.
SPEAK TO Roger Nosworthy.
SEE Silver.

PETER STANTON
The Old Pottery, Chapel Hill, Truro,
Cornwall TR1 3BN
TEL   0872 70262
OPEN   9–5 Mon–Fri.

Specialise in restoring 17th and 18th
century furniture and upholstery.

PROVIDE Home Inspections. Free
Estimates. Chargeable
Collection/Delivery Service.
SPEAK TO Peter Stanton.

TUDOR ROSE DEVELOPMENTS
Court Cottage, Higher Porthpean, St
Austell, **Cornwall PL26 6AY**
TEL   0726 75653
OPEN   9–4 Mon–Fri.

Specialise in restoring English and some
Continental furniture.

PROVIDE Home Inspections. Chargeable
Estimates. Chargeable
Collection/Delivery Service.
SPEAK TO Christopher Pascoe.
Also give restoration tuition.

PETER HALL & SON
Danes Road, Staveley, Kendal, **Cumbria LA8 9PL**
TEL   0539 821633
FAX   0539 821905
OPEN   9–5 Mon–Fri.

Specialise in restoring antique furniture, structural and inlay repair, repolishing, gilding, carving, marquetry, metalwork and traditional re-upholstery, recaning and rushing, repair of locks and brassware.

PROVIDE Local Home Inspections. Free Estimates. Chargeable Collection/Delivery Service.
SPEAK TO Jeremy Hall.

This workshop is included on the register of conservators maintained by the Conservation Unit of the Museums and Galleries Commission.

JOSEPH JAMES ANTIQUES
Corney Square, Penrith, **Cumbria CA11 7PX**
TEL   0768 62065
OPEN   9–5.30 Mon–Sat; closed Wed.

Specialise in repairing antique furniture, French polishing and re-upholstering.

PROVIDE Home Inspections. Free Estimates. Free Local Collection/Delivery Service.
SPEAK TO Gordon Walker.

Also have soft furnishings workrooms.

SHIRE ANTIQUES
The Post House, High Newton, Newton-in-Carmel, Nr. Grange-over-Sands, **Cumbria LA11 6JQ**
TEL   05395 31431
OPEN   9.30–5 Mon, Wed–Sat; 10–4 Sun; closed Tues. Telephone first.

Specialise in restoring 16th–18th century furniture.

PROVIDE Home Inspections. Free Estimates. Free Local Collection/Delivery Service.
SPEAK TO Brian or Jean Shire.

R. UDALL
Merlin Cragg, Howgill, Sedbergh, **Cumbria LA10 5HU**
TEL   05396 20719
OPEN   10–5 Daily.

Specialise in restoring period furniture.

PROVIDE Free Estimates. Chargeable Collection/Delivery Service.
SPEAK TO Mr R. Udall.

CANE AND RUSH SEATING
50 Ashbourne Road, Derby, **Derbyshire DE22 3AD**
TEL   0332 44363
OPEN   10–4 Mon–Fri.

Specialise in replacing cane and rush in chairs, settees, bedheads. All patterns of cane can be reproduced, including single set, double set, sunset patterns, blind holes. Chairs which have been upholstered because nobody could be found to re-cane or rush them may be restored to their original appearance. Fine rush a speciality.

PROVIDE Home Inspections, Free Estimates.
SPEAK TO Joan Gilbert.

K. CHAPPELL ANTIQUES AND FINE ART
King Street, Bakewell, **Derbyshire DE4 1DZ**
TEL   0629 812496
FAX   0629 814531
OPEN   9.30–5.30 Mon–Sat.

Specialise in restoring antique and other furniture.

PROVIDE Home Inspections. Free Estimates. Free Local Collection/Delivery Service.

SPEAK TO W. N. Chappell.
Member of the Guild of Master
Craftsmen.
SEE Clocks.

D. W. & J. E. FODDY

Derby Antique Centre, 11 Friargate,
Derby, **Derbyshire DE1 1BU**
TEL 0332 385002
OPEN 10–5.30 Mon–Sat.

Specialise in restoring antique furniture.

PROVIDE Home Inspections. Chargeable
Estimates. Free Collection/Delivery.
SPEAK TO Mr Foddy.
SEE Clocks.

MELBOURNE HALL FURNITURE RESTORERS

The Old Saw Mill, Melbourne Hall Craft
Centre, Melbourne Hall, **Derbyshire
DE7 1EN**
TEL 0332 864131
OPEN 9–5 Mon–Fri; 10–5 Sat; 1.30–5
Sun, but phone first.

Specialise in furniture repairs, including
hand polishing.

PROVIDE Home Inspections.
Free/Refundable Estimates.
Collection/Delivery Service.
SPEAK TO Neil Collumbell.

PENROSE AND RIETBERG

Broome's Barnes, Pilsey Lane, Pilsley
Village, Nr. Bakewell, **Derbyshire
DE4 1PF**
TEL 0246 583444
FAX 0246 583360
OPEN 9–5.30 Mon–Fri; 10–4 Sat.

Specialise in restoring traditionally
upholstered fine quality antique chairs,
sofas, settees. They also recover modern
upholstered sofas and chairs, and offer a
full interior design service.

PROVIDE Home Inspections. Free Local

Estimates. Free Local
Collection/Delivery Service.
SPEAK TO Mark A. von Rietberg, Rory
D. F. Penrose or Brian Rosen.

STEPHEN SIMMONS AND HELEN MILES

Broadstones, Main Road, Wensley,
Matlock, **Derbyshire DE4 2LH**
TEL 0629 732227
OPEN 10–4 Mon–Sat By Appointment.

Specialise in restoring antique furniture
and offer a range of services from light
cleaning to the challenge of re-building
and re-finishing pieces in very poor
condition. Also hand French polishing.

PROVIDE Home Inspections. Free
Estimates. Free Local
Collection/Delivery Service.
SPEAK TO Stephen Simmons or Helen
Miles.

NIGEL F. THOMPSON

Antiques Warehouse, 25 Lightwood
Road, Buxton, **Derbyshire**
TEL 0298 72967
OPEN 10–5 Mon–Sat.

Specialise in restoring brass and brass
and iron bedsteads and some furniture,
mainly Victorian mahogany and
Georgian oak, also re-upholstery, recaning and rushing.

PROVIDE Home Inspections.
Discretionary Estimates. Chargeable
Collection/Delivery Service.
SPEAK TO Nigel Thompson.

WATER LANE ANTIQUES

Water Lane, Bakewell, **Derbyshire
DE4 1EU**
TEL 062981 4161
OPEN 9.30–5 Mon–Sat.

Specialise in the restoration of antique
furniture.

PROVIDE Home Inspections. Free

Estimates. Free Collection/Delivery
Service
SPEAK TO Michael Pembery.

D. J. BENT
Stonecourt, Membland, Newton Ferrers,
Plymouth, **Devon PL8 1HP**
TEL   0752 872 831
OPEN   By Appointment.

Specialise in restoring antique English
and Continental furniture, particularly
oak, walnut and mahogany.

PROVIDE Home Inspections. Free
Estimates. Chargeable
Collection/Delivery Service.
SPEAK TO Mr D. J. Bent.
Mr Bent teaches furniture restoration
and is a member of BAFRA and UKIC.
This workshop is included on the register
of conservators maintained by the
Conservation Unit of the Museums and
Galleries Commission.

BRITANNIA RESTORATIONS
Old Britannia House, Castle Street,
Combe Martin, Nr. Ilfracombe,
Devon EX34 0JF
TEL   0271 882887
OPEN   9–5.30 Mon–Sat or By
        Appointment.

Specialise in restoring traditional
Windsor chairs, farmhouse furnishings,
non-caustic strip and polish service, brass
and ironware.

PROVIDE Home Inspections. Free
Estimates. Chargeable
Collection/Delivery Service.
SPEAK TO Stephen Lloyd Malsom.
Member of the Guild of Master
Craftsmen.

RODERICK BUTLER
Marwood House, Honiton, **Devon
EX14 8PY**
TEL   0404 42169
OPEN   9.30–5.30 Mon–Sat.

Specialise in restoring antique furniture
and works of art.

PROVIDE Home Inspections. Free
Estimates. Chargeable
Collection/Delivery Service.
SPEAK TO Roderick Butler.

CLIVE AND LESLEY COBB
Newhouse Farm, Bratton Fleming,
Barnstaple, **Devon EX31 4RT**
TEL   0598 710465
OPEN   9–5.30 Mon–Sun.

Specialise in restoring lacquer work,
chinoiserie and decorative painted
artefacts. Also create individual
decorative items to customers'
requirements.

PROVIDE Home Inspections. Free
Estimates. Chargeable
Collection/Delivery Service.
SPEAK TO Clive Cobb.

Member of UKIC and the Guild of
Master Craftsmen. This workshop is
included on the register of conservators
maintained by the Conservation Unit of
the Museums and Galleries Commission.
SEE Clocks.

J. COLLINS AND SON
63 High St, Bideford, **Devon
EX39 2AN**
TEL   0237 473103
FAX   0237 475658
OPEN   9.30–5 Mon–Sat; closed Wed.

Specialise in restoring antique furniture.

PROVIDE Home Inspections. Free
Estimates. Free Local
Collection/Delivery Service.
SPEAK TO Mr J. C. Biggs.
Established 1953. Member of UKIC.

This workshop is included on the register maintained by the Conservation Unit of the Museums and Galleries Commission.

MICHAEL HURST
326 Old Laira Road, Plymouth, **Devon PL3 6AQ**
TEL   0752 221161 (Answerphone out of hours)
OPEN   8.30–5 Mon–Fri; 9–12 Sat.

Specialise in restoring all antique and modern (1900 plus) furniture, including rush, sea-grass and cane work with a complete upholstery workshop using traditional methods and materials.

PROVIDE Home Inspections. Free Local Estimates. Free Collection/Delivery Service.
SPEAK TO Michael Hurst or Elizabeth Powles.

LOVE'S FURNITURE RESTORATIONS
The Workshop, South Street, Axminster, **Devon EX13 5AD**
TEL   0297 35059
OPEN   8.30–5 Mon–Sat. Closed Wed.

Specialise in restoring and repairing antique and grand furniture, French polishing, rushing, caning and re-upholstery.

PROVIDE Home Inspections. Free Estimates. Chargeable Collection/Delivery Service.
SPEAK TO Jamie Love.

Members of the Guild of Master Craftsmen; the family has been trading in Axminster since 1873.

PETER MOORE
The Workshop, 56 Sherwell Lane, Torquay, **Devon TQ2 6BE**
TEL   0803 605334
OPEN   8.30–5 Mon–Sat.

Specialise in restoring antique and solid timber furniture.

PROVIDE Home Inspections. Free Estimates. Chargeable Collection/Delivery Service.
SPEAK TO Peter Moore.

Member of the Guild of Master Craftsmen and Guild of Woodworkers.

PETTICOMBE MANOR ANTIQUES
Petticombe Manor, Monkleigh, Bideford, **Devon EX39 5JR**
TEL   0237 475605
OPEN   9–6 Daily.

Specialise in restoring antique furniture, including cabinet work, French polishing and upholstery.

PROVIDE Home Inspections by arrangement. Free Estimates. Chargeable Collection/Delivery Service.
SPEAK TO Mr O. Wilson.

TONY VERNON
15 Follett Road, Topsham, **Devon EX3 0JP**
TEL   0392 874635
OPEN   9–6 Mon–Fri.

Specialise in restoring and conserving antique English and Continental furniture, marquetry inlay, Boulle work, gilding, re-veneering and French polishing.

PROVIDE Home Inspections. Refundable Estimates. Chargeable Collection/Delivery Service.
SPEAK TO Tony Vernon.

MICHAEL BARRINGTON
The Old Rectory, Warmwell, Dorchester, **Dorset DT2 8HQ**
TEL   0305 852104
OPEN   8.30–5.30 or By Appointment.

Specialise in restoring antique furniture and associated metalwork, gilding, painting, marquetry, organ casework and pipe gilding.

PROVIDE Free Local Estimates.

Free/Chargeable Collection/Delivery
Service.
SPEAK TO Michael Barrington.
Member of BAFRA.
SEE Clocks, Collectors (Toys).

BLACKWOODS
805 Christchurch Road, Boscombe,
Bournemouth, **Dorset BH7 6AP**
TEL   0202 434800
OPEN   9–5 Mon–Fri.

Specialise in restoring antique English
furniture, including marquetry, inlay,
carving, turning and gilding; also
upholstery and all types of polishing.

PROVIDE Home Inspections.
Free/Refundable Estimates. Free
Collection/Delivery Service.
SPEAK TO Richard Owen.
Member of BAFRA and UKIC. This
workshop is included on the register
maintained by the Conservation Unit of
the Museums and Galleries Commission.

RICHARD BOLTON
Ash Tree Cottage, Whitecross,
Netherbury, Bridport, **Dorset**
DT6 5NH
TEL   030 888 474
OPEN   8.30–6 Mon–Fri.

Specialise in all aspects of sympathetic
furniture restoration using traditional
cabinetmaking and polishing techniques.
Desk and table leathers supplied and
fitted, upholstery, caning, rushing, brass
casting and gilding services available.

PROVIDE Home Inspections. Free
Estimates. Free Collection/Delivery
Service.
SPEAK TO Richard Bolton.
Member of BAFRA.

PETER BRAZIER
Nash Court Farmhouse, Marnhull,
Sturminster Newton, **Dorset**
DT10 1JZ
TEL   0258 820255
OPEN   8.30–5.30 Mon–Fri or By
       Appointment.

Specialise in all aspects of furniture
restoration and finishing, excluding
gilding. Also run a non-ferrous foundry
where missing mounts can be cast using
the lost wax method.

PROVIDE Home Inspections. Free
Estimates. Free Local
Collection/Delivery Service.
SPEAK TO Peter Brazier.
Member of BAFRA.

THE CHETTLE GUILD
The Stables, Chettle House, Chettle,
Blandford, **Dorset DT11 8DB**
TEL   0258 89576
OPEN   9–6 Mon–Sat.

Specialise in restoring furniture,
including metalwork, fine gilding and oil
and water gilding.

PROVIDE Home Inspections. Free
Estimates. Free Local
Collection/Delivery Service.
SPEAK TO Alastair or Andrew Arnold.
SEE Arms, Clocks, Collectors (Scientific
Instruments).

MRS CATHERINE
MATHEW
Kiwi Cottage, Maperton Road, Charlton
Horethorne, Sherborne, **Dorset**
DT9 4NT
TEL   096 322 595
OPEN   9–6 Mon–Fri or By
       Appointment.

Specialise in repairing furniture,
cleaning, regilding, cane seating.

PROVIDE Home Inspections. Free
Estimates. Free Collection/Delivery
Service.

SPEAK TO Catherine Mathew.
SEE Picture Frames, Porcelain.

G. A. MATTHEWS
The Cottage Workshop, 174
Christchurch Road, Parley Cross,
Wimborne, **Dorset BH22 8SS**
TEL   0202 572665
OPEN   9–5 Mon–Fri.

Specialise in restoring antique furniture,
all types of finishing and both modern
and antique cabinetmaking.

PROVIDE Home Inspections. Free
Estimates. Chargeable
Collection/Delivery Service.
SPEAK TO G. A. Matthews.

OLD BARN ANTIQUES CO.
Flamberts, Trent, Sherborne, **Dorset
DT9 4SS**
TEL   0935 850648
OPEN   By Appointment.

Specialise in restoring and repairing
18th and 19th century furniture,
including upholstery. Individual items
made to order.

PROVIDE Home Inspections. Free
Estimates. Free/Chargeable
Collection/Delivery Service.
SPEAK TO Geoffrey Mott.

TOLPUDDLE ANTIQUE RESTORERS
The Stables, Tolpuddle, Dorchester,
Dorset DT2 7HF
TEL   0305 848739
OPEN   9–6 Mon–Fri; 12–5 Sat.

Specialise in restoring antique furniture.

PROVIDE Home Inspections. Free
Estimates. Free Collection/Delivery
Service.
Member of BAFRA.
SEE Clocks.

THE COLLECTOR
Douglas House, 23–25 The Bank,
Barnard Castle, **Durham DL12 8PH**
TEL   0833 37783
OPEN   10–5 or By Appointment.

Specialise in restoring early oak and
period furniture, including metalwork.

PROVIDE Home Inspections. Refundable
Estimates. Chargeable
Collection/Delivery Service.
SPEAK TO Robert Jordan or Paul Hunter.

Also provide a full design service.
SEE Clocks.

CLIVE BEARDALL
104B High Street, Maldon, **Essex
CM9 7ET**
TEL   0621 857890
FAX   0621 857565
OPEN   8–6 Mon–Fri; 8–1 Sat.

Specialise in restoring period furniture,
including marquetry, carving, gilding,
leather desk lining, traditional hand
French polishing and wax finishing. Do
rush and cane seating.

PROVIDE Home Inspections.
Free/Chargeable Estimates.
Free/Chargeable Collection/Delivery
Service.
SPEAK TO Clive Beardall.
Member of BAFRA and UKIC. This
workshop is included on the register of
conservators maintained by the
Conservation Unit of the Museums and
Galleries Commission.

S. BOND & SON
14/15 North Hill, Colchester, **Essex
CO1 1DZ**
TEL   0206 572925
OPEN   9–5 Mon–Sat.

Specialise in restoring antique and
Victorian furniture.

PROVIDE Home Inspections. Free

Estimates. Free Local
Collection/Delivery Service.
SPEAK TO Robert Bond.
This family firm has been established 140
years and is run by the fifth generation.
SEE Oil Paintings.

DAVID, JEAN & JOHN ANTIQUES

587 London Road, Westcliff, **Essex
SS0 9PQ**
TEL   0702 339106
FAX   0268 560563
OPEN   10–5 Mon–Sat; closed Wed.

Specialise in restoring Victorian and
Edwardian furniture.

PROVIDE Home Inspections. Refundable
Estimates. Free Collection/Delivery
Service.
SPEAK TO David Howard.
SEE Clocks.

A. DUNN & SON

The White House, 8 Wharf Road,
Chelmsford, **Essex CM3 4XL**
TEL   0245 354452
FAX   0245 494991
OPEN   7–5 Mon–Fri; Sat a.m. telephone
         first.

Specialise in restoring antique furniture
of all periods, especially marquetry and
Boulle. Will also make new panels.

PROVIDE Home Inspections. Free Local
Estimates. Collection/Delivery Service
available.
SPEAK TO Bob Dunn.
This third-generation firm was started in
1896. They made the marquetry panels
for the VSOE Orient Express and liners
including the *Queen Mary* and *Queen
Elizabeth*.

FORGE STUDIO WORKSHOPS

Stour Street, Manningtree, **Essex
CO11 1BE**
TEL   0206 396222
OPEN   8.30–5 Mon–Fri; 9–12 Sat.

Specialise in restoring fine antique
furniture, bespoke cabinetmaking, chair
matching, church and heraldic carving.

PROVIDE Home Inspections.
Free/Chargeable Estimates. Chargeable
Collection/Delivery Service.
SPEAK TO Dick Patterson.
Member of BAFRA.

TERRY HILLIARD

The Barn, Master Johns, Thoby Lane,
Mountnessing, Brentwood, **Essex
CM15 0JY**
TEL   0277 354717
OPEN   By Appointment.

Specialise in restoring gilded furniture,
mirror frames and carving and gilding.

PROVIDE Home Inspections. Free
Estimates. Free Collection/Delivery
Service.
SPEAK TO Terry Hilliard.
Member of the Guild of Master
Craftsmen.
SEE Picture Frames.

LITTLEBURY ANTIQUES

58–60 Fairycroft Road, Saffron Walden,
Essex CB10 1LZ
TEL   0799 27961
FAX   0799 27961
OPEN   8.30–5.15 Mon–Fri; Sat By
         Appointment.

Specialise in restoring furniture of all
periods.

PROVIDE Home Inspections. Free
Estimates. Free/Chargeable
Collection/Delivery Service.
SPEAK TO N. H. D'Oyly.
SEE Clocks.

GREVILLE MARCHANT
Coach House (Courtyard), Market Place, Abridge, **Essex RM4 1UA**
TEL   0992 812996
FAX   0992 814300
OPEN   8.30–6 Mon to Fri; 10–5.30 Sun.

Specialise in restoring all types of furniture, especially chairs. Copies made to match existing pieces; also architectural joinery.

PROVIDE Home Inspections. Free Estimates. Free Collection/Delivery Service.
SPEAK TO Greville Marchant.

Mr Marchant holds a Licentiateship to the City & Guilds.

MILLERS ANTIQUES KELVEDON
46 High Street, Kelvedon, Colchester, **Essex CO5 9AG**
TEL   0376 570098
FAX   0376 572186
OPEN   9–5.30 Mon–Fri; 10–4 Sat.

Specialise in restoring antique furniture, French polishing, carving and gilding, desk and table-top relining, upholstery and bespoke furniture making.

PROVIDE Home Inspections. Free Estimates. Chargeable Collection/Delivery Service.
SPEAK TO Mr R. C. Miller.

ANTONY PALMER ANTIQUES
169 St Mary's Lane, Upminster, **Essex**
TEL   04022 26620
OPEN   9.30–5.30 Tues–Sat.

Specialise in repairing and restoring Victorian furniture.

PROVIDE Home Inspections. Free Estimates. Free/Chargeable Collection/Delivery Service.
SPEAK TO Antony Palmer.

SEE Clocks.

SKILLCRAFTS
10 Park Street, Thaxted, Great Dunmow, **Essex CM6 2ND**
TEL   0371 830162
OPEN   9–6 Mon–Sat.

Specialise in complete restoration of antique and traditional furniture, including an upholstery service.

PROVIDE Home Inspections. Free Local Estimates. Free/Refundable Collection/Delivery Service.
SPEAK TO Michael L. Rickwood.

Member of UKIC. This workshop is included on the register of conservators maintained by the Conservation Unit of the Museums and Galleries Commission.

THOMAS STAFFORD
44 Marcos Road, Canvey Island, **Essex SS8 7LE**
TEL   0268 680929
OPEN   8.30–6 Mon–Sat.

Specialise in all aspects of furniture restoration and wood finishing employing traditional and shellac waxed finishes and modern spray techniques. Other services include cabinet manufacturing and joinery designed to individual requirements.

PROVIDE Home Inspections. Free Estimates. Free Collection/Delivery Service.
SPEAK TO Thomas Stafford.

Member of the Guild of Master Craftsmen.

TAYLOR'S FURNITURE RESTORATIONS
The Terminus, Prince Edward Road, Billericay, **Essex CM11 2LD**
TEL   0277 657867
OPEN   9–5 Mon–Fri or By Appointment.

Specialise in restoration of antique furniture.

PROVIDE Home Inspections. Free Local

Estimates. Free Local
Collection/Delivery Service.
SPEAK TO Mr B. C. Taylor.

Member of the Guild of Master
Craftsmen.

TURPINS ANTIQUES
4 Stoney Lane, Thaxted, **Essex**
TEL   0371 830495 or 0860 883302
OPEN   10–5 Mon–Sat.

Specialise in restoring 18th century
English furniture.

PROVIDE Home Inspections. Free
Estimates. Chargeable
Collection/Delivery Service.
SPEAK TO John Braund.

WEDMID & SIMPSON LTD
232–234 High Street, Epping, **Essex**
CM16 7PW
TEL   0378 560309
FAX   0378 73027
OPEN   10–5.30 Daily.

Specialise in restoring furniture and
French polishing.

PROVIDE Home Inspections. Free
Estimates. Free Collection/Delivery
Service.
SPEAK TO Mr Levan.

ANTIQUE FURNITURE RESTORATION
Gloucester Antique Centre, 1 Severn
Road, Gloucester, **Gloucestershire**
GL1 2LE
TEL   0452 529716
FAX   0452 307161
OPEN   9.30–5 Mon–Sat; 1–5 Sun.

Specialise in restoring Georgian and
Regency furniture as well as marquetry.

PROVIDE Home Inspections. Free
Estimates. Free Collection/Delivery
Service.
SPEAK TO Mr C. A. Cook.

KEITH BAWDEN
Mews Workshop, Montpellier Retreat,
Cheltenham, **Gloucestershire**
GL50 2XG
TEL   0242 230320
OPEN   7–4.30 Mon–Fri.

Specialise in conserving and restoring
antique furniture and upholstery.

PROVIDE Free Estimates. Home
Inspections. Local Collection/Delivery
Service.
SPEAK TO Keith Bawden
SEE Clocks, Oil Paintings, Porcelain,
Silver.

FORUM ANTIQUES
20 West Way, Cirencester,
Gloucestershire GL7 1JA
TEL   0285 658406
OPEN   9–5.30 Mon–Sat.

Specialise in restoring 17th century oak
furniture.

PROVIDE Home Inspections. Free
Estimates. Free Collection/Delivery
Service.
SPEAK TO Weston Mitchell.

G. M. S. RESTORATIONS
The Workshops (rear of Bell Passage
Antiques), High Street, Wickwar,
Gloucestershire GL12 8NP
TEL   0454 294251
FAX   0454 294251
OPEN   8–5 Mon–Fri.

Specialise in restoring furniture,
polishing, carving, gilding and
traditional upholstery.

PROVIDE Home Inspections. Refundable
Estimates. Chargeable
Collection/Delivery Service.
SPEAK TO Mr G. M. St George-Stacey.
Member of LAPADA, Association of
Master Upholsterers, Guild of Master
Craftsmen, Guild of Woodcarvers, Guild
of Antique Dealers and Restorers.
SEE Oil Paintings.

MRS JANET GIBBS
The Hope, Ampney St Peter,
Cirencester, **Gloucestershire GL7 5SH**
TEL   0285 851227
OPEN   By Appointment.

Specialise in chair caning and rushing.

PROVIDE Home Inspections, Free
Estimates.
SPEAK TO Janet Gibbs.

ALAN HESSEL
The Old Town Workshop, St George's
Close, Moreton-in-Marsh,
Gloucestershire GL56 0LP
TEL   0608 50026
OPEN   8–5 Mon–Fri or By
    Appointment.

Specialise in restoring 17th–early 19th
century English furniture, including
marquetry, parquetry and oyster work
with an emphasis on patina retention.

PROVIDE Home Inspections. Free
Estimates. Free/Chargeable
Collection/Delivery Service.
SPEAK TO Alan Hessel.

Member of BAFRA and UKIC.

STEPHEN HILL
No. 5 Cirencester Workshops, Brewery
Court, Cirencester, **Gloucestershire
GL7 2HA**
TEL   0285 658817
OPEN   9–5.30 Mon–Fri, Sat a.m. or By
    Appointment.

Specialise in all types of furniture
restoration, especially 18th century
walnut, oak and mahogany and pre-1900
furniture. Full traditional re-upholstery,
rush and cane seating.

PROVIDE Home Inspections. Free
Estimates. Free Local
Collection/Delivery Service.
SPEAK TO Stephen Hill.
Member of BAFRA.

HUNT AND LOMAS
Village Farm Workshops, Preston,
Cirencester, **Gloucestershire GL7 5PR**
TEL   0285 640111
OPEN   8.30–6. Mon–Fri or By
    Appointment.

Specialise in all aspects of furniture
restoration, including carving and
gilding.

PROVIDE Home Inspections. Free
Estimates. Free Local
Collection/Delivery Service.
SPEAK TO Christian Macduff-Hunt.
Member of BAFRA and BADA.

DONALD HUNTER
The Old School Room, Shipton Oliffe,
Cheltenham, **Gloucestershire
GL54 4JQ**
TEL   0242 820755
OPEN   8–6 Mon–Fri.

Specialise in carving, gilding and painted
finishes to mirror frames, lacquer work
and antique furniture.

PROVIDE Home Inspections.
Free/Chargeable Estimates.
Collection/Delivery Service by
arrangement.
SPEAK TO Donald Hunter.

Member of BAFRA.

ANDREW LELLIOTT
6 Tetbury Hill, Avening, Tetbury,
Gloucestershire GL8 8LT
TEL   045 383 5783
OPEN   By Appointment.

Specialise in restoring 18th century
English furniture, including walnut,
mahogany, satinwood.

PROVIDE Home Inspections. Free
Estimates. Free Collection/Delivery
Service.
SPEAK TO Andrew Lelliott.

Member of BAFRA. This workshop is
included on the register of conservators

maintained by the Conservation Unit of the Museums and Galleries Commission. SEE Clocks.

A. J. PONSFORD ANTIQUES
51–53 Dollar Street, Cirencester, **Gloucestershire GL7 2AS**
TEL   0285 652355
OPEN   8.30–5.30 Mon–Fri.

Specialise in restoring antique furniture and upholstery.

PROVIDE Home Inspections. Free Estimates. Free Collection/Delivery Service.
SPEAK TO A. J. Ponsford.
SEE Oil Paintings.

ANGUS STEWART
Sycamore Barn, Bourton Industrial Park, Bourton-on-the-Water, Cheltenham, **Gloucestershire GL54 2HQ**
TEL   0451 21611
OPEN   8–5.30 Mon–Fri.

Specialise in restoring antique furniture, works of art, gilded and lacquered furniture and mirrors.

PROVIDE Home Inspections. Free Estimates. Chargeable Collection/Delivery Service.
SPEAK TO Angus Stewart.
Member of BAFRA.

UEDELHOVEN AND CAMPION
Post Office, Gretton, Cheltenham, **Gloucestershire GL54 5EP**
TEL   0242 602306
OPEN   9–5.30 Mon–Fri; Sat a.m.

Specialise in restoring furniture, including Boulle work, brass inlays, turning. Also make up a chair to match a set or another piece of furniture.

PROVIDE Home Inspections. Free Estimates. Free/Chargeable Collection/Delivery Service.

SPEAK TO Mr Uedelhoven or Mr Campion.

GUY BAGSHAW
Plain Farm, Old Dairy, East Tisted, Alton, **Hampshire GU34 3RT**
TEL   0420 58362
OPEN   8–6 Mon–Fri or By Appointment.

Specialise in 18th and early 19th century English furniture copy pieces.

PROVIDE Home Inspections. Free/Chargeable Estimates. Free Local Collection/Delivery Service.
SPEAK TO Guy Bagshaw.
Member of BAFRA. This workshop is included on the register of conservators maintained by the Conservation Unit of the Museums and Galleries Commission.

CORFIELD RESTORATIONS LTD
120 High Street, Lymington, **Hampshire SO41 9AQ**
TEL   0590 673532
OPEN   9.15–5.30 Mon–Sat.

Specialise in all furniture restoration, including gilding and upholstery.

PROVIDE Home Inspections. Free Estimates. Local Free Collection/Delivery Service.
SPEAK TO Alan Bloomfield or Michael Corfield.
Also at Setters Farm, Lymington. 0590 671977.
SEE Oil Paintings, Picture Frames.

DYER AND FOLLETT LTD
Coward Road, Alverstoke, Gosport, **Hampshire PO12 2LD**
TEL   0705 582204
OPEN   9–12.45, 2.15–5.30 Mon–Fri; 9.15–12.45, 2.15–5 Sat.

Specialise in restoring antique English and Continental furniture, French polishing, upholstery.

PROVIDE Local Home Inspections.
Refundable Estimates, Free Local
Collection/Delivery Service.
SPEAK TO Mr E. A. Dyer.

JAMES FLAVELL BOOKBINDER AND RESTORER
26 Foreland Road, Bembridge, Isle of
Wight, **Hampshire PO35 5XW**
TEL   0983 872856
OPEN   9–5.30 Mon–Fri, 9–12.30 Sat.

Specialise in inlaying and replacement of
leather-covered tables and desk tops.

PROVIDE Home Inspections. Free
Estimates. Free Collection/Delivery
Service.
SPEAK TO James Flavell.

Mr Flavell is City and Guilds qualified,
Member of the Society of Bookbinders,
Associate Member of Designer
Bookbinders. This workshop is included
on the register of conservators
maintained by the Conservation Unit of
the Museums and Galleries Commission.
SEE Oil Paintings, Books.

A. FLEMING (SOUTHSEA) LTD
The Clock Tower, Castle Road,
Southsea, **Hampshire PO5 3DE**
TEL   0705 822934
OPEN   8.30–5 Mon–Fri; 8.30–1 Sat.

Specialise in a full restoration service for
antique furniture.

PROVIDE Home Inspections. Free
Estimates. Free Collection/Delivery
Service.
SPEAK TO A. Fleming or J. Harris.

This family firm was founded in 1908
and is now run by the third generation.
Member of BADA.

GAYLORDS ANTIQUES
75 West Street, Titchfield, Fareham,
Hampshire PO14 4DG
TEL   0329 43402
OPEN   10–4 Mon–Sat.

Specialise in restoring antique furniture,
French polishing and upholstery.

PROVIDE Home Inspections. Free
Estimates. Free Collection/Delivery
Service.
SPEAK TO Mr Hebbard.

JOHN HAYWARD
Cane and Woodcraft Centre, 57 High
Street, Beaulieu, **Hampshire
SO42 7YA**
TEL   0590 612211
OPEN   10–1, 2–5 Wed–Sat; 12–5 Sun.

Specialise in restoring antique and
modern cane, rush and seagrass seats.
Blind, double, fan, medallions, close and
pre-woven canework undertaken.

PROVIDE Local Home Inspections. Free
Estimates. Free Local
Collection/Delivery Service.
SPEAK TO John Hayward.

Member of the Basketmakers'
Association. Mr Hayward gives talks and
demonstrations.

DAVID C. E. LEWRY
'Wychelms', 66 Gorran Avenue, Rowner,
Gosport, **Hampshire PO13 ONF**
TEL   0329 286901
OPEN   By Appointment.

Specialise in conserving and restoring
17th and 18th century furniture.

PROVIDE Home Inspections. Refundable
Estimates. Free/Chargeable
Collection/Delivery Service.
SPEAK TO David Lewry.

Member of BAFRA.

DOUGLAS J. LINCOLN

Athgarvan House, Shawford,
Winchester, **Hampshire SO21 2AA**
TEL   0962 712662
OPEN   By Appointment.

Specialise in providing engraving
services for decorated furniture,
especially Boulle.

PROVIDE Local Home Inspections. Free
Estimates. Chargeable Local
Collection/Delivery Service.
SPEAK TO Douglas Lincoln.

Visiting tutor at West Dean. This
workshop is included on the register of
conservators maintained by the
Conservation Unit of the Museums and
Galleries Commission.
SEE Silver.

J. A. PRADO (PRADO CABINETMAKER AND RESTORER)

Great Weir House, The Great Weir,
Alresford, **Hampshire SO24 9DB**
TEL   0962 732896
FAX   0962 734233
OPEN   By Appointment.

Specialise in restoring English furniture
1660 to 1815 with emphasis on
marquetry and brass inlay.

PROVIDE Home Inspections. Free
Estimates. Chargeable
Collection/Delivery Service.
SPEAK TO Mr J. A. Prado.

This workshop is included on the register
of conservators maintained by the
Conservation Unit of the Museums and
Galleries Commission.
SEE Clocks.

HUMPHREY SLADDEN FINE FURNITURE RESTORATION

Yard House, South Harting, Petersfield,
Hampshire GU31 5NS
TEL   0730 825339
OPEN   8–4.30 Mon–Fri; 8–12 Sat.

Specialise in restoring 18th and early
19th century English furniture,
cabinetwork, veneering, polishing,
turning.

PROVIDE Home Inspections by
arrangement. Free/Chargeable
Estimates.
SPEAK TO H. P. Sladden or John Birkett.

Mr Sladden is currently a tutor at West
Dean.
Although the postal address is
Hampshire, Harting is actually in West
Sussex.

MR D. J. SMITH

34 Silchester Road, Pamber Heath, Nr.
Basingstoke, **Hampshire RG26 6EF**
TEL   0734 700595
OPEN   8–6 Mon–Sat or By
            Appointment.

Specialise in restoration and
reproduction of fine 18th century carved
and giltwood furniture. Fine carving in
wood and oil or water gilding and
distressing.

PROVIDE Local Home Inspections. Free
Estimates. Free Local
Collection/Delivery Service.
SPEAK TO Douglas Smith.

THE TANKERDALE WORKSHOP

Tankerdale Farm, Steep Marsh,
Petersfield, **Hampshire GU32 2BH**
TEL   0730 893839
FAX   0730 894523
OPEN   8–6 Mon–Fri.

Specialise in conserving and restoring
furniture, including carving, gilding,
lacquer work, japanning and
cabinetmaking.

PROVIDE Home Inspections. Refundable
Estimates. Chargeable
Collection/Delivery Service.
SPEAK TO John Hartley.

THE BAROMETER SHOP
4 New Street, Leominster, **Hereford & Worcester HR6 8BT**
TEL   0568 613652
OPEN   9–5.30 Mon–Sat, closed Wed.

Specialise in restoring furniture, including hand French polishing, hand engraving, metalware. Mirrors re-silvered.

PROVIDE Home Inspections. Free Estimates. Free Collection/Delivery Service.
SPEAK TO Richard Cookson.
CMBHI.
SEE Clocks, Collectors (Scientific Instruments).
SEE **Avon**

I. AND J. L. BROWN LTD
58 Commercial Road, Hereford, **Hereford & Worcester HR1 2BP**
TEL   0432 358895
FAX   0432 275338
OPEN   9–5.30 Mon–Sat.

Specialise in restoring English country and French provincial furniture, chair rush work.

PROVIDE Free/Chargeable Estimates. Free/Chargeable Collection/Delivery Service.
SPEAK TO Ian Brown.
SEE **London SW6**.

B. R. HONEYBORNE
The Whyle Cottage, Pudleston, Leominster, **Hereford & Worcester HR6 ORE**
TEL   056887 250
OPEN   9–5 Mon–Sat.

Specialise in restoring antique furniture.

PROVIDE Home Inspections. Free Estimates. Chargeable Collection/Delivery Service.
SPEAK TO B. R. Honeyborne.

JENNINGS & JENNINGS
30 Bridge Street, Leominster, **Hereford & Worcester HR6 9JQ**
TEL   05448 586
OPEN   By Appointment.

Specialise in conserving and restoring gilded items, including furniture and mirror frames.

PROVIDE Home Inspections. Free Estimates. Free/Chargeable Collection/Delivery Service.
SPEAK TO Sabina Jennings.
SEE Picture Frames.

H. W. KEIL LTD
Tudor House, Broadway, **Hereford & Worcester WR12 7DP**
TEL   0386 852408
OPEN   9.15–12.45, 2.15–5.30 Mon–Sat; closed Thur p.m.

Specialise in restoring 17th, 18th and sometimes 20th century furniture, mainly in oak and mahogany.

PROVIDE Refundable Estimates. Free Local Collection/Delivery Service.
SPEAK TO P. J. W. Keil.

KIMBER AND SON
6 Lower Howsell Road, Malvern Link, **Hereford & Worcester WR14 1EF**
TEL   0684 574339
OPEN   8.30–1, 2–5 Mon–Fri; 9–12.30 Sat.

Specialise in restoring fine 18th and 19th century furniture.

PROVIDE Home Inspections. Free Estimates. Free Collection/Delivery Service.
SPEAK TO Mr E. M. Kimber.

MALVERN STUDIOS
56 Cowleigh Road, Malvern,
Hereford & Worcester WR14 1QD
TEL   0684 574913
OPEN   9–5 Mon–Thur; 9–4.45 Fri, Sat.

Specialise in restoring antique furniture, hand polishing, Boulle and gilt work.

PROVIDE Home Inspections. Refundable Estimates. Chargeable Collection/Delivery Service.
SPEAK TO Mr L. M. Hall.
Member of BAFRA and UKIC. This workshop is included on the register of conservators maintained by the Conservation Unit of the Museums and Galleries Commission.

MERIDIEN ANTIQUES
41 Upper Tything, Worcester,
Hereford & Worcester WR1 1JT
TEL   0905 29014
OPEN   9–5.30 Mon–Sat.

Specialise in restoring antique furniture, particularly dining tables and desks. Also do traditional French polishing and upholstery work.

PROVIDE Home Inspections. Free Estimates. Free Collection/Delivery Service.
SPEAK TO Robert Hubbard.

NEIL POSTONS RESTORATIONS
29 South Street, Leominster,
Hereford & Worcester HR6 8JQ
TEL   0568 616677
OPEN   8.30–5.30 Mon–Fri.

Specialise in restoring period furniture, carving, tooling, carcase work, French polishing, re-leathering desk tops.

PROVIDE Home Inspections. Free Local Estimates. Chargeable Collection/Delivery Service.
SPEAK TO Neil Postons.

BRYAN WIGINGTON
Chapel Schoolroom, 1 Heolydwr, Hay-on-Wye, via Hereford, **Hereford & Worcester HR3 5AT**
TEL   0497 820545
OPEN   By Appointment Only.

Specialise in restoring a wide range of period furniture from Tudor oak to Edwardian mahogany, with associated metalwork. They have a large stock of antique timbers plus salvaged sundries.

PROVIDE Home Inspections. Free Estimates. Free Local Collection/Delivery Service.
SPEAK TO Bryan Wigington.

Established in 1899, this is a third-generation family business.

WOODLAND FINE ART
16 The Square, Alvechurch, **Hereford & Worcester B48 7LA**
TEL   021 445 5886
OPEN   10–6 Mon–Sat.

Specialise in restoring furniture.

PROVIDE Home Inspections, Free Estimates, Free Collection/Delivery Service.
SPEAK TO C. J. Haynes.
SEE Oil Paintings.

BECKWITH & SON
St Nicholas Hall, St Andrew Street, Hertford, **Hertfordshire SG14 1HZ**
TEL   0992 582079
OPEN   9–1, 2–5.30 Mon–Sat.

Specialise in restoring antique English furniture, cabinetmaking and polishing.

PROVIDE Home Inspections. Chargeable Estimates. Free Local Collection/Delivery Service.
SPEAK TO G. Gray.

CENTRE OF RESTORATION AND ARTS
11–15 Victoria Street, St Albans, **Hertfordshire AL1 3JJ**
TEL   0727 51555
FAX   0727 811508
OPEN   8.30–5.30 Mon–Fri.

Specialise in chair caning.

PROVIDE Local Home Inspections. Free/Chargeable Estimates. Chargeable Collection/Delivery Service.
SPEAK TO Paul Roe.

FARRELLY ANTIQUE RESTORATION
The Long Barn, 50 High Street, Tring, **Hertfordshire HP23 5AG**
TEL   0442 891905
OPEN   9–4 Mon–Fri.

Specialise in restoring cabinets and chairs, carving, gilding, upholstery, polishing.

PROVIDE Home Inspections. Free Estimates. Chargeable Collection/Delivery Service.
SPEAK TO Paul Farrelly.

GRISS AND BUTLER
2 Lord Street, Hoddesdon, **Hertfordshire EN11 8NA**
TEL   0992 465244
OPEN   7.30–6.30 Mon–Fri.

Specialise in restoration of carved and gilded antiques, all aspects of period furniture and mirror restoration.

PROVIDE Home Inspections. Free Estimates. Free Collection/Delivery Service.
SPEAK TO Mr Griss or Mr Butler.

HERTFORDSHIRE CONSERVATION SERVICE
Seed Warehouse, Maidenhead Yard, The Wash, Hertford, **Hertfordshire SG14 1PX**
TEL   0992 588966
FAX   0992 588971
OPEN   9–6 Mon–Fri By Appointment.

Specialise in restoring furniture and other items of wood of any period.

PROVIDE Home Inspections. Free/Chargeable Estimates. Chargeable Collection/Delivery Service.
SPEAK TO J. M. MacQueen.

This workshop is included on the register of conservators maintained by the Conservation Unit of the Museums and Galleries Commission.
SEE Carpets, Collectors (Dolls), Lighting, Porcelain, Oil Paintings, Picture Frames.

CHARLES PERRY RESTORATIONS LTD
Praewood Farm, Hemel Hempstead Road, St Albans, **Hertfordshire AL3 6AA**
TEL   0727 53487
FAX   0727 46668
OPEN   Mon–Fri 8.30–6; By Appointment Sat.

Specialise in furniture restoration and allied trades including gilding, carving, polishing, marquetry, lacquerwork, marble, traditional upholstery, caning and rushing and expert advice and reports to clients intending to purchase at auction.

PROVIDE Home Inspections. Free Estimates. Chargeable Collection/Delivery Service.
SPEAK TO John Carr.
Mr Carr is a Member of BAFRA and the Guild of Master Craftsmen.
By Appointment to HM Queen Elizabeth II Antique Furniture Restorers.
SEE Clocks.

R. J. PERRY ANTIQUES
37–38 Bridge Street, Hitchin,
Hertfordshire SG5 2DF
TEL   0462 434525
OPEN   10–5.30 Mon–Sat.

Specialise in restoring furniture to a very high standard, re-veneering, re-polishing, replacement where required of applied metal beading. Brass, copper and spelter repaired and re-polished where appropriate.

PROVIDE Home Inspections. Free Estimates. Free Local Collection/Delivery Service.
SPEAK TO Ronald Perry.
Member of LAPADA.

PHILLIPS OF HITCHIN
The Manor House, Hitchin,
Hertfordshire SG5 1JW
TEL   0462 432067
OPEN   9–5.30 Mon–Sat.

Specialise in restoring English and Continental furniture.

PROVIDE Home Inspections. Free/Chargeable Estimates. Chargeable Collection/Delivery Service.
SPEAK TO Jerome Phillips.
SEE Specialist Booksellers.

GRAHAM PORTER
Graham Porter Antiques, 31 Whitehorse Street, Baldock, **Hertfordshire SG7 6QF**
TEL   0462 895351
FAX   0462 892711
OPEN   9.30–5 Mon–Sat; 11–4 Sun.

Specialise in restoring antique furniture, especially country pieces and period pine.

PROVIDE Home Inspections. Collection/Delivery Service.
SPEAK TO Graham Porter.

JOHN RUSH
39 Christchurch Road, Tring,
Hertfordshire HP23 4EH
TEL   044282 5387
OPEN   10.30–1 Mon–Sat or By Appointment.

Specialise in restoring all types of upholstered furniture, re-upholstery and frame restoration.

PROVIDE Home Inspections. Free Estimates. Free/Chargeable Collection/Delivery Service.
SPEAK TO John Rush.
Fellow of the Association of Master Upholsterers. This workshop is included on the register of conservators maintained by the Conservation Unit of the Museums and Galleries Commission.

ST OUEN ANTIQUES LTD
Vintage Corner, Old Cambridge Road, Puckeridge, **Hertfordshire SG11 1SA**
TEL   0920 821336
FAX   0920 822877
OPEN   10–5 Mon–Sat.

Specialise in restoring 18th and 19th century English, Continental and gilded furniture and 19th century paintings.

PROVIDE Home Inspections. Refundable Estimates. Chargeable Collection/Delivery Service.
SPEAK TO Tim or John Blake.
SEE Oil Paintings.

TRACY'S FRENCH POLISHING CONTRACTORS
55 Great North Road, Brookmans Park, **Hertfordshire AL9 6LA**
TEL   0707 52144
FAX   0707 45153
OPEN   8–5 Mon–Fri.

Specialise in all aspects of original hand-rubbed French polishing and wood-finishing.

PROVIDE Home Inspections. Free

Estimates. Free Collection/Delivery
Service.
SPEAK TO Susan Tracy.
They prefer to carry out their work in
situ.

VICTOR WHINES
29 River Close, Waltham Cross,
Hertfordshire EN8 7QR
TEL   0992 712246
OPEN   9–5.30 Mon–Fri.

Specialise in restoring antique painted
furniture and Chinese lacquer. Also do
graining, marbling and gilding.

PROVIDE Home Inspections. Free
Estimates.
SPEAK TO Victor Whines.

WREN-OVATIONS
8 Hemel Hempstead Road, Redbourn,
Hertfordshire AL3 7NL
TEL   0923 260666
OPEN   8–6 Mon–Fri.

Specialise in restoring antique and
modern furniture, French polishing and
spray finishes.

PROVIDE Home Inspections. Free
Estimates. Free Local Collection/
Delivery Service.
SPEAK TO Barbara Murphy or David
Withers.

55 ANTIQUES
55–57 Spring Bank, Hull, **North
Humberside HU3 1AG**
TEL   0482 224510
OPEN   9–6 Mon–Sat.

Specialise in restoring antique furniture,
garden furniture and papier mâché.

PROVIDE Home Inspections. Estimates.
Collection/Delivery Service by
arrangement.
SPEAK TO Gerald Etherington.

If shop is closed the owner can be
contacted at No. 57.

OLD ROPERY ANTIQUES
East Street, Kilham, Nr. Driffield, **North
Humberside YO25 0ST**
TEL   026282 233
OPEN   9.30–5 Mon–Sat.

Specialise in restoring furniture.

PROVIDE Home Inspections. Chargeable
Estimates. Chargeable
Collection/Delivery Service.
SPEAK TO John Butterfield.

SEE Clocks, Collectors (Scientific
Instruments).

ADRIAN J. BLACK
36A Freeman Street, Grimsby, **South
Humberside DN32 7AG**
TEL   0472 824823 and 355668
OPEN   By Appointment.

Specialise in restoring English antique
furniture and cabinetmaking.

PROVIDES Home Inspections. Free
Estimates. Chargeable
Collection/Delivery Service.
SPEAK TO Adrian Black.

T. M. AKERS PERIOD FURNITURE RESTORATIONS
39 Chancery Lane, Beckenham, **Kent
BR3 2NR**
TEL   081 650 9179
OPEN   9–6 Mon–Fri.

Specialise in restoring English period
furniture up to 1900.

PROVIDE Home Inspections. Free
Estimates. Free Local
Collection/Delivery Service.
SPEAK TO Tim Akers.

Member of BAFRA, LAPADA and
UKIC. This workshop is included on the
register of conservators maintained by
the Conservation Unit of the Museums
and Galleries Commission.

WILLIAM ANTHONY BIRCH

Tenterden Rushcraft, Station Road, Tenterden, **Kent TN30 6JB**
TEL   05806 3326
OPEN   9.15–5 Mon–Sat, 9.15–1 Wed.

Specialise in restoring cane and rush furniture and repairing all woodwork.

PROVIDE Local Home Inspections. Free Estimates in workshop. Chargeable Collection/Delivery Service.
SPEAK TO W. A. Birch.

This workshop is included on the register of conservators maintained by the Conservation Unit of the Museums and Galleries Commission.

ROBERT COLEMAN

The Oasthouse, Three Chimneys, Biddenden, **Kent TN27 8LW**
TEL   0580 291520
OPEN   By Appointment.

Specialise in restoring mahogany and walnut English furniture.

PROVIDE Home Inspections. Free Estimates. Free Collection/Delivery Service.
SPEAK TO Robert Coleman.
Member of BAFRA and the Guild of Master Craftsmen.

FORGE ANTIQUES AND RESTORATION

Rye Road, Sandhurst, Hawkhurst, **Kent TN18 5JG**
TEL   0580 850308 and 850665
OPEN   9–5 Daily.

Specialise in repairing and polishing furniture, wood turning, carving, veneering.

PROVIDE Home Inspections. Free Estimates. Chargeable Collection/Delivery Service.
SPEAK TO James Nesfield.

GILTWOOD RESTORATION

71 Bower Mount Road, Maidstone, **Kent ME16 8AS**
TEL   0622 752273
OPEN   9–6 Mon–Fri.

Specialise in restoring fine gilded furniture, frames and architectural ornament, water-gilded or oil-gilded.

PROVIDE Home Inspections. Free Estimates. Free Collection/Delivery Service.
SPEAK TO Martin Body.

ANTHONY HARRINGTON

Squerryes Court Workshops, Squerryes Court, Westerham, **Kent TN16 ISJ**
TEL   0959 64936
FAX   0959 64936
OPEN   9–5 Mon–Fri.

Specialise in restoring antique wood carving and gilding.

PROVIDE Home Inspections. Free Estimates. Free Collection/Delivery Service.
SPEAK TO Anthony Harrington.

RICKY HOLDSTOCK

Hillside Cottage, The Forstal, Hernhill, Faversham, **Kent ME13 9JQ**
TEL   0227 751204
FAX   0227 751204
OPEN   9–5 Mon–Fri.

Specialise in replacing chair seats and panels in cane, rush and Danish cord.

PROVIDE Home Inspections. Free Estimates. Free/Chargeable Estimates.
SPEAK TO Ricky Holdstock.

LANGOLD ANTIQUES
Oxon Hoath, Tonbridge, **Kent**
TEL   0737 810577
OPEN   9–5 Mon, Thur, Fri.

Specialise in restoring furniture.

PROVIDE Free Collection/Delivery Service.
SPEAK TO Mr Bayne-Powell.

TIMOTHY LONG RESTORATION
26 High Street, Seal, Nr. Sevenoaks, **Kent TN15 0AP**
TEL   0732 62606
OPEN   By Appointment.

Specialise in restoring 18th and 19th century English and Continental furniture.

PROVIDE Home Inspections. Free Local Estimates. Free Local Collection/Delivery Service.
SPEAK TO Tim Long.
Member of BAFRA. This workshop is included on the register of conservators maintained by the Conservation Unit of the Museums and Galleries Commission.

MANDARIN GALLERY
32 London Road, Riverhead, Sevenoaks, **Kent TN13 2DE**
TEL   0732 457399
OPEN   9.30–5 Mon–Sat; closed Wed.

Specialise in restoring 18th–19th century Chinese hardwood furniture.

PROVIDE Free Estimates. Free Collection/Delivery Service.
SPEAK TO Joseph Liu.

R. M. RESTORATIONS
Chaddesden Barn, Morants Court Road, Dunton Green, **Kent TN13 2TR**
TEL   0732 741604
OPEN   7.30–5.30 Mon–Sat.
Specialise in restoring English furniture from 1700–1830.

PROVIDE Home Inspections. Free Estimates. Chargeable Collection/Delivery Service.
SPEAK TO Richard Marson.
Member of BAFRA.

J. T. RUTHERFORD & SON
55 Sandgate High Street, Folkestone, **Kent CT20 3AH**
TEL   0303 49515
OPEN   8.30–6 Mon–Sat or By Appointment.

Specialise in restoring period furniture.

PROVIDE Home Inspections. Refundable Estimates. Free/Chargeable Collection/Delivery Service.
SPEAK TO John Rutherford.

R. G. SCOTT
Furniture Mart, Bath Place and Grotto Hill, Margate, **Kent CT9 2BU**
TEL   0843 220653
FAX   0843 227207
OPEN   9.30–1, 2–5 Mon–Sat; closed Wed.

Specialise in restoring furniture, veneering, cabinet work, marquetry.

PROVIDE Home Inspections. Free Estimates. Free Local Collection/Delivery Service.
SPEAK TO Ron Scott.

ALAN GRICE ANTIQUES
106 Aughton Street, Ormskirk, **Lancashire L39 3BS**
TEL   0695 572007
OPEN   10–6 Mon–Sat.

Specialise in restoring English and Continental antique furniture.

PROVIDE Home Inspections. Free/Chargeable Estimates. Chargeable Collection/Delivery Service.
SPEAK TO Alan Grice.

ROBERT BINGLEY ANTIQUES
Church Street, Wing, Oakham,
Leicestershire LE15 8RS
TEL   057 285 725 or 314
OPEN   9–5 Mon–Sat; 11–4 Sun.

Specialise in restoring antique furniture,
including walnut, oak, mahogany and
rosewood.

PROVIDE Home Inspections. Free
Estimates. Free Collection/ Delivery
Service.
SPEAK TO Robert Bingley.

JOHN GARNER
51–53 High Street East, Uppingham,
Leicestershire LE15 9PY
TEL   0572 823607
FAX   0572 821654
OPEN   9–5.30 Mon–Sat; Sun By
        Appointment.

Specialise in restoring antique furniture,
mainly 18th and 19th century.

PROVIDE Home Inspections. Free
Collection/Delivery Service.
SPEAK TO John or Wendy Garner.

SEE Oil Paintings.

ALEXANDER A. JESSOP
(address withheld by request),
Leicestershire LE16 8LS
TEL   0858 433590
OPEN   By Appointment Only.

Specialise in restoring antique furniture,
including French polishing, wood-
carving, wood-turning and leather-
lining.

PROVIDE Home Inspections. Free
Estimates. Free Collection/Delivery
Service.
SPEAK TO Alexander Jessop.

E. & C. ROYALL
10 Waterfall Way, Medbourne, Nr.
Market Harborough, **Leicestershire
LE15 8EE**
TEL   0858 83744
OPEN   8.30–5 Mon–Fri.

Specialise in restoring antique English,
Continental and Oriental furniture,
including lacquer, Boulle and inlay work,
carving, veneering, French polishing and
mouldings.

PROVIDE Home Inspections. Free
Estimates. Chargeable
Collection/Delivery Service.
SPEAK TO C. Royall.
SEE Porcelain.

TATTERSALL'S
14 Orange Street, 2 Bear Yard, Orange
Street, Uppingham, **Leicestershire
LE15 9SQ**
TEL   0572 821171
OPEN   9.30–5 Tues–Sat; closed Mon &
        Thur.

Specialise in restoring upholstered
furniture and mirrors. Specialist restorers
of rush and cane furniture.

PROVIDE Home Inspections. Free
Estimates. Chargeable
Collection/Delivery Service.
SPEAK TO Janice Tattersall.
SEE Carpets.

BURGHLEY FINE ART CONSERVATION
Burghley House, Stamford,
Lincolnshire PE9 3JY
TEL   0780 62155
OPEN   By Appointment.

Specialise in conserving and restoring
painted furniture, European lacquer,
mirror frames and gilding.

PROVIDE Home Inspections. Free
Estimates. Chargeable
Collection/Delivery Service.
SPEAK TO Michael Cowell.

135

Any work undertaken is fully documented.
SEE Oil Paintings, Picture Frames.

E. CZAJKOWSKI & SON
96 Tor-O-Moor Road, Woodhall Spa, **Lincolnshire LN10 6SB**
TEL   0526 352895
OPEN   9–5 Mon–Fri.

Specialise in restoring antique furniture, including marquetry, lacquerwork, carving, gilding and upholstery. Also copy furniture.

PROVIDE Home Inspections. Free Estimates. Free Local Collection/Delivery Service.
SPEAK TO Mr M. J. Czajkowski.
Member of COSIRA.
SEE Clocks.

LINCOLN CONSERVATION STUDIO
c/o Museum of Lincolnshire Life, Burton Road, Lincoln, **Lincolnshire LN1 3LY**
TEL   0522 533207
OPEN   9–5 Mon–Fri.

Specialise in restoring gilding and frames to museum conservation standards.

PROVIDE Home Inspections. Free/Chargeable Estimates. Chargeable Collection/Delivery Service.
SPEAK TO John Hurd, Stephanie Margrett or David Fisher.
Members of UKIC. This workshop is included on the register of conservators maintained by the Conservation Unit of the Museums and Galleries Commission.
SEE Arms, Porcelain, Lighting.

RODDY McVITTIE
24 Bow Bridge House, 19–21 Payne Road, **London E3**
TEL   081 981 4083
OPEN   8–6 Mon–Fri.

Specialise in restoring and conserving 17th, 18th and 19th century furniture, both English and Continental.

PROVIDE Home Inspections. Free Estimates. Free Collection/Delivery Service.
SPEAK TO Roddy McVittie.
SEE Clocks.

I. & P. PRITCHARD
17 Heathcote Grove, **London E4 6RZ**
TEL   081 529 2884
OPEN   By Appointment.

Specialise in restoring chairs, re-caning, rushing, Danish cord, some Victorian garden furniture.

PROVIDE Home Inspections. Free Estimates. Free/Chargeable Collection/Delivery Service.
SPEAK TO Iorwerth or Phyllis Pritchard.
Member of Basketmakers Association and the Guild of Master Craftsmen. This workshop is included on the register of conservators maintained by the Conservation Unit of the Museums and Galleries Commission.

ELMER–MENAGE
78A Cecilia Road, **London E8 2ET**
TEL   071 923 1338
OPEN   9–6 Mon–Fri.

Specialise in restoring 18th–19th century rosewood furniture. Will also undertake marquetry restoration including Boulle.

PROVIDE Refundable Home Inspections. Chargeable Collection/Delivery Service.
SPEAK TO Chris Elmer.

MICHAEL PERRY
278 Richmond Road, **London E8 3QW**
TEL   081 533 5270
OPEN   By Appointment.

Specialise in restoration and reproduction of looking-glass frames.

PROVIDE Home Inspections. Free
Estimates. Free Local
Collection/Delivery Service within
London.
SPEAK TO Michael Perry.
SEE Picture Frames.

DAVID TURNER
4 Atlas Mews, Ramsgate Street, **London
E8 2NA**
TEL 071 249 2379
OPEN 10–6 Mon–Fri.

Specialise in restoring small pieces of
furniture and leather screens.

PROVIDE Home Inspections. Free
Estimates. Free Collection/Delivery
Service.
SEE Porcelain, Silver.

CANE AND RUSH SEATING
47 Spratt Hall Road, **London E11 2RP**
TEL 081 530 7052
OPEN By Appointment.

Specialise in restoring cane and rush
seating of antique and modern furniture.

PROVIDE Home Inspections. Estimates.
Free/Chargeable Collection/Delivery
Service.
SPEAK TO Jane Swan.
Also at rear of 2 Voluntary Place,
Wanstead, **London E11 2RQ**

YOUNG'S FRENCH POLISHING
570–572–574 Commercial Road,
London E14 7JD
TEL 071 790 4474 and 790 4691
FAX 071 265 9476
OPEN 9.30–6 Mon–Sat; closed Thur.

Specialise in polishing, renovating,
repairing, French polishing, door-
barring and glazing. Leather-lining tables
and desk-tops, upholstery repairs and
coverings.

PROVIDE Home Inspections. Free

Estimates. Chargeable
Collection/Delivery Service.
SPEAK TO Mr S. R. Young.

HOMEGUARD LIMITED
80–84 St Mary Road, **London E17 9RE**
TEL 081 520 4464
FAX 081 520 8335
OPEN 9–12.15, 1.30–5 Mon–Fri.

Specialise in restoring and
manufacturing locks and keys to
products dating back to the 15th century.
They can make presentation keys to
customers' designs and modify old locks
to bring them up to current standards.

PROVIDE Home Inspections. Chargeable
Estimates.
SPEAK TO J. E. A. Camfield or Alan
Camfield.
Established over forty-five years. This
workshop is included on the register of
conservators maintained by the
Conservation Unit of the Museums and
Galleries Commission.

MICHAEL PARFETT
Unit 407, Clerkenwell Workshops, 31
Clerkenwell Close, **London EC1R 0AT**
TEL 071 490 8768
OPEN By Appointment.

Specialise in all aspects of restoration to
furniture and mirror frames inclusive of
on-site architectural carving and gilding.
No upholstery work.

PROVIDE Home Inspections. Free
Estimates. Local Free
Collection/Delivery Service.
SPEAK TO Michael Parfett.

Licenciate of the City and Guilds of
London, Member of UKIC. This
workshop is included on the register of
conservators maintained by the
Conservation Unit of the Museums and
Galleries Commission.
SEE Collectors (Musical Instruments),
Picture Frames.

BOSWELL AND DAVIS
The Holywell Centre, 1 Phipp Street,
London EC2A 4PS
TEL   071 739 5738
FAX   071 729 9882
OPEN   9–6 Mon–Fri.

Specialise in restoring English and
Continental furniture, including
cabinetmaking, French polishing,
turning, marquetry work, leather desk
lining, gilding, upholstery, cane and rush
seating. Locks repaired and keys made.
Lost wax casting.

PROVIDE Home Inspections. Free
Estimates. Free Collection/Delivery
Service
SPEAK TO David Boswell.
SEE Clocks.

PETER CHAPMAN ANTIQUES
Incorporating **CHAPMAN RESTORATIONS**
10 Theberton Street, **London N1 0QX**
TEL   071 226 5565
FAX   081 348 4846
OPEN   9.30–6 Mon–Sat.

Specialise in restoring period furniture,
cabinetmaking, French polishing and
wax finishing, upholstery and repairing
gesso and composition frames. Specialise
in Arts and Crafts, Gothic Revival and
Aesthetic Movement furniture.

PROVIDE Home Inspections. Refundable
Estimates. Chargeable
Collection/Delivery Service.
SPEAK TO Peter Chapman or Tony
Holohan.
Members of LAPADA.
SEE Oil Paintings, Picture Frames,
Porcelain, Silver.

MATTHEW CRAWFORD FURNITURE RESTORATION
Basement, 74–77 White Lion Street,
London N1 1QP
TEL   071 278 7146
OPEN   9–5 Mon–Fri.

Specialise in restoring 16th–early 20th
century English furniture, including
inlay, recarving, leather, cane and
upholstery. Can also copy existing pieces.

PROVIDE Home Inspections. Free
Estimates. Free Collection/Delivery
Service.
SPEAK TO Matthew Crawford.

JULIAN KELLY
26A Gopsall Street, **London N1**
TEL   071 739 2949
FAX   071 739 2949
OPEN   9–5 Mon–Fri.

Specialise in wood carving, making
chairs to match existing ones and general
restoration work.

PROVIDE Free Estimates.
SPEAK TO Julian Kelly.

RICHARD G. PHILLIPS (RESTORATIONS) LTD
3 Ardleigh Road, **London N1 4HS**
TEL   071 923 0921 or 0922
FAX   071 923 3668
OPEN   8–5 Mon–Fri.

Specialise in restoring antique furniture.

PROVIDE Home Inspections. Refundable
Estimates. Chargeable
Collection/Delivery Service.
SPEAK TO Richard Phillips.

RILEY ANTIQUES
Mall Antique Arcade, 359 Upper Street,
London N1 0PD
TEL   071 226 0939 and 354 1719
OPEN   10–4 Wed; 10–5 Sat.

Specialise in restoring Victorian and
Edwardian furniture.

PROVIDE Home Inspections. Chargeable
Estimates. Free Collection/Delivery
Service.
SPEAK TO George Riley.
SEE **London N5**

VICTORIA ILLINGWORTH
Petherton Antiques, 124 Petherton
Road, **London N5 2RT**
TEL   071 226 6597
OPEN   10–6 Tues–Sat.

Specialise in restoring furniture,
especially marquetry and veneered
pieces, but excluding gilding and lacquer
work.

PROVIDE Free Estimates. Free Local
Collection/Delivery Service.
SPEAK TO Victoria Illingworth.

RILEY ANTIQUES
233 Blackstock Road, **London N5**
TEL   071 354 1719 and 226 0939
OPEN   10–4 Mon–Fri.

Specialise in restoring Victorian and
Edwardian furniture.

PROVIDE Home Inspections. Chargeable
Estimates. Free Collection/Delivery
Service.
SPEAK TO George Riley.
SEE **London N1**

ALEXANDER LEY & SON
13 Brecknock Rd, **London N7 0BL**
TEL   071 267 3645
FAX   071 267 4462
OPEN   8–6 Mon–Fri.

Specialise in restoring antique frames,
gilt furniture and mirrors. Also
reproduction carving and gilding.

PROVIDE Home Inspections. Free
Estimates. Free Collection/Delivery
Service.

SPEAK TO Alexander or Anthony Ley.
SEE Picture Frames.

B. S. H. RESTORERS LTD
7a Tynemouth Terrace, Tynemouth
Road, **London N15 4AP**
TEL   081 808 7965
OPEN   7–3.30 Mon–Fri.

Specialise in restoring antique English
and Continental furniture.

PROVIDE Home Inspections.
Free/Chargeable Estimates. Free
Collection/Delivery Service.
SPEAK TO Barry Howells.

CLIFFORD J. TRACY
6–40 Durnford Street, **London
N15 5NQ**
TEL   081 800 4773 or 4774
FAX   081 800 4351
OPEN   7.30–5 Mon–Thur; 7.30–4 Fri.

Specialise in restoring furniture,
including carving, marquetry, Boulle,
leather-lining and re-upholstery.

PROVIDE Home Inspections. Free
Estimates. Free Collection/Delivery
Service.
SPEAK TO Clifford Tracy.

Member of BAFRA and UKIC. Will do
minor repairs on site.
SEE Clocks.

THE COLLECTORS WORKSHOP
Heathrow House, Factory Lane,
London N17 9BY
TEL   081 808 1920
OPEN   8–5 Mon–Fri; Sat By
       Appointment.

Specialise in restoring fine English and
Continental furniture.

PROVIDE Home Inspections. Free
Estimates. Free Collection/Delivery
Service.
SPEAK TO Barrie Branwan.

Member of the Guild of Master Craftsmen.

A. J. BRETT & CO. LTD
Blenheim Works, 168C Marlborough Road, **London N19 4NP**
TEL 071 272 8462
FAX 071 272 5102
OPEN 7–4.30 Mon–Fri.

Specialise in restoring antique furniture, including upholstery, metalwork, gilding and decorating, French polishing, table-lining.

PROVIDE Home Inspections. Free Estimates. Free Collection/Delivery Service.
SPEAK TO Emma Whitley.

Members of the Guild of Master Craftsmen. Successfully restored the furniture damaged in the fire at Hampton Court.

MAX E. OTT LTD
1A Southcote Road, **London N19 5BJ**
TEL 071 607 1384
FAX 071 607 3506
OPEN 6.30–8.30 Mon–Fri.

Specialise in restoring antique furniture of all periods. Also copy period furniture.

PROVIDE Home Inspections. Free Estimates. Free Collection/Delivery Service.
SPEAK TO Max Ott.

ROCHEFORT ANTIQUES LTD
32–34 The Green, **London N21 1AX**
TEL 081 886 4779 or 363 0910
OPEN 10–6 Mon, Tues, Thur, Sat.

Specialise in restoring furniture.

PROVIDE Home Inspections. Free Estimates. Chargeable Collection/Delivery Service.
SPEAK TO L. W. Stevens-Wilson.
SEE Porcelain, Silver.

PHILIP J. WOLFF
4 Esther Close, **London N21 1AW**
TEL 081 364 0024
OPEN By Appointment.

Specialise in restoring carved and gilded antiques and fine furniture, decorative and architectural gilding, specialising in matte and burnish water gilding, powder gilding (water base) and oil gilding.

PROVIDE Home Inspections by arrangement. Estimates by agreement.
SPEAK TO Philip J. Wolff.

Mr Wolff has had forty-five years' experience. He is an Hon. Member of the Guild of Master Craftsmen.

K. RESTORATIONS
2A Ferdinand Place, **London NW1 8EE**
TEL 071 482 402
FAX 071 267 6712
OPEN 8–6 Mon–Fri.

Specialise in restoring all antique furniture including French polishing and renovation of leather upholstery and the supply of desk leathers,

PROVIDE Home Inspections. Free Estimates. Chargeable Collection/Delivery Service.
SPEAK TO David Peston.

Member of the Guild of Antique Dealers and Restorers.

THE MORLEY UPHOLSTERY WORKS LTD
82–86 Troutbeck, Albany Street, **London NW1 4EJ**
TEL 071 387 3846 and 388 0651
OPEN 8–4.30 Mon–Fri.

Specialise in renovating antique and modern upholstery.

PROVIDE Home Inspections. Chargeable Estimates. Free Collection/Delivery Service.
SPEAK TO Mr E. G. Vidler.

MURGA CANDLER LTD
57 Bayham Place, **London NW1 0ET**
TEL   071 387 7830
OPEN   8–5 Mon–Fri.

Specialise in leather-lining of desk and table-tops, loose leathers, upholstery in suede and leather.

PROVIDE Free Estimates.
SPEAK TO John Murga.

A. SPIGARD
236 Camden High Street, **London NW1 8QS**
TEL   071 485 4095
OPEN   9–6 Mon–Sat.

Specialise in restoring antique furniture.

PROVIDE Refundable Estimates. Chargeable Collection/Delivery Service.
SPEAK TO A. Spigard.

JOHN SZAKALY
2 Chartley Avenue, **London NW2 7RA**
TEL   081 450 5882
OPEN   9–6 Mon–Fri.

Specialise in restoration of antique furniture and polishing.

PROVIDE Home Inspections. Free Estimates. Free Collection/Delivery Service.
SPEAK TO John Szakaly.

ANTIQUE LEATHERS
4 Park End, South Hill Park, **London NW3 2SE**
TEL   071 435 8582
FAX   071 435 7799
OPEN   8–5 Mon–Fri.

Specialise in restoring leather work of all kinds, upholstery, bellows, desk-tops with gold tooling, screens, backgammons.

PROVIDE Free Estimates.

Free/Chargeable Collection/Delivery Service.
SPEAK TO Jackie Crisp or Roy Holliday.

J. CRISP
48 Roderick Road, **London NW3 2NL**
TEL   081 340 0668
FAX   071 485 8566
OPEN   10–6 Mon–Fri.

Specialise in restoring antique and modern and office furniture, leather work, staining, polishing, reviving bookshelf leather, loose leathers.

PROVIDE Home Inspections. Refundable Estimates. Free/Chargeable Collection/Delivery Service.
SPEAK TO Mr J. Crisp.

ROSS ANTHONY FULLER
23 Rosecroft Avenue, **London NW3 7QA**
TEL   071 435 4562
OPEN   Mon–Sat By Appointment.

Specialise in restoration and conservation of antique furniture particularly wood carving and finishing.

PROVIDE Home Inspections. Free/Chargeable Estimates. Free Local Collection/Delivery Service.
SPEAK TO Ross Anthony Fuller.
This workshop is included on the register of conservators maintained by the Conservation Unit of the Museums and Galleries Commission.
SEE Porcelain.

PARKHILL RESTORATIONS
11 Park End, South Hill Park, **London NW3 2ST**
TEL   071 794 5624
OPEN   10–6 Mon–Fri or By Appointment.

Specialise in restoring antique furniture, carving, gilding, rushing, caning, upholstering.

PROVIDE Home Inspections. Free
Estimates. Chargeable
Collection/Delivery Service.
SPEAK TO Peter Colgin.

RODERIC COWING
Unit 12, Liddell Road, **London**
NW6 2EW
TEL 071 328 6025
OPEN 10–6 Mon–Fri.

Specialise in upholstery restoration.

PROVIDE Home Inspections.
Chargeable/Refundable Estimates.
Chargeable Collection/Delivery Service.
SPEAK TO Roderic Cowing.

JOHN CHAMBERS
4 Nugent Terrace, **London NW8 9QB**
TEL 071 289 1393
OPEN 9–5 Mon–Fri.

Specialise in restoring and repairing
English 17th and 18th century oak,
walnut and mahogany furniture.

PROVIDE Home Inspections. Free
Estimates in Central London only.
Chargeable Collection/Delivery Service.
SPEAK TO John Chambers.

ROD JONES
Basement, Alfie's Antique Market, 13–
25 Church Street, **London NW8 8DT**
TEL 071 724 3437
OPEN 1–5 Tues–Sat By Appointment.

Specialise in restoring mirror frames
using original materials where possible.

PROVIDE Home Inspections. Free
Estimates. Free Local
Collection/Delivery Service.
SPEAK TO Rod Jones.
SEE Picture Frames.

WELLINGTON GALLERY
1 St John's Wood High Street, **London**
NW8 7NG
TEL 071 586 2620
OPEN 10–5.30 Mon–Sat.

Specialise in restoring furniture.

PROVIDE Home Inspections. Free
Estimates. Chargeable
Collection/Delivery Service.
SPEAK TO Mrs Maureen Barclay or Mr
K. J. Barclay.
Member of LAPADA.
SEE Oil Paintings, Porcelain, Silver.

BALLANTYNE BOOTH LTD
Cadogan House, Hythe Road, **London**
NW10 6RS
TEL 081 960 3255
FAX 081 960 4567
OPEN 8–6 Mon–Fri.

Specialise in restoring all antique
furniture and related items, including
cabinetmaking, veneering, turning,
leatherwork, carving, gilding, polishing
and metalwork.

PROVIDE Home Inspections. Free
Estimates. Chargeable
Collection/Delivery Service.
SPEAK TO Helen Mark.
Member of UKIC. This workshop is
included on the register of conservators
maintained by the Conservation Unit of
the Museums and Galleries Commission.

ADAMS & SHERIDAN
7 Ashbourne Parade, Finchley Road,
London NW11 0AD
TEL 081 455 6970
OPEN 9–5.30 Mon–Sat.

Specialise in repairing antique and
modern furniture, French polishing and
re-covering.

PROVIDE Home Inspections.
Free/Refundable Estimates.
Collection/Delivery Service.

142

SPEAK TO Mrs Healy.
Member of the Association of Master Upholsterers.

JEREMY CZERKAS
103 Wentworth Road, **London NW11 0RH**
TEL   081 458 5140
OPEN   By Appointment.

Specialise in restoring antique furniture, including traditional upholstery and caning.

PROVIDE Home Inspections. Free Estimates. Free/Chargeable Collection/Delivery Service.
SPEAK TO Jeremy Czerkas.

ELIZABETH LAWRENCE
107 Wentworth Road, **London NW11 0RH**
TEL   081 455 1691
OPEN   By Appointment.

Specialise in traditional upholstery and re-upholstery, refurbishment and restoration.

PROVIDE Home Inspections. Free/Chargeable Collection/Delivery Service.
SPEAK TO Elizabeth Lawrence.

PHOENIX ANTIQUE FURNITURE RESTORATION LIMITED
96 Webber Street, **London SE1 0QN**
TEL   071 928 3624
OPEN   By Appointment.

Specialise in restoring and conserving furniture, including cabinetmaking, polishing, upholstery, metalwork, desk lining. Specialist chair doctors and can make furniture to order.

PROVIDE Home Inspections. Free Estimates. Chargeable Collection/Delivery Service.
SPEAK TO David Battle.

PARAGON FURNITURE
Unit 2C, Ashleigh Commercial Estate, Westmoor Street, **London SE7 8NQ**
TEL   081 305 2332
OPEN   8–5 Mon–Fri.

Specialise in restoring antique furniture and conversions.

PROVIDE Home Inspections. Free Estimates. Free Collection/Delivery Service.
SPEAK TO G. Matthews or I. Watson.

GREENWICH CONSERVATION WORKSHOPS
Spread Eagle Antiques of Greenwich, 8–9 Nevada Street, **London SE10 9JL**
TEL   081 305 1666
OPEN   10–5.30 Mon–Sat.

Specialise in restoring furniture.

PROVIDE Home Inspections. Refundable Estimates. Free/Chargeable Collection/Delivery Service.
SPEAK TO Richard Moy.

SEE Oil Paintings.

RELCY ANTIQUES
9 Nelson Road, **London SE10 9JB**
TEL   081 858 2812
FAX   081 293 4135
OPEN   10–6 Mon–Sat.

Specialise in restoring 18th and 19th century English and Continental furniture.

PROVIDE Home Inspections. Free/Chargeable Estimates. Collection/Delivery Service by arrangement.
SPEAK TO Robin Challis.

SEE Collectors (Scientific Instruments), Oil Paintings, Silver.

A. FAGIANI
30 Wagner Street, **London SE15 1NN**
TEL   071 732 7188
OPEN   8–5.30 Mon–Fri.

Specialise in repairing and restoring antique English and Continental furniture and polishing.

PROVIDE Home Inspections. Free Estimates. Free Collection/Delivery Service.
SPEAK TO Mr A. Fagiani

SOPHIE LEVENE GILDING AND RESTORATION
63A Cheltenham Road, Peckham Rye, **London SE15 3AF**
TEL   071 639 5735
FAX   081 299 0923
OPEN   10–6 Mon–Fri.

Specialise in restoring all styles of gilded decoration to period furniture, frames, architectural features, objets d'art etc. They also provide a range of services including repair and reproduction of composition mouldings, carving and paint finishes carried out on site or in their London studio.

PROVIDE Home Inspections. Free Estimates. Chargeable Collection/Delivery Service.
SPEAK TO Sophie Levene.

Member of UKIC. This workshop is included on the register of conservators maintained by the Conservation Unit of the Museums and Galleries Commission.
SEE Picture Frames.

J. T. GROSSE LTD
12 Verney Road, **London SE16 3DH**
TEL   071 231 7969
OPEN   7.30–5.30 Mon–Fri; Sat By
        Appointment.

Specialise in renovation of antique and other quality furniture.

PROVIDE Home Inspections. Free

Estimates. Free Collection/Delivery Service.
SPEAK TO A. F. Grosse.

This family business has been established since 1911.

GLEN'S ANTIQUE RESTORATION
36 Romola Road, **London SE24 9AZ**
TEL   081 671 1880
FAX   081 671 1880
OPEN   9–6 Mon–Fri.

Specialise in restoring painted furniture, gilding and wood-carving, French polishing.

PROVIDE Home Inspections. Free Estimates. Chargeable Collection/Delivery Service.
SPEAK TO Glen Beckford.
SEE Picture Frames.

CRAWLEY STUDIOS
39 Wood Vale, **London SE23 3DS**
TEL   081 299 4121
FAX   081 299 0756
OPEN   9–6.15 Mon–Fri.

Specialise in restoring painted furniture, lacquer, gilding, papier mâché and polishing.

PROVIDE Home Inspections. Free Estimates. Chargeable Collection/Delivery Service.
SPEAK TO Marie Louise Crawley.

Member of BAFRA, UKIC and the Guild of Master Craftsmen.
SEE Silver.

OSSWOSKI WORKSHOP
83 Pimlico Road, **London SW1W 8PH**
and at 595 Kings Road, **London SW6 2EL**
TEL   071 730 3256 and 731 0334
OPEN   10–6 Mon–Fri; 10–1 Sat.

Specialise in restoring and gilding 18th century giltwood mirrors, furniture and carvings. Water-gilding only; no oil-gilding, small repairs or touching-up jobs.

PROVIDE Free Estimates.
SPEAK TO Mark or Matthew Ossowski.

PETER DUDGEON LTD
Brompton Place, **London SW3 1QE**
TEL   071 589 0322
FAX   071 589 1910

Specialise in restoring upholstered furniture, French chairs etc.

PROVIDE Home Inspections. Free Estimates. Collection/Delivery Service.
SPEAK TO Hugh Garforth-Bles or William Dudgeon.
They have been established for over forty years.

M. P. GERVAL & ASSOCIATES
28 Cheyne Walk, **London SW3 5HH**
TEL   071 351 2840
FAX   071 351 5374
OPEN   9.30–6 By Appointment.

Specialise in restoring carved, composition and other types of frames and mirrors, gilt or otherwise finished.

PROVIDE Home Inspections. Free Estimates. Free Local Collection/Delivery Service.
SPEAK TO Marie-Pierre Gerval.
Member of UKIC. This workshop is included on the register of conservators maintained by the Conservation Unit of the Museums and Galleries Commission.
SEE Picture Frames.

JOANNA PIOTROWSKA
A. & J. Restoration, Chenil Galleries F3–J4, 181–183 Kings Road, **London SW3 5EB**
TEL   071 352 2704 and 081 578 9688
OPEN   11–5 Thur, Fri, Sat.

Specialise in restoring gilt mirrors and furniture, gilding, lacquering and painting.

PROVIDE Home Inspections. Free Estimates. Collection/Delivery Service.
SPEAK TO Joanna or Andrew Piotrowska.

JOHN HEAP
No. 1 The Polygon, **London SW4**
TEL   071 627 4498
OPEN   By Appointment.

Specialise in restoring painted antique furniture, gesso work and gilding.

PROVIDE Home Inspections. Free Estimates. Free Collection/Delivery Service.
SPEAK TO John Heap.
SEE Porcelain, Silver.

DAVID ALEXANDER ANTIQUES & KATE THURLOW
102 Waterford Road, **London SW6 2HA**
TEL   071 731 4644
OPEN   By Appointment.

Specialise in restoring 16th–17th century European furniture.

PROVIDE Home Inspections. Chargeable Collection/Delivery Service.
SPEAK TO Kate Thurlow or Rodney Robertson.

I. AND J. L. BROWN LTD
636 Kings Road, **London SW6 2DU**
TEL   071 736 4141
OPEN   9–5.30 Mon–Sat.

Specialise in restoring English country and French Provincial furniture. Also undertake chair rush work.

PROVIDE Free/Chargeable Estimates. Free/Chargeable Collection/Delivery Service.
SPEAK TO Peter Baker-Place
SEE Hereford & Worcester.

145

JOHN CLAY ANTIQUES
263 New Kings Road, **London**
SW6 4RB
TEL   071 731 5677
OPEN   9–6 Mon–Sat.

Specialise in restoring antique furniture.

PROVIDE Home Inspections. Refundable Estimates. Chargeable Collection/Delivery Service.
SPEAK TO John Clay.

PETER L. JAMES
681 Fulham Road, **London SW6 5PZ**
TEL   071 736 0183
OPEN   7.30–5.30 Mon–Fri.

Specialise in restoring lacquer, painted and gilded furniture and mirror frames.

PROVIDE Home Inspections. Refundable Estimates. Chargeable Collection/Delivery Service.
SPEAK TO Peter L. James.
SEE Picture Frames.

CHRISTOPHER J. LEWIS
464A Fulham Road, **London SW6 6HY**
TEL   071 386 5669
OPEN   10–6 Mon–Fri.

Specialise in restoring all aspects of furniture, except for upholstery, as well as offering a design and construction service.

PROVIDE Home Inspections. Refundable Estimates.
SPEAK TO Christopher Lewis.

MICHAEL MARRIOTT LTD
588 Fulham Road, **London SW6 5NT**
TEL   071 736 3110
FAX   071 731 2632
OPEN   9.30–5.30 Mon–Fri.

Specialise in restoring furniture, including traditional upholstery.

PROVIDE Home Inspections in **London,** outside London for major restorations only. Free Estimates. Collection/Delivery Service.
SPEAK TO Michael Marriott.
SEE Picture Frames.

AUBREY BROCKLEHURST
124 Cromwell Road, **London SW7 4ET**
TEL   071 373 0319
OPEN   9–1, 2–5.30 Mon–Fri; 10–1 Sat.

Specialise in restoring and repairing antique furniture.

PROVIDE Home Inspections. Free Estimates. Chargeable Collection/Delivery Service.
SPEAK TO Aubrey Brocklehurst, Ms Gill or Mrs Leonard.

Mr Brocklehurst is a member of BADA and he, Ms Gill and Mrs Leonard are all FBHIs.
SEE Clocks.

R. HORNSBY
33 Thurloe Place, **London SW7 2HQ**
TEL   071 225 2888
FAX   071 225 2888
OPEN   8.30–6 Mon–Fri; 8.30–2 Sat.

Specialise in restoring furniture, including French polishing, chair repairs, cabinet work and repairs, traditional upholstery.

PROVIDE Home Inspections. Free Estimates. Collection/Delivery Service Available.
SPEAK TO Mr R. Gough.

Established 1890.

PETER AND FRANCES BINNINGTON
65 St Johns Hill, **London SW11 1SX**
TEL   071 223 9192
FAX   071 924 1668
OPEN   8.30–5.30 Mon–Fri.

Specialise in restoring all kinds of antique furniture, including surfaces decorated in marquetry, paint, carving and gilding.

PROVIDE Home Inspections. Free Estimates. Chargeable Collection/Delivery Service.
SPEAK TO Joanne Neal.
SEE Porcelain.

CALLANAN LTD
Unit 7, Parkfields Industrial Estate, Culvert Place, Culvert Road, **London** SW11 5BA
TEL   071 828 7577
OPEN   9–6.30 Mon–Fri.

Specialise in restoring mirror frames.

PROVIDE Home Inspections. Free Estimates. Chargeable Collection/Delivery Service.
SPEAK TO David Callanan.
SEE Picture Frames.

W. J. COOK AND SONS
167 Battersea High Street, **London** SW11 3JS
TEL   071 736 5329
OPEN   8–7 Mon–Fri.

Specialise in restoring all types of furniture, late 17th century to present day, including gilding, carving, leathering, upholstery and marquetry.

PROVIDE Home Inspections. Free Estimates. Free Local Collection/Delivery Service.
SPEAK TO Mr Cook.
This is a family business established over thirty years.
SEE **Wiltshire.**

RUPERT BEVAN
75 Lower Richmond Road, **London** SW15 1ET
TEL   081 780 1190
OPEN   9–6 Mon–Fri.

Specialise in restoring gilded furniture and mirror frames.

PROVIDE Home Inspections. Free

Estimates. Chargeable Collection/Delivery Service.
SPEAK TO Rupert Bevan.
SEE Picture Frames.

ROGER BOARD DESIGNS
273 Putney Bridge Road, **London** SW15 2PT
TEL   081 789 0046
FAX   081 789 0047
OPEN   9–6 Mon–Fri.

Specialise in restoring antique furniture and panelling.

PROVIDE Home Inspections. Free Estimates. Free Local Collection/Delivery Service.
SPEAK TO Roger Board.

DELIA BRAIN
136 Putney Bridge Road, **London** SW15 2NQ
TEL   081 874 1678
OPEN   9–5 Mon–Fri.

Specialise in restoring 18th and 19th century painted furniture and specialist paint techniques such as marbling and graining.

PROVIDE Home Inspections. Free/Refundable Estimates. Chargeable Collection/Delivery Service.
SPEAK TO Delia Brain.

Ms Brain also restores and retouches scenic wallpaper on site.

ALAN S. STONE
3 Wadham Road, **London** SW15
TEL   081 870 1606
OPEN   9–4.30 Mon–Fri; 9–2.30 Sat.

Specialise in restoring 18th and 19th century furniture.

PROVIDE Home Inspections. Free Estimates. Free Collection/Delivery Service.
SPEAK TO Alan S. Stone.

WEAVER NEAVE & DAUGHTER
17 Lifford Street, **London SW15 1NY**
TEL   081 785 2464
OPEN   9–6 Mon–Fri.

Specialise in all cane and rush work for antique furniture.

PROVIDE Home Inspections. Free Estimates. Collection/Delivery Service by arrangement.
SPEAK TO Rosslyn Neave.

E. & A. WATES LTD
82–84 Mitcham Lane, **London SW16 6NR**
TEL   081 769 2205
FAX   081 677 4766
OPEN   9–6 Mon–Sat; 9–7 Thur.

Specialise in repairing fine furniture including re-upholstery, French polishing, caning and carving.

PROVIDE Home Inspections. Free/Refundable Estimates.
SPEAK TO Mr R. D. Wates.
Established 1900.

CARVERS & GILDERS
9 Charterhouse Works, Eltringham Street, **London SW18 1TD**
TEL   081 870 7047
FAX   081 874 0470
OPEN   By Appointment.

Specialise in restoring wood-carving and gilding, particularly of ornate applied ornament. Also design and make new pieces.

PROVIDE Home Inspections. Free Estimates.
SPEAK TO Anna Baker.

SERENA CHAPLIN
32 Elsynge Road, **London SW18 2HN**
TEL   081 870 9455
OPEN   By Appointment.

Specialise in restoring mirror frames and other gilded objects as well as restoring and conserving antique lacquer such as screens, cabinets and trays.

PROVIDE Free Estimates.
SPEAK TO Serena Chaplin.
Ms Chaplin also runs gilding courses.
SEE Picture Frames.

COMPTON HALL RESTORATION
Unit A, 133 Riverside Business Centre, Haldane Place, **London SW18 4UQ**
TEL   081 874 0762
OPEN   9–5 Mon–Fri.

Specialise in restoring painted furniture, lacquer, gilding, papier mâché, penwork, Tôle.

PROVIDE Home Inspections. Free Estimates. Collection/Delivery Service by arrangement.
SPEAK TO Lucinda Compton, Jane Hall or Henrietta Hohler.

Member of BAFRA and UKIC. This workshop is included on the register maintained by the Conservation Unit of the Museums and Galleries Commission.
SEE Silver.

PLOWDEN AND SMITH LTD
190 St Ann's Hill, **London SW18 2RT**
TEL   081 874 4005
FAX   081 874 7248
OPEN   9–5.30 Mon–Fri.

Specialise in restoring and conserving fine furniture and upholstery.

PROVIDE Home Inspections. Free Estimates. Chargeable Collection/Delivery Service.
SPEAK TO Bob Butler.
They also advise on conservation

strategy, environmental control and microclimates for collections as well as installing, mounting and displaying temporary and permanent exhibitions. SEE Oil Paintings, Silver, Porcelain.

CONNOLLY LEATHER LTD
Wandle Bank, **London SW19 1DW**
TEL   081 542 5251 and 543 4611
FAX   081 543 7455
OPEN   9–12.45, 1.30–4 Mon–Fri.

Specialise in restoring leather chairs, screens, wallpanelling. Also carry out gold embossing.

PROVIDE Home Inspections. Free Estimates. Free Collection/Delivery Service.
SPEAK TO Mr C. Carron.
SEE Lighting.

W. R. HARVEY & CO. (ANTIQUES) LTD
5 Old Bond Street, **London W1X 3TA**
TEL   071 499 8385
FAX   071 495 0209
OPEN   10–5.30 Mon–Sat.

Specialise in restoring fine English period (1650–1830) furniture and works of art.

PROVIDE Home Inspections. Free Estimates. Free Collection/Delivery Service.
SPEAK TO Mr D. Watkinson or Mr D. Harvey.

Member of BADA and the Guild of Master Craftsmen. This workshop is included on the register of conservators maintained by the Conservation Unit of the Museums and Galleries Commission.

RICHARD KERLEY
6 York Mansions, 84 Chiltern Street, **London W1M 1PT**
TEL   071 486 6483
OPEN   By Appointment.

Specialise in restoring furniture; Boulle work and carving, English water gilding. Also copy chairs and mirror frames to match clients' own pieces.

PROVIDE Home Inspections. Chargeable Estimates. Chargeable Collection/Delivery Service.
SPEAK TO Richard Kerley.

MATTEI RADEV
10 Ogle Street, **London W1P 7LQ**
TEL   071 580 4704
OPEN   8–5 Mon–Fri.

Specialise in restoring antique mirror frames and gilded furniture.

PROVIDE Home Inspections. Free Estimates. Collection/Delivery Service by arrangement.
SPEAK TO Mattei Radev or Charles Rhodes.
SEE Picture Frames.

M. TURPIN LTD
27 Bruton Street, **London W1X 7DB**
TEL   071 493 3275
FAX   071 408 1869
OPEN   10–5.30 Mon–Fri.

Specialise in repairing 17th–early 19th century furniture and giltwood mirrors.

PROVIDE Home Inspections. Chargeable Estimates. Chargeable Collection/Delivery Service.
SPEAK TO M. Turpin.

G. D. WARDER AND SONS LTD
14 Hanway Place, **London W1P 9DG**
TEL   071 636 1867
OPEN   9–4.30 Mon–Fri.

Specialise in water gilding and carving, gilding and restoration of period mirrors, antique furniture, frames and bijoutiers. Reproduction Regency mirrors made to order.

PROVIDE Free Estimates. Chargeable
Collection/Delivery Service.
SPEAK TO David or Robert Warder.

BOURLET
32 Connaught Street, **London W2 2AY**
TEL   071 724 4837
OPEN   11–5.30 Mon–Fri and most Sats.

Specialise in restoring furniture.

PROVIDE Home Inspections. Free
Estimates. Collection/Delivery Service.
SPEAK TO Gabrielle Rendell.

SEE Oil Paintings, Picture Frames.

H. J. HATFIELD & SON
42 St Michael's Street, **London
W2 1QP**
TEL   071 723 8265
FAX   071 706 4562
OPEN   9–1, 2–5 Mon–Fri.

Specialise in restoring English and
French 17th–19th century furniture.

PROVIDE Home Inspections. Free
Estimates.
SPEAK TO Philip Astley-Jones.
SEE Silver.

LESLEY WILSON
14 Dordrecht Road, **London W3 7TE**
TEL   081 743 0909
OPEN   By Appointment.

Specialise in the restoration of
upholstered furniture, working closely
with wood and textile conservators.

PROVIDE Home Inspections. Free
Estimates. Free/Chargeable
Collection/Delivery Service.
SPEAK TO Lesley Wilson.
Member of UKIC. This workshop is
included on the register of conservators
maintained by the Conservation Unit of
the Museums and Galleries Commission.

THE OLD CINEMA
160 Chiswick High Road, **London
W4 1PR**
TEL   081 995 4166
OPEN   10–6 Daily.

Specialise in comprehensive restoration
and upholstery service for antique and
Victorian furniture.

PROVIDES Free Estimates. Free
Collection/Delivery Service.
SPEAK TO Martin Hanness.

PETER JAMES AVERSON-MAUNDER
73 Queen Anne's Grove, **London
W5 3XP**
TEL   081 567 6586
OPEN   9–5.30 Mon–Fri By
        Appointment Only.

Specialise in restoring rush and cane in
antique and modern furniture, excluding
settees. Minor repairs to framework and
re-seating in Danish cord and pre-woven
cane.

PROVIDE Local Home Inspections. Free
Estimates. Chargeable
Collection/Delivery Service.
SPEAK TO Peter James Averson-Maunder.
Member of the Guild of Master
Craftsmen.

BADGER ANTIQUES
12 St Mary's Road, **London W5 5ES**
TEL   081 567 5601
OPEN   10–6 Mon–Sat.

Specialise in restoring furniture.

PROVIDE Home Inspections. Free
Estimates. Free Collection/Delivery
Service.
SPEAK TO Michael Allders.
SEE Clocks.

C. J. G. GILDERS & CARVERS
Unit 10, Sandringham Mews, **London W5 5DF**
TEL   081 579 2341
FAX   081 571 9022
OPEN   10–5 Mon–Sat.

Specialise in restoring antique mirrors and gilt furniture.

PROVIDE Home Inspections. Free Estimates. Free Collection/Delivery Service within London.
SPEAK TO Chris Gostonski or Richard Kosmala.
SEE Picture Frames.

BARNET ANTIQUES
79 Kensington Church Street, **London W8 4BG**
TEL   071 376 2817
OPEN   10–5.30 Mon–Sat.

Specialise in all aspects of furniture restoration, including cabinet repairs, carving, gilding, turning, decoration, metalwork, keys and locks, straightening warped items, polishing, fretwork, Boulle and brass inlay.

PROVIDE Home Inspections. Free Estimates. Chargeable Collection/Delivery Service.
SPEAK TO Richard Gerry.

DON HOLMES ANTIQUES
47C Earls Court Road (in Abingdon Villas), **London W8 6EE**
TEL   071 937 6961 or 020 888 0254
OPEN   2–7 Fri; 9.30–5.30 Sat or By Appointment.

Specialise in restoring and repairing 18th and 19th century furniture, mainly mahogany.

PROVIDE Home Inspections. Refundable Estimates. Chargeable Collection/Delivery Service.
SPEAK TO Don or Sarah Holmes.

ARTHUR SEAGER
25A Holland Street, **London W8 4NA**
TEL   071 937 3262
FAX   071 937 3262
OPEN   10–5.30 Mon–Sat.

Specialise in restoring 17th and 18th century oak furniture.

PROVIDE Home Inspections. Free Estimates. Free/Chargeable Collection/Delivery Service.
SPEAK TO Arthur Seager.

LAWRENCE BRASS AND SON
154 Sutherland Avenue, **London W9**
TEL   071 636 3401
OPEN   8–5 Mon–Fri.

Specialise in restoring fine furniture, including metalwork, gilding, upholstery. They cast furniture mounts in all metals and do fire gilding and specialise in difficult or impossible commissions.

PROVIDE Home Inspections. Free/Chargeable Estimates. Free Collection/Delivery Service.
SPEAK TO Mr Murray.

Member of BAFRA, UKIC. This workshop is included on the register of conservators maintained by the Conservation Unit of the Museums and Galleries Commission.
SEE **Avon.**

TITIAN STUDIO
326 Kensal Road, **London W10 5BN**
TEL   081 960 6247 and 969 6126
OPEN   9–6 Mon–Fri.

Specialise in carving, gilding, furniture restoration and lacquer polishing.

PROVIDE Home Inspections. Free/Chargeable Estimates. Chargeable Collection/Delivery Service.
SPEAK TO Rod Titian or Elizabeth Porter.

151

DAVID HORDERN RESTORATIONS LIMITED

1A Codrington Mews, Blenheim Crescent, **London W11 2EH**

TEL   071 727 8855
FAX   071 792 9164
OPEN   9–6 Mon–Fri.

Specialise in restoring quality antique furniture, including Boulle cabinetwork, carving, gilding, ivory, lacquer, leather, marble, marquetry, metalwork, ormolu, polishing and upholstery.

PROVIDE Home Inspections. Free Estimates. Chargeable Collection/Delivery Service available.
SPEAK TO David Hordern.

Member of UKIC and BAFRA. This workshop is included on the register of conservators maintained by the Conservation Unit of the Museums and Galleries Commission.

WARWICK DE WINTER c/o WYNYARDS ANTIQUES

5 Ladbroke Road, **London W11 3PA**

TEL   071 221 7936
OPEN   10–6 Tues–Fri; 1.30–6 Mon & Sat.

Specialise in repairing and restoring furniture, upholstery, recaning, rush seating.

PROVIDE Home Inspections. Free Estimates. Free/Chargeable Collection/Delivery Service.
SPEAK TO Warwick de Winter.

ROSEMARY COOK RESTORATION

78 Stanlake Road, **London W12 7HJ**

TEL   081 749 7977
OPEN   By Appointment.

Specialise in restoring painted furniture, caning and rush seating.

PROVIDE Home Inspections. Free

Estimates. Free Collection/Delivery Service in London.
SPEAK TO Rosemary Cook.
SEE Porcelain, Silver.

COUTTS GALLERIES

75 Blythe Road, **London W14 0HD**

TEL   071–602–3980
OPEN   10–5 Mon–Fri.

Specialise in restoration of decorative antique furniture, including gilding, carving, modelling, lacquerwork, cabinetwork, French polishing.

PROVIDE Home Inspections, Free Estimates, Free Collection/Delivery Service.
SPEAK TO Seabury Burdett-Coutts.
SEE Oil Paintings, Picture Frames.

FELLOWES AND SAUNDERSON

116 Blythe Road, **London W14 0UH**

TEL   071 603 7475
OPEN   9.30–5.30 Tues–Fri, 10–4 Sat.

Specialise in restoration of antique mirrors. They have their own range of gilded and hand-finished frames.

PROVIDE Home Inspections. Free Estimates. Free Collection/Delivery Service.
SPEAK TO Joan Burdett-Coutts.
SEE Picture Frames.

PAUL FERGUSON

Unit 20, 21 Wren Street, **London WC1X 0HF**

TEL   071 278 8759
FAX   071 278 8759
OPEN   9–5.30 Mon–Fri.

Specialise in restoring carved and gilded furniture, girandoles, torchères.

PROVIDES Home Inspections. Free Estimates. Collection/Delivery Service by arrangement.
SPEAK TO Paul Ferguson.
SEE Picture Frames.

S. H. JEWELL
26 Parker Street, **London WC2B 5PH**
TEL   071 405 8520
OPEN   9–5.30 Mon–Fri; Sat By
Appointment.

Specialises in 19th and 20th century English furniture repairs and polishing, table-lining and upholstery.

PROVIDES Home Inspections. Free Estimates. Chargeable Collection/Delivery Service.
SPEAK TO S. H. Jewell.

ALBION ANTIQUES
643 Stockport Road, Longsight,
Greater Manchester M12 4QA
TEL   061 225 4957
OPEN   9–6 Mon–Fri or By
Appointment.

Specialise in restoring antique and period furniture and timber items.

PROVIDE Chargeable Home Inspections. Refundable Estimates. Chargeable Collection/Delivery Service.
SPEAK TO Tony Collins.

CASEMENTS THE CABINETMAKERS
Slack Lane Works, Pendlebury, Salford,
Greater Manchester M27 2QT
TEL   061 794 1610
OPEN   8–6 Mon–Fri; 8–1 Sat.

Specialise in antique restoration, including veneering, French polishing and turning. One-off copy pieces.

PROVIDE Home Inspections Refundable Estimates. Chargeable Collection/Delivery Service.
SPEAK TO D. Casement.

TREEN ANTIQUES
Treen House, 72 Park Road, Prestwich,
Greater Manchester M25 8FA
TEL   061 740 1063
FAX   061 720 7244
OPEN   By Appointment.

Specialise in restoring antique English furniture, particularly regional furniture with an emphasis on finishes and coating technology.

PROVIDE Home Inspections. Free Estimates. Free Local Collection/Delivery.
SPEAK TO Simon Feingold.
Member of FHS, GADAR, UKIC and RFS.

MICHAEL BENNETT
100 Market Street, Hoylake, Wirral,
Merseyside L47 3BE
TEL   051 632 4331
FAX   051 632 6220
OPEN   9–5.30 Mon–Fri and By
Appointment.

Specialise in invisible repairs of late 17th–early 18th century furniture with emphasis on blending in both colour and patina repairs. Also Boulle and marquetry work.

PROVIDE. Home Inspections. Mostly Free Estimates. Collection/Delivery Service by arrangement.
SPEAK TO Michael Bennett.

PILGRIMS PROGRESS
1A–3A Bridgewater Street, Liverpool,
Merseyside L1 OAR
TEL   051 708 7515
FAX   051 709 1465
OPEN   9–5 Mon–Fri; 1–4 Sat.

Specialise in restoring antique furniture, including cabinet-work, French polishing, re-upholstery.

PROVIDE Home Inspections. Free
Estimates. Free/Chargeable
Collection/Delivery Service.
SPEAK TO Selwyn Hyams.

WELLINGTON CRAFTS (1980)
121A/123A St John's Road, Waterloo,
Liverpool, **Merseyside L22 9QE**
TEL   051 920 5511
OPEN   9.30–5 Mon, Tues; 9.30–2 Wed;
9.30–5.30 Thur–Sat.

Specialise in cane, rush and bergère
restoration.

PROVIDE Home Inspections. Refundable
Estimates. Chargeable
Collection/Delivery Service.
SPEAK TO Neville Hymus.
SEE Picture Frames.

H. AKSERALIAN
79 Mollison Way, Edgware, **Middlesex
HA8 5QU**
TEL   081 952 6432 evenings.
OPEN   By Appointment.

Specialise in chair caning, repairs to cane
work, reseating, staining cane work and
sea-grass seating, including bergère
suites.

PROVIDE Home Inspections. Free
Estimates. Chargeable
Collection/Delivery Service.
SPEAK TO Harry Akseralian.

ANTIQUE RESTORATIONS
45 Windmill Road, Brentford,
Middlesex TW8 0QQ
TEL   081 568 5249
OPEN   8–5 Mon–Fri.

Specialise in restoring and conserving
painted and gilded furniture, Oriental
lacquer and japanning.

PROVIDE Home Inspections.

Free/Chargeable Estimates. Free Local
Collection/Delivery Service.
SPEAK TO Reginald Dudman.

R. BECKFORD
4 Elms Lane, Wembley, **Middlesex
HA0 2NH**
TEL   081 904 4735
OPEN   9.30–6 Mon–Fri.

Specialise in repairing and restoring all
types of furniture, polishing and
refinishing.

PROVIDE Home Inspections. Free
Estimates. Chargeable
Collection/Delivery Service.
SPEAK TO R. Beckford.

CHURCH LANE RESTORATIONS
1 Church Lane, Teddington, **Middlesex
TW11 8PA**
TEL   081 977 2526
OPEN   7.30–5 Mon–Thur; 7.30–4 Fri.

Specialise in restoring period furniture
and French polishing.

PROVIDE Home Inspections. Free
Estimates. Free Collection/Delivery
Service.
SPEAK TO Mr Vincent.
Member of LAPADA.

MARIA J. LESIAK
Leliwa, 71 St Anne's Avenue, Stanwell,
Staines, **Middlesex TW19 7RL**
TEL   0784 257401
FAX   0784 257401
OPEN   By Appointment.

Specialise in restoring decorative
objects, including lacquerwork.

PROVIDE Home Inspections. Free
Estimates. Free Local
Collection/Delivery Service.
SPEAK TO Maria J. Lesiak.

Member of UKIC and an Associate
Member of ABPR. This workshop is
included on the register of conservators

maintained by the Conservation Unit of
the Museums and Galleries Commission.
SEE Picture Frames, Oil Paintings.

R. V. MORGAN & CO.
Unit 41, 26–28 The Queensway,
Ponders End, Enfield, **Middlesex
EN3 5UU**
TEL   081 805 0353
OPEN   8–5.30 Mon–Fri and 8–3 Sat.

Specialise in all aspects of furniture
restoration, specialist cabinetmaking and
French polishing.

PROVIDE Home Inspections.
Free/Chargeable Estimates. Chargeable
Collection/Delivery Service.
SPEAK TO Mr R. V. Morgan.

PHELPS LTD
133–135 St Margarets Road,
Twickenham, **Middlesex TW1 1RG**
TEL   081 892 1778
FAX   081 892 3661
OPEN   9–5.30 Mon–Sat.

Specialise in restoring 19th and early
20th century furniture.

PROVIDE Home Inspections. Free
Estimates. Chargeable
Collection/Delivery Service.
SPEAK TO R. Phelps.

BARNT GREEN ANTIQUES
93 Hewell Road, Barnt Green,
Birmingham, **West Midlands B45 8NL**
TEL   021 445 4942
OPEN   9–5.30 Mon–Fri; 9–1 Sat.

Specialise in restoring and conserving
antique furniture, gilding.

PROVIDE Home Inspections. Free
Estimates. Chargeable
Collection/Delivery Service.
SPEAK TO Mr N. Slater.

Member of BAFRA.
SEE Clocks.

HAMPTON UTILITIES (B'HAM) LTD
15 Pitsford Street, Hockley,
Birmingham, **West Midlands B18 6LJ**
TEL   021 554 1766
OPEN   9–5 Mon–Thur; 9–4 Fri.

Specialise in restoring and repairing
mirror frames, including gilding.

PROVIDE Free Estimates. Chargeable
Collection/Delivery Service.
SPEAK TO B. Levine.

SEE Picture Frames, Silver.

HARBORNE PLACE UPHOLSTERY
22–24 Northfield Road, Harborne,
Birmingham, **West Midlands B17 0SU**
TEL   021 427 5788
OPEN   9–6 Mon–Sat.

Specialise in all types of furniture
restoration and upholstery,
including deep buttoning using
traditional materials.

PROVIDE Home Inspections. Refundable
Estimates. Free Collection/Delivery
Service.
SPEAK TO Peter Hubbard.

GEOFFREY HASSALL ANTIQUES
20 New Road, Solihull, **West Midlands
B91 3DP**
TEL   021 705 0068
OPEN   9.30–1, 2–5.30 Tues–Sat.

Specialise in restoring all periods of
furniture.

PROVIDE Home Inspections. Free
Estimates. Free/Chargeable
Collection/Delivery Service.
SPEAK TO Geoffrey Hassall.

PHIL HILL (ROCKING HORSES)

188 Alcester Road South, Kings Heath, Birmingham, **West Midlands B14 6DE**
TEL   021 444 0102
OPEN   9.30–6 Mon–Fri or By Appointment.

Specialise in restoring furniture, including all aspects of wood carving, gesso, painting, wax/oil finish.

PROVIDE Home Inspections. Free Estimates. Free Collection/Delivery Service.
SPEAK TO Phil Hill.
SEE Collectors (Toys).

JOHN HUBBARD ANTIQUES

224–226 Court Oak Road, Harborne, Birmingham, **West Midlands B32 2EG**
TEL   021 426 1694
FAX   021 428 1214
OPEN   9–6 Mon–Sat.

Specialise in restoring 18th and 19th century fine furniture and decorative items, including carving, veneering, polishing and leather lining.

PROVIDE Home Inspections. Refundable Estimates. Collection/Delivery Service.
SPEAK TO John Hubbard or David Taplin.

ARK ANTIQUE RESTORATIONS

Morton Peto Road, Gapton Hall Industrial Estate, Great Yarmouth, **Norfolk NR3 0LT**
TEL   0493 653357
FAX   0493 658405
OPEN   9–5.30 Mon–Fri; 9–1 Sat.

Specialise in restoring fine English and Continental furniture.

PROVIDE Home Inspections. Chargeable Estimates. Free Local Collection/Delivery Service.
SPEAK TO Ben Deveson.
SEE Clocks.

DAVID BARTRAM FURNITURE

The Raveningham Centre, Castell Farm, Beccles Road, Raveningham, Nr. Norwich, **Norfolk NR14 6NU**
TEL   050 846 721
OPEN   10–6 Daily.

Specialise in comprehensive antique restoration service in their own workshops covering furniture, gilding, upholstery.

PROVIDE Home Inspections. Free Estimates. Free Collection/Delivery Service.
SPEAK TO David Bartram.

Member of BAFRA and UKIC. This workshop is included on the register of conservators maintained by the Conservation Unit of the Museums and Galleries Commission.
SEE Silver, Clocks.

ERIC BATES & SONS

Melbourne House, Bacton Road, North Walsham, **Norfolk NR28 0RA**
TEL   0692 403221
OPEN   8.30–4.30 Mon–Fri.

Specialise in restoring antique furniture and upholstery. They also hand make period style oak furniture.

PROVIDE Home Inspections. Refundable Estimates. Collection/Delivery Service by arrangement.
SPEAK TO Eric Bates.

DAVID BOHN

The Old Rectory, Bradenham, **Norfolk IP25 7QL**
TEL   0362 820918
FAX   0362 820918
OPEN   9–5.30 Mon–Fri or by Appointment.

Specialise in all aspects of the conservation and restoration of giltwood furniture.

PROVIDE Home Inspections. Chargeable

Estimates. Chargeable
Collection/Delivery Service.
SPEAK TO David Bohn.

They have had over thirty years
experience. This workshop is included
on the register of conservators
maintained by the Conservation Unit of
the Museums and Galleries Commission.

BROCKDISH ANTIQUES (M. & L. E. PALFREY)

Commerce House, Brockdish, Diss,
Norfolk IP21 4JL
TEL   03975 498
OPEN   9–5.30 Mon–Sat; closed Wed.

Specialise in sympathetic restoration of
antique furniture, including antique
upholstery, using only traditional
methods.

PROVIDE Home Inspections. Free
Estimates. Free Collection/Delivery
Service.
SPEAK TO Michael Palfrey.
This is a three-generation family business.

J. C. DAWES

The Street, Corpusty, Norwich, **Norfolk
NR11 6QP**
TEL   026387 512
FAX   026387 512
OPEN   By Appointment.

Specialise in conservation of carved,
moulded, veneered wood or parquetry,
stained and polished using traditional or
modern methods, working when
necessary with other specialist art
conservators.

PROVIDE Home Inspections.
Refundable/Chargeable Estimates
Chargeable Collection/Delivery Service.
SPEAK TO J. C. Dawes.

DISS ANTIQUES RESTORATION SERVICES

2–3 Market Place, Diss, **Norfolk
IP22 3JT**
TEL   0379 642213
FAX   0379 642213
OPEN   8–5 Mon–Sat.

Specialise in all antique furniture
restoration, as well as copper and brass.
They undertake to finish with care by
hand every individual piece to retain its
age and patina.

PROVIDE Home Inspections. Free
Estimates. Collection/Delivery Service.
SPEAK TO Brian Wimshurst.

Member of the Guild of Master
Craftsmen and LAPADA.
SEE Clocks.

PETER HOWKINS

39–40 King Street, Great Yarmouth,
Norfolk NR30 2PQ
TEL   0493 851180
OPEN   9–5.30 Mon–Sat or By
       Appointment.

Specialise in restoring antique furniture.

PROVIDE Home Inspections.
SPEAK TO Peter Howkins, Thomas Burn
or Matthew Higham.

Member of NAG.
SEE Silver (different address).

JASPER ANTIQUES

11A Hall Road, Snettisham, King's
Lynn, **Norfolk PE31 7LU**
TEL   0485 541485 (Home 0485
       540604)
OPEN   10.30–1 Mon, Wed, Fri; 10.30–
       1, 2–4 Sat.

Specialise in repairing gilt mirrors.

PROVIDE Home Inspections. Free
Estimates. Free Collection/Delivery
Service.
SPEAK TO Mrs A. Norris.
SEE Clocks, Porcelain, Silver.

RODERICK LARWOOD
The Oaks, Station Road, Larling,
Norwich, **Norfolk NR16 2QS**
TEL   0953 717937
OPEN   8–6 Mon–Fri.

Specialise in restoring 18th century
furniture, brass inlay.

PROVIDE Home Inspections. Free Local
Estimates. Free Collection/Delivery
Service.
SPEAK TO Roderick Larwood.
Member of BAFRA.

PENNY LAWRENCE
Fairhurst Gallery, Bedford Street,
Norwich, **Norfolk NR2 1AS**
TEL   0603 632064
OPEN   9–5 Mon–Fri.

Specialise in restoring and conserving
painted furniture.

PROVIDE Home Inspections. Free
Estimates. Free/Chargeable
Collection/Delivery Service.
SPEAK TO Penny Lawrence.
This workshop is included on the register
of conservators maintained by the
Conservation Unit of the Museums and
Galleries Commission.
SEE Oil Paintings, Picture Frames, Silver.

CLASSIC UPHOLSTERY
Estate Yard, Upper Harlestone,
Northampton, **Northamptonshire
NN7 4EH**
TEL   0604 584556
OPEN   8.30–5 Mon–Fri.

Specialise in traditionally restoring and
renovating upholstered furniture.

PROVIDE Home Inspections. Free
Estimates. Free Collection/Delivery
Service.
SPEAK TO Mark Austin.

Member of the Association of Master
Upholsterers.

THE LEATHER CONSERVATION CENTRE
34 Guildhall Road, Northampton,
Northamptonshire NN1 1EW
TEL   0604 232723
FAX   0604 602070
OPEN   9–6 Mon–Fri.

Specialise in conservation of all types of
leather objects, especially decorated
screens and wall hangings and furniture
upholstery. Advice given on sources of
appropriate specialist leather and
conservation materials.

PROVIDE Home Inspections. Chargeable
Estimates. Chargeable
Collection/Delivery Service.
SPEAK TO Christopher Calnan.
SEE Carpets, Lighting.

DOMENICO LUCISANO 'THE WOODCARVER'
The Grange Farm, Sywell,
Northamptonshire NN6 0BE
TEL   0604 755068
OPEN   8–5 Mon–Fri.

Specialise in any restoration involving
woodcarving.

PROVIDE Home Inspections. Free
Estimates. Chargeable
Collection/Delivery Service.
SPEAK TO Domenico Lucisano.

BRYAN PERKINS ANTIQUES
52 Cannon Street, Wellingborough,
Northamptonshire NN8 4DT
TEL   0933 228812
OPEN   9–5.30 Mon–Fri; 10–12.30 Sat.

Specialise in restoring antique furniture
and French polishing, especially chests
of drawers and mahogany dining tables.

PROVIDE Home Inspections. Free
Estimates. Chargeable
Collection/Delivery Service.
SPEAK TO B. or J. Perkins.

J. A. & T HEDLEY
3 St Mary's Chare, Hexham,
Northumberland NE46 1NQ
TEL   0434 602317
OPEN   9–5 Mon–Sat; 9–12 Thur.

Specialise in restoring antique furniture
and French polishing.

PROVIDE Free Estimates. Chargeable
Collection/Delivery Service.
SPEAK TO D. Hall or W. H. Jewitt.
SEE Picture Frames.

**JOHN SMITH OF
ALNWICK LTD**
West Cawledge Park, Alnwick,
Northumberland NE66 2HJ
TEL   0665 604363
OPEN   10–5 Daily (Gallery).

Specialise in restoring antique English
and Continental furniture.

PROVIDE Home Inspections. Chargeable
Estimates. Chargeable
Collection/Delivery Service.
SPEAK TO Mr P. J. Smith.

T. S. BARROWS & SON
Hamlyn Lodge, Station Road, Ollerton,
Nr. Newark, **Nottinghamshire**
NG22 9BN
TEL   0623 823600
OPEN   8.30–5 Mon–Fri.

Specialise in restoring furniture, French
polishing, cabinetmaking.

PROVIDE Home Inspections. Chargeable
Collection/Delivery Service.
SPEAK TO Norman Barrows.
A three-generation family business.

**FLORENCE
CONSERVATION &
RESTORATION**
102 Nottingham Road, Long Eaton,
Nottingham, **Nottinghamshire**
NG10 2BZ
TEL   0602 733625
OPEN   8–5 Mon–Fri; 9–12 Sat.

Specialise in restoring gesso frames,
gilding and gold leafing. They also repair
and restore marquetry, painted and inlaid
furniture.

PROVIDE Home Inspections. Refundable
Estimates. Chargeable
Collection/Delivery Service.
SPEAK TO Ron Florence.
SEE Oil Paintings, Porcelain.

THE KEYHOLE
Dragonwyck, Far Back Lane, Farnsfield,
Newark, **Nottinghamshire**
NG22 8JX
TEL   0623 882590
OPEN   By Appointment.

Specialise in restoring locks and keys,
anything from a jewel box to a church
door key. They also supply period locks
and keys, duplicate keys, composite keys
and lock servicing.

PROVIDE Home Inspections. Estimates by
negotiation. Chargeable
Collection/Delivery Service.
SPEAK TO George or Valerie Olifent.

Member of the Master Locksmiths
Association. This workshop is included
on the register of conservators
maintained by the Conservation Unit of
the Museums and Galleries Commission.

BARBARA BIBB
149 Kingston Road, Oxford,
Oxfordshire OX2 6RP
TEL   0865 56444
OPEN   9–5 Mon–Sat.

Specialise in restoring gilded frames and
mirrors, lacquer tables and screens etc.

PROVIDE Home Inspections. Free
Estimates. Free Local
Collection/Delivery Service.
SPEAK TO Barbara Bibb.

Member of ABPR. This workshop is
included on the register of conservators
maintained by the Conservation Unit of
the Museums and Galleries Commission.
SEE Oil Paintings, Picture Frames.

COUNTRY CHAIRMEN
Home Farm, Ardington, Wantage,
Oxfordshire OX12 8PY
TEL   0235 833614
OPEN   8.30–5.30 Mon–Fri; 10–1 Sat.

Specialise in restoring and repairing
antique furniture, rush and cane seating
of chairs.

PROVIDE Home Inspections. Free
Estimates. Free Collection/Delivery
Service.
SPEAK TO Tony Handley.

ALISTAIR FRAYLING-CORK
2 Mill Lane, Wallingford, **Oxfordshire
OX10 0DH**
TEL   0491 26221
OPEN   10–6 Mon–Fri, Sat by
            arrangement.

Specialise in restoring fine antique
furniture and brass fittings.

PROVIDE Home Inspections. Free
Estimates. Chargeable
Collection/Delivery Service.
SPEAK TO Alistair Frayling-Cork.
Member of BAFRA.
SEE Clocks, Collectors (Musical
Instruments).

LA CHAISE ANTIQUE
30 London Street, Faringdon,
Oxfordshire SN7 7AA
TEL   0367 240427
OPEN   9.30–5.30 Mon–Sat.

Specialise in restoring and re-
upholstering 18th and 19th century
furniture using traditional materials,
deep buttoning, leather table-liners.

PROVIDE Home Inspections. Free
Estimates. Free Collection/Delivery
Service.
SPEAK TO Roger Clark.
Member of the Guild of Master
Craftsmen.

MANOR FARM FURNITURE RESTORATIONS
Nettlebed, **Oxfordshire, OX14 4QX**
TEL   0491 641186
OPEN   By appointment.

Specialise in the proper restoration of
fine furniture, including Boulle and
marquetry, gilding and decorated work.

PROVIDE Home Inspection. Free
Estimates. Chargeable Collection and
Delivery Service.

SPEAK TO Nicola Shreeve.

ROY D. STRATTON
Wayside, Great Coxwell, Faringdon,
Oxfordshire SN7 7NB
TEL   0367 240030
OPEN   8–8 Daily.

Specialise in restoring all types of
antique furniture except Boulle work and
gilded furniture.

PROVIDE Home Inspections. Free
Estimates. Free Collection/Delivery
Service.
SPEAK TO Roy Stratton.
Member of BAFRA.

TERENCE C. J. WALSH
Park Farmhouse, Hook Norton,
Banbury, **Oxfordshire OX15 5LR**
TEL   0608 730293
OPEN   Mon–Sat By Appointment.

Specialise in restoring 17th–19th
century furniture, including Boulle and
marquetry. They also do upholstery,
including four-poster beds and
headboards.

PROVIDE Home Inspections. Chargeable
Collection/Delivery Service.
SPEAK TO Terence Walsh.

WEAVES AND WAXES
53 Church Street, Bloxham, Banbury,
Oxfordshire OX15 4ET
TEL   0295 721535
FAX   0295 271867
OPEN   9–1, 2–5.30 Tues–Fri; 9–1, 2–4
Sat.

Specialise in restoring antique furniture,
including polishing, veneering, general
repairs, gilding, rush and cane seating,
brass facsimilies, upholstery, leather
skivers.

PROVIDE Home Inspections.
Free/Chargeable Estimates. Chargeable
Collection/Delivery Service.
SPEAK TO Laurie Grayer.
SEE Clocks.

WITNEY RESTORATIONS
Workshop: Unit 17, Hanborough
Business Park, Main Road, Long
Hanborough, **Oxfordshire OX7 2LH**
Accounts and Enquiries: 96–100 Corn
Street, Witney, **Oxfordshire OX8 7BU**
TEL   0993 703902 accounts and
enquiries
0993 883336 workshop
FAX   0993 779852
OPEN   9.30–5 Mon–Fri.

Specialise in restoring and conserving
fine antique furniture as well as
decorative furniture and objects.

PROVIDE Home Inspections. Free
Estimates. Chargeable
Collection/Delivery Service.
SPEAK TO Mr A. Smith or Mrs J. Jarrett.
SEE Clocks.

RICHARD HIGGINS
The Old School, Longnor, Nr.
Shrewsbury, **Shropshire SY5 7PP**
TEL   074373 8162
OPEN   8–6 Mon–Fri.

Specialise in restoring antique furniture,
including Boulle, marquetry, rosewood,
mahogany, oak, walnut.

PROVIDE Home Inspections.
Free/Chargeable Estimates.
Collection/Delivery Service by
arrangement.
SPEAK TO Richard Higgins.

Member of BAFRA and UKIC. This
workshop is included on the register of
conservators maintained by the
Conservation Unit of the Museums and
Galleries Commission.
SEE Clocks, Collectors (Mechanical
Music).

C. J. PRITCHARD
143a Belle Vue Road, Shrewsbury,
Shropshire SY3 7NN
TEL   0743 362854
OPEN   8.15–1, 2.15–4 Mon–Fri.

Specialise in restoring and conserving
antique furniture.

PROVIDE Home Inspections. Refundable
Estimates. Chargeable
Collection/Delivery Service.
SPEAK TO Mr A. W. Jones.

ST MARY'S ANTIQUES AND CABINETMAKERS
2 Lower Bar, Newport, **Shropshire
TF10 1BQ**
TEL   0952 811549
OPEN   9–6 Mon–Fri; 9–12 Sat.

Specialise in restoring antique furniture.

PROVIDE Home Inspections. Free
Estimates. Free/Chargeable
Collection/Delivery Service.
SPEAK TO Ray Edwards.

T. R. BAILEY
11 St Andrew's Road, Stogursey,
Bridgwater, **Somerset TA5 1TE**
TEL   0278 732887
OPEN   By Appointment.

Specialise in restoring small items of
English furniture.

PROVIDE Free Estimates.

Collection/Delivery Service by arrangement.
SPEAK TO Tim Bailey.
SEE Silver.

BOXWOOD ANTIQUE RESTORERS
67 High Street, Wincanton, **Somerset BA9 9JZ**
TEL   0963 33988
OPEN   8.30–6 Mon–Sat.

Specialise in restoring fine furniture, French polishing, wax polishing, carving, metalwork.

PROVIDE Home Inspections. Free Estimates. Free Collection/Delivery Service.
SPEAK TO Alan Stacey.
Member of BAFRA. Delivers regularly to London.

NICHOLAS BRIDGES
68 Lower Street, Merriot, **Somerset TA16 5NN**
TEL   0460 74672
OPEN   By Appointment.

Specialise in all aspects of furniture restoration and finishing, including marquetry, carving, French polishing, turning, gilding, brass casting, caning and rushing, upholstery, desk and table leathers.

PROVIDE Home Inspections. Free Estimates. Free Local Collection/Delivery Service.
SPEAK TO Nicholas Bridges.
Member of BAFRA.

J. BURRELL
Westerfield House, Seavington St Mary, Ilminster, **Somerset TA19 OQR**
TEL   0460 40610
OPEN   By Appointment.
Specialise in restoring antique furniture, including structural repairs, veneering, marquetry, lacquer work, carving, wax polishing.

PROVIDE Home Inspections. Refundable Estimates. Chargeable Collection/Delivery Service.
SPEAK TO J. Burrell.

Member of BAFRA. This workshop is included on the register of conservators maintained by the Conservation Unit of the Museums and Galleries Commission.

CASTLE HOUSE
Unit 1, Bennetts Field Estate, Moor Lane, Wincanton, **Somerset BA9 9DT**
TEL   0963 33884
OPEN   8.30–5.30 Mon–Fri.

Specialise in restoring antique and Continental furniture, Boulle work, marquetry and period finishes.

PROVIDE Home Inspections. Free/Chargeable Estimates. Free/Chargeable Collection/Delivery Service.
SPEAK TO Michael Durkee.
Member of BAFRA.

G. J. DICK-READ
Duxhams, Dulverton, **Somerset TA22 9EJ**
TEL   0398 23460
OPEN   By Appointment.

Specialise in restoring furniture of any period, including painted and gilded furniture, Tunbridge ware, wood turning, upholstery. They do not include Boulle work.

PROVIDE Home Inspections. Free Local Estimates. Chargeable Collection/Delivery Service.
SPEAK TO John Dick-Read.
This workshop is included on the register of conservators maintained by the Conservation Unit of the Museums and Galleries Commission.
SEE Porcelain.

162

CLARE HUTCHISON
1A West Street, Ilminster, **Somerset TA19 9AA**
TEL   0460 53369
OPEN   10–3 Mon–Fri; 10–1 Sat; closed
       Thur.

Specialise in restoring antique mirror frames.

PROVIDE Free Estimates.
SPEAK TO Clare Hutchison.

SEE Picture Frames.

JENNIFER M. JOHN
Myrtle Cottage, Merryfield Lane, Ilton,
Ilminster,
Somerset TA19 9EZ
TEL   0460 53963
OPEN   9–5 Mon–Sat or By
       Appointment.

Specialise in cane seating, including medallions, blind and close caning as well as seating in sea-grass rush and string.

PROVIDE Home Inspections. Free
Estimates. Free Local Collection/
Delivery Service.
SPEAK TO Jennifer John.

Member of the Basketmakers
Association.

RECTORY RESTORATIONS
Raddington, Nr. Wiveliscombe,
Taunton, **Somerset TA4 2QW**
TEL   03986 271
OPEN   By Appointment.

Specialise in restoring all types of antique furniture.

PROVIDE Home Inspections. Free
Estimates. Free Local
Collection/Delivery Service.
SPEAK TO Simon Coates.

EDWARD VENN ANTIQUE RESTORATIONS
52 Long Street, Williton, Taunton,
Somerset TA4 4QU
TEL   0984 32631
OPEN   8.30–5.30 Mon–Fri.

Specialise in restoring antique furniture up to 1900. They also replace mirror glass and restore frames.

PROVIDE Chargeable Estimates.
Chargeable Collection/Delivery
Service.
SPEAK TO Mr Venn.
SEE Clocks.

THE ANTIQUE RESTORATION STUDIO
The Old Post Office, Haughton,
Staffordshire ST18 9JH
TEL   0785 780424
FAX   0785 780157
OPEN   9–5 Mon–Fri.

Specialise in restoring antique and modern furniture.

PROVIDE Home Inspections. Free
Estimates. Free Collection/Delivery
Service.
SPEAK TO D. P. Albright.

SEE Porcelain, Oil Paintings, Carpets.

ANTIQUES WORKSHOP
43–45 Hope Street, Hanley, Stoke-on-
Trent, **Staffordshire ST1 5BT**
TEL   0782 273645
OPEN   9–5 Mon–Fri; 10–4 Sat.

Specialise in repairing and restoring oak and mahogany and French polishing of the latter.

PROVIDE Home Inspections. Free
Estimates. Chargeable
Collection/Delivery Service.
SPEAK TO Howard Oakes.

163

JALNA ANTIQUES
'Jalna', Coley Lane, Little Haywood, Nr. Stafford, **Staffordshire ST18 0UP**
TEL   0889 881381
OPEN   9–5 Daily.

Specialise in restoring upholstery, carving, veneering and French polishing.

PROVIDE Home Inspections. Free Estimates. Free Collection/Delivery Service.
SPEAK TO Geoff Hancox.

STEPHEN MASSEY CANE AND RUSH RESTORATION
143 Leek Road, Shelton, Stoke-on-Trent, **Staffordshire ST4 2BW**
TEL   0782 48852
OPEN   By Appointment Only.

Specialise in restoring cane and rush seating and panel restoration.

PROVIDE Home Inspections. Free Estimates. Free Local Collection/Delivery Service.
SPEAK TO Stephen Massey.

A. C. PRALL RESTORATIONS
Highfield Farm, Uttoxeter Road, Draycott, **Staffordshire ST11 9AE**
TEL   0782 399022
OPEN   9–7 Mon–Fri.

Specialise in restoring Georgian furniture.

PROVIDE Free Estimates. Free/Chargeable Collection/Delivery Service.
SPEAK TO Mr Prall.
SEE Clocks.

GRAHAM WHEELER PERIOD INTERIORS
24 Radford Street, Stone, **Staffordshire ST15 8DA**
TEL   0785 875000
FAX   0785 875015
OPEN   9–5 Mon–Fri.

Specialise in restoring antique furniture and creating period interiors.

PROVIDE Home Inspections. Refundable Estimates. Chargeable Collection/Delivery Service.
SPEAK TO Graham Wheeler.

ROGER & SYLVIA ALLAN
The Old Red Lion, Bedingfield, Eye, **Suffolk IP23 7LQ**
TEL   0728 76 491
OPEN   By Appointment.

Specialise in restoring antique furniture, carved objects and treen.

PROVIDE Home Inspections. Free Estimates.
SPEAK TO Roger Allan.
SEE Oil Paintings, Silver.

ANTIQUE RESTORATION
Unit 3, Bench Barn Farm, Clare, **Suffolk**
TEL   0787 277635
OPEN   8–5 Mon–Fri, 8–12 Sat.

Specialise in restoring furniture. Will also design and manufacture furniture to commission.

PROVIDE Home Inspections. Free Estimates. Free Local Collection/Delivery Service.
SPEAK TO Terry Wheeler.

BALLYBEG RESTORATIONS AND HARCOURT ANTIQUES
101 Kingsway, Mildenhall, **Suffolk IP28 7HS**
TEL   0638 712378
OPEN   By Appointment.

Specialise in restoring antique furniture, including upholstery, gilding, painted furniture, marquetry, veneering, French polishing.

PROVIDE Home Inspections. Free Estimates. Free Collection/Delivery Service.
SPEAK TO Mr P. B. Bailey.

BED BAZAAR
29 Double Street, Framlingham, Woodbridge, **Suffolk IP13 9BN**
TEL   0728 723756
FAX   0728 724626
OPEN   By Appointment.

Specialise in restoring antique brass and iron beds and supply mattresses and bed spring bases.

PROVIDE Home Inspections. Free Estimates. Chargeable Collection/Delivery Service.
SPEAK TO Ben Goodbrey.

JOHN GAZELEY ASSOCIATES FINE ART
17 Fonnereau Road, Ipswich, **Suffolk IP1 3JR**
TEL   0473 252420
OPEN   By Appointment.

Specialise in gilding and repairing mirror frames as well as making reproduction frames.

PROVIDE Free Estimates.
SPEAK TO Dr. John Gazeley.
SEE Oil Paintings, Picture Frames.

THE MENDLESHAM FURNITURE WORKSHOP
Elms Farm, Mendlesham, Stowmarket, **Suffolk IP14 5RS**
TEL   0449 767107
OPEN   By Appointment.

Specialise in restoring English antique furniture, particularly Mendlesham chairs, woodcarving, French polishing and some upholstery work.

PROVIDE Home Inspections. Chargeable Estimates. Chargeable Collection/Delivery Service.
SPEAK TO Roy Clement-Smith.
Member of the Guild of Master Craftsmen.

NETTLE HALL RESTORATION
Unit 1, Corner Farm, Sibton, Saxmundham, **Suffolk IP17 2NE**
TEL   072 879 550 and 205.
OPEN   9–5 Mon–Sat.

Specialise in restoring and conserving antique furniture, inlay work, marquetry, cabinetmaking, French polishing, gilding.

PROVIDE Home Inspections. Free Estimates. Chargeable Collection/Delivery Service.
SPEAK TO Thomas Mark Spirling.

JULIA PARK, CONSERVATION SERVICES
9 Cardigan Street, Ipswich, **Suffolk IP1 3PF**
TEL   0473 216862
OPEN   9–5 Mon–Fri.

Specialise in restoring lacquer and Chinoiserie furniture and objects.

PROVIDE Home Inspections. Free/Chargeable Estimates. Chargeable Collection/Delivery Service.
SPEAK TO Julia Park.
Member of IIC. This workshop is included on the register of conservators maintained by the Conservation Unit of the Museums and Galleries Commission.

PEASENHALL ART & ANTIQUES GALLERY
Peasenhall, Nr. Saxmundham, **Suffolk IP17 2HJ**
TEL   072 879 224
OPEN   9–6 Daily.

Specialise in restoring antique furniture.

165

They also make and repair walking sticks.

PROVIDE Local Home Inspections. Free Estimates. Free Local Collection/Delivery Service.
SPEAK TO Mike Wickins.
SEE Oil Paintings.

PEPPERS PERIOD PIECES
23 Churchgate Street, Bury St Edmunds, **Suffolk IP33 1RG**
TEL   0284 768786
OPEN   10–5 Mon–Sat.

Specialise in restoring furniture.

PROVIDE Home Inspections. Refundable Estimates. Free/Chargeable Collection/Delivery Service.
SPEAK TO M. E. Pepper.
SEE Clocks.

MARK PETERS ANTIQUES
Green Farm Cottage, Thurston, Bury St. Edmunds, **Suffolk IP31 3SN**
TEL   0359 30888
OPEN   8.30–6 Mon–Fri, 8.30–1 Sat.

Specialise in all aspects of period furniture restoration.

PROVIDE Home Inspections. Chargeable Estimates. Chargeable Collection/Delivery Service.
SPEAK TO Mark Peters.
Member of UKIC. This workshop is included on the register of conservators maintained by the Conservation Unit of the Museums and Galleries Commission.

A. G. SMEETH
Clock House, Locks Lane, Leavenheath, Colchester, **Suffolk CO6 4PF**
TEL   0206 262187
OPEN   By Appointment.

Specialise in restoring furniture.

PROVIDE Home Inspections. Free Estimates. Free Collection/Delivery Service.

SPEAK TO A. G. Smeeth.
SEE Clocks.

MICHAEL ADDISON ANTIQUES
28–30 Godstone Road, Kenley, **Surrey CR8 5JE**
TEL   081 668 6714
OPEN   10–5 Mon–Sat.

Specialise in restoring antique furniture and upholstery.

PROVIDE Home Inspections. Free Estimates. Free Collection/Delivery Service.
SPEAK TO M. Addison.

A. E. BOOTH & SON
9 High Street, Ewell, Epsom, **Surrey KT17 1SG**
TEL   081 393 5245
OPEN   9–5 Mon–Fri.

Specialise in repairs to chairs, antique and reproduction furniture, including polishing, gilding and upholstery.

PROVIDE Home Inspections. Free/Refundable Estimates.Free Collection/Delivery Service.
SPEAK TO D. J. Booth.

Member of BAFRA.
SEE Clocks.

IAN CALDWELL
9A The Green, Dorking Road, Tadworth, **Surrey KT20 5SQ**
TEL   0737 813969
OPEN   10–5.30 Mon–Sat; closed Wed.

Specialise in restoring furniture, including gilding, lacquer work and upholstery.

PROVIDE Home Inspections. Free Collection/Delivery Service.
SPEAK TO Ian Caldwell.
Member of LAPADA.

COURTLANDS RESTORATION
Courtlands, Park Road, Banstead,
Surrey SM7 3EF
TEL   0737 352429
OPEN   8–6 Mon–Sat.

Specialise in restoring antique furniture,
including traditional and French
polishing, simulation effects,
cabinetmaking, turning and carving,
veneer repairs, gilding, metal repairs.

PROVIDE Home Inspections. Free
Estimates. Free Collection/Delivery
Service.
SPEAK TO David Sayer.
Member of BAFRA.

DAVID EMBLING
45 Fairfield, Farnham, **Surrey**
GU9 8AG
TEL   0252 712660
OPEN   8–1, 2–5 Mon–Fri.

Specialise in restoring antique and
modern furniture, French polishing,
lacquering, gilding.

PROVIDE Home Inspections. Free
Estimates. Chargeable
Collection/Delivery Service.
SPEAK TO David Embling.
SEE Picture Frames.

G. & R. FRASER SINCLAIR
11 Orchard Works, Streeters Lane,
Beddington, **Surrey SM6 7ND**
TEL   081 669 5343
OPEN   8–5.30 Mon–Fri.

Specialise in restoring 18th century
English furniture.

PROVIDE Home Inspections. Free
Estimates. Free Collection/Delivery
Service.
SPEAK TO Glen Sinclair.

Member of BAFRA.

HEARN-COOPER LTD
46 Park Hill Road, Wallington, **Surrey**
SM6 0SB
TEL   081 395 5498
OPEN   8.30–5.30 Mon–Fri; Sat By
Appointment

Specialise in restoring Oriental lacquer
and European lacquered furniture.

PROVIDE Home Inspections. Estimates.
Collection/Delivery Service Available.
SPEAK TO Richard Hearn-Cooper.

HEATH-BULLOCK
8 Meadrow, Godalming, **Surrey**
GU7 3HN
TEL   0483 422562
FAX   0483 426077
OPEN   10–1, 2–4 Mon–Sat.

Specialise in restoring and upholstering
antique furniture. They have a long
tradition in leather upholstery.

PROVIDE Home Inspections. Free
Estimates. Chargeable
Collection/Delivery Service.
SPEAK TO Roger Heath-Bullock.

MICHAEL HEDGECOE
Rowan House, 21 Burrow Hill Green,
Chobham, Woking, **Surrey GU24 8QS**
TEL   0276 858206
OPEN   8–5 Mon–Fri.

Specialise in restoring top quality
English and French 18th and 19th
century furniture, as well as best quality
upholstery.

PROVIDE Home Inspections. Free
Estimates. Chargeable
Collection/Delivery Service.
SPEAK TO Michael Hedgecoe.

Member of LAPADA.

JOHN KENDALL
156 High Street, Old Woking, **Surrey
GU21 9JH**
TEL   0483 771310
OPEN   9–5 Mon–Fri.

Specialise in restoring frames and furniture, including marquetry.

PROVIDE Home Inspections. Free Estimates. Chargeable Collection/Delivery Service.
SPEAK TO John Kendall.

SEE Clocks.

RICHARD LAWMAN–WARWICK ANTIQUE RESTORATIONS
32 Beddington Lane, Croydon, **Surrey
CR0 4TB**
TEL   081 688 4511
OPEN   9–6 Tues–Sat.

Specialise in restoring fine furniture, leathering, caning, rushing, upholstery.

PROVIDE Home Inspections. Free Estimates. Free Collection/Delivery Service.
SPEAK TO Richard Lawman.

Member of the Guild of Master Craftsmen. This workshop is included on the register of conservators maintained by the Conservation Unit of the Museums and Galleries Commission.
SEE Clocks.

TREVOR LAWRENCE FURNITURE
Rectory Barn, High Street, Limpsfield, Oxted, **Surrey RH8 0DG**
TEL   0883 730300 or 730301
FAX   0883 730300
OPEN   8–5 Mon–Fri, 9–1 Sat.

Specialise in all aspects of furniture restoration and finishing. Traditional upholstery and re-upholstery.

PROVIDE Home Inspections. Free Estimates. Chargeable Collection/Delivery Service.
SPEAK TO Trevor Lawrence.

MANOR ANTIQUES AND RESTORATIONS
2 New Shops, High Street, Old Woking, **Surrey GU22 9JW**
TEL   0483 724666
OPEN   10–5 Mon–Fri; 10–4.30 Sat.
Specialise in restoring furniture, including French polishing, inlay work, chair-caning and rush work.

PROVIDE Home Inspections. Free Estimates. Collection/Delivery Service.
SPEAK TO Alan Wellstead or Paul Thomson.

Member of the Guild of Master Craftsmen.
SEE Clocks, Picture Frames.

SIMON MARSH RESTORATIONS
The Old Butchers Shop, High Street, Bletchingley, **Surrey RH1 4PA**
TEL   0883 743350
OPEN   By Appointment.

Specialise in restoring fine furniture.

PROVIDE Home Inspections. Free/Refundable Estimates. Chargeable Collection/Delivery Service.
SPEAK TO Mrs Marsh.

Member of BAFRA.

TIMOTHY NAYLOR ASSOCIATES
26B Dunstable Road, Richmond, **Surrey TW9 1UH**
TEL   081 332 0444
OPEN   8–5.30 Mon–Fri.

Specialise in restoring 18th century English furniture, including marquetry and carving.

PROVIDE Home Inspections. Free

Estimates. Collection/Delivery Service by arrangement.
SPEAK TO Timothy Naylor.

N. J. NEWMAN
22 Eastcroft Road, West Ewell, **Surrey KT19 9TX**
TEL   081 393 0538
OPEN   By Appointment.

Specialise in restoring English and Continental furniture.

PROVIDE Home Inspections. Free/Chargeable Estimates. Chargeable Collection/Delivery Service.
SPEAK TO Nick Newman.

Member of BAFRA. This workshop is included on the register of conservators maintained by the Conservation Unit of the Museums and Galleries Commission.

CHARLES OWEN RESTORATIONS (GILDER)
The Studio, 1 Hillrise, Shere Road, West Horsley, **Surrey KT24 6EF**
TEL   04865 5271
OPEN   By Appointment.

Specialise in restoring gilt furniture and overmantels.

PROVIDE Home Inspections. Free Estimates.
SPEAK TO Charles Owen.
SEE Picture Frames.

SAGE ANTIQUES & INTERIORS
High Street, Ripley, **Surrey GU23 6BB**
TEL   0483 224396
FAX   0483 211996
OPEN   9.30–5.30 Mon–Sat.

Specialise in restoring furniture 1600–1840, including oak, walnut, mahogany and fruitwood.

PROVIDE Free Estimates. Free Collection/Delivery Service.
SPEAK TO Howard or Chrissie Sage.

Member of LAPADA and the Guild of Master Craftsmen.
SEE Oil Paintings, Porcelain.

R. SAUNDERS
71 Queens Road, Weybridge, **Surrey KT13 9UQ**
TEL   0932 842601
OPEN   9.15–5 Mon–Sat; closed Wed.

Specialise in repairing good quality English furniture pre-1830.

PROVIDE Home Inspections. Free Estimates. Free Collection/Delivery Service.
SPEAK TO J. B. Tonkinson.
SEE Oil Paintings, Porcelain, Silver.

MICHAEL SCHRYVER ANTIQUES
The Granary, 10 North Street, Dorking, **Surrey RH4 1DN**
TEL   0306 881110
FAX   0306 876168
OPEN   8.30–5.30 Mon–Fri; 8.30–12.30 Sat.

Specialise in restoring fine quality period furniture, including metalwork, period and contemporary upholstery.

PROVIDE Home Inspections. Free Estimates. Free Collection/Delivery Service.
SPEAK TO Michael Schryver.

JUDITH WETHERALL
trading as **J.B. SYMES**
28 Silverlea Gardens, Horley, **Surrey RH6 9BB**
TEL   0293 775024
OPEN   8.30–5.30 By Appointment Only.

Specialise in restoring painted and gilded furniture and japanned and lacquered boxes.

PROVIDE Free Local Home Inspections. Free Estimates. Chargeable Collection/Delivery Service.

169

SPEAK TO Judith Wetherall.
Member of UKIC and IIC. This workshop is included on the register of conservators maintained by the Conservation Unit of the Museums and Galleries Commission.
SEE Clocks, Picture Frames, Porcelain.

CHARLES WRIGHT
Lark Rise, Glendine Avenue, East Horsley, **Surrey KT24 5AY**
TEL 04865 2904
OPEN By Appointment.

Specialise in restoring furniture of all periods.

PROVIDE Chargeable Home Inspections. Free Estimates.
SPEAK TO Charles Wright.
Mr Wright was Head of the Furniture Conservation Department at the Victoria and Albert Museum for thirty-six years.

BRAGGE & SONS
Landgate House, Rye, **East Sussex TN31 7LH**
TEL 0797 223358
FAX 0797 225143
OPEN 9–5 Mon–Fri; Tues & Sat 9–12.

Specialise in restoring 18th century English and French furniture.

PROVIDE Free Estimates.
SPEAK TO J. Bragge.

KEVIN C. BUTCHER
1 Lucknow Cottage, Northbridge Street, Robertsbridge, **East Sussex TN32 5NP**
TEL 0580 881864
OPEN 9–6 Mon–Sat.

Specialise in restoring all pre-1850 furniture, woodwork only and surface restoration. Also fine furniture made to customers' specifications. Timbers are always carefully matched from a large stock of old wood.

PROVIDE Home Inspections. Chargeable Estimates. Free Local Collection/Delivery Service.
SPEAK TO Kevin Butcher.

JOHN COWDEROY ANTIQUES
42 South Street, Eastbourne, **East Sussex BN21 4XB**
TEL 0323 20058
FAX 0323 410163
OPEN 9.30–1, 2.30–5 Mon–Fri; 9.30–1 Wed, Sat.

Specialise in restoring furniture and French polishing.

PROVIDE Home Inspections. Free Estimates. Chargeable Collection/Delivery Service.
SPEAK TO John, Ruth, David or Richard Cowderoy.
Member of LAPADA.
SEE Clocks, Collectors (Mechanical Music).

FIRELEAD LTD
Banff Farm, Upper Clayhill, Uckfield Road, Ringmer, Lewes, **East Sussex BN8 5RR**
TEL 0273 890918
FAX 0273 890691
OPEN 8–5.30 Mon–Fri By Appointment.

Specialise in full antique restoration, including re-leathering writing surfaces, upholstery, re-silvering mirrors, keys made for old locks, marquetry repairs, water-gilding. Also duplicate items to match other pieces.

PROVIDE Local Home Inspections. Local Free Estimates. Chargeable Collection/Delivery Service.
SPEAK TO David Gilbert.
SEE Oil Paintings.

GOLDEN FISH GILDING & RESTORATION
94 Gloucester Road, Brighton, **East Sussex BN1 4AP**
TEL   0273 691164
FAX   0273 691164
OPEN   9–5 Mon–Fri.

Specialise in gilding and restoring mirror frames and furniture, including carving.

PROVIDE Home Inspections. Free Estimates. Free Collection/Delivery Service.
SPEAK TO Marianne Hatchwell.

Also teaches gilding techniques.
SEE Picture Frames, Porcelain.

JOHN HARTNETT & SON
2 Victoria Street, Brighton, **East Sussex BN1 3FP**
TEL   0273 28793
OPEN   9–6 Mon–Fri.

Specialise in restoring fine furniture, including French polishing, upholstery, leather insets, lacquer and japanning marquetry and inlay, caning and rushing, carving, gilding.

PROVIDE Home Inspections. Free Estimates. Chargeable Collection/Delivery Service.
SPEAK TO John Hartnett.

SIMON HATCHWELL ANTIQUES
94 Gloucester Road, Brighton, **East Sussex BN1 4AP**
TEL   0273 691164
FAX   0273 691164
OPEN   9–1.30, 2.30–5 Mon–Fri; Sat By Appointment.

Specialise in restoring English and Continental furniture, Empire and Biedermeier.

PROVIDE Home Inspections. Free

Estimates. Free Local Collection/Delivery Service.
SPEAK TO Simon or Allan Hatchwell.
Member of LAPADA.
SEE Clocks.

D. J. MATTHEWS
20–21 Newark Place, Brighton, **East Sussex BN2 2NT**
TEL   0273 602427
OPEN   7.30–5 Mon–Fri.

Specialise in restoring antique furniture, particularly that which has a painted finish, including trays, small boxes, screens and papier mâché items.

PROVIDE Local Home Inspections. Free Estimates.
SPEAK TO D. J. Matthews.
Member of the Guild of Master Craftsmen.

MORE RESTORATIONS
The Old Booking Hall, Hove Park Villas, Hove, **East Sussex BN3 6HP**
TEL   0273 25380
OPEN   8.30–5 Mon–Fri.

Specialise in restoring period (1700–1850) English furniture and some Continental marquetry.

PROVIDE Home Inspections. Free Estimates. Collection/Delivery Service by arrangement.
SPEAK TO Arthur Moore.
SEE Clocks.

THE OLD BAKERY FURNISHING COMPANY
Punetts Town, Nr. Heathfield, **East Sussex TN21 9DS**
TEL   0435 830608
OPEN   9–5 Mon–Fri; 9–1 Sat.

Specialise in restoring antique furniture, including tapestry work and traditional upholstery.

PROVIDE Free/Chargeable Home

Inspections. Estimates. Chargeable Collection/Delivery Service.
SPEAK TO Ann Spencer.

SPEAK TO Mr or Mrs B. R. Higgins. Member of LAPADA.
SEE Silver.

GRAHAM PRICE ANTIQUES LTD

Unit 4, Chaucer Industrial Estate, Polegate, **East Sussex BN26 6JD**
TEL   0323 487167 and 485301
FAX   0323 483904
OPEN   8–6 Mon–Fri.

Specialise in restoring antique furniture, especially 17th–19th century English and Continental furniture.

PROVIDE Home Inspections. Free Estimates. Collection/Delivery Service.
SPEAK TO G. J. Price or C. M. Springett.

CAROL BANKS AND SON

September Cottage, 88 Victoria Road, Shoreham-by-Sea, **West Sussex BN4 5WS**
TEL   0273 461647
OPEN   By Appointment.

Specialise in conservation and restoration of carved and gilded finished mirror frames, columns, brackets, console tables.

PROVIDE Local Home Inspections. Free Estimates.
SPEAK TO Carol Banks.
SEE Picture Frames, Porcelain.

PETER SEMUS CRAFTING ANTIQUES

The Warehouse, Gladstone Land, Portslade, **East Sussex BN41 1LJ**
TEL   0273 420154
FAX   0273 430355
OPEN   8–6 Mon–Fri.

Specialise in restoring antique furniture, making bespoke furniture and reproduction furniture.

PROVIDE Home Inspections. Refundable Estimates. Free Collection/Delivery Service.
SPEAK TO Peter Semus.

RICHARD AND SUE BEALE CONSERVATION

West Chiltington, **West Sussex**
TEL   0798 813380
OPEN   9.30–5 Mon–Fri.

Specialise in conserving and restoring antique furniture, including English japanned, Oriental lacquer, French vernis Martin, gilded and painted furniture, frames and related objets d'art.

PROVIDE Home Inspections. Free Estimates. Chargeable Collection/Delivery Service.
SPEAK TO Richard or Sue Beale.

YELLOW LANTERN ANTIQUES LTD

34 & 34B Holland Road, Hove, **East Sussex BN3 1JL**
TEL   0273 771572
OPEN   9.30–1, 2.15–5.30 Mon–Fri; 9–1, 2.15–4.30. Sat.

Specialise in cleaning of ormolu and bronze and restoring furniture.

PROVIDE Home Inspections. Free Estimates. Free Collection/Delivery Service.

P. G. CASEBOW

Pilgrims, Mill Lane, Worthing, **West Sussex BN13 3DE**
TEL   0903 264045
OPEN   By Appointment.

Specialise in restoring period furniture, fretwork, inlay and marquetry.

PROVIDE Home Inspections. Free Estimates. Chargeable Collection/Delivery Service.

172

SPEAK TO Peter Casebow.
Member of BAFRA.

SONIA DEMETRIOU
The Studio, Tillington Cottage,
Tillington, Petworth, **West Sussex**
GU28 0RA
TEL   0798 44113
OPEN   9.30–6 Mon–Fri.

Specialise in cleaning and restoring all
types of decorated furniture and objets
d'art, including japanned work and Tôle
ware.

PROVIDE Local Home Inspections. Free
Local Estimates.
SPEAK TO Sonia Demetriou.

GARNER & CO.
Stable Cottage, Steyning Road, Wiston,
West Sussex BN44 3DD
TEL   0903 814565
OPEN   By Appointment (Tel Mon–Fri
9–5.30).

Specialise in conserving fine period
(1600–1850) English and Continental
furniture and works of art, including
painted furniture and gilded frames.

PROVIDE Home Inspections. Estimates.
SPEAK TO Sid Garner.
SEE Clocks, Porcelain, Silver.

NOEL & EVA-LOUISE PEPPERALL
Dairy Lane Cottage, Walberton,
Arundel, **West Sussex BN18 0PT**
TEL   0243 551282
OPEN   By Appointment.

Specialise in restoring antique furniture,
including painted furniture and gilding.

PROVIDE Home Inspections. Free
Estimates. Chargeable
Collection/Delivery Service.
SPEAK TO Noel or Eva-Louise Pepperall.
Mr Pepperall is a member of BAFRA.
This workshop is included on the register
of conservators maintained by the

Conservation Unit of the Museums and
Galleries Commission.

ALBERT PLUMB
31 Whyke Lane, Chichester, **West Sussex**
PO19 2JS
TEL   0243 788468
OPEN   9.30–5 Mon–Sat.

Specialise in antique furniture
restoration.

PROVIDE Home Inspections. Free
Estimates. Chargeable
Collection/Delivery Service.
SPEAK TO Albert Plumb.
SEE Lighting.

THAKEHAM FURNITURE
Rock Road, Storrington, **West Sussex**
RH20 3AE
TEL   0903 745464
OPEN   8.30–5 Mon–Fri.

Specialise in restoring 18th and 19th
century furniture, including marquetry,
veneering, cabinetwork and French
polishing.

PROVIDE Home Inspections.
Free/Chargeable Estimates.
Free/Chargeable Collection/Delivery
Service.
SPEAK TO Mr Chavasse.
Member of BAFRA.

WEST DEAN COLLEGE
West Dean, Chichester, **West Sussex**
PO18 0OZ
TEL   0243 63 301
FAX   0243 63 342
OPEN   9–5 Mon–Fri.

Specialise in training conservators and
restorers in the fields of antique
furniture. They will also undertake
restoration work.

PROVIDE Local Home Inspections. Free
Estimates.
SPEAK TO Peter Sarginson.
SEE Books, Clocks, Porcelain, Silver.

DAVID WESTON
East Lodge, Woldringfold, Lower
Beeding, Horsham, **West Sussex
RH13 6NJ**
TEL   0403 891617
OPEN   By Appointment.

Specialise in restoring composition
frames and gilding.

PROVIDE Free Estimates.
SPEAK TO David Weston.

Also make reproduction composition
frames.
SEE Picture Frames.

WILSON ANTIQUES
57–59 Broadwater Road, Worthing,
West Sussex BN14 8AH
TEL   0903 202059
OPEN   9–5 Mon–Sat.

Specialise in restoring antique furniture.

PROVIDE Home Inspections. Free
Estimates. Free Collection/Delivery
Service.
SPEAK TO Frank Wilson.

ABERCROMBIES
140–142 Manor House Road, Jesmond,
Newcastle-upon-Tyne, **Tyne & Wear
NE2 2NA**
TEL   091 281 7182
FAX   091 281 7183
OPEN   10–6 Tues–Fri; 10–4 Sat.

Specialise in traditional re-upholstery
and furniture restoration.

PROVIDE Home Inspections. Free
Estimates. Collection/Delivery Service.
SPEAK TO Mr C. N. Stell.

The showroom has an extensive
collection of archive wallpaper and
fabrics.

ANNA HARRISON ANTIQUES
Grange Park, Great North Road,
Gosforth, Newcastle-upon-Tyne,
Tyne & Wear NE3 2DQ
TEL   091 284 3202
FAX   091 284 6689
OPEN   10–5 Mon–Sat.

Specialise in restoring furniture and
upholstery.

PROVIDE Home Inspections. Free
Estimates. Chargeable
Collection/Delivery Service.
SPEAK TO Anna Harrison.

OWEN HUMBLE ANTIQUES
11–12 Clay Road, Jesmond, Newcastle-
upon-Tyne, **Tyne & Wear NE2 4RP**
TEL   091 281 4602
OPEN   10–5 Mon–Sat.

Specialise in restoring 18th and 19th
century furniture.

PROVIDE Home Inspections. Free
Estimates. Free Collection/Delivery
Service.
SPEAK TO Michael Humble.
Member of LAPADA.

TAYLOR & BROOK RE-UPHOLSTERY LTD
5 Greenhill Street, Stratford upon Avon,
Warwickshire CV37 6LF
TEL   0789 269604
OPEN   9–5 Mon–Sat.

Specialise in re-upholstering antique
and quality traditional furniture, recaning and supply of all upholstery
sundries and materials for DIY.

PROVIDE Home Inspections, Free
Estimates, Free Collection/Delivery
Service all within a ten-mile radius.
SPEAK TO Collin Brook.

PERCY F. WALE
32 & 34 Regent Street, Leamington Spa, **Warwickshire CV32 5EG**
TEL   0926 421288
OPEN   9–1, 2–5.30 Mon–Sat.

Specialise in restoring fine old and antique furniture, including cabinet repairs, French polishing, desk-lining and re-upholstery.

PROVIDE Home Inspections. Free Estimates. Chargeable Collection/Delivery Service.
SPEAK TO Peter G. Barton.

BRADFORD FURNITURE WORKSHOPS
Unit 20, Longs Yard, Trowbridge Road, Bradford-on-Avon, **Wiltshire BA15 1EE**
TEL   02216 4551
OPEN   9–5.30 Mon–Fri; 9–12 Sat

Specialise in restoring antique and general furniture, cabinet-work and French polishing.

PROVIDE Home Inspections. Refundable Estimates. Free Collection/Delivery Service.
SPEAK TO I. Blackshaw.

CHAIRPERSONS OF MARSHFIELD
40 High Street, Marshfield, Nr. Chippenham, **Wiltshire SN14 8LP**
TEL   0225 891431
OPEN   By Appointment.

Specialise in cane and rush seating. Also repair wicker, rattan, bamboo and willow chairs and can arrange for chair frames to be repaired.

PROVIDE Home Inspections. Free Estimates. Free Delivery/Collection Service to Bath/Bristol.
SPEAK TO Michael Pitts.

W. J. COOK AND SONS LTD
High Trees House, Savernake Forest, Marlborough, **Wiltshire SN8 3JS**
TEL   0672 513017
FAX   0672 514455
OPEN   8–7 Mon–Fri.

Specialise in restoring all types of furniture, late 17th century to present day, including gilding, carving, leathering, upholstery and marquetry.

PROVIDE Home Inspections. Free Estimates. Free Local Collection/Delivery Service.
SPEAK TO Mr Cook.

This is a family business established over thirty years.
SEE **London SW11.**

PHILIP HAWKINS
The Old School Workshop, High Street, Maiden Bradley, Warminster, **Wiltshire BA12 7JG**
OPEN   By Appointment.

Specialise in restoring early oak, country and period furniture.

PROVIDE Home Inspections. Free Estimates. Free Collection/Delivery Service.
SPEAK TO Philip Hawkins.

Member of BAFRA.

MAC HUMBLE ANTIQUES
7–9 Woolley Street, Bradford-on-Avon, **Wiltshire BA15 1AD**
TEL   02216 6329
OPEN   9–6 Mon–Sat.

Specialise in restoring 18th and 19th century furniture and decorative objects.

PROVIDE Home Inspections. Refundable Estimates. Free Collection/Delivery Service.
SPEAK TO Mac Humble.
SEE Carpets, Silver.

ROD NAYLOR
208 Devizes Road, Hilperton,
Trowbridge, **Wiltshire BA14 7QP**
TEL   0225 754497
OPEN   By Appointment.

Specialise in restoring fine quality wood-carving and cabinetwork, including gilding, marquetry etc. Also supply hard-to-find items for restorers such as three-dimensional copying machines, embossed lining paper and small replica knobs suitable for tea caddies, boxes and secretaires.

PROVIDE Home Inspections. Free Estimates. Free Collection/Delivery Service.
SPEAK TO Rod Naylor.
SEE Lighting, Porcelain.

MARCO PITT
Staple House, High Street, Tisbury,
Wiltshire SP3 6LD
TEL   0747 870420
OPEN   9–6 Mon–Sat.

Specialise in restoring carving, gilding, Boulle work, all types of finishes, furniture metalwork, locks, painted furniture. They are cabinetmakers and can restore any type and style of antique furniture.

PROVIDE Home Inspections. Free Estimates. Free Collection/Delivery Service.
SPEAK TO Marco Pitt.
Member of BAFRA.

RESTORATIONS UNLIMITED
Pinkney Park, Malmesbury, **Wiltshire SN16 0NX**
TEL   0666 840888
OPEN   8.30–5 Mon–Fri and By
       Appointment Sat and Sun.

Specialise in restoring antique furniture, veneering, inlay, rush and cane seating and will also make furniture to match existing pieces.

PROVIDE Home Inspections. Free Estimates. Free Collection/Delivery Service.
SPEAK TO Richard Pinchis.
SEE Oil Paintings, Porcelain, Clocks.

ROOTHS OF BRADFORD-ON-AVON
18 Market Street, Bradford-on-Avon,
Wiltshire BA15 1LL
TEL   02216 4191
OPEN   9.30–1, 2.15–6 Mon–Sat.

Specialise in restoring gilded furniture.

PROVIDE Home Inspections. Free Estimates. Collection/Delivery Service.
SPEAK TO Edward Rooth or Julia Rooth.
SEE Picture Frames.

SHENSTONE RESTORATIONS
23 Lansdown Road, Swindon, **Wiltshire SN1 3NE**
TEL   0793 644980
OPEN   By Appointment.

Specialise in restoring smaller decorative items, including marquetry, inlay and veneering. They work in bone, mother-of-pearl, ebony and ivory and its substitutes. They also do Boulle marquetry and marble restoration.

PROVIDE Local Home Inspections. Chargeable Estimates. Chargeable Collection/Delivery Service.
SPEAK TO Blair Shenstone.
SEE Silver.

JOHN TIGHE
One Oak, Lights Lane, Alderbury,
Salisbury, **Wiltshire SP5 3AL**
TEL   0722 710231
OPEN   By Appointment.

Specialise in restoring 18th and 19th century furniture and gilding.

PROVIDE Home Inspections. Free Estimates.

SPEAK TO John Tighe.
Member of BAFRA.

PAUL WINSTANLEY
213 Devizes Road, Salisbury, **Wiltshire
SP2 9LT**
TEL   0722 337383
OPEN   8.30–5.30 Mon–Fri.

Specialise in restoring antique furniture, particularly marquetry and veneers.

PROVIDE Home Inspections. Free Estimates. Chargeable Collection/Delivery Service.
SPEAK TO Paul Winstanley.

NIDD HOUSE ANTIQUES
Nidd House, Bogs Lane, Harrogate, **North Yorkshire HG1 4DY**
TEL   0423 884739
OPEN   9–5 Mon–Fri or By
        Appointment.

Specialise in restoring furniture and upholstery, cane and rush seats, leaf and powder gilding, gesso work, inlay.

PROVIDE Home Inspections. Free Local Estimates. Chargeable Collection/Delivery Service.
SPEAK TO Mr D. Preston.

Member of the Guild of Master Craftsmen and UKIC. This workshop is included on the register of conservators maintained by the Conservation Unit of the Museums and Galleries Commission.
SEE Collectors (Scientific Instruments), Porcelain, Silver.

T. L. PHELPS
8 Mornington Terrace, Harrogate, **North Yorkshire HG1 5DH**
TEL   0423 524604
OPEN   8.30–6 Mon–Fri or By
        Appointment.

Specialise in restoring fine English and Continental furniture.

PROVIDE Home Inspections. Free

Estimates. Chargeable Collection/Delivery Service.
SPEAK TO Timothy Phelps.
Member of BAFRA.

ANDREW G. PODMORE & SON
49A East Mount Road, York, **North Yorkshire YO2 2BD**
TEL   0904 627717
OPEN   8.30–5 Mon–Fri.

Specialise in restoring antique furniture, French polishing and upholstery.

PROVIDE Home Inspections. Free Estimates. Free/Chargeable Collection/Delivery Service.
SPEAK TO David Podmore.

G. SHAW RESTORATIONS
Jansville, Quarry Lane, New Park, Harrogate, **North Yorkshire HG1 3HR**
TEL   0423 503590
OPEN   7–6 Mon–Fri or By
        Appointment.

Specialise in restoring antique furniture and copying furniture to customers' requirements.

PROVIDE Home Inspections. Free Estimates.
SPEAK TO G. or M. G. S. Shaw.

DOVETAIL RESTORATIONS
112–114 London Road, Sheffield, **South Yorkshire S2 4LR**
TEL   0742 700273
OPEN   9–4.30 Mon–Sat.

Specialise in restoring furniture, including French polishing and stripping by hand.

PROVIDE Home Inspections. Free Estimates. Free Collection/Delivery Service.
SPEAK TO Darren Beedle.

JULIE GODDARD ANTIQUES

7–9 Langsett Road South,
Oughtibridge, Sheffield,
South Yorkshire S30 3GY
TEL   0742 862261
OPEN   By Appointment; closed Wed.

Specialise in restoring antique furniture.

PROVIDE Home Inspections. Free
Estimates. Chargeable
Collection/Delivery Service.
SPEAK TO Julie Goddard.

A. E. JAMESON & CO.

257 Glossop Road, Sheffield, **South
Yorkshire S10 2GZ**
TEL   0742 723846
OPEN   8–6 Mon–Fri; 9.30–5 Sat.

Specialise in restoring Georgian and
Victorian furniture.

PROVIDE Home Inspections. Chargeable
Estimates. Free Collection/Delivery
Service.
SPEAK TO Mr Jameson.
Established 1883.

NEIL TRINDER

Burrowlee House, Broughton Road,
Sheffield, **South Yorkshire S6 2AS**
TEL   0742 852428
OPEN   9–5 Mon–Fri.

Specialise in restoring furniture,
woodwork, Boulle work, marquetry,
carving and gilding.

PROVIDE Home Inspections. Free
Estimates. Chargeable
Collection/Delivery Service.
SPEAK TO Neil Trinder.

Member of UKIC and BAFRA. This
workshop is included on the register of
conservators maintained by the
Conservation Unit of the Museums and
Galleries Commission.

J. H. COOPER & SON (ILKLEY) LTD

33–35 Church Street, Ilkley, **West
Yorkshire LS29 9DR**
TEL   0943 608020
OPEN   9–1, 2–5.30 Mon–Sat.

Specialise in restoration of antique
furniture and works of art.

PROVIDE Home Inspections. Free
Estimates. Free Collection/Delivery
Service.
SPEAK TO Charles Cooper Jr.

GEARY ANTIQUES

114 Richardshaw Lane, Pudsey, Leeds,
West Yorkshire LS28 6BN
TEL   0532 564122
OPEN   10–5.30 Mon–Sat; closed Wed.

Specialise in conserving and restoring
furniture and upholstery and allied skills.

PROVIDE Home Inspections. Free
Estimates. Free Collection/Delivery
Service.
SPEAK TO J. A. Geary.

RODNEY FARMER KEMBLE

16 Crag Vale Terrace, Glusburn, Nr.
Keighley, **West Yorkshire BD20 8QU**
TEL   0535 636954 or 633702
OPEN   8.30–5.30 Mon–Fri, 8.30–12
Sat or By Appointment.

Specialise in all aspects of furniture
restoration and finishing, including
upholstery and cabinet repairs.

PROVIDE Home Inspections. Free
Estimates. Free Collection/Delivery
Service.
SPEAK TO Rodney Kemble.

Member of BAFRA.

THE SCAGLIOLA COMPANY

Chapeltown Business Centre, 231
Chapeltown Road, Leeds, **West Yorkshire LS7 3DX**
TEL   0532 626811
FAX   0532 625448
OPEN 9–5 Mon–Fri.

Specialise in restoring scagliola
(traditional marble-finish based on a
plaster recipe) on table surfaces, columns,
pedestals, panels, floors and inlays.

PROVIDE Home Inspections. Free
Estimates. Chargeable
Collection/Delivery Service.
SPEAK TO Michael Koumbouzis.

This workshop is included on the register
of conservators maintained by the
Conservation Unit of the Museums and
Galleries Commission.

THOMAS H. KEARNEY AND SONS

Treasure House Antiques, 123
University Street, Belfast, **Co. Antrim BT7 1HP.**
TEL   0232 231055
OPEN 8–6 Mon–Fri.

Specialise in restoring antique furniture
of all types, upholstery, polishing.

PROVIDE Home Inspections. Free
Estimates.
SPEAK TO Thomas Kearney.

FIONA CHICHESTER-CLARK

186 Loughgall Road, Portadown,
Craigavon, **Co. Armagh BT62 4EQ**
TEL   0762 335848
OPEN 8–5 Mon–Fri.

Specialise in restoring antique English
and Irish furniture and cane seating.

PROVIDE Home Inspections. Free
Estimates. Free Collection
Delivery/Service.
SPEAK TO Fiona Chichester-Clark.

MARION CAFFERKEY-BYRNE

Deerfield, Paulville, Tullow, **Co. Carlow**
TEL   0503 51750
OPEN By Appointment.

Specialise in restoring gilding on mirror
frames.

PROVIDE Home Inspections. Free
Estimates. Chargeable
Collection/Delivery Service.
SPEAK TO Marion Cafferkey.
Member of IPCRA and IGS.
SEE Picture Frames.

PATRICK CABOURNE-BASSET

The Farm House, Sarsfield's Court,
Glanmire, **Co. Cork**
TEL   021 821076
OPEN By Appointment.

Specialise in restoring Georgian and
Victorian furniture and some Boulle
repairs.

PROVIDE Home Inspections. Free
Estimates.
SPEAK TO Member of IPCRA.

T. J. MITCHELL LTD

4 Lower Pembroke Street, Dublin 2,
Co. Dublin
TEL   01 766881
OPEN 9–12.45, 2–5.30 Mon–Fri.

Specialise in restoring English and Irish
furniture.

PROVIDE Home Inspections. Refundable
Estimates. Collection/Delivery Service
by arrangement.
SPEAK TO Tommy Mitchell.

JENNY SLEVIN
China Restoration Studio, Monkstown,
Co. Dublin
TEL   01 280 3429
OPEN   By Appointment.

Specialise in restoring lacquerwork on screens, furniture, boxes. Will also clean and repair mirror frames.

PROVIDE Home Inspections.
Free/Chargeable Estimates.
Collection/Delivery Service by arrangement.
SPEAK TO Jenny Slevin.

Member of IPCRA.
SEE Carpets, Porcelain, Picture Frames, Collectors (Wax).

GLEBE STUDIO
Straffan, **Co. Kildare**
TEL   01 6271129
OPEN   10–4 Mon–Fri.

Specialise in restoring water and oil gilded mirror frames and furniture.

PROVIDE Chargeable Home Inspections.
Free Estimates. Collection/Delivery at Automobile Club, Dublin.
SPEAK TO Phillipa Hynde, Dominique Synott or Esen Philcox.

Member of IPCRA and UKIC.
SEE Porcelain, Picture Frames.

SUSAN MULHALL
Blackwood, Robertstown, Naas,
Co. Kildare
TEL   045 60336
OPEN   By Appointment.

Specialise in restoring furniture and mirror frames, including gilding and gessowork.

PROVIDE Home Inspections.
Free/Chargeable Estimates.
Collection/Delivery Service by arrangement.

SPEAK TO Susan Mulhall.
Member of IPCRA.
SEE Picture Frames.

WLODEK SZUSTKIEWICZ
Stacumny House, Celbridge,
Co. Kildare
TEL   01 628 8345 ex. 10
OPEN   By Appointment.

Specialise in restoring brown wood furniture and mirror frames, including carving and gilding, gesso work.

PROVIDE Home Inspections. Free Estimates. Free Collection/Delivery Service.
SPEAK TO Wlodek Szustkiewicz.

Member of IPCRA.
SEE Picture Frames.

KARL AND CLAIRE DAVENPORT
Kilbrook, Enfield, **Co. Meath**
TEL   0405 41214
OPEN   By Appointment.

Specialise in restoring good antique furniture, including marquetry, inlay, wood-carving.

PROVIDE Home Inspections.
Free/Chargeable Estimates. Chargeable Collection/Delivery Service.
SPEAK TO Karl or Claire Davenport.
Member of IPCRA.

EMILY NAPER
Loughcrew, Oldcastle, **Co. Meath**
TEL   049 41356
FAX   049 41722
OPEN   By Appointment.

Specialise in restoring water and oil gilded mirror frames and gilt furniture, gesso painted finishes and marbling.

PROVIDE Home Inspections. Free

Estimates. Chargeable Local
Collection/Delivery Service.
SPEAK TO Emily Naper.
Member of IPCRA.
SEE Picture Frames.

ANNE HYLAND
Beechmount, Roscrea, **Co. Tipperary**
TEL   0503 22310
OPEN   By Appointment.

Specialise in conserving gilded furniture
and mirror frames, including oil and
water gilding, eglomisé, gessowork.

PROVIDE Home Inspections. Free
Estimates. Chargeable
Collection/Delivery Service.
SPEAK TO Anne Hyland.
Member of IPCRA.
SEE Picture Frames.

VALERIE McCOY
Fan-na-Greine, Glendalough,
Co. Wicklow
TEL   0404 45125
OPEN   By Appointment.

Specialise in restoring and gilding
mirror frames.

PROVIDE Home Inspections.
Free/Chargeable Estimates. Free
Collection/Delivery Service.
SPEAK TO Valerie McCoy.
Member of IPCRA.
SEE Porcelain, Picture Frames.

ST JAMES'S GALLERY LTD
Smith Street, St Peter Port, **Guernsey,
Channel Islands**
TEL   0481 720070
OPEN   9–5.30 Mon–Sat or By
         Appointment.

Specialise in restoring 18th and 19th
century English and Continental
furniture, Edwardian furniture.

PROVIDE Home Inspections. Chargeable

Estimates. Collection/Delivery Service
by arrangement.
SPEAK TO Mrs Whittam.
SEE Clocks, Porcelain.

CHISHOLME ANTIQUES
5 Orrock Place, Hawick, **Borders**
TD9 0HQ
TEL   0450 76928
OPEN   9–6 Mon–Fri.

Specialise in restoring antique furniture,
including veneering, tortoiseshell, ivory,
gilding and composition work, rush
seating, caning and upholstery.

PROVIDE Home Inspections. Free
Estimates. Chargeable
Collection/Delivery Service.
SPEAK TO Mr Roberts.
SEE Carpets.

GRANT LEES
98 Gala Park, Galashiels, Selkirkshire,
Borders TD1 1EZ
TEL   0896 3721
OPEN   9–6 Mon–Sat, closed Wed and
         Sat a.m.

Specialise in restoring old and antique
locks.

PROVIDE Home Inspections. Free
Estimates. Chargeable
Collection/Delivery Service.
SPEAK TO Grant Lees.
This workshop is in the Scottish
Conservation Directory.
SEE Clocks, Collectors (Mechanical
Music).

LYNWOOD REPRODUCTIONS
Lynwood, Eskdalemuir, Langholm,
Dumfriesshire, **Dumfries & Galloway**
DG13 0QH
TEL   03873 73211
OPEN   9–6 Mon–Fri.

Specialise in restoring carved and gilded

wood furniture and frames. They also have the facility to make copies of most wood-carvings and can undertake gilding of any sort.

PROVIDE Home Inspections. Free Estimates. Chargeable Collection/Delivery Service.
SPEAK TO John or Nancy Chinnery.

Member of SSCR and the Guild of Master Craftsmen.
SEE Picture Frames.

JUDITH A. LIVINGSTON
Willowbrae, 3 Pittenweem Road, Anstruther, **Fife KY10 3DS**
TEL   0333 310 425
OPEN   By Appointment.

Specialise in restoring antique furniture, veneering, French polishing, carving and mouldings.

PROVIDE Home Inspections. Free/Chargeable Estimates.
SPEAK TO Judith Livingston.

Member of SSCR. This workshop is in the Scottish Conservation Directory.

JOHN McWILLIAM BEATON
16 Fingal Place, Portree, Isle of Skye, **Highland IV51 9ND**
TEL   0478 3290
OPEN   By appointment.

Specialise in restoring furniture, including wood-carving such as making replica pieces and pieces from photographs.

PROVIDE Home Inspections. Free Estimates. Chargeable Collection/Delivery Service.
SPEAK TO Ian Beaton.
Member of SSCR. This workshop is in the Scottish Conservation Directory.

PETER DAVIS
Unit 5, Glen Nevis Place, Fort William, **Highland PH33 6DA**
TEL   0397 704039
OPEN   8–5 Mon–Fri.

Specialise in handmade furniture and furniture repair and restoration, wood-turning.

PROVIDE Home Inspections. Free Estimates. Chargeable Collection/Delivery Service.
SPEAK TO Peter Davis.

GILES PEARSON
Brightmony House, Auldern, **Highland IV12 5HZ**
TEL   0667 55550
OPEN   9–6 Daily.

Specialise in rush and cane work for chairs, stools and bergère suites.

PROVIDE Home Inspections. Free Estimates. Collection/Delivery Service by arrangement.
SPEAK TO Giles Pearson.

This workshop is in the Scottish Conservation Directory.
SEE Silver.

STABLE WORKSHOP
Foddalty by Dingwall, **Highland IV15 9UE**
TEL   0997 21606
OPEN   9–5 Mon–Sat.

Specialise in restoring antique furniture and will make furniture on commission.

PROVIDE Chargeable Estimates. Free Local Collection/Delivery Service.
SPEAK TO Dennis Manson.

LUIGI M. VILLANI
Traditional Antique Restoration and Consultancy Service, The Stable, Altyre, Forres, **Highland IV36 0SH**
TEL   0309 672572
OPEN   8 a.m.–10 p.m. Mon–Fri.

Specialise in repair and restoration of antique furniture, frames and fittings, including marquetry (structural, inlay and finish), marble (furniture and fittings).

PROVIDE Home Inspections. Estimates. SPEAK TO Luigi M. Villani or Rosalie Stuart.
Run a consultancy and training service on restoration, wood stains and finishes and also give lectures.
SEE Porcelain.

G. A. WHITE
High Street, Nairn, **Highland IV12 4QD**
TEL   0667 52201
FAX   0667 56033
OPEN   9–5.30 Mon–Fri.

Specialise in restoring antique furniture and upholstery.

PROVIDE Home Inspections. Free Estimates. Chargeable Collection/Delivery Service.
SPEAK TO W. G. White.

CAROL CARSTAIRS
67 George Street, Edinburgh, **Lothian EH2 2JG**
TEL   031 220 3931
OPEN   9.30–6 Mon–Fri or By Appointment.

Specialise in conservation and restoration of gilding on furniture and architectural projects plus carving and lacquer work.

PROVIDE Home Inspections. Free Local Estimates. Chargeable Collection/Delivery Service.
SPEAK TO Carol Carstairs.

Member of SSCR. This workshop is in the Scottish Conservation Directory.

PAUL COUTS LTD
Linkfield House, 8–10 High Street, Musselburgh, **Lothian EH21 7BN**
TEL   031 665 7759
FAX   031 665 0836
OPEN   9–5 Mon–Fri; Sat a.m. By Appointment.

Specialise in conserving and restoring fine English furniture.

PROVIDE Home Inspections. Free/Chargeable Estimates. Chargeable Collection/Delivery Service.
SPEAK TO Julian Labarre.

This workshop is in the Scottish Conservation Directory.

ANSELM FRASER
The Carthouse, Crauchie, East Linton, **Lothian EH40 3EB**
TEL   0620 860067
OPEN   9–4.30 Mon–Fri.

Specialise in restoring antique furniture, including veneer repairs, wood-carving and turning, Boulle and marquetry work, inlays, gilding, gesso mouldings, grain simulation, metal repairs, French polishing, simple upholstery, carcase repairs.

PROVIDE Home Inspections. Free Estimates. Free/Chargeable Collection/Delivery Service.
SPEAK TO Anselm Fraser.

This workshop is in the Scottish Conservation Directory.

J. & J. HARDIE ANTIQUES LTD
222–224 Newhaven Road, Edinburgh, **Lothian EH6 4JY**
TEL   031 552 7080
OPEN   8.30–5.30 Mon–Fri; 9–4.30 Sat.

Specialise in restoring all periods of fine furniture up to 1930s, including Continental pieces.

PROVIDE Home Inspections. Free

Estimates. Chargeable
Collection/Delivery Service.
This workshop is in the Scottish
Conservation Directory.

BARBARA HOPE
5 Barclay Terrace, Edinburgh, **Lothian
EH10 4HP**
TEL   031 445 3606
FAX   031 445 3606
OPEN   By Appointment.

Specialise in restoring giltwood
furnishing with especial interest in verre
eglomisé and simulated finishes.

PROVIDE Home Inspections.
Free/Chargeable Estimates.
SPEAK TO Barbara Hope.
Member of UKIC and SSCR. This
workshop is in the Scottish Conservation
Directory.

HOUNDWOOD ANTIQUES RESTORATION
7 West Preston Street, Edinburgh,
Lothian EH8 9PX
TEL   031 667 3253
OPEN   By Appointment.

Specialise in restoring antique furniture.

PROVIDE Home Inspections. Free
Estimates. Chargeable
Collection/Delivery Service.
SPEAK TO Mr A Gourlay.
SEE Porcelain, Silver.

W. R. MARTIN
Bowden Springs Fishery, Linlithgow,
Lothian EH49 6QE
TEL   0506 847269
OPEN   9–5 Daily or By Appointment.

Specialise in restoring solid wood
furniture and objects. They also make
copies and specialise in designs by Charles
Rennie Mackintosh.

PROVIDE Home Inspections. Free

Estimates. Chargeable
Collection/Delivery Service.
SPEAK TO Wil Martin.
This workshop is in the Scottish
Conservation Directory.

TRIST & McBAIN
9 Cannongate Venture, New Street,
Edinburgh, **Lothian EH8 8VH**
TEL   031 557 3828
OPEN   8.30–5.30 Mon–Fri; By
        Appointment Sat.

Specialise in conserving and restoring
period furniture, including Boulle,
marquetry, wood-turning, French
polishing. They also do cane and rush
seating and desk leathers.

PROVIDE Home Inspections. Free
Estimates. Free Collection/Delivery
Service.
SPEAK TO William Trist or Andrew
McBain.
This workshop is in the Scottish
Conservation Directory.

WHYTOCK & REID
Sunbury House, Belford Mews,
Edinburgh, **Lothian EH4 3DN**
TEL   031 226 4911
FAX   031 226 4595
OPEN   9–5.30 Mon–Fri; 9–12.30 Sat.

Specialise in restoring 18th and 19th
century furniture, re-upholstery,
polishing and gilding.

PROVIDE Home Inspections. Free
Estimates. Collection/Delivery Service
available.
SPEAK TO David Reid.
This workshop is in the Scottish
Conservation Directory.
SEE Carpets.

DAPHNE FRASER
Glenbarry, 58 Victoria Road, Lenzie,
Glasgow, **Strathclyde G66 5AP**
TEL   041 776 1281
OPEN   By Appointment.

Specialise in restoring ornate mirror frames.

PROVIDE Free Estimates.
SPEAK TO Daphne Fraser.
This workshop is in the Scottish Conservation Directory.
SEE Collectors (Dolls; Toys), Oil Paintings, Picture Frames.

ROBERT HOWIE AND SON
19 High Street, Mauchline, **Strathclyde**
TEL 0290 50556
OPEN 8–5 Mon–Fri.

Specialise in restoring painted furniture, specialised finishes.

PROVIDE Home Inspections. Free Estimates. Chargeable Collection/Delivery Service.
SPEAK TO Robert Howie.
This workshop is in the Scottish Conservation Directory.

PIERS KETTLEWELL CABINETMAKERS
10 Robertson Street, Barrhead, **Strathclyde G78 1QW**
TEL 041 881 8166
OPEN By Appointment.

Specialise in restoring antique furniture and making furniture to commission.

PROVIDE Home Inspections. Free Estimates. Collection/Delivery Service by arrangement.
SPEAK TO Piers Kettlewell.
This workshop is in the Scottish Conservation Directory.

FRAN MALLOY
Suite 1, 66 Dora Street, Glasgow, **Strathclyde G40 4DP**
TEL 041 551 0616
OPEN 8.30–6 Mon–Sat.

Specialise in restoring antique furniture of all periods.

PROVIDE Home Inspections.
Free/Chargeable Estimates.
Free/Chargeable Collection/Delivery Service.
SPEAK TO Fran Malloy.
This workshop is in the Scottish Conservation Directory.

THE OLD CURIOSITY SHOP
27–29 Crown Street, Ayr, **Strathclyde KA8 8AG**
TEL 0292 280222
OPEN 8–5 Mon–Fri; 10–4 Sat.

Specialise in restoring antique furniture, repairs, re-upholstery and polishing. Also manufacture hand made furniture.

PROVIDE Home Inspections. Refundable Estimates. Free Collection/Delivery Service locally.
SPEAK TO Brian Kelly.
This workshop is in the Scottish Conservation Directory.

GREYCROFT ANTIQUES
Station Road, Errol, **Tayside PH2 7SN**
TEL 0821 642221
OPEN 11–5 Mon–Sat.

Specialise in restoring pre-1840 furniture sympathetically.

PROVIDE Home Inspections. Refundable Estimates.
SPEAK TO David or June Pickett.

KINGS OF KINBUCK
Old Mill, Kinbuck, **Tayside FK15 0NQ**
TEL 0786 822915
FAX 0786 822915
OPEN 10–5 Mon–Fri; 10–2 Sat.

Specialise in restoring upholstered items, including chaises longues, Victorian and Edwardian sofas and chairs.

PROVIDE Free Estimates. Free Collection/Delivery Service.
SPEAK TO Hilda King.

NEIL LIVINGSTONE
3 Old Hawkhill, Dundee, **Tayside
DD1 5EU**
TEL   0382 21751
OPEN   9–5 Mon–Fri.

Specialise in restoring antique furniture and wood-carving.

PROVIDE Free Estimates. Chargeable Collection/Delivery Service.
SPEAK TO Neil Livingstone.
SEE Arms, Oil Paintings, Picture Frames, Silver.

IRENA ANTIQUES
111 Broad Street, Barry, **South
Glamorgan CF6 8SX**
TEL   0446 747626 or 732517
OPEN   10–4 Mon–Fri.

Specialise in restoring antique furniture, including painted and lacquer work. Their specialist service includes trompe l'oeil, marbling, gold leaf and gilding and painting of Pontypool tin ware.

PROVIDE Free Estimates. Free Collection/Delivery Service.
SPEAK TO Irena Halabuda.

Mrs Halabuda is a specialist in painted work in the manner of Angelica Kaufmann.
SEE Porcelain.

SNOWDONIA ANTIQUES
Station Road, Llanrwst, **Gwynedd
LL26 QEP**
TEL   0492 640789
OPEN   9–5.30 Mon–Sat or By Appointment.

Specialise in restoring period furniture.

PROVIDE Home Inspections. Chargeable Estimates. Chargeable Collection/Delivery Service.
SPEAK TO Mr J. Collins.
SEE Clocks.

CLOCKS, WATCHES, BAROMETERS

DO

Identify weights when moving longcase clocks so that they can go back on the same pulley
Allow hours to strike when moving hands forward
Use wax polish, not silicon sprays, on wooden cases
Keep fitted boxes for clocks and watches, as this can enhance resale value
For insurance purposes, keep a photograph and details such as serial numbers of all clocks and watches you own

DON'T

Turn hands backwards
Move any clock without securing or removing the pendulum
Clean carriage clocks or gilt cases with metal polish
Clean brass inlay on wood with metal polish
Touch silvered chapter rings – fingermarks may result

THE BAROMETER SHOP
2 Lower Park Row, Bristol, **Avon**
BS1 5BJ
TEL   0272 272565
OPEN   9–5.30 Mon, Wed, Fri; 9–1 Sat.

Specialise in restoring barometers and
clocks.

PROVIDE Home Inspections. Free
Estimates. Free Collection/Delivery
Service.
SPEAK TO Mrs Honey.
SEE Furniture, Collectors (Scientific
Instruments).

D. J. DAVIS
13 Castle Street, Thornbury, Bristol,
Avon BS12 1HA
TEL   0454 412430
OPEN   By Appointment.

Specialise in restoring clock cases,
including wood-turning, locks, some
metalwork and clock movement repairs.
All aspects of cleaning, polishing and
finishing covered.

PROVIDE Home Inspections. Free
Estimates. Free Local
Collection/Delivery Service.
SPEAK TO David Davis.
Mr Davis is a member of the Guild of
Master Craftsmen and a director of the
local museum.
SEE Furniture.

JOHN AND CAROL HAWLEY
'The Orchard', Clevedon Lane, Clapton
Wick, Clevedon, **Avon BS21 7AG**
TEL   0275 852052
OPEN   By Appointment.

Specialise in repairing and restoring all
types of antique clocks. Do not
undertake watches.

PROVIDE Home Inspections. Free Local
Estimates. Free Collection/Delivery
Service.
SPEAK TO John or Carol Hawley.
They are CMBHI and MBWCG.

ASHLEY ANTIQUES AND FURNITURE
129 High Street, Hungerford, **Berkshire**
RG17 0DL
TEL   0488 682771
OPEN   10–1, 2–5 Mon–Fri; 11–1, 2–5
       Sat.

Specialise in restoring clocks.

PROVIDE Home Inspections. Free
Estimates. Free Local
Collection/Delivery Service.
SPEAK TO Robert Duff.

SEE Furniture.

D. N. CARD
1A Chester Street, Caversham, Reading,
Berkshire RG4 8JH
TEL   0734 470777
OPEN   9–12.30, 2–5 Mon–Fri or By
       Appointment.

Specialise in restoring antique clocks,
watches and barometers.

PROVIDE Home Inspections. Free
Estimates. Chargeable
Collection/Delivery Service.
SPEAK TO David Card.

Mr Card is CMBHI. This workshop is
included on the register of conservators
maintained by the Conservation Unit of
the Museums and Galleries Commission.
SEE Collectors (Mechanical Music).

THE CLOCK WORKSHOP
17 Prospect Street, Caversham, Reading,
Berkshire RG4 8JB
TEL   0734 470741
FAX   0734 474194
OPEN   9.30–5.30 Mon–Fri; 10–1 Sat.

Specialise in restoring antique clocks,
including grande-sonnerie striking, pull
quarter repeating and chronometers.
They also restore barometers.

PROVIDE Home Inspections. Free Estimates. Collection/Delivery Service by arrangement.
SPEAK TO John Yealland FBHI.

HAMILTON HAVERS
58 Conisboro Avenue, Caversham Heights, Reading, **Berkshire RG4 7JE**
TEL   0734 473379
OPEN   By Appointment.

Specialise in restoring Boulle, marquetry, ivory, tortoiseshell, mother-of-pearl, brass, lapis lazuli and malachite on clock-cases.

PROVIDE Free/Chargeable Estimates.
SPEAK TO Hamilton Havers.
SEE Furniture, Silver.

S. J. BIRT & SON
21 Windmill Street, Brill, Aylesbury, **Buckinghamshire HP18 9TG**
TEL   0844 237440
OPEN   By Appointment.

Specialise in restoring clocks, barometers and tower clocks.

PROVIDE Home Inspections. Free Estimates. Free Collection/Delivery Service.
SPEAK TO Mr S. J. Birt.
SEE Collectors (Mechanical Music).

CHESS ANTIQUE RESTORATIONS
85 Broad Street, Chesham, **Buckinghamshire HP5 3EF**
TEL   0494 783043
FAX   0494 791302
OPEN   8–5 Mon–Sat.

Specialise in restoration of clocks.

PROVIDE Home Inspections. Chargeable Estimates. Chargeable Collection/Delivery Service.
SPEAK TO T. F. Chapman.
SEE Furniture, Oil Paintings.

HERITAGE RESTORATIONS
36B High Street, Great Missenden, **Buckinghamshire HP16 OAU**
TEL   02406 5710
OPEN   10–5 Mon–Sat.

Specialise in restoring clocks and watches.

PROVIDE Free Estimates. Home Inspections.
SPEAK TO John Wilshire.
SEE Furniture, Porcelain.

ALAN MARTIN
Farthing Cottage, Clickers Yard, Yardley Road, Olney, **Buckinghamshire MK46 5DX**
TEL   0234 712446
OPEN   9–5 Mon–Sat; Sun By Appointment.

Specialise in repairing antique clocks and pocket watches.

PROVIDE Home Inspections. Free/Chargeable Estimates. Free Collection/Delivery Service.
SPEAK TO Alan Martin.

Mr Martin is MBHI and a Member of the Clock and Watchmakers' Guild.

TINGEWICK ANTIQUES CENTRE
Main Street, Tingewick, **Buckinghamshire MK18 4PB**
TEL   0280 847922
OPEN   10.30–5 Mon–Sat; 11–5 Sun.

Specialise in restoring metalware on clocks.

PROVIDE Home Inspections. Free Estimates. Collection/Delivery Service by arrangement.
SPEAK TO Rosemarie or Barry Smith.
SEE Furniture.

DODDINGTON HOUSE ANTIQUES

2 Benwick Road, Doddington, Nr. March, **Cambridgeshire PE15 OTG**

TEL   0354 740755
OPEN   10–6 Mon–Sat.

Specialise in restoring clock-cases and barometers.

PROVIDE Refundable Estimates. Free Collection/Delivery Service.
SPEAK TO Brian or Lynette Frankland.
SEE Furniture.

A.F.DUDLEY trading as 'THE FURNITURE CLINIC'.

Vine House, Reach, **Cambridgeshire CB5 OJD**

TEL   0638 741989
FAX   0638 743239
OPEN   By Appointment.

Specialise in restoring barometers and clocks.

PROVIDE Home Inspections. Free Estimates. Free Collection/Delivery Service.
SPEAK TO Mr A. Dudley.

Members of the Guild of Master Craftsmen and the Association of Master Upholsterers.
SEE Collectors (Dolls, Toys, Mechanical Music), Furniture.

PETER JOHN

38 St Mary's Street, Eyresbury, St Neots, **Cambridgeshire PE19 2TA**

TEL   0480 216297
OPEN   9–5 Mon–Sat.

Specialise in restoring antique English and French clocks.

PROVIDE Home Inspections. Free Estimates. Chargeable Collection/Delivery Service.
SPEAK TO Kym or Peter John.
SEE Silver.

A. ALLEN ANTIQUE RESTORERS

Buxton Rd, Newtown, Newmills, Via Stockport, **Cheshire SK12 3JS**

TEL   0663 745274
OPEN   8–5 Mon–Fri; 9–12 Sat.

Specialise in designing and copying clocks.

PROVIDE Home Inspections. Free/Chargeable Estimates. Collection/Delivery Service.
SPEAK TO Tony Allen.

SEE Furniture, Picture Frames, Silver.

PETER D. BOSSON

10B Swan St, Wilmslow, **Cheshire SK9 1HE**

TEL   0625 525250 and 527857
OPEN   10–12.45, 2.15–5 Tues–Sat.

Specialise in restoring barographs, barometers, clocks.

PROVIDE Home Inspections. Free Estimates. Free Local Collection/Delivery Service.
SPEAK TO Peter Bosson.

SEE Collectors (Scientific Instruments).

COPPELIA ANTIQUES

Holford Lodge, Plumley Moor Road, Plumley, **Cheshire WA16 9RS**

TEL   0565 722197
OPEN   By Appointment.

Specialise in restoring longcase and other clocks.

PROVIDE Home Inspections and Estimates by arrangement. Chargeable Collection/Delivery Service.
SPEAK TO K. R. Clements.

SEE Furniture.

MILL FARM ANTIQUES
50 Market Street, Disley, Stockport, **Cheshire SK12 2DT**
TEL   0663 764045
OPEN   9–6 Mon–Sat.

Specialise in restoring antique clocks and barometers.

PROVIDE Home Inspections. Free Estimates. Free Collection/Delivery Service.
SPEAK TO F. E. Berry.
SEE Collectors (Mechanical Music).

DEREK RAYMENT ANTIQUES
Orchard House, Barton Road, Barton, Nr. Farndon, **Cheshire SY14 7HT**
TEL   0829 270 429
OPEN   By Appointment.

Specialise in repairing and restoring antique barometers.

PROVIDE Home Inspections. Free Estimates.
SPEAK TO Derek or Tina Rayment.
Member of BADA.

THE OLD MAN ANTIQUES
Coniston, **Cumbria LA21 8DU**
TEL   05394 41389
OPEN   9.30–5.30 Daily from Easter to 5 November. Phone calls advised during winter months.

Specialise in repairing and restoring wheel (mercury) barometers.
SPEAK TO Ron or Yvonne Williams.

JOHN M. PENDLEBURY
4 Meadow Grove, Grange-over-Sands, **Cumbria LA11 7AT**
TEL   05395 35201
OPEN   9–5 Mon–Fri By Appointment Only.

Specialise in restoring clocks and barometers.

PROVIDE Home Inspections. Free Local Estimates. Free Collection/Delivery Service.
SPEAK TO John M. Pendlebury.
Mr Pendlebury is MBHI.

DERBYSHIRE CLOCKS
104 High Street West, Glossop, **Derbyshire SK13 8BB**
TEL   0457 862677
OPEN   1–5 Mon–Sat, closed Tues; 1–4.30 Sun.

Specialise in restoring antique clocks and barometers.

PROVIDE Home Inspections. Refundable Estimates. Free Collection/Delivery Service.
SPEAK TO Terence Peter Lees.

D. W. & J. E. FODDY
Derby Antique Centre, 11 Friargate, Derby, **Derbyshire DE1 1BU**
TEL   0332 385002
OPEN   10–5.30 Mon–Sat.

Specialise in restoring antique clock-cases.

PROVIDE Home Inspections. Chargeable Estimates. Free Collection/Delivery.
SPEAK TO Mr Foddy.
SEE Furniture.

C. REYNOLDS
The Spindles, Tonge, Melbourne, **Derbyshire DE7 1BD**
TEL   0332 862609 and 0836 752602
OPEN   By Appointment.

Specialise in restoring verge movement watches 1780–1880.

PROVIDE Home Inspections. Chargeable Estimates.
SPEAK TO Mr T. Reynolds.

JOHN SMITH & SONS
Midland Clock Works, 27 Queen Street, Derby, **Derbyshire DE1 3DY**
TEL   0332 45569
FAX   0332 290642
OPEN   8–5 Mon–Fri.

Specialise in restoring clocks and barometers, expert in longcase, bracket and case restoration.

PROVIDE Home Inspections. Free Estimates (in workshop). Chargeable Collection/Delivery Service.
SPEAK TO Mr David Higginbotham.

Mr Higginbotham is CMBHI. This workshop is included on the register of conservators maintained by the Conservation Unit of the Museums and Galleries Commission.

CLIVE AND LESLEY COBB
Newhouse Farm, Bratton Fleming, Barnstaple, **Devon EX31 4RT**
TEL   0598 710465
OPEN   9–5.30 Daily.

Specialise in restoring painted clock dials.

PROVIDE Home Inspections. Free Estimates. Chargeable Collection/Delivery Service.
SPEAK TO Clive Cobb.

Established over twenty years. Member of UKIC and the Guild of Master Craftsmen. This workshop is included on the register of conservators maintained by the Conservation Unit of the Museums and Galleries Commission.
SEE Furniture.

MERTON ANTIQUES
Quicksilver Barn, Merton, Okehampton, **Devon EX20 3DS**
TEL   08053 443
OPEN   8–5 Mon–Sat.

Specialise in restoring antique barometers.

PROVIDE Home Inspections by arrangement. Free Estimates. Chargeable Collection/Delivery Service.
SPEAK TO Philip Collins.

Member of BAFRA. This workshop is included on the register of conservators maintained by the Conservation Unit of the Museums and Galleries Commission.
SEE Furniture.

LAURIE PENMAN
Castle Workshop, 61 High Street, Totnes, **Devon TQ9 5PB**
TEL   0803 866344
OPEN   7a.m.–10p.m. Mon–Sat; By Appointment Sun.

Specialise in repairing and restoring clocks.

PROVIDE Home Inspections. Free Estimates.
SPEAK TO Laurie Penman.

Also provide workshop tuition and a correspondence course.

TEMPUS FUGIT
16C Fore Street, Shaldon, Teignmouth, **Devon TQ14 0DE**
TEL   0626 872752
OPEN   10–1, 2–5 Mon–Sat.

Specialise in repairing barometers, watches and clocks.

PROVIDE Home Inspections. Free Estimates. Usually Free Collection/Delivery Service.
SPEAK TO Roger Walkley.

Established 1982.

LAURENCE G. WOOTTON
2 Church Street, South Brent, **Devon TQ10 9AB**
TEL   0364 72553
OPEN   By Appointment (telephone between 9.30a.m.–12.30p.m.)

Specialise in repairing clocks and watches.

PROVIDE Home Inspections.
SPEAK TO Laurence Wootton.

MICHAEL BARRINGTON
The Old Rectory, Warmwell, Dorchester, **Dorset DT2 8HQ**
TEL   0305 852104
OPEN   By Appointment.

Specialise in restoring longcase clock-cases.

PROVIDE Free Estimates Locally.
Free/Chargeable Collection/Delivery Service.
SPEAK TO Michael Barrington.

Member of BAFRA.
SEE Collectors (Musical Instruments, Toys), Furniture.

THE CHETTLE GUILD
The Stables, Chettle House, Chettle, Blandford, **Dorset DT11 8DB**
TEL   0258 89576
OPEN   9–6 Mon–Sat.

Specialise in restoring clocks.

PROVIDE Home Inspections. Free Estimates. Free Local Collection/Delivery Service.
SPEAK TO Alastair or Andrew Arnold.

SEE Arms, Furniture, Collectors (Scientific Instruments).

D. J. JEWELLERY
166–168 Ashley Road, Parkstone, Poole, **Dorset BH14 9BY**
TEL   0202 745148
OPEN   9.30–5 Mon–Sat.

Specialise in repairing antique clocks.

PROVIDE Home Inspections. Free Estimates. Chargeable Collection/Delivery Service.
SPEAK TO Dennis O'Sullivan.

SEE Silver.

GOOD HOPE ANTIQUES
2 Hogshill Street, Beaminster, **Dorset DT8 3AE**
TEL   0308 862119
OPEN   9.30–5 Mon–Sat; closed Wed.

Specialise in restoring barometers and clocks, especially longcase, bracket and English wall clocks.

PROVIDE Chargeable Estimates.
Chargeable Collection/Delivery Service.
SPEAK TO David Beney.

TOLPUDDLE ANTIQUE RESTORERS
The Stables, Tolpuddle, Dorchester, **Dorset DT2 7HF**
TEL   0305 848739
OPEN   9–6 Mon–Fri; 12–5 Sat.

Specialise in restoring clocks and barometers.

PROVIDE Home Inspections. Free Estimates. Free Collection/Delivery Service.
Member of BAFRA.
SEE Furniture.

MAURICE YARHAM
Holly Cottage, Birdsmoorgate, Paynes Downe, Nr. Bridport, **Dorset DT6 5PL**
TEL   02977 377
OPEN   7–7 Mon–Fri.

Specialise in repairing, restoring and conserving antique clocks; particularly bracket and longcase clocks. Will also repair turret (stable) clocks.

PROVIDE Home Inspections. Free Estimates. Chargeable Collection/Delivery Service
SPEAK TO Maurice Yarham.

Mr Yarham is CMBHI.
SEE Collectors (Mechanical Music).

THE COLLECTOR
Douglas House, 23–25 The Bank,
Barnard Castle, **Durham DL12 8PH**
TEL   0833 37783
OPEN   10–5 or By Appointment.

Specialise in restoring clocks.

PROVIDE Home Inspections. Refundable
Estimates. Chargeable
Collection/Delivery Service.
SPEAK TO Robert Jordan or Paul Hunter.

Also provide a full design service.
SEE Furniture.

DAVID, JEAN & JOHN ANTIQUES
587 London Road, Westcliff, **Essex SS0 9PQ**
TEL   0702 339106
FAX   0268 560563
OPEN   10–5 Mon–Sat; closed Wed.

Specialise in clock and watch repairs.

PROVIDE Home Inspections. Refundable
Estimates. Free Collection/Delivery
Service.
SPEAK TO David Howard.

SEE Furniture.

LITTLEBURY ANTIQUES
58–60 Fairycroft Road, Saffron Walden,
Essex CB10 1LZ
TEL   0799 27961
FAX   0799 27961
OPEN   8.30–5.15 Mon–Fri; Sat By
        Appointment.

Specialise in restoring clocks and
barometers of all periods.

PROVIDE Home Inspections. Free
Estimates. Free/Chargeable
Collection/Delivery Service.
SPEAK TO N. H. D'Oyly.

SEE Furniture.

SMALLCOMBE CLOCKS
Gee House, Globe Industrial Estate,
Rectory Road, Grays, **Essex RM17 6ST**
TEL   0375 379980
FAX   0375 390286
OPEN   8.30–5 Mon–Fri.

Specialise in repairing and restoring
longcase clocks.

PROVIDE Home Inspections. Free
Estimates. Free/Chargeable
Collection/Delivery Service.
SPEAK TO Brett Smallcombe or Tony
Holland.

ANTONY PALMER ANTIQUES
169 St. Mary's Lane, Upminster, **Essex**
TEL   04022 26620
OPEN   9.30–5.30 Tues–Sat.

Specialise in repairing and restoring
Victorian clocks.

PROVIDE Home Inspections. Free
Estimates. Free/Chargeable
Collection/Delivery Service.
SPEAK TO Antony Palmer.
SEE Furniture.

KEITH BAWDEN
Mews Workshop, Montpellier Retreat,
Cheltenham, **Gloucestershire GL50 2XG**
TEL   0242 230320
OPEN   7–4.30 Mon–Fri.

Specialise in conserving and restoring
antique clocks.

PROVIDE Free Estimates. Home
Inspections. Local Collection/Delivery
Service.
SPEAK TO Keith Bawden.

SEE Furniture, Oil Paintings, Porcelain,
Silver.

WILLIAM COOK CABINETMAKER
Primrose Cottage, 11 Northfield Road, Tetbury, **Gloucestershire GL8 8HD**
TEL 0666 502877
OPEN 9–5 Mon–Fri.

Specialise in restoring clock-cases, including gilding.

PROVIDE Free Estimates.
SPEAK TO William or Ruth Cook.

KEITH HARDING'S WORLD OF MECHANICAL MUSIC
Oak House, High Street, Northleach, **Gloucestershire GL54 3EU**
TEL 0451 60181
FAX 0451 61133
OPEN 10–6 Daily.

Specialise in restoring clocks.

PROVIDE Home Inspections. Free Estimates. Free Local Collection/Delivery Service.
SPEAK TO Keith Harding.

SEE Collectors (Mechanical Music).

ANDREW LELLIOTT
6 Tetbury Hill, Avening, Tetbury, **Gloucestershire GL8 8LT**
TEL 045 383 5783
OPEN By Appointment.

Specialise in restoring 18th century English clock-cases.

PROVIDE Home Inspections. Free Estimates. Free Collection/Delivery Service.
SPEAK TO Andrew Lelliott.

Member of BAFRA. This workshop is included on the register of conservators maintained by the Conservation Unit of the Museums and Galleries Commission.
SEE Furniture.

BRYAN CLISBY ANTIQUE CLOCKS
Andwells Antiques, The Row, Hartley Wintney, **Hampshire RG27 8NY**
TEL 025126 2305
OPEN 9–5.30 Mon–Sat.

Specialise in restoring antique clocks and barometers.

PROVIDE Home Inspections. Free Estimates. Chargeable Collection/Delivery Service.
SPEAK TO Bryan Clisby.

EVANS AND EVANS
40 West Street, Alresford, **Hampshire SO24 9AU**
TEL 0962 732170
OPEN 9–1, 2–5 Fri–Sat; Mon–Thur By Appointment.

Specialise in restoring good English and French clocks.

PROVIDE Home Inspections. Refundable Estimates. Free Collection/Delivery Service.
SPEAK TO David or Noel Evans.

GERALD MARSH ANTIQUE CLOCKS LTD
32A The Square, Winchester, **Hampshire SO23 9EX**
TEL 0962 844443
OPEN 9.30–5 Mon–Sat.

Specialise in restoring antique English and French clocks, watches and barometers.

PROVIDE Home Inspections. Free Estimates. Free Collection/Delivery Service.
SPEAK TO Gerald Marsh.

Member of Worshipful Company of Clockmakers, Fellow of British Horological Institute, Member of NAWCC (USA) and BADA.
SEE **Oxfordshire**.

A. W. PORTER
High St, Hartley Wintney, Nr.
Basingstoke, **Hampshire RG27 8NY**
TEL   025 126 2676
FAX   025 126 2064
OPEN   9–5.30 Mon–Fri; 9.30–5 Sat.

Specialise in restoring antique clocks,
watches and barometers.

PROVIDE Home Inspections. Free
Estimates. Chargeable
Collection/Delivery Service.
SPEAK TO Mr Porter.

Established 1844.
SEE Silver.

J. A. PRADO (PRADO CABINETMAKER AND RESTORER)
Great Weir House, The Great Weir,
Alresford, **Hampshire SO24 9DB**
TEL   0962 732896
FAX   0962 734233
OPEN   By Arrangement.

Specialise in restoring English clock-
cases 1660 to 1815 with emphasis on
marquetry and brass inlay.

PROVIDE Home Inspections. Free
Estimates. Chargeable
Collection/Delivery Service.
SPEAK TO Mr J. A. Prado.

This workshop is included on the register
of conservators maintained by the
Conservation Unit of the Museums and
Galleries Commission.
SEE Furniture.

THE BAROMETER SHOP
4 New Street, Leominster, **Hereford & Worcester HR6 8BT**
TEL   0568 613652
OPEN   9–5.30 Mon–Sat, closed Wed.

Specialise in restoring barometers and
clocks.

PROVIDE Home Inspections. Free
Estimates. Free Collection/Delivery
Service.
SPEAK TO Richard Cookson.

Mr Cookson is CMBHI.
SEE Furniture, Collectors (Scientific
Instruments).

BEARWOOD MODELS
20 Westminster Road, Malvern Wells,
Hereford & Worcester WR14 4EF
TEL   0684 568977
OPEN   By Appointment.

Specialise in repairing and restoring old
clocks.

PROVIDE Free Estimates.
SPEAK TO R. W. Chester-Lamb.
SEE Collectors (Toys).

HANSEN CHARD ANTIQUES
126 High Street, Pershore, **Hereford & Worcester WR10 1EA**
TEL   0386 553423
OPEN   10–5 Tues, Wed, Fri, Sat or By
        Appointment.

Specialise in restoring clocks and
barometers.

PROVIDE Home Inspections. Free
Estimates. Free Local
Collection/Delivery Service.
SPEAK TO P. W. Ridler.

Member of BHI.

THE CLOCK SHOP
161 Victoria Street, St Albans,
Hertfordshire AL1 3TA
TEL   0727 56633
OPEN   10.30–6.30 Mon–Fri; 10.30–4
        Sat; closed Thur.

Specialise in restoring antique and
modern clocks, watches and barometers.

PROVIDE Free Estimates. Chargeable
Collection/Delivery Service.
SPEAK TO Mr P. E. Setterfield.

COUNTRY CLOCKS
3 Pendley Bridge Cottages, Tring Station, Tring, **Hertfordshire HP23 5QU**
TEL   044282 5090
OPEN   By Appointment.

Specialise in restoring antique clocks, including movements, dials and cases. No watch repairs.

PROVIDE Home Inspections. Free Estimates. Free Local Collection/Delivery Service.
SPEAK TO Terence Cartmell.

W. B. GATWARD & SON LTD
20 Market Place, Hitchin, **Hertfordshire SG5 1DU**
TEL   0462 434273
OPEN   9.15–5.15 Mon–Sat, closed Wed.

Specialise in repairing and restoring antique clocks and watches.

PROVIDE Local Home Inspections. Free Estimates. Chargeable Collection/Delivery Service.
Speak to Miss Gatward or Mr Hunter.
SEE Silver.

HOWARD ANTIQUE CLOCKS
33 Whitehorse Street, Baldock, **Hertfordshire SG7 6QF**
TEL   0462 892385
OPEN   9.30–5 Tues–Sat.

Specialise in restoring and repairing antique clocks.

PROVIDE Home Inspections. Free Estimates. Free Local Collection/Delivery Service.
SPEAK TO Mr D. Howard.

Mr Howard is CMBHI.

CHARLES PERRY RESTORATIONS LTD
Praewood Farm, Hemel Hempstead Road, St Albans, **Hertfordshire AL3 6AA**
TEL   0727 53487
FAX   0727 46668
OPEN   Mon–Fri 8.30–6; Sat By Appointment.

Specialise in restoring clocks,

PROVIDE Home Inspections. Free Estimates. Chargeable Collection/Delivery Service.
SPEAK TO John Carr.
Mr. Carr is a member of BAFRA and the Guild of Master Craftsmen. By Appointment to HM Queen Elizabeth II, Antique Furniture Restorers.
SEE Furniture.

OLD ROPERY ANTIQUES
East Street, Kilham, Nr. Driffield, **North Humberside YO25 0ST**
TEL   026282 233
OPEN   9.30–5 Mon–Sat.

Specialise in restoring antique clocks.

PROVIDE Home Inspections. Chargeable Estimates. Chargeable Collection/Delivery Service.
SPEAK TO John Butterfield.
SEE Collectors (Scientific Instruments), Furniture.

ROBIN FOWLER (PERIOD CLOCKS)
Washingdales, Washing Dale Lane, Aylesby, Grimsby, **South Humberside DN37 7LH**
TEL   0472 883264
OPEN   By Appointment.

Specialise in restoring antique clocks and barometers, also supply and restore all types of turret clocks.

PROVIDE Home Inspections. Free

Estimates. Free Collection/Delivery
Service.
SPEAK TO Robin Fowler.
Work guaranteed for five years in the case
of spring-driven movements and ten
years for weight-driven movements.

A. & S. ALLEN
40 Clarendon Way, Chislehurst, **Kent
BR7 6RF**
TEL   0689 826345
OPEN   9–5 Mon–Fri.

Specialise in restoring clock dials.

PROVIDE Free Estimates.
Collection/Delivery Service by
arrangement.
SPEAK TO Adrian Allen.
SEE Porcelain.

ANTIQUE RESTORATIONS
The Old Wheelwright's Shop, Brasted
Forge, Brasted, Westerham, **Kent
TN16 1JL**
TEL   0959 563863
FAX   0959 561262
OPEN   9–5 Mon–Fri; 10–1 Sat.

Specialise in restoring longcase and
bracket clocks.

PROVIDE Refundable Estimates. Free
Collection/Delivery Service.
SPEAK TO Raymond Konyn.

Member of BAFRA.
SEE Furniture, Lighting.

GURNEY C. CRANE
Clockcase Maker, North Grove Road,
Hawkhurst, **Kent TN18 4AP**
TEL   0580 754054
OPEN   By Appointment.

Specialise in restoring all casework,
period longcase movements. Specialist in
new period cases to suit antique
movement.

PROVIDE Local Home Inspections. Free

Estimates. Chargeable Collection
Service.
SPEAK TO Gurney Crane.

Member of UKIC. This workshop is
included on the register of conservators
maintained by the Conservation Unit of
the Museums and Galleries Commission.

KEITH DAVIS
14 Little Buckland Avenue, Maidstone,
Kent ME16 0BG
TEL   0622 679034
OPEN   8.30–5.30 Mon–Fri.

Specialise in restoring antique clocks
and barometers.

PROVIDE Home Inspections. Free
Estimates. Free Local
Collection/Delivery Service.
SPEAK TO Keith Davis.
Member of AHS and Freeman of the
Clockmakers' Company. This workshop
is included on the register of conservators
maintained by the Conservation Unit of
the Museums and Galleries Commission.

ANTHONY GRAY
South Goodwin House, St Margaret's
Bay, **Kent CT15 6DT**
TEL   0304 853287
FAX   0304 853488
OPEN   By Appointment.

Specialise in restoring antique clocks,
watches, barometers and barographs.
Clock and barometer case restoration, re-
silvering, parts made to order.
Reproduction barographs made to order.

PROVIDE Home Inspections. Free
Estimates. Free Local
Collection/Delivery Service.
SPEAK TO Anthony Gray.

Mr Gray is MBHI and a member of
UKIC.

B. V. M. SOMERSET
The Dial, Stags Head, Stafford Road, Tonbridge, **Kent TN9 1HT**
TEL   0732 352017
OPEN   11–8 Daily.

Specialise in restoring antique clocks and watches. Clock-cases can be repaired, also French polishing.

PROVIDE Home Inspections. Free Collection/Delivery Service.
SPEAK TO B. Somerset.
Mr Somerset is MBHI.

GEORGE WILBY
32 West Reach, Whitstable, **Kent CT5 1EG**
TEL   0227 274736
OPEN   By Appointment.

Specialise in restoring longcase and painted clock dials.

PROVIDE Free Estimates.
SPEAK TO Gerry Wilby.
Member of UKIC. This workshop is included on the register of conservators maintained by the Conservation Unit of the Museums and Galleries Commission.

DROP DIAL ANTIQUES
Last Drop Village, Hospital Road, Bolton, **Lancashire**
TEL   0204 57186
OPEN   12–5 Daily.

Specialise in restoring antique clocks, including dials and movements, although casework is limited. Restoring mercury but not aneroid barometers.

PROVIDE Free Estimates.
SPEAK TO Mr or Mrs I. Roberts.

COLIN D. FISHER
61 High Street, Chapeltown, Turton, Bolton, **Lancashire BL7 OEW**
TEL   0204 853428
OPEN   9–5 Mon, Wed, Fri, Sat or By Appointment.

Specialise in restoring antique clocks, especially longcase and Vienna and bracket clocks. Parts can be made to order and dials restored.

PROVIDE Home Inspections. Free Estimates. Collection/Delivery Service.
SPEAK TO C. D. Fisher.

Member of the British Watch and Clockmakers' Guild and the Antiquarian Horological Association. This workshop is included on the register of conservators maintained by the Conservation Unit of the Museums and Galleries Commission.

HARROP FOLD CLOCKS
Harrop Fold, Bolton-by-Bowland, Nr. Clitheroe, **Lancashire BB7 4PJ**
TEL   02007 665
OPEN   By Appointment.

Specialise in restoring antique longcase clocks.

PROVIDES Home Inspections. Free Estimates. Free Collection/Delivery Service.
SPEAK TO Mr F. Robinson.

N. BRYAN-PEACH ANTIQUES
28 Far Street, Wymeswold, Loughborough, **Leicestershire LE12 6TZ**
TEL   0509 880425
OPEN   9–6 Mon–Sat.

Specialise in restoring clocks and barometers, re-silvering, dial repair.

PROVIDE Home Inspections.
SPEAK TO Mr N. Bryan-Peach.

CHARLES ANTIQUES
3 Market Place, Whitwick,
Leicestershire LE6 4AE
TEL   0530 36932
OPEN   10–5 Tues, Thur–Sat.

Specialise in repairing and restoring clocks.

PROVIDE Home Inspections. Free Estimates. Chargeable Collection/Delivery Service.
SPEAK TO N. Haydon.

ELLIOTT NIXON
5 Alexandra Road, Stoneygate, Leicester,
Leicestershire LE2 2BB
TEL   0533 705713
OPEN   9–6 Mon–Sat.

Specialise in a full restoration and conservation service for clocks and watches.

PROVIDE Home Inspections. Free Estimates. Free Local Collection/Delivery Service.
SPEAK TO Elliott Nixon

Mr Nixon is FBHI. This workshop is included on the register of conservators maintained by the Conservation Unit of the Museums and Galleries Commission.
SEE Collectors (Scientific Instruments).

E. CZAJKOWSKI & SON
96 Tor-O-Moor Road, Woodhall Spa,
Lincolnshire LN10 6SB
TEL   0526 352895
OPEN   9–5 Mon–Fri.

Specialise in restoring clocks and barometers.

PROVIDE Home Inspections. Free Estimates. Free Local Collection/Delivery Service.
SPEAK TO Mr M. J. Czajkowski.

Member of COSIRA and West Dean trained.
SEE Furniture.

GRANTHAM CLOCKS
30 Lodge Way, Grantham, **Lincolnshire NG31 8DD**
TEL   0476 61784
OPEN   By Appointment.

Specialise in repairing and restoring all types of antique clocks.

PROVIDE Home Inspections. Free Estimates. Free Collection/Delivery Service.
SPEAK TO Roy Conder.
Member of BHI.

RODDY McVITTIE
24 Bow Bridge House, 19–21 Payne Road, **London E3**
TEL   081 981 4083
OPEN   8–6 Mon–Fri.

Specialise in restoring and conserving 17th, 18th and 19th century clocks and barometers, both English and Continental.

PROVIDE Home Inspections. Free Estimates. Free Collection/Delivery Service.
SPEAK TO Roddy McVittie.

SEE Furniture.

O. COMITTI & SON LTD
656 Forest Road, **London E17 3ED**
TEL   081 509 0011
FAX   081 521 3320
OPEN   9–5 Mon–Fri.

Specialise in repairing and restoring mercury and aneroid barometers and clocks, including casework.

PROVIDE Free Estimates.
SPEAK TO Simon Barker.

Established 1850.

ALBION CLOCKS
4 Grove End, Grove Hill, **London
E18 2LE**
TEL   081 530 5570 and 0860 487830
OPEN   7.30–7 Mon–Sat.

Specialise in restoring fine antique
clocks.

PROVIDE Home Inspections. Free
Estimates. Free Collection/Delivery
Service.
SPEAK TO C.·D. Bent.
Mr Bent is CMBHI. This workshop is
included on the register maintained by
the Conservation Unit of the Museums
and Galleries Commission.

THE CONSERVATION STUDIO
Unit 21, Pennybank Chambers, 33–35
St Johns Square, **London EC1M 4DS**
TEL   071 251 6853
OPEN   9.30–5 Mon–Fri.

Specialise in restoring enamel watch
dials.

PROVIDES Home Inspections (large items
only). Refundable Estimates.
Chargeable Collection/Delivery Service.
SPEAK TO Sandra Davison.
SEE Silver, Porcelain.

BOSWELL AND DAVIS
The Holywell Centre, 1 Phipp Street,
London EC2A 4PS
TEL   071 739 5738
FAX   071 729 9882
OPEN   9–6 Mon–Fri.

Specialise in restoring longcase clocks.

PROVIDE Home Inspections. Free
Estimates. Free Collection/Delivery
Service.
SPEAK TO David Boswell.

SEE Furniture.

NORTH LONDON CLOCK SHOP LTD
72 Highbury Park, **London N5 2XE**
TEL   071 226 1609
OPEN   9–6 Mon–Fri.

Specialise in repairing and restoring all
types of antique clocks and barometers.

PROVIDE Home Inspections. Free
Estimates.
SPEAK TO Derek Tomlin.

Mr Tomlin is CMBHI.

CLIFFORD J. TRACY
6–40 Durnford Street, **London
N15 5NQ**
TEL   081 800 4773 or 4774
FAX   081 800 4351
OPEN   7.30–5 Mon–Thur; 7.30–4 Fri.

Specialise in restoring clock-cases and
movements.

PROVIDE Home Inspections. Free
Estimates. Free Collection/Delivery
Service.
SPEAK TO Clifford Tracy.

Member of BAFRA and the UKIC. Will
do minor repairs on site.
SEE Furniture.

W. PAIRPOINT & SONS LTD
10 Shacklewell Road, **London N16 7TA**
TEL   071 254 6362
FAX   071 254 7175
OPEN   8.30–5.30 Mon–Fri.

Specialise in regilding carriage clocks.

PROVIDE Free Estimates. Free
Collection/Delivery Service in the
London area.
SPEAK TO Eric Soulard.
SEE Silver.

PARKHILL RESTORATIONS
11 Park End, South Hill Park, **London NW3 2ST**
TEL   071 794 5624
OPEN   10–6 Mon–Fri or By Appointment.

Specialise in restoring small bracket and longcase clocks.

PROVIDE Home Inspections. Free Estimates. Chargeable Collection/Delivery Service.
SPEAK TO Peter Colgin.
SEE Furniture.

B. C. METALCRAFTS
69 Tewkesbury Gardens, **London NW9 OQU**
TEL   081 204 2446
FAX   081 206 2871
OPEN   By Appointment.

Specialise in restoring and repairing French clocks and clock sets.
SPEAK TO F. Burnell or M. A. Burnell.
SEE Silver.

R. E. ROSE
731 Sidcup Rd, **London SE9 3SA**
TEL   081 859 4754
OPEN   8.30–5.30 Mon–Sat; closed Thur.

Specialise in restoring antique clocks and barometers.

PROVIDE Free Estimates.
SPEAK TO Ron Rose.
Mr Rose is FBHI.

NEWCOMBE & SON
89 Maple Rd, Penge, **London SE20 8UL**
TEL   081 778 0816
OPEN   7.15–5.30 Mon–Fri.

Specialise in repairing and restoring antique clocks and barometers, including silvering and gilding service, enamel and painted clock faces, brass and wood frets, clock hands in brass or steel.

PROVIDE Home Inspections. Free Estimates. Free Collection/Delivery Service.
SPEAK TO Mike Newcombe.

N. BLOOM & SON (KNIGHTSBRIDGE)
Harrod's Fine Jewellery Room, **London SW1 1XL**
TEL   071 730 1234 ext. 4062 or 4072
FAX   071 589 0655
OPEN   Mon–Sat 10–6, Wed 10–8.

Specialise in restoring carriage clocks, good mechanical watches.

PROVIDE Free Estimates.
SPEAK TO Heidi McKeown.
Member of LAPADA.
SEE Silver.

SOMLO ANTIQUES
7 Piccadilly Arcade, **London SW1Y 6NA**
TEL   071 499 6526
FAX   071 499 0603
OPEN   10–5.30 Mon–Fri.

Specialise in repairing vintage wristwatches, antique pocket watches, technical and decorative enamel watches.

PROVIDE Home Inspections. Free/Chargeable Estimates.
SPEAK TO George Somlo.

BIG BEN CLOCKS
5 Broxholme House, New Kings Road, **London SW6 4AA**
TEL   071 736 1770
FAX   071 384 1957
OPEN   9–5 Mon–Fri.

Specialise in repairing and overhauling all types of antique clocks. They are not undertaking restoration work at present.

PROVIDE Home Inspections. Chargeable Collection/Delivery Service.

SPEAK TO Roger Lascelles.
SEE Silver.

AUBREY BROCKLEHURST
124 Cromwell Road, **London SW7 4ET**
TEL   071 373 0319
OPEN   9–1, 2–5.30 Mon–Fri; 10–1 Sat.

Specialise in restoring and repairing antique English and French clocks.

PROVIDE Home Inspections. Free Estimates. Chargeable Collection/Delivery Service.
SPEAK TO Aubrey Brocklehurst, Ms Gill or Mrs Leonard.

Mr Brocklehurst is a member of BADA and he and Ms Gill and Mrs Leonard are all FBHIs.
SEE Furniture.

CAPITAL CLOCKS
190 Wandsworth Road, **London SW8 2JU**
TEL   071 720 6372
OPEN   9–5 Tues–Sat.

Specialise in restoring pre-1900 clocks, longcase, bracket and carriage, restoration of barometers, new mercury tubes, Boulle and enamel work.

PROVIDE Free Estimates. Chargeable Collection/Delivery Service.
SPEAK TO Robert McMillan.

THE CLOCK CLINIC LTD
85 Lower Richmond Road, **London SW15 1EU**
TEL   081 788 1407
FAX   081 780 2838
OPEN   9–6 Tues–Fri; 9–1 Sat.

Specialise in restoring antique clocks, barometers and barographs.

PROVIDE Chargeable Home Inspections. Free Estimates in shop. Chargeable Collection/Delivery Service.
SPEAK TO Robert Pedler.
Mr Pedler is FBHI.

JOHN WALKER
64 South Molton Street, **London W1Y 1HH**
TEL   071 629 3487
OPEN   8.30–5.15 Mon–Fri.

Specialise in repairing and restoring antique and modern clocks and watches.

PROVIDE Home Inspections. Free Estimates. Chargeable Collection/Delivery Service.
SPEAK TO John Walker or Steve Martin.

This family firm was established in 1830. Mr Walker is FBHI.
SEE Silver.

WILLIAM MANSELL
24 Connaught Street, **London W2 2AF**
TEL   071 723 4154
OPEN   9–6 Mon–Fri and Sat a.m.

Specialise in repairing and restoring antique clocks, wrist-watches, pocket watches.

PROVIDE Home Inspections. Free Estimates. Free Collection/Delivery Service.
SPEAK TO Bill Salisbury.

This is a small, established business which dates back to 1864.
SEE Silver.

BADGER ANTIQUES
12 St Mary's Road, **London W5 5ES**
TEL   081 567 5601
OPEN   10–6 Mon–Sat.

Specialise in restoring clocks and pocket watches.

PROVIDE Home Inspections. Free Estimates. Free Collection/Delivery Service.
SPEAK TO Michael Allders.
SEE Furniture.

ROY BENNETT
22 Cuckoo Lane, **London W7 3EY**
TEL　　081 840 6911
OPEN　By Appointment.

Specialise in restoring antique clocks and watches.

PROVIDE Free Estimates, Chargeable Collection/Delivery Service.
SPEAK TO Roy Bennett.

Member of BWCMG.

RODERICK ANTIQUE CLOCKS
23 Vicarage Gate, **London W8 4AA**
TEL　　071 937 8517
FAX　　071 937 8517
OPEN　10–5.15 Mon–Fri, 10–4 Sat, By Appointment.

Specialise in restoring antique clocks, including carriage, bracket, skeleton and decorative French, ormolu and longcase clocks.

PROVIDE Free Estimates.
SPEAK TO Roderick Mee.

Mr Mee is a member of LAPADA.

IGOR TOCIAPSKI
39 Ledbury Road, **London W11 2AA**
TEL　　071 229 8317
OPEN　10–5 Tues–Fri.

Specialise in repairing antique clocks.

PROVIDE Home Inspections. Free Estimates. Chargeable Collection/Delivery Service.
SPEAK TO Igor Tociapski.

BAROMETER FAIR
18 Bury Place, **London WC1A 2JR**
TEL　　071 404 4521
FAX　　071 831 9150

Specialise in restoring barometers.

PROVIDE Home Inspections. Chargeable Estimates. Free Local Collection/Delivery Service.
SPEAK TO John Forster.

DAVID NEWELL
55 Shelton Street, **London WC2H 9HE**
TEL　　071 836 1000
OPEN　By Appointment.

Specialise in restoring antique clocks and watches, particularly French clocks. Barometers and barographs are also restored.

PROVIDE Free Estimates.
SPEAK TO David Newell.
Mr Newell is FBHI.
SEE Collectors (Mechanical Music).

J. G. TREVOR-OWEN
181–193 Oldham Rd, Rochdale, **Greater Manchester OL16 5QZ**
TEL　　0706 48138
OPEN　1.30–7 Mon–Fri or By Appointment.

Specialise in restoring clocks.

PROVIDE Home Inspections, Refundable Estimates.
SPEAK TO J. G. Trevor-Owen.
SEE Furniture, Oil Paintings, Collectors (Musical Instruments).

R. W. BAXTER
Joel House, 43 Hoghton Street, Southport, **Merseyside PR9 0PG**
TEL　　0704 537377
OPEN　9–10, 2–5.30 Mon–Fri.

Specialise in restoring antique clocks, carriage, longcase, bracket, French. Brass dials resilvered and pocket watches and modern clocks and watches repaired.

PROVIDE Home Inspections. Free Estimates. Free Collection/Delivery Service.
SPEAK TO R. W. Baxter.

Mr Baxter is FBHI. This workshop is included on the register of conservators maintained by the Conservation Unit of the Museums and Galleries Commission.

THE CLOCK SHOP
7 The Quadrant, Hoylake, Wirral, **Merseyside L47 2AY**
TEL   051 632 1888
OPEN   9–5.30 Mon–Fri.

Specialise in restoring antique clocks.

PROVIDE Home Inspections. Free Estimates. Collection/Delivery Service by arrangement.
SPEAK TO Kevin Whay.
Mr Whay is MBHI and MBWCG.

ARTBRY'S ANTIQUES
44 High Street, Pinner, **Middlesex HA5 5PW**
TEL   081 868 0834
OPEN   9.15–5.30 Mon–Sat; Wed 9.15–1.

Specialise in restoring bracket, longcase and carriage clocks.

PROVIDE Home Inspections. Free Estimates. Free Collection/Delivery Service.
SPEAK TO Mr A. H. Davies.

MICHAEL ALLEN (WATCHMAKERS)
76A Walsall Road, Four Oaks, Sutton Coldfield, **West Midlands B74 4QY**
TEL   021 308 6117
OPEN   9–5.30 Mon–Sat. Closed last two weeks in August.

Specialise in restoring all wrist, pocket and complicated watches and all clocks from longcase to carriage. They can repair any timepiece with no exceptions.

PROVIDE Home Inspections. Free Estimates. Free Collection/Delivery Service.
SPEAK TO Michael Allen.

BARNT GREEN ANTIQUES
93 Hewell Road, Barnt Green, Birmingham, **West Midlands B45 8NL**
TEL   021 445 4942
OPEN   9–5.30 Mon–Fri; 9–1 Sat.

Specialise in restoring and conserving longcase clocks, gilding.

PROVIDE Home Inspections. Free Estimates. Chargeable Collection/Delivery Service.
SPEAK TO Mr N. Slater.
Member of BAFRA.
SEE Furniture.

F. S. BUGGINS trading as FIELDHOUSE BROS.
40 Castlecroft Gardens, Wolverhampton, **West Midlands WV3 8LN**
TEL   0902 761148
OPEN   9–5 Mon, Tues, Wed, Fri, Sat.

Specialise in restoring antique longcase clocks.

PROVIDE Home Inspections. Free Estimates. Free Collection/Delivery Service.
SPEAK TO Mr Buggins.
Mr Buggins is a CMBHI. This workshop is included on the register of conservators maintained by the Conservation Unit of the Museums and Galleries Commission.

GEOSTRAN ANTIQUES
Middle Lane, Whitacre Heath, Coleshill, Birmingham, **West Midlands B46 2HX**
TEL   0675 81483
OPEN   10–5 Mon–Fri or By Appointment.

Specialise in restoring antique clocks.

PROVIDE Home Inspections. Free Estimates. Free/Chargeable Collection/Delivery Service.
SPEAK TO Anthony Potter.
They are CMBHI.
SEE Furniture.

THE OLD CLOCK SHOP

32 Stephenson Street, Birmingham,
West Midlands B2 4BH
TEL   021 632 4864
OPEN   9 30–5 Mon–Fri; 10–3 Sat.

Specialise in restoring wrist-watches,
including Patek Phillipe, Rolex,
precision pocket watches, also longcase,
bracket and carriage clocks.

PROVIDE Home Inspections. Free
Estimates. Chargeable
Collection/Delivery Service.
SPEAK TO M. L. or S. R. Durham.
They are MBHI.

OSBORNES ANTIQUES

91 Chester Road, New Oscott, Sutton
Coldfield, **West Midlands B73 5BA**
TEL   021 355 6667
FAX   021 354 7166
OPEN   9–1 Mon; 9–1, 2–5 Tues, Wed;
       9–1, 2–5.30 Thur, Fri; 9.15–12
       Sat.

Specialise in repairing and restoring
antique barometers, scientific glass-
blowers and manufacture of replacement
barometer parts.

PROVIDE Free Estimates.
SPEAK TO Mrs Osborne.
Member of BSSG.

ARK ANTIQUE RESTORATIONS

Morton Peto Road, Gapton Hall
Industrial Estate, Great Yarmouth,
Norfolk NR3 0LT
TEL   0493 653357
FAX   0493 658405
OPEN   9–5.30 Mon–Fri; 9–1 Sat.

Specialise in restoring clocks.

PROVIDE Home Inspections. Chargeable
Estimates. Free Local
Collection/Delivery Service.
SPEAK TO Ben Deveson.
SEE Furniture.

'AS TIME GOES BY'

Wrights Court, Elm Hill, Norwich,
Norfolk NR3 1HQ
TEL   0603 666508
FAX   0603 665508
OPEN   9.30–5 Mon–Fri; 10–4 Sat.

Specialise in restoring antique clocks.
Also make fine walnut longcase clocks.

PROVIDE Home Inspections. Free
Estimates. Free/Chargeable
Collection/Delivery Service.
SPEAK TO Stephen or Catherine Phillips.
Member of BHI.

DAVID BARTRAM FURNITURE

The Raveningham Centre, Castell Farm,
Beccles Road, Raveningham, Nr.
Norwich, **Norfolk NR14 6NU**
TEL   050 846 721
OPEN   10–6 daily.

Specialise in comprehensive antique
restoration service, including clock cases.

PROVIDE Home Inspections. Free
Estimates. Free Collection/Delivery
Service.
SPEAK TO David Bartram.

Mr Bartram is a member of BAFRA and
UKIC. This workshop is included on
the register of conservators maintained
by the Conservation Unit of the
Museums and Galleries Commission.
SEE Silver, Furniture.

DISS ANTIQUES RESTORATION SERVICES

2–3 Market Place, Diss, **Norfolk
IP22 3JT**
TEL   0379 642213
FAX   0379 642213
OPEN   8–5 Mon–Sat.

Specialise in restoring barometers and
clocks. They undertake to finish with
care by hand every individual piece to
retain its age and patina.

PROVIDE Home Inspections. Free
Estimates. Collection/Delivery Service.
SPEAK TO Brian Wimshurst.
Member of the Guild of Master
Craftsmen and LAPADA.

TONY GROVER, FAKENHAM ANTIQUES CENTRE
14 Norwich Road, Fakenham, **Norfolk NR21 8AZ**
TEL   0328 862941 or 0953 83654
OPEN   10–5 Mon–Sat.

Specialise in restoring antique English
bracket and longcase clocks.

PROVIDE Home Inspections. Free
Estimates. Chargeable
Collection/Delivery Service.
SPEAK TO Tony Grover.

HARRISONS OF NORWICH
3 Capitol House, Heigham Street,
Norwich, **Norfolk NR2 4TE**
TEL   0603 767573
OPEN   9–1, 2–5.30 Mon–Fri.

Specialise in restoring antique clock dials
of all descriptions.

PROVIDE Free Estimates.
SPEAK TO Mr Roger L. Moll.
CMBHI, MBWCMG. This workshop is
included on the register of conservators
maintained by the Conservation Unit of
the Museums and Galleries Commission.

HUMBLEYARD FINE ART
3, Fish Hill, Holt, **Norfolk NR25 6BD**
TEL   0263 713362
OPEN   10–5 Mon–Thur; 10–5 Sat.

Specialise in repairing and restoring
barometers.

PROVIDE Home Inspections. Free
Estimates. Chargeable Collection/
Delivery Service.
SPEAK TO James Layte.
SEE Collectors (Scientific Instruments).

JASPER ANTIQUES
11A Hall Road, Snettisham, King's
Lynn, **Norfolk PE31 7LU**
TEL   0485 541485 and 540604
OPEN   10.30–1 Mon, Wed, Fri; 10.30–
        1, 2–4 Sat.

Specialise in repair service for clocks and
watches.

PROVIDE Home Inspections. Free
Estimates. Free Collection/Delivery
Service.
SPEAK TO Mrs A. A. Norris.
SEE Porcelain, Silver.

PARRISS
20 Station Road, Sheringham, **Norfolk NR26 8RE**
TEL   0263 822661
OPEN   9.30–1, 2.15–5 Mon–Fri.

Specialise in repairing antique clocks.

PROVIDE Home Inspections. Chargeable
Estimates. Free/Chargeable
Collection/Delivery Service.
SPEAK TO J. H. Parriss.

R. PINDER
20 Recreation Road, Hethersett,
Norwich, **Norfolk NR9 3EF**
TEL   0603 8118641
OPEN   By Appointment.

Specialise in restoring and repairing
antique English and French clocks and
barometers. He also repairs case work.

PROVIDE Home Inspections.
Free/Chargeable Estimates.
Free/Chargeable Collection/Delivery
Service.
SPEAK TO R. Pinder.
Mr Pinder is MBHI and MBWCMG.

THOMAS TILLETT & CO.
17 Saint Giles Street, Norwich, **Norfolk NR2 1JL**
TEL   0603 625922 or 620372
FAX   0603 620372
OPEN   9–5.30 Mon–Sat.

Specialise in repairing antique and modern watches.

PROVIDE Home Inspections. Free Estimates. Free Collection/Delivery Service.
SPEAK TO Mr T. Scally or Lorraine Scally.
This firm was established in 1908.
SEE Silver.

WICKENDEN CLOCKS
53 Gorse Rd, Thorpe St Andrew, Norwich, **Norfolk NR7 OAY**
TEL   0603 32179
OPEN   9–5 Daily.

Specialise in restoring clocks and barometers.

PROVIDE Home Inspections. Free Estimates. Free Local Collection/Delivery Service.
SPEAK TO Eric Wickenden.

SEE Collectors (Mechanical Music).

R. C. WOODHOUSE
(Antiquarian Horologist),
10 Westgate, Hunstanton, **Norfolk PE36 5AL**
TEL   0485 532903
OPEN   11–5 Wed, Fri, Sat or By Appointment.

Specialise in restoring longcase, bracket and other good clocks from a carriage clock to a church/stable clock. Barometers also undertaken and small locks repaired and keys made.

PROVIDE Home Inspections. Free Estimates. Collection/Delivery Service.
SPEAK TO R. C. Woodhouse.
Member of the UKIC, BHI and BWCMG.

GOODACRE ENGRAVING LTD
Thrumpton Avenue (off Chatsworth Avenue), Meadow Lane, Long Eaton, Nottingham, **Nottinghamshire NG10 2GB**
TEL   0602 734387
FAX   0602 461193
OPEN   8.30–5 Mon–Thur; 8.30–1.30 Fri.

Specialise in restoration of antique dials and movements, including painted dials.

PROVIDE Free Estimates.
Can produce castings on a one-off basis.

ALISTAIR FRAYLING-CORK
2 Mill Lane, Wallingford, **Oxfordshire OX10 ODH**
TEL   0491 26221
OPEN   10–6 Mon–Fri, Sat by arrangement.

Specialise in restoring clock-cases.

PROVIDE Home Inspections. Free Estimates. Chargeable Collection/Delivery Service.
SPEAK TO Alistair Frayling-Cork.
Member of BAFRA.
SEE Furniture, Collectors (Musical Instruments).

GERALD MARSH ANTIQUE CLOCKS LTD
Jericho House, North Aston, **Oxfordshire OX5 4HX**
TEL   0869 40080
OPEN   9.30–5 Mon–Sat.

Specialise in restoring antique English and French clocks, watches and barometers.

PROVIDE Home Inspections. Free Estimates. Free Collection/Delivery Service.
SPEAK TO Gerald Marsh.
Member of Worshipful Company of

Clockmakers, Fellow of British
Horological Institute, Member of
NAWCC (USA) and BADA.
SEE **Hampshire**.

PETER A. MEECHAM
The Malt House, Milton-Under-
Wychwood, **Oxfordshire OX7 6JT**
TEL   0993 830215
FAX   0993 830039
OPEN   8.30–5 Mon–Fri.

Specialise in restoring and repairing
antique clocks, including verge
reconversions and the making of
replacement parts in a traditional and
sympathetic manner.

PROVIDE Home Inspections. Free
Estimates. Free Collection/Delivery
Service.
SPEAK TO P. A. Meecham.

Mr Meecham is CMBHI.

ROSEMARY AND TIME
42 Park Street, Thame, **Oxfordshire
OX9 3HR**
TEL   084421 6923
OPEN   9–12.30, 1.30–6 Mon–Sat.

Specialise in restoring clocks and all
mechanical items.

PROVIDE Home Inspections. Free
Estimates. Chargeable
Collection/Delivery Service.
SPEAK TO Tom Fletcher.

WEAVES AND WAXES
53 Church Street, Bloxham, Banbury,
Oxfordshire OX15 4ET
TEL   0295 721535
FAX   0295 271867
OPEN   9–1, 2–5.30 Tues–Fri; 9–1, 2–4
        Sat.

Specialise in restoring clocks.

PROVIDE Home Inspections.
Free/Chargeable Estimates. Chargeable

Collection/Delivery Service.
SPEAK TO Laurie Grayer.
SEE Furniture.

PETER WIGGINS
Raffles, Southcombe, Chipping Norton,
Oxfordshire OX7 5QH
TEL   0608 642652
OPEN   9–6 Mon–Fri.

Specialise in restoring barometers and
clocks.

PROVIDE Home Inspections. Free
Estimates. Chargeable
Collection/Delivery Service.
SPEAK TO Peter Wiggins.
SEE Collectors (Scientific Instruments).

WITNEY RESTORATIONS
Workshop: Unit 17, Hanborough
Business Park, Main Road, Long
Hanborough, **Oxfordshire OX7 2LH**
Accounts and Enquiries: 96–100 Corn
Street, Witney, **Oxfordshire OX8 7BU**
TEL   0993 703902 accounts and
        enquiries
        0993 883336 workshop
FAX   0993 779852
OPEN   9.30–5 Mon–Fri.

Specialise in restoring and conserving
fine antique clocks.

PROVIDE Home Inspections. Free
Estimates. Chargeable
Collection/Delivery Service.
SPEAK TO Mr A. Smith or Mrs J. Jarrett.
SEE Furniture.

RICHARD HIGGINS
The Old School, Longnor, Nr.
Shrewsbury, **Shropshire SY5 7PP**
TEL   074373 8162
OPEN   8–6 Mon–Fri.

Specialise in restoring bracket, longcase
and carriage clocks, including specialist
works to movements, dials and cases.
Also restore barometers.

PROVIDE Home Inspections.

Free/Chargeable Estimates.
Collection/Delivery Service by
arrangement.
SPEAK TO Richard Higgins.

Member of BAFRA and UKIC. This
workshop is included on the register of
conservators maintained by the
Conservation Unit of the Museums and
Galleries Commission.
SEE Furniture, Collectors (Mechanical
Music).

F. C. MANSER & SON LTD
53–54 Wyle Cop, Shrewsbury,
Shropshire SY1 1XJ
TEL   0743 351120
FAX   0743 271047
OPEN   9–5.30 Mon, Tues, Wed, Fri; 9–
         10 Thur; 9–5 Sat.

Specialise in restoring clocks,
barometers, Boulle work.

PROVIDE Home Inspections. Free
Estimates. Chargeable
Collection/Delivery Service.
SPEAK TO Paul Manser.
Member of LAPADA and the Guild of
Master Craftsmen.
SEE Porcelain, Silver.

EDWARD VENN ANTIQUE RESTORATIONS
52 Long Street, Williton, Taunton,
Somerset TA4 4QU
TEL   0984 32631
OPEN   8.30–5.30 Mon–Fri.

Specialise in restoring barometers and
longcase clocks.

PROVIDE Chargeable Estimates.
Chargeable Collection/Delivery
Service.
SPEAK TO Mr Venn.
SEE Furniture.

A. C. PRALL RESTORATIONS
Highfield Farm, Uttoxeter Road,
Draycott, **Staffordshire ST11 9AE**
TEL   0782 399022
OPEN   9–7 Mon–Fri.

Specialise in restoring clocks, including
longcase and mantel.

PROVIDE Free Estimates.
Free/Chargeable Collection/Delivery
Service.
SPEAK TO Mr Prall.
SEE Furniture.

ANTIQUE CLOCKS BY SIMON CHARLES
The Limes, 72 Melford Road, Sudbury,
Suffolk CO10 6LT
TEL   0787 75931
OPEN   10–6 Mon–Sat.

Specialise in restoring early English
clocks, including movements and cases.

PROVIDE Home Inspections. Free
Estimates. Chargeable
Collection/Delivery Service.
SPEAK TO Simon Charles.
Member of BWCMG.

E. T. MANSON
8 Market Hill, Woodbridge, **Suffolk
IP12 4LU**
TEL   0394 380235
OPEN   10–5 Thur and Sat or By
         Appointment.

Specialise in restoring antique clocks,
including wheel and pinion cutting,
remaking of missing parts, repeating
work.

PROVIDE Home Inspections. Free
Estimates. Free Collection/Delivery
Service.
SPEAK TO E. T. Manson.

PEPPERS PERIOD PIECES
23 Churchgate Street, Bury St Edmunds, **Suffolk IP33 1RG**
TEL   0284 768786
OPEN   10–5 Mon–Sat.

Specialise in restoring clocks.
PROVIDE Home Inspections. Refundable Estimates. Free/Chargeable Collection/Delivery Service.
SPEAK TO M. E. Pepper.
Their restorers are West Dean trained.
SEE Furniture.

A. G. SMEETH
Clock House, Locks Lane, Leavenheath, Colchester, **Suffolk CO6 4PF**
TEL   0206 262187
OPEN   By Appointment.

Specialise in restoring antique clocks.
PROVIDE Home Inspections. Free Estimates. Free Collection/Delivery Service.
SPEAK TO A. G. Smeeth.
SEE Furniture.

A. E. BOOTH & SON
9 High Street, Ewell, Epsom, **Surrey KT17 1SG**
TEL   081 393 5245
OPEN   9–5 Mon–Fri.

Specialise in restoration of clocks.
PROVIDE Home Inspections. Free/Refundable Estimates. Free Collection/Delivery Service.
SPEAK TO D. J. Booth.
Member of BAFRA.
SEE Furniture.

B. S. ANTIQUES
39 Bridge Road, East Molesey, **Surrey KT8 9ER**
TEL   081 941 1812
OPEN   10–5 Mon–Sat; closed Wed.

Specialise in repairing and restoring antique clocks and barometers.
PROVIDE Home Inspections. Free Estimates. Collection/Delivery Service by arrangement.
SPEAK TO Stephen Anderman.

THE CLOCK SHOP
64 Church Street, Weybridge, **Surrey KT13 8DL**
TEL   0932 840407 and 855503
OPEN   9.45–5.45 Mon–Sat.

Specialise in restoring antique clocks and barometers, including casework.
PROVIDE Home Inspections. Free Estimates. Free Collection/Delivery Service.
SPEAK TO Mr Forster.

ROGER A. DAVIS
19 Dorking Rd, Great Bookham, **Surrey KT23 4PU**
TEL   0372 457655 and 453167
OPEN   9.30–5.30 Tues, Thur, Sat.

Specialise in restoring antique clocks.
PROVIDE Home Inspections. Free Estimates. Free Collection/Delivery Service.
SPEAK TO Roger Davis.
Mr Davis is MBHI and MBWCMG.

E. HOLLANDER LTD
The Dutch House, Horsham Road, South Holmwood, Dorking, **Surrey RH5 4NF**
TEL   0306 888921
OPEN   8–4.50 Mon–Fri; Sat By Appointment.

Specialise in restoring 17th–19th century clocks and watches as well as barometers.
PROVIDE Home Inspections. Free Estimates. Collection/Delivery Service by arrangement.
SPEAK TO David Pay.
BADA and MBHI.

HOROLOGICAL WORKSHOPS
204 Worplesdon Road, Guildford, **Surrey GU2 6UY**
TEL   0483 576496
OPEN   8.30–5.30 Mon–Fri; 9–12.30 Sat.

Specialise in repairing antique clocks, watches and barometers and restoring turret clocks.

PROVIDE Home Inspections, Free Estimates. Chargeable Collection/Delivery Service.
SPEAK TO Mr M. D. Tooke.
Member of BADA.

JOHN KENDALL
156 High St, Old Woking, **Surrey GU21 9JH**
TEL   0483 771310
OPEN   9–5 Mon–Fri.

Specialise in restoring clocks, especially 17th century and barometers.

PROVIDE Home Inspections. Free Estimates. Chargeable Collection/Delivery Service.
SPEAK TO John Kendall.
SEE Furniture.

RICHARD LAWMAN–WARWICK ANTIQUE RESTORATIONS
32 Beddington Lane, Croydon, **Surrey CR0 4TB**
TEL   081 688 4511
OPEN   9–6 Tues–Sat.

Specialise in clock restoration.

PROVIDE Home Inspections. Free Estimates. Free Collection/Delivery Service.
SPEAK TO Richard Lawman.

Member of the Guild of Master Craftsmen. This workshop is included on the register of conservators

maintained by the Conservation Unit of the Museums and Galleries Commission.
SEE Furniture.

MANOR ANTIQUES AND RESTORATIONS
2 New Shops, High Street, Old Woking, **Surrey GU22 9JW**
TEL   0483 724666
OPEN   10–5 Mon–Fri; 10–4.30 Sat.

Specialise in clock repairs.

PROVIDE Home Inspections. Free Estimates. Collection/Delivery Service.
SPEAK TO Alan Wellstead or Paul Thomson.
Member of the Guild of Master Craftsmen.
SEE Furniture, Picture Frames.

SURREY CLOCK CENTRE
3 Lower Street, Haslemere, **Surrey GU27 2NY**
TEL   0428 651313
OPEN   9–5 Wed; 9–1 Sat.

Specialise in restoring antique clocks and barometers.

PROVIDE Home Inspections. Free Estimates. Chargeable Collection/Delivery Service.
SPEAK TO C. Ingrams or S. Haw.

JUDITH WETHERALL
trading as **J.B. SYMES**
28 Silverlea Gardens, Horley, **Surrey RH6 9BB**
TEL   0293 775024
OPEN   8.30–5.30 Daily By Appointment Only.

Specialise in restoring japanned and lacquered clock-cases, Boulle and inlay.

PROVIDE Free Local Home Inspections. Free Estimates. Chargeable Collection/Delivery Service.
SPEAK TO Judith Wetherall.
Member of UKIC and IIC. This workshop is included on the register of

conservators maintained by the Conservation Unit of the Museums and Galleries Commission.

SEE Furniture, Picture Frames, Porcelain.

W. BRUFORD & SON LTD

11–13 Cornfield Road, Eastbourne, **East Sussex BN21 3NA**

TEL   0323 25452
OPEN   9–1, 2–5.30 Mon–Fri; 9–1, 2–5 Sat.

Specialise in repairing and restoring 19th century bracket and carriage clocks and pocket watches.

PROVIDE Free Estimates.
SPEAK TO N. Bruford or J. Burgess.
SEE Silver.

JOHN COWDEROY ANTIQUES

42 South Street, Eastbourne, **East Sussex BN21 4XB**

TEL   0323 20058
FAX   0323 410163
OPEN   9.30–1, 2.30–5 Mon, Tues, Thur, Fri; 9.30–1 Wed, Sat.

Specialise in restoring antique English and French clocks.

PROVIDE Home Inspections. Free Estimates. Chargeable Collection/Delivery Service.
SPEAK TO John, Ruth, David or Richard Cowderoy.
Member of LAPADA.
SEE Collectors (Mechanical Music), Furniture.

EASTBOURNE CLOCKS

9 Victoria Drive, Eastbourne, **East Sussex BN20 8JR**

TEL   0323 642650
OPEN   8.30–12.30, 2–5 Mon–Fri; 8.30–12.30 Sat.

Specialise in restoring and repairing antique and good quality clocks. They

will make clocks and movements to order.

PROVIDE Home Inspections. Free Estimates. Free Collection/Delivery Service.
SPEAK TO Philip Wardale.
Mr Wardale is CMBHI.

SIMON HATCHWELL ANTIQUES

94 Gloucester Rd, Brighton, **East Sussex BN1 4AP**

TEL   0273 691164
FAX   0273 691164
OPEN   9–1.30, 2.30–5 Mon–Fri; Sat By Appointment.

Specialise in restoring barometers.

PROVIDE Home Inspections. Free Estimates. Free Local Collection/Delivery Service.
SPEAK TO Simon or Allan Hatchwell.
Member of LAPADA.
SEE Furniture.

MORE RESTORATIONS

The Old Booking Hall, Hove Park Villas, Hove, **East Sussex BN3 6HP**

TEL   0273 25380
OPEN   8.30–5 Mon–Fri.

Specialise in restoring English dial clocks, barometers, barographs and their casework.

PROVIDE Home Inspections. Free Estimates. Collection/Delivery Service by arrangement.
SPEAK TO Arthur Moore.
SEE Furniture.

ANTIQUE CLOCK RESTORATION

23 Greenacres Ring, Angmering, **West Sussex BN16 4BU**

TEL   0903 786203
OPEN   9–5 Mon–Sat.

Specialise in repairing and restoring

English and French antique clocks and
pocket watches.

PROVIDE Home Inspections. Free
Estimates. Chargeable
Collection/Delivery Service.
SPEAK TO C. Houston.
Mr Houston is a MBHI.

T. P. BROOKS
Sycamores, School Lane, Lodsworth,
Petworth, **West Sussex GU28 9DH**
TEL   07985 248
OPEN   9–6 Mon–Fri or By
        Appointment.

Specialise in restoring 17th to 19th
century clocks and barometers.

PROVIDE Home Inspections. Free
Estimates. Free Collection/Delivery
Service.
SPEAK TO Mr T. P. Brooks.
Member of BHI and UKIC. This
workshop is included on the register of
conservators maintained by the
Conservation Unit of the Museums and
Galleries Commission.
SEE Collectors (Mechanical Music).

GARNER & CO.
Stable Cottage, Steyning Road, Wiston,
West Sussex BN44 3DD
TEL   0903 814565
OPEN   By Appointment (Tel Mon–Fri
        9–5.30).

Specialise in restoring clocks and dials.

PROVIDE Home Inspections. Estimates.
SPEAK TO Sid Garner.
SEE Furniture, Porcelain, Silver.

ROB GILLIES
38 Maltravers Street, Arundel, **West
Sussex BN18 9BU**
TEL   0903 882574
OPEN   8–5 Daily.

Specialise in restoring painted and silver
clock dials, re-painting and rewriting
wall dials and cleaning and restoring

longcase dials, re-silvering and re-
numbering brass dials.

PROVIDE Free Estimates.
Collection/Delivery Service by
arrangement.
SPEAK TO Rob Gillies.
This workshop is included on the register
of conservators maintained by the
Conservation Unit of the Museums and
Galleries Commission.

WEST DEAN COLLEGE
West Dean, Chichester, **West Sussex
PO18 00Z**
TEL   0243 63 301
FAX   0243 63 342
OPEN   9–5 Mon–Fri.

Specialise in training conservators and
restorers in the field of antique clocks.
They will also undertake restoration
work.

PROVIDE Local Home Inspections. Free
Estimates.
SPEAK TO Peter Sarginson.
SEE Books, Furniture, Porcelain, Silver.

T. P. ROONEY
CLOCKMAKER AND
RESTORER
191 Sunderland Road, Harton Village,
South Shields, **Tyne & Wear
NE34 6AQ**
TEL   091 456 2950
OPEN   By Appointment.

Specialise in restoring and repairing
antique and quality clocks, except turret
and carriage, and will hand-make
traditional clocks to commission.

PROVIDE Home Inspections. Free
Estimates. Free Collection/Delivery
Service.
SPEAK TO T. P. Rooney.
This workshop is included on the register
of conservators maintained by the
Conservation Unit of the Museums and
Galleries Commission.

W. MAHONEY CLOCK & WATCH RESTORATION

15 Meadow Road, Newbold-on-Avon, Nr. Rugby, **Warwickshire CV21 1ER**

TEL   0788 546985

OPEN   6–6 Mon–Sat.

Specialise in restoring clocks and watches, including movements, dials, cases, silvering dials, painted dials, recutting wheels, pinions.

PROVIDE Home Inspections. Chargeable Estimates. Chargeable Collection/Delivery Service.

SPEAK TO William Mahoney.

TIME IN HAND

11 Church Street, Shipston-on-Stour, **Warwickshire CV36 4AP**

TEL   0608 62578

OPEN   9–1, 2–5.30 Mon–Sat.

Specialise in restoring fine clocks, barometers and antique mechanisms.

PROVIDE Home Inspections. Free Estimates. Chargeable Collection/Delivery Service.

SPEAK TO Francis Bennett or Alyson Clossick.

COSBY FINE CLOCKS RESTORER

The Park House, Tockenham Wick, Nr. Wootton Bassett, Swindon, **Wiltshire SN4 7PQ**

TEL   0793 848945

OPEN   9–6 Mon–Sat By Appointment Only.

Specialise in restoring fine quality antique clocks, longcase, bracket, French mantel and table clocks, carriage clocks etc. Also automata clocks. Specialists in proper restoration of mechanical tower and stable (turret) clocks.

PROVIDE Local Home Inspections. Free/Chargeable Estimates. Chargeable Collection/Delivery Service.

SPEAK TO Mr Julian C. S. F. Cosby.

MBWCG, Associate Member of the BHI, Member of the Antiquarian Horological Society. This workshop is included on the register of conservators maintained by the Conservation Unit of the Museums and Galleries Commission.

RESTORATIONS UNLIMITED

Pinkney Park, Malmesbury, **Wiltshire SN16 0NX**

TEL   0666 840888

OPEN   8.30–5 Mon–Fri; Sat & Sun By Appointment.

Specialise in restoring longcase and bracket clocks.

PROVIDE Home Inspections. Free Estimates. Free Collection/Delivery Service.

SPEAK TO Richard Pinchis.

SEE Furniture, Oil Paintings, Porcelain.

TIME RESTORED & CO.

18–20 High Street, Pewsey, **Wiltshire SN9 5AQ**

TEL   0672 63544

FAX   0672 63544

OPEN   By Appointment.

Specialise in restoring antique English and French clocks and barometers.

PROVIDE Home Inspections. Free Estimates. Free Collection/Delivery Service.

SPEAK TO J. H. Bowler-Reed.

SEE Collectors (Mechanical Music).

CHRIS WADGE CLOCKS

142 Fisherton Street, Salisbury, **Wiltshire SP2 7QT**

TEL   0722 334467

OPEN   9–5 Tues–Sat.

Specialise in repairing most types of clocks, especially anniversary clocks 1880–1970. They also repair barometers, barographs and pocket watches.

PROVIDE Home Inspections. Free

Estimates. Chargeable
Collection/Delivery Service.
SPEAK TO Chris or Patrick Wadge.

ALVERTON ANTIQUES
7 South Parade, Northallerton, **North Yorkshire DL7 OSE**
TEL   0609 780402
OPEN   10–5.30 Wed, Fri, Sat or By
Appointment.

Specialise in repairing and restoring British longcase clocks.

PROVIDE Home Inspections. Free Estimates. Chargeable Collection/Delivery Service.
SPEAK TO Mrs Matson.

HAWORTH ANTIQUES
Harrogate Road, Huby, Nr. Leeds,
North Yorkshire LS17 OEF
and 26 Cold Bath Road, Harrogate,
North Yorkshire HG2 ONA
TEL   0423 734293
       0423 521401
OPEN   9–6 Tues–Sat or By
Appointment.

Specialise in restoring clocks, including white and brass dial movements and casework.

PROVIDE Home Inspections. Free Estimates. Chargeable Collection/Delivery Service.
SPEAK TO Glynn or June White.
They are MBWCMG.

G. D. HOPPER
Clock Work, 27 Elm Road, Ripon,
North Yorkshire HG4 2PE
TEL   0765 602606
OPEN   9–5 Mon–Fri or By
Appointment.

Specialise in restoring all types of antique and modern clocks and watches. Also service time-lock mechanisms and other special timers.

PROVIDE Home Inspections. Free

Estimates. Chargeable
Collection/Delivery Service.
SPEAK TO David Hopper.
CMBHI. This workshop is included on the register of conservators maintained by the Conservation Unit of the Museums and Galleries Commission.

DAVID MASON & SON
7–9 Westmoreland Street, Harrogate,
North Yorkshire HG1 5AY
TEL   0423 567305
OPEN   9–5 Mon–Sat.

Specialise in repair of clocks, watches and barometers.

PROVIDE Home Inspections. Free Estimates. Chargeable Collection/Delivery Service.
SPEAK TO John Mason.
Member of NAG, Yorkshire Goldsmiths Association, FGA.
SEE Silver.

JOHN PEARSON ANTIQUE CLOCK RESTORATION
Church Cottage, Birstwith, Harrogate,
North Yorkshire HG3 2NG
TEL   0423 770828
OPEN   By Appointment.

Specialise in dial restoration, complete clock restoration including movement, case and dial.

PROVIDE Home Inspections. Refundable Estimates. Collection/Delivery Service.
SPEAK TO John Pearson.

DAVID BARKER
Antique Clock Restoration, Inglenook, Ferncliffe Drive, Utley, Keighley, **West Yorkshire BD20 6HN**
TEL   0535 606306
OPEN   Mon–Sat By Appointment.

Specialise in restoring antique clocks.

PROVIDE Home Inspections. Free

Estimates. Free/Chargeable
Collection/Delivery Service.
SPEAK TO David Barker.
SEE Collectors (Mechanical Music).

HARRY GILMORE
75 Osborne Park, Belfast, **Co. Antrim
BT9 6JQ**
TEL 0232 084 661580
OPEN By Appointment.

Specialise in restoring French and
English antique clocks, some American,
including bracket, longcase and carriage
clocks.

PROVIDE Home Inspections.
Free/Chargeable Estimates.
Collection/Delivery Service by
arrangement.
SPEAK TO Harry Gilmore.

Member of IPCRA, MBHI and
BCWMG.

ROBERT E. BARFOOT
9 York Parade, Belfast, **Co. Antrim
BT15 3QZ**
TEL 0232 773108
OPEN By Appointment.

Specialise in restoring English bracket
clocks and French Boulle and ormolu
clocks.

PROVIDE Home Inspections. Free
Estimates. Free Collection/Delivery
Service.
SPEAK TO Robert Barfoot.
Member of IPCRA and BHI.

T. M. TUKE
18 Main Street, Greyabbey,
Newtownards, **Co. Down**
TEL 024774 416
FAX 024774 250
OPEN 11–5 Mon–Sat; closed Thur.

Specialise in restoring antique clocks
and watches.

PROVIDE Home Inspections. Free

Estimates. Free Collection/Delivery
Service.
SPEAK TO Tom Tuke.
Mr Tuke is MBHI.
SEE Silver.

K. AND M. NESBITT
21 Tobermore Road, Magherafelt,
Co. Londonderry BT45 5HB
TEL 0648 32713
OPEN By Appointment.

Specialise in restoring antique clocks
and watches.

PROVIDE Home Inspections. Free
Estimates. Chargeable
Collection/Delivery Service.
SPEAK TO Mr K. Nesbitt.

THE CLOCK CENTRE
71 York Road, Dun Laoghaire,
Co. Dublin
TEL 01 2803667
OPEN 9.30–5 Mon–Fri; 9.30–1 Sat.

Specialise in restoring and repairing
clocks but not watches.

PROVIDE Home Inspections. Free
Estimates.
SPEAK TO Patrick Healey.

DAVID HEATH
'Fontaine', Sarshill, Kilmore,
Co. Wexford
TEL 053 29722
OPEN By Appointment.

Specialise in restoring antique English
and American longcase, bracket and
carriage clocks.

PROVIDE Home Inspections. Free
Estimates. Collection/Delivery Service
by arrangement.
SPEAK TO David Heath.
Member of IPCRA.

ST JAMES'S GALLERY LTD

Smith Street, St Peter Port, **Guernsey, Channel Islands**
TEL   0481 720070
OPEN   9–5.30 Mon–Sat or By
        Appointment.

Specialise in clock repairs.

PROVIDE Home Inspections. Chargeable
Estimates. Collection/Delivery Service
by arrangement.
SPEAK TO Mrs Whittam.
SEE Furniture, Porcelain.

GRANT LEES

98 Gala Park, Galashiels, Selkirkshire,
Borders TD1 1EZ
TEL   0896 3721
OPEN   9–6 Mon–Sat, closed Wed and
        Sat a.m.

Specialise in restoring antique clocks,
barometers, vintage wrist-watches.

PROVIDE Home Inspections. Free
Estimates. Chargeable
Collection/Delivery Service.
SPEAK TO Grant Lees.
This workshop is in the Scottish
Conservation Directory.
SEE Furniture, Collectors (Mechanical
Music).

J. TUBBECKE

Antique Clocks, 11 Island Street,
Galashiels, **Borders TD1 1NZ**
TEL   0896 58958
OPEN   10–5 Mon, Tues, Thur, Fri; 10–
        1.30 Sat.

Specialise in restoring antique clocks
and watches, including gear cutting, dial
painting, case restoration. Missing parts
hand-made.

PROVIDE Home Inspections. Free
Estimates. Free Collection/Delivery
Service.
SPEAK TO J. Tubbecke or T. Treeby.

This workshop is in the Scottish
Conservation Directory.
SEE Collectors (Mechanical Music).

HAMILTON AND INCHES

87 George Street, Edinburgh, **Lothian
EH2 3EY**
TEL   031 225 4898
FAX   031 220 6994
OPEN   9–5 Mon–Fri; 9–12.30 Sat.

Specialise in repairing clocks and
watches.

PROVIDE Home Inspections. Free
Estimates. Chargeable
Collection/Delivery Service.
SPEAK TO Densil Skinner.

Member of NAG.
SEE Silver.

SIMON LOWMAN

112 Gilmore Place, Edinburgh, **Lothian
EH3 9PL**
TEL   031 229 2129
OPEN   9–6 Mon–Fri.

Specialise in repairing and restoring
18th century English and French bracket
and longcase clocks as well as carriage
clocks.

PROVIDE Home Inspections. Free
Estimates. Chargeable
Collection/Delivery Service.
SPEAK TO Simon Lowman.

Mr Lowman is a MBHI. This workshop
is in the Scottish Conservation
Directory.

WILIAM MITCHELL CLOCK REPAIRER

42 Dundas Street, Edinburgh, **Lothian
EH3 6JN**
TEL   031 556 8000
OPEN   9–1, 2–5 Mon–Sat or By
        Appointment.

Specialise in restoring clocks, antique and modern mechanical but not quartz.

PROVIDE Home Inspections. Free Estimates. Chargeable Collection/Delivery Service.
SPEAK TO William Mitchell.

This workshop is in the Scottish Conservation Directory.

KENNETH CHAPELLE ANTIQUE CLOCK RESTORER
26 Otago Lane, Glasgow, **Strathclyde G12 8PB**.
TEL   041 334 7766
OPEN   8.30–4.30 Mon–Fri; 8.30–1 Sat.

Specialise in restoring fine antique clocks.

PROVIDE Home Inspections. Free Estimates. Chargeable Collection/Delivery Service.
SPEAK TO Kenneth Chapelle.

Mr Chapelle is FBHI. This workshop is in the Scottish Conservation Directory.

TIM BRAMELD
Howell's House, Grosmont, **Gwent NP7 8BP**
TEL   0981 240 940
OPEN   By Appointment.

Specialise in repairing and restoring antique clocks, particularly regulators.

PROVIDE Home Inspections. Free Estimates. Chargeable Collection/Delivery Service.
SPEAK TO Tim Brameld.

SNOWDONIA ANTIQUES
Station Road, Llanrwst, **Gwynedd LL26 QEP**
TEL   0492 640789
OPEN   9–5.30 Mon–Sat or By Appointment.

Specialise in restoring longcase clocks.

PROVIDE Home Inspections. Chargeable Estimates. Chargeable Collection/Delivery Service.
SPEAK TO Mr J. Collins.
SEE Furniture.

SILVER, JEWELLERY, OBJECTS OF VERTU AND METALWORK

SILVER

DO

Clean with soft rags and soap and water
Keep silver in felt bags
Store in a dry environment
Avoid stacking in cupboards
Use a soft toothbrush for cast ornament
Beware of wetting any items containing other materials such as iron or steel

DON'T

Overclean hallmarks
Leave salt, mustard etc in condiments
Put away cutlery while still warm from washing
Put rubber bands round cutlery
Put plated items in the dishwasher
Use liquid polish on inlaid items such as tortoiseshell, wood etc
Clean with any abrasive

JEWELLERY

DO

Remember that pearls are very sensitive to abrasion and corrosion – always store and wrap them separately and polish gently with a soft cloth after wearing
Keep all fitted boxes which bear a maker's or retailer's name
Have bead necklaces regularly restrung with silk
Keep insurance valuations up to date and understand exactly what is covered and where: losses overseas are often not

DON'T

Do the gardening or any other manual task while wearing jewellery
Waste gin on cleaning jewellery: warm water and a little detergent are preferable, applied with a soft toothbrush
Clean anything except gemstones and gold or platinum yourself
Apply hairspray or scent while wearing jewellery, particularly pearls

IAN AND DIANNE McCARTHY

Arcadian Cottage, 112 Station Road, Clutton, **Avon BS18 4RA**
TEL   0761 53188
OPEN   By Appointment.

Specialise in restoring metalware, including table lamps.

PROVIDE Home Inspections. Free Estimates. Chargeable Collection/Delivery Service.
SPEAK TO Ian or Dianne McCarthy.
SEE Furniture, Porcelain.

ANNE FINNERTY

62 Gainsborough Road, Southcote, Reading, **Berkshire RG3 3BZ**
TEL   0734 588274
OPEN   By Appointment.

Specialise in restoring antique beadwork, pearl and bead re-threading.

PROVIDE Home Inspections. Free Estimates. Postal Collection/Delivery Service.
SPEAK TO Anne Finnerty.

HAMILTON HAVERS

58 Conisboro Avenue, Caversham Heights, Reading, **Berkshire RG4 7JE**
TEL   0734 473379
OPEN   By Appointment.

Specialise in restoring Boulle, marquetry, ivory, tortoiseshell, mother-of-pearl, brass, lapis-lazuli and malachite objets d'art.

PROVIDE Free/Chargeable Estimates.
SPEAK TO Hamilton Havers.
SEE Clocks, Furniture.

STYLES SILVER

12 Bridge Street, Hungerford, **Berkshire RG17 0EH**
TEL   0488 683922

Specialise in repairing and cleaning English 18th–20th century silverware

PROVIDE Free Estimates.
SPEAK TO Derek Styles.

JOHN ARMISTEAD

Malham Cottage, Bellingdon, Nr. Chesham, **Buckinghamshire HP5 2UR**
TEL   0494 758209
OPEN   9–5 Mon–Fri.

Specialise in repairing metalwork, including brass candlesticks, chandeliers, fire irons, polishing, plating, casting.

PROVIDE Home Inspections, Free Estimates. Collection/Delivery Service by arrangement.
SPEAK TO John Armistead.

Member of the Guild of Master Craftsmen and UKIC. This workshop is included on the register of conservators maintained by the Conservation Unit of the Museums and Galleries Commission.
SEE Furniture.

BUCKIES JEWELLERS

31 Trinity Street, Cambridge, **Cambridgeshire CB2 1TB**
TEL   0223 357910
OPEN   9.45–5 Tues–Sat.

Specialise in repairing and restoring jewellery and silverware.

PROVIDE Home Inspections. Refundable Estimates. Chargeable Collection/Delivery Service.
SPEAK TO Peter R. Buckie.

IAN FALCON HAMMOND

50 Kings Road, Eaton Socon, St Neots, **Cambridgeshire PE19 3DB**
TEL   0480 212794
OPEN   By Appointment.

Specialise in restoring Oriental and European ivories, tortoiseshell, mother-of-pearl, fans, meerschaum pipes, snuff boxes, Japanese shibyama and netsuke.

PROVIDE Home Inspections. Chargeable

Estimates. Chargeable
Collection/Delivery Service.
SPEAK TO Ian Hammond.

PETER JOHN
38 St Mary's Street, Eyresbury, St Neots,
Cambridgeshire PE19 2TA
TEL   0480 216297
OPEN   9–5 Mon–Sat.

Specialise in restoring antique jewellery.

PROVIDE Home Inspections. Free
Estimates. Chargeable
Collection/Delivery Service.
SPEAK TO Kym or Peter John.
SEE Clocks.

A. ALLEN ANTIQUE RESTORERS
Buxton Rd, Newtown, Newmills, Via
Stockport, **Cheshire SK12 3JS**
TEL   0663 745274
OPEN   8–5 Mon–Fri; 9–12 Sat.

Specialise in restoring Boulle work,
inlay, gilding and metalwork.

PROVIDE Home Inspections.
Free/Chargeable Estimates.
Collection/Delivery Service.
SPEAK TO Tony Allen.
SEE Clocks, Furniture, Picture Frames.

THE TEXTILE RESTORATION STUDIO
20 Hargreaves Road, Timperley,
Altrincham, **Cheshire WA15 7BB**
TEL   061 904 9944
FAX   061 903 9144
OPEN   9.30–5 Mon–Fri.

Specialise in cleaning, conserving and
repairing of antique fans. They also
undertake framing and mounting for
display.

PROVIDE Home Inspections. Free
Estimates. Collection/Delivery Service
by arrangement.

SPEAK TO Jacqueline Hyman.
SEE Carpets, Collectors (Dolls), Lighting.

ST AUSTELL ANTIQUES CENTRE
(formerly The Furniture Store)
37/39 Truro Road, St Austell, **Cornwall
PL25 5JE**
TEL   0726 63178 and 0288 81548
OPEN   10–5 Mon–Sat or By
        Appointment.

Specialise in restoring metalwork.

PROVIDE Home Inspections. Free
Estimates. Free Local
Collection/Delivery Service.
SPEAK TO Roger Nosworthy.
SEE Furniture.

THE LANTERN SHOP
4 New Street, Sidmouth, **Devon
EX10 8AP**
TEL   0395 516320
OPEN   9.45–12.45, 2.15–4.45 Mon–
        Sat; closed Mon and Sat p.m.

Specialise in restoring antique items of
lighting and conversion to electricity.

PROVIDE Home Inspections. Free
Estimates. Chargeable
Collection/Delivery Service.
SPEAK TO Julia Creeke.
SEE Oil Paintings, Porcelain.

D. J. JEWELLERY
166–168 Ashley Road, Parkstone, Poole,
Dorset BH14 9BY
TEL   0202 745148
OPEN   9.30–5 Mon–Sat.

Specialise in repairing antique jewellery.

PROVIDE Home Inspections. Free
Estimates. Chargeable
Collection/Delivery Service.
SPEAK TO Dennis O'Sullivan.
SEE Clocks.

GEORGIAN GEMS
28 High Street, Swanage, **Dorset**
BH19 2NU
TEL 0929 424697
OPEN 9.30–1, 2.15–5 Daily; closed Sun summer; closed Mon p.m. and Thur winter.

Specialise in repairing antique jewellery.

PROVIDE Home Inspections. Free Estimates. Chargeable Collection/Delivery Service.
SPEAK TO Brian Barker.

Member of the Gemmological Association.

HEIRLOOMS ANTIQUE JEWELLERS
21 South Street, Wareham, **Dorset**
BH20 4LR
TEL 0929 554207
OPEN 9–5 Mon–Sat; closed Wed.

Specialise in restoring and repairing antique jewellery and silver, except watches.

PROVIDE Free Estimates.
SPEAK TO Michael or Gabrielle Young.

GEO. A. PAYNE & SON LTD
742 Christchurch Road, Boscombe, Bournemouth, **Dorset BH7 6BZ**
TEL 0202 394954
OPEN 9–5.30 Mon–Sat.

Specialise in repairing and restoring jewellery and silverware.

PROVIDE Home Inspections. Free Estimates. Chargeable Collection/Delivery Service.
SPEAK TO Nicholas G. Payne.

Fellow of the Gemmological Association and member of NAG.

DAVANA INTERIORS
88 Hythe Hill, Colchester, **Essex**
CO1 2NH
TEL 0206 577853
OPEN 8–5 Mon–Fri.

Specialise in restoring antique lights and antique metalware.

PROVIDE Home Inspections. Free Estimates.
SPEAK TO Mr D. Donnelly.

MILLSIDE ANTIQUE RESTORATION
Parndon Mill, Parndon Mill Lane, Harlow, **Essex CM20 2HP**
TEL 0279 428148
FAX 0279 415075
OPEN 10–5 Mon–Fri.

Specialise in cleaning and restoring enamels, including snuff boxes and cloisonné work as well as ivory enamelling.

PROVIDE Home Inspections. Free/Chargeable Estimates. Chargeable Collection/Delivery Service.
SPEAK TO David Sparks or Angela Wickliffe-Philp.
SEE Oil Paintings, Picture Frames, Porcelain.

PETER SHORER
40 Devonshire Road, Ilford, **Essex**
IG2 7EW
TEL 081 590 8364
OPEN By Appointment.

Specialise in restoring and reconstructing items of adornment and small metalwork, antiquities.

PROVIDE Chargeable Home Inspections. Free/Chargeable Estimates. Chargeable Collection/Delivery Service.
SPEAK TO Peter Shorer or Michael Shorer.

This workshop is included on the register of conservators maintained by the Conservation Unit of the Museums and Galleries Commission.

KEITH BAWDEN
Mews Workshop, Montpellier Retreat, Cheltenham, **Gloucestershire GL50 2XS**
TEL   0242 230320
OPEN   7–4.30 Mon–Fri.

Specialise in conserving and restoring all aspects of metalwork.

PROVIDE Free Estimates. Home Inspections. Local Collection/Delivery Service.
SPEAK TO Keith Bawden.
SEE Clocks, Furniture, Oil Paintings, Porcelain.

ATELIER FINE ART CASTINGS LTD
Hulfords Lane, Nr. Hartley Witney, **Hampshire RG27 8AG**
TEL   0252 844388
OPEN   8.30–5 Mon–Fri.

Specialise in restoring bronze, brass, copper and lead art work. Bronze casting and restoration of most other metalwork undertaken.

PROVIDE Home Inspections. Free Estimates. Chargeable Collection/Delivery Service.
SPEAK TO Mrs A. Wills.

Work can be collected in London from The Sladmore Gallery, 32 Bruton Place, London W1X 7AA
TEL   071 499 0365.
SEE Porcelain.

DOUGLAS J. LINCOLN
Athgarvan House, Shawford, Winchester, **Hampshire SO21 2AA**
TEL   0962 712662
OPEN   By Appointment.

Specialise in restoring silverware, especially engraved and chased work. They can also provide engraving services for lettered plaques.

PROVIDE Local Home Inspections. Free

Estimates. Chargeable Local Collection/Delivery Service.
SPEAK TO Douglas Lincoln.
Visiting Tutor at West Dean. This workshop is included on the register of conservators maintained by the Conservation Unit of the Museums and Galleries Commission.
SEE Furniture.

A. W. PORTER
High Street, Hartley Witney, Nr. Basingstoke, **Hampshire RG27 8NY**
TEL   025 126 2676
FAX   025 126 2064
OPEN   9–5.30 Mon–Fri; 9.30–5 Sat.

Specialise in restoring jewellery and silverware.

PROVIDE Home Inspections. Free Estimates. Chargeable Collection/Delivery Service.
SPEAK TO Mr Porter.
Established since 1844.
SEE Clocks.

STANLEY THORNE
Hursley Antiques, Hursley, Nr. Winchester, **Hampshire SO21 2JY**
TEL   0962 75488
OPEN   10–6 Mon–Sat.

Specialise in repairs and restoration to brass, copper, spelter, bronze, pewter, commissions taken, vases lamped, brass or lead liners made, lanterns made to pattern or sketch.

PROVIDE Local Home Inspections. Free Estimates. Local Free Collection/Delivery Service.
SPEAK TO Stanley Thorne.

HOWARDS OF BROADWAY
27A The High Street, Broadway, **Hereford & Worcester WR12 7DP**
TEL   0386 858924
OPEN   9.30–5.30 Daily.

Specialise in repairing antique and modern silver and jewellery. They will remodel antique or modern pieces to either a customer's own designs or those by their own designer.

PROVIDE Home Inspections. Free Estimates. Free Collection/Delivery Service.
SPEAK TO Robert Allport.

W. B. GATWARD & SON LTD
20 Market Place, Hitchin,
Hertfordshire SG5 1DU
TEL   0462 434273
OPEN   9.15–5.15 Mon–Sat; closed
         Wed.

Specialise in repairing and restoring antique jewellery and silver.

PROVIDE Local Home Inspections. Free Estimates. Chargeable Collection/Delivery Service.
SPEAK TO Miss Gatward or Mr Hunter.
SEE Clocks.

WILLIAM H. STEVENS
8 Eton Avenue, East Barnet,
Hertfordshire EN4 8TU
TEL   081 449 7956
OPEN   9–5.30 Mon–Fri.

Specialise in restoring Japanese and Chinese works of art, including enamels, lacquer, ivory, horn, mother-of-pearl, soapstone and jade. They also restore Blue John.

PROVIDES Home Inspections. Free Estimates. Free Collection/Delivery Service.
SPEAK TO John Robin or Daniel Stevens.

This is the fifth generation of a family firm founded in 1836.
SEE Porcelain.

BEEBY & POWELL
2–6 Basement, Victoria Street,
Rochester, **Kent ME1 1XH**
TEL   0634 830764
OPEN   By Appointment.

Specialise in restoring antique silver and gold objects.

PROVIDE Home Inspections. Free Estimates. Free Collection/Delivery Service.
SPEAK TO Jonathan Beeby or Jim Powell.
Member of the Guild of Master Craftsmen.

HENWOOD DECORATIVE METAL STUDIOS
The Bayle, Folkestone, **Kent CT20 1SQ**
TEL   0303 50911
FAX   0303 850224
OPEN   8.30–5 Mon–Fri.

Specialise in restoring any non-ferrous metalwork; antiques, church altarware, door furniture and domestic tableware. They can undertake any service allied to non-ferrous metals i.e. repairs, replacement, re-polishing, electro-plating, lacquering, engraving. Can also manufacture to suit client's own requirements, either small run or one off.

PROVIDE Local Home Inspections. Free Estimates. Local Free Collection/Delivery Service.
SPEAK TO Mr P. J. Rose.
Member of UKIC, Federation of Master Craftsmen and National Church Craft Association.
SEE Porcelain.

SARGEANT RESTORATIONS
21 The Green, Westerham, **Kent TN16 1AX**
TEL   0959 62130
OPEN   8.30–5.30 Mon–Sat.

Specialise in restoring, cleaning and

wiring metal chandeliers, candelabra and general light fittings.

PROVIDE Home Inspections. Free Estimates. Chargeable Collection/Delivery Service.
SPEAK TO Ann, David or Denys Sargeant.
SEE Porcelain.

CHARLES HOWELL JEWELLER
2 Lord Street, Oldham, **Lancashire OL1 3EY**
TEL   061 624 1479
OPEN   9.15–5 Mon–Sat.

Specialise in restoring Victorian and Edwardian jewellery and silverware.

PROVIDE Free Estimates.
SPEAK TO Mr N. G. Howell.
Member of NAG.

WILLIAM DICKENSON
Home Farm, Burley On The Hill, Oakham, **Leicestershire LE15 7SX**
TEL   0572 757333
OPEN   By Appointment.
Specialise in cleaning brass and copper objects.

PROVIDE Home Inspections. Chargeable Estimates. Chargeable Collection/ Delivery Service.
SPEAK TO William Dickenson.

BARRY M. WITMOND
42 Wragby Road, Bardney, **Lincolnshire LN3 5XL**
TEL   0526 398338 and 071 409 2335
OPEN   By Appointment.

Specialise in restoring English and Continental silver plate.

PROVIDE Home Inspections. Free/Chargeable Estimates. Collection/Delivery Service Available.
SPEAK TO Barry Witmond.

DAVID LAWTON LTD
P. O. Box 1702, **London E8 3LW**
TEL   071 254 8708
OPEN   By Appointment Only.

Specialise in restoring silver and silver plate. Replating, gilding, rebristling of hairbrushes, cigarette boxes relined, frames rebacked, cutlery rebladed, new handles on tea or coffee pots. Blue glass liners supplied.

PROVIDE Home Inspections. Free Estimates. Free Local/Collection Delivery Service. Chargeable Postal Service outside London.
SPEAK TO Richard Lawton.

DAVID TURNER
4 Atlas Mews, Ramsgate Street, **London E8 2NA**
TEL   071 249 2379
OPEN   10–6 Mon–Fri.

Specialise in restoring metalwork and metal light fittings.

PROVIDE Home Inspections. Free Estimates. Free Collection/Delivery Service.
SEE Furniture, Porcelain.

RUPERT HARRIS
Studio 5, 1 Fawe Street, **London E14 6PD**
TEL   071 987 6231 and 515 2020
FAX   071 987 7994
OPEN   9–6 Mon–Fri.

Specialise in conserving fine and decorative metalwork. Advice also given on display, storage, environmental control, security of outdoor sculpture, emergency and disaster planning and salvage.

PROVIDE Home Inspections. Chargeable Estimates. Chargeable Collection/Delivery Service.
SPEAK TO Rupert Harris.

Member of UKIC and IIC. This workshop is included on the register of

conservators maintained by the
Conservation Unit of the Museums and
Galleries Commission.
SEE Porcelain.

EDWARD BARNARD & SONS LTD
54 Hatton Garden, **London**
EC1N 8HN
TEL   071 405 5677
FAX   071 405 6604
OPEN   9–5 Mon–Fri.

Specialise in repairing and restoring
antique and modern silver and gold
ware.

PROVIDE Home Inspections. Free
Estimates, Free Collection/Delivery
Service in Central London.
SPEAK TO C. Ashenden or J. Padgett.

THE CONSERVATION STUDIO
Unit 21, Pennybank Chambers, 33–35
St John's Square, **London EC1M 4DS**
TEL   071 251 6853
OPEN   9.30–5 Mon–Fri.

Specialise in restoring enamels including
snuff boxes, jewellery and watch dials.
They will also repair objects in ivory and
tortoiseshell.

PROVIDE Home Inspections (large items
only). Refundable Estimates.
Chargeable Collection/Delivery Service.
SPEAK TO Sandra Davison.

SEE Clocks, Porcelain.

R. HOLT & CO. LTD
98 Hatton Garden, **London**
EC1N 8NX
TEL   071 405 5286 or 0197
FAX   071 430 1279
OPEN   9.30–5.30 Mon–Fri.

Specialise in cutting and re-cutting
gemstones and restoring and repairing
gemset items and carvings.

PROVIDE Home Inspections. Free
Estimates.
SPEAK TO R. Holt or M. R. Howard.

Members of Guild of Master Craftsmen,
British Jewellers Association and the
Gemmological Association of Great
Britain. Members of the London
Diamond Bourse.

ANDREW R. ULLMAN LTD
10 Hatton Garden, **London**
EC1N 8AH
TEL   071 405 1877
OPEN   9–5.30 Mon–Sat.

Specialise in restoring antique jewellery.

PROVIDE Free Estimates.
SPEAK TO J. S. Ullman or J. Pinkus.

KEMPSON AND MAUGER
Studio 26, 63 Clerkenwell Road,
London EC1M 5NP
TEL   071 251 0578
OPEN   By Appointment.

Specialise in restoring enamel on
precious metals.

PROVIDE Free Estimates.
SPEAK TO Mr Hamilton.

C. J. VANDER LTD
Dunstan House, 14A St Cross Street,
London EC1N 8XD
TEL   071 831 6741
FAX   071 831 9695
OPEN   9–5.30 Mon–Fri.

Specialise in repairing and restoring high
quality antique and second-hand silver
and Victorian electroplate.

PROVIDE Free Estimates.
SPEAK TO Mr R. F. H. Vander.

This firm was established in 1886.

DON BAKER
3 Canonbury Park South, **London
N1 2JR**
TEL   071 226 2314
OPEN   By Appointment.

Specialise in restoring Indian
miniatures.

PROVIDE Free Estimates.
SPEAK TO Don Baker.
SEE Books.

PETER CHAPMAN ANTIQUES
Incorporating **CHAPMAN
RESTORATIONS**
10 Theberton Street, **London N1 0QX**
TEL   071 226 5565
FAX   081 348 4846
OPEN   9.30–6 Mon–Sat.

Specialise in repairing bronze and other
metalwork and will convert objects into
lamps.

PROVIDE Home Inspections. Refundable
Estimates. Chargeable
Collection/Delivery Service.
SPEAK TO Peter Chapman or Tony
Holohan.
SEE Furniture, Oil Paintings, Picture
Frames, Porcelain.

CHARLOTTE DE SYLLAS
28 Park Avenue North, **London
N8 7RT**
TEL   081 348 7181
OPEN   By Appointment.

Specialise in restoring hard stone
carvings, particularly jade.

PROVIDE Home Inspections. Free
Estimates. Collection/Delivery Service
by arrangement.
SPEAK TO Charlotte de Syllas.

Charlotte de Syllas can also be
commissioned to make one-off pieces of
jewellery.

W. PAIRPOINT & SONS LTD
10 Shacklewell Road, **London N16 7TA**
TEL   071 254 6362
FAX   071 254 7175
OPEN   8.30–5.30 Mon–Fri.

Specialise in restoring Old Sheffield and
EPNS plate.

PROVIDE Free Estimates, Free Local
Collection/Delivery Service.
SPEAK TO Eric Soulard.
SEE Clocks.

WAKELEY AND WHEELER LTD
10 Shacklewell Road, **London N16 7TA**
TEL   071 254 6362
FAX   071 254 7175
OPEN   8.30–9.30 Mon–Fri.

Specialise in restoring and repairing
antique and other silverware.

PROVIDE Free Estimates
SPEAK TO F. J. P. Legget
They have been established for 200 years.

ROCHEFORT ANTIQUES LTD
32–34 The Green, **London N21 1AX**
TEL   081 886 4779 or 363 0910
OPEN   10–6 Mon, Tues, Thur, Sat.

Specialise in restoring silver.

PROVIDE Home Inspections. Free
Estimates. Chargeable
Collection/Delivery Service.
SPEAK TO L. W. Stevens-Wilson.
SEE Furniture, Porcelain.

STAMFORD SILVER REPAIRS
The Workshop, Scope Antiques
Emporium, 64–66 Willesden Lane,
London NW6 7SX
TEL   071 328 5833
OPEN   10–6 Mon–Sat.

Specialise in repairing silver, including

removing dents and engravings, replacing missing parts. They will also repair good quality brass and copper objects.

PROVIDE Free Estimates.
SPEAK TO Donald Stamford.

WELLINGTON GALLERY
1 St John's Wood High Street, **London NW8 7NG**
TEL   071 586 2620
OPEN   10–5.30 Mon–Sat.

Specialise in restoring silver and Sheffield plate.

PROVIDE Home Inspections. Free Estimates. Chargeable Collection/ Delivery Service.
SPEAK TO Mrs Maureen Barclay or Mr K. J. Barclay.
Member of LAPADA.
SEE Porcelain, Oil Paintings, Furniture.

B. C. METALCRAFTS
69 Tewkesbury Gardens, **London NW9 0QU**
TEL   081 204 2446
FAX   081 206 2871
OPEN   By Appointment.

Specialise in restoring and repairing antique lighting decor and all types of conversion to electricity.
SPEAK TO F. Burnell or M. A. Burnell. They are Members of DLA.
SEE Clocks.

VERDIGRIS ART METALWORK RESTORERS
Arch 280 or 290, Crown Street, **London SE5 0UR**
TEL   071 703 8373
OPEN   9–5 Mon–Fri.

Specialise in restoring bronzes, chandeliers, door furniture, ormolu, pewter and spelter, monumental bronzes, including modern works.

PROVIDE Free Estimates.
SPEAK TO Gerard Bacon.

R. WILKINSON & SON
5 Catford Hill, **London SE6 4NU**
TEL   081 314 1080
FAX   081 690 1524
OPEN   9–5 Mon–Fri.

Specialise in restoring chandeliers.

PROVIDE Home Inspections. Free Estimates. Chargeable Collection/Delivery Service.
SPEAK TO Peter Prickett, Jane Milnes or David Wilkinson.

SEE Porcelain.

THE FAN MUSEUM
12 Crooms Hill, **London SE10 8ER**
TEL   081 858 7879 or 305 1441
OPEN   By Appointment.

Specialise in conserving and restoring all types of fans.

PROVIDE Home Inspections. Free Estimates. Postal Collection/Delivery Service.
SPEAK TO Mrs Alexander.

RELCY ANTIQUES
9 Nelson Road, Greenwich, **London SE10 9JB**
TEL   081 858 2812
FAX   081 293 4135
OPEN   10–6 Mon–Sat.

Specialise in restoring antique metalwork, including copper, brass, silver and ormolu.

PROVIDE Home Inspections. Free/Chargeable Estimates. Collection/Delivery Service by arrangement.
SPEAK TO Robin Challis.

SEE Collectors (Scientific Instruments), Furniture, Oil Paintings.

CRAWLEY STUDIOS
39 Wood Vale, **London SE23 3DS**
TEL   081 299 4121
FAX   081 299 0756
OPEN   9–6.15 Mon–Fri.

Specialise in restoring Tôle and papier mâché objects.

PROVIDE Home Inspections. Free Estimates. Chargeable Collection/ Delivery Service.
SPEAK TO Marie Louise Crawley.

Member of BAFRA, UKIC and the Guild of Master Craftsmen.
SEE Furniture.

N. BLOOM & SON (KNIGHTSBRIDGE)
Harrod's Fine Jewellery Room, **London SW1X 7XL**
TEL   071 730 1234 ext. 4062 or 4072
FAX   071 589 0655
OPEN   Mon–Sat 10–6, Wed 10–8.

Specialise in restoring old jewellery, antique and Victorian silver, enamel repairs.

PROVIDE Free Estimates.
SPEAK TO Heidi McKeown.

Member of LAPADA.
SEE Clocks.

CLARE HOUSE LIMITED
35 Elizabeth Street, **London SW1W 9RP**
TEL   071 730 8480
FAX   071 259 9752
OPEN   9.30–5.30 Mon–Fri.

Specialise in restoring objects of vertu.

PROVIDE Home Inspections. Free Estimates. Chargeable Collection/ Delivery Service.
SPEAK TO Elizabeth Hanley.
SEE Porcelain.

BOURBON–HANBY ANTIQUES
Chelsea Antiques Market, 245–253 Kings Road, **London SW3 5EL.**
TEL   071 352 2106
OPEN   10–6 Mon–Sat.

Specialise in repairing antique jewellery.

PROVIDE Home Inspections. Free Estimates. Free Collection/Delivery Service.
SPEAK TO Mr Barrett.

CHRISTINE SCHELL
15 Cale Street, **London SW3 3QS**
TEL   071 352 5563
OPEN   10–5.30 Mon–Fri; 10–1 Sat.

Specialise in restoring tortoiseshell, silver and pique work, refurbishing dressing-table sets and photograph frames.

PROVIDE Home Inspections. Free/Chargeable Estimates.
SPEAK TO Christine Schell.

JOHN HEAP
No.1 The Polygon, **London SW4**
TEL   071 627 4498
OPEN   By Appointment.

Specialise in restoring enamels, cane handles.

PROVIDE Home Inspections. Free Estimates. Free Collection/Delivery Service.
SPEAK TO John Heap.
SEE Furniture, Porcelain.

CHRISTOPHER WRAY'S LIGHTING EMPORIUM
600 Kings Road, **London SW6 2DX**
TEL   071 736 8434
FAX   071 731 3507
OPEN   9.30–6 Mon–Sat.

Specialise in restoring original Victorian and Edwardian light fittings.

PROVIDE Free Estimates. Chargeable Collection/Delivery Service.
SPEAK TO Christopher Wray.
SEE Porcelain.

COLIN BOWLES LTD
Unit 15, Heliport Estate, Bridges Court, **London SW11 3RE**
TEL   071 738 2559
OPEN   9–4 Mon–Fri.

Specialise in restoring antiquities and works of art.

PROVIDE Home Inspections. Free Estimates. Free Collection/Delivery Service.
SPEAK TO Colin Bowles.

COMPTON HALL RESTORATION
Unit A, 133 Riverside Business Centre, Haldane Place, **London SW18 4UQ**
TEL   081 874 0762
OPEN   9–5 Mon–Fri.

Specialise in restoring Tôle, papier mâché and penwork.

PROVIDE Home Inspections. Free Estimates. Collection/Delivery Service by arrangement.
SPEAK TO Lucinda Compton, Jane or Henrietta Hohler.
Member of BAFRA and UKIC.
SEE Furniture.

PLOWDEN AND SMITH LTD
190 St Ann's Hill, **London SW18 2RT**
TEL   081 874 4005
FAX   081 874 7248
OPEN   9–5.30 Mon–Fri.

Specialise in restoring and conserving gold and silver.

PROVIDE Home Inspections. Free Estimates. Chargeable Collection/Delivery Service.
SPEAK TO Bob Butler.

They also advise on conservation

strategy, environmental control and microclimates for collections as well as installing, mounting and displaying temporary and permanent exhibitions.
SEE Oil Paintings, Furniture, Porcelain.

BLOOMFIELD CERAMIC RESTORATIONS LTD
4th Floor, 58 Davies Street, **London W1Y 1LB**
TEL   071 580 5761
FAX   071 636 1625
OPEN   By Appointment.

Specialise in restoring antique European and Oriental objets d'art.

PROVIDE Free Estimates.
SPEAK TO Steven P. Bloomfield.
SEE Porcelain.

A. & B. BLOOMSTEIN
Bond Street Silver Galleries, 111–112 New Bond Street, **London W1Y 0BQ**
TEL   071 493 6180
FAX   071 495 3493
OPEN   9–5 Mon–Fri.

Specialise in restoring antique silver, Victorian plate and old Sheffield plate.

PROVIDE Free Estimates. Free Collection/Delivery Service.
SPEAK TO Alfred Bloomstein.
Member of LAPADA and BADA.

BRUFORD & HEMING LTD
28 Conduit Street, **London W1R 9TA**
TEL   071 499 7644
FAX   071 493 5879
OPEN   9.30–5.30 Mon–Fri.

Specialise in restoring antique jewellery and antique domestic silver, especially flatware. They also specialise in matching up missing items of antique cutlery.

PROVIDE Home Inspections. Free Estimates. Free Collection/Delivery Service.
SPEAK TO Alan Kinsey.

Member of BADA and NAG, this business has traded from the same address since 1858.

HADLEIGH JEWELLERS
30A Marylebone High Street, **London W1M 3PP**
TEL   071 935 4074
OPEN   9.30–5.30 Mon–Fri; 9.30–5 Sat.

Specialise in repairing and restoring antique jewellery and stones.

PROVIDE Home Inspections. Refundable Estimates.
SPEAK TO Mr J. Aldridge.

GEOFFREY HAGGER
58 Davies Street, **London W1Y 1LB**
TEL   071 409 1418
OPEN   9.30–4 Daily.

Specialise in restoring all types of jewellery.

PROVIDE Home Inspections. Free Estimates. Free Collection/Delivery Service.
SPEAK TO Geoffrey Hagger.

HARVEY AND GORE
4 Burlington Gardens, **London W1X 1LH**
TEL   071 493 2714
FAX   071 493 0324
OPEN   9.30–5 Mon–Fri.

Specialise in restoring antique, period and fine jewellery and antique silver and old Sheffield plate.

PROVIDE Free/Chargeable Estimates.
SPEAK TO Brian Norman.
Member of BADA. Established in 1723.

HENNELL SILVER LTD
12 New Bond Street, **London W1Y OH6**
TEL   071 629 6888
FAX   071 493 8158
OPEN   9.30–5.30 Tues–Sat.

Specialise in restoring modern and antique silver, old Sheffield plate.

PROVIDE Home Inspections. Free Estimates. Free Collection/Delivery Service.
SPEAK TO A. C. Kaufmann.

SEE Collectors (Scientific Instruments).

MYRA ANTIQUES
Bond Street Antiques Centre, 124 New Bond Street, **London W1**
TEL   071 408 1508
FAX   071 409 1317
OPEN   10–5.30 Mon–Fri.

Specialise in restoring jewellery.
SPEAK TO Myra Sampson.

W. SITCH & CO. LTD
48 Berwick Street, **London W1V 4JD**
TEL   071 437 3776
OPEN   8.30–5.30 Mon–Fri; 9–10 Sat.

Specialise in restoring late 19th century lighting.

PROVIDE Home Inspections. Free Estimates. Free/Chargeable Collection/Delivery Service.
SPEAK TO Ron Sitch.

SEE Porcelain.

JOHN WALKER
64 South Molton Street, **London W1Y 1HH**
TEL   071 629 3487
OPEN   8.30–5.15 Mon–Fri.

Specialise in repairing and restoring antique and modern jewellery.

PROVIDE Home Inspections. Free Estimates. Chargeable Collection/Delivery Service.
SPEAK TO John Walker or Steve Martin.

FBHI. Established in 1830.
SEE Clocks.

YOUNG & STEPHENS LTD
1 Burlington Gardens, **London**
W1X 1LD
TEL 071 499 7927
FAX 071 495 0570
OPEN 9.30–5.30 Mon–Fri; 10.30–4.30 Sat.

Specialise in repairing and restoring fine antique and period jewellery.

PROVIDE Home Inspections. Free Estimates. Chargeable Collection/Delivery Service.
SPEAK TO Stephen Burton or Duncan Semmens.

H. J. HATFIELD & SON
42 St Michael's Street, **London**
W2 1QP
TEL 071 723 8265
FAX 071 706 4562
OPEN 9–1 and 2–5 Mon–Fri.

Specialise in restoring metalwork and lacquer.

PROVIDE Home Inspections. Free Estimates.
SPEAK TO Philip Astley-Jones.
SEE Furniture.

WILLIAM MANSELL
24 Connaught Street, **London W2 2AF**
TEL 071 723 4154
OPEN 9–6 Mon–Fri and 10–1 Sat.
Specialise in repairing and restoring silverware and antique jewellery.

PROVIDE Home Inspections. Free Estimates. Free Collection/Delivery Service.
SPEAK TO Bill Salisbury.

Established in 1864.
SEE Clocks.

S. LAMPARD & SON LTD
32 Notting Hill Gate, **London**
W11 3HX
TEL 071 229 5457
OPEN 9–4.30 Mon–Fri.

Specialise in restoring antique jewellery and silver.

PROVIDE Home Inspections. Free Estimates.
SPEAK TO Mr J. R. Barnett.

ROSEMARY COOK RESTORATION
78 Stanlake Road, **London W12 7HJ**
TEL 081 749 7977
OPEN By Appointment.

Specialise in restoring painted objects.

PROVIDE Home Inspections. Free Estimates. Free Local Collection/Delivery Service.
SPEAK TO Rosemary Cook.
SEE Furniture, Porcelain.

S. J. SHRUBSOLE LTD
43 Museum Street, **London**
WC1A 1LY
TEL 071 405 2712
OPEN 9–5.30 Mon–Fri.

Specialise in repairing antique silver and old Sheffield plate.

PROVIDE Free Estimates. Free Collection/Delivery Service.
SPEAK TO Mr C. J. Shrubsole. Member of the Antique Plate Committee, Goldsmith Hall.

RICKETT & CO. ANTIQUES
Church Square, Shepperton, **Middlesex**
TW17 8JN
TEL 0932 243571
OPEN 9–5 Mon–Sat.

Specialise in repairing and restoring 18th and 19th century metal items, including fenders, fire grates, fire tools, fire dogs and candlesticks.

PROVIDE Free Estimates.
SPEAK TO A. Spencer.

ROGERS OF LONDON
344 Richmond Road, East Twickenham, **Middlesex TW1 2DU**
TEL   081 891 2122
OPEN   081 891 6418

Specialise in restoring period lighting.

PROVIDE Home Inspections. Chargeable Estimates. Collection/Delivery Service by arrangement.
SPEAK TO Joy or Charles Lolcoma.

HAMPTON UTILITIES (B'HAM) LTD
15 Pitsford Street, Hockley, Birmingham, **West Midlands B18 6LJ**
TEL   021 554 1766
OPEN   9–5 Mon–Thur; 9–4 Fri.

Specialise in restoring and repairing antique and modern silver, including plating and gilding.

PROVIDE Free Estimates. Chargeable Collection/Delivery Service.
SPEAK TO B. Levine.
SEE Furniture, Picture Frames.

WILLIAM ALLCHIN
22–24 St Benedict's Street, Norwich, **Norfolk NR2 4AQ**
TEL   0603 660046
FAX   0603 660046
OPEN   10.30–5 Mon–Sat.

Specialise in restoring period lighting, including metal chandeliers and wall brackets.

PROVIDE Home Inspections. Free Estimates.
SPEAK TO William Allchin.

SEE Porcelain.

DAVID BARTRAM FURNITURE
The Raveningham Centre, Castell Farm, Beccles Road, Raveningham, Nr. Norwich, **Norfolk**
TEL   050 846 721
OPEN   10–6 Daily.

Specialise in comprehensive antique restoration, including metalwork.

PROVIDE Home Inspections. Free Estimates. Free Collection/Delivery Service.
SPEAK TO David Bartram.

SEE Clocks, Furniture.

PETER HOWKINS
135 King Street, Great Yarmouth, **Norfolk NR30 2PQ**
TEL   0493 844639
OPEN   9–5.30 Mon–Sat or By Appointment.

Specialise in restoring antique jewellery and silver.

PROVIDE Home Inspections.
SPEAK TO Peter Howkins, Thomas Burn or Matthew Higham.
Member of NAG.
SEE Furniture (different address).

JASPER ANTIQUES
11A Hall Road, Snettisham, King's Lynn, **Norfolk PE31 7LU**
TEL   0485 541485 (Home 0485 540604)
OPEN   10.30–1 Mon, Wed, Fri; 10.30–1, 2–4 Sat.

Specialise in repair service for silver, silver plating and jewellery.

PROVIDE Home Inspections. Free Estimates. Free Collection/Delivery Service.
SPEAK TO Mrs A. A. Norris.

SEE Clocks, Porcelain.

PENNY LAWRENCE
Fairhurst Gallery, Bedford Street,
Norwich, **Norfolk NR2 1AS**
TEL   0603 632064
OPEN   9–5 Mon–Fri.

Specialise in restoring and conserving
objets d'art.

PROVIDE Home Inspections. Free
Estimates. Free/Chargeable
Collection/Delivery Service.
SPEAK TO Penny Lawrence.
This workshop is included on the
register of conservators maintained by
the Conservation Unit of the Museums
and Galleries Commission.
SEE Furniture, Oil Paintings, Picture
Frames.

MARIANNE MORRISH
South Cottage Studio, Union Lane,
Wortham Ling, Diss, **Norfolk
IP22 ISP**
TEL   0379 643831
OPEN   10–4 Mon–Fri.

Specialise in restoring objets d' art.

PROVIDE Home Inspections. Free
Estimates. Chargeable
Collection/Delivery Service.
SPEAK TO Marianne Morrish.
Member of the Guild of Master
Craftsmen.
SEE Porcelain.

THOMAS TILLETT & CO.
17 St Giles Street, Norwich, **Norfolk
NR2 1JL**
TEL   0603 625922 or 620372
FAX   0603 620372
OPEN   9–5.30 Mon–Sat.

Specialise in all types of jewellery repairs
and restoration.

PROVIDE Home Inspections. Free
Estimates. Free Collection/Delivery
Service.
SPEAK TO Mr T. Scally or Lorraine Scally.
SEE Clocks.

ARTISTRY AND METAL
Sherwood Forge, Oakset Drive,
Welbeck, Nr. Worksop,
Nottinghamshire S80 3LW
TEL   0909 486029
OPEN   8–5 Mon–Fri.

Specialise in interior iron and metalwork
repoussage and relevage, fine knives and
damascus, restoration and conservation
of architectural ironwork, etching.

PROVIDE Home Inspections. Refundable
Estimates. Chargeable
Collection/Delivery Service.
SPEAK TO F. J. M. Craddock.
Mr Craddock is a Master Bladesmith and
a Member of UKIC and BABA.

HOWARDS OF BURFORD
51 High Street, Burford, **Oxfordshire
OX18 4QA**
TEL   0993 823172
OPEN   9.30–5.30 Sun–Sat.

Specialise in repairing and restoring
antique and modern silver and jewellery.

PROVIDE Home Inspections. Free
Estimates. Free Collection/Delivery
Service.
SPEAK TO Robert Light.

F. C. MANSER & SON LTD
53–54 Wyle Cop, Shrewsbury,
Shropshire SY1 1XJ
TEL   0743 351120
FAX   0743 271047
OPEN   9–5.30 Mon–Wed, Fri; 9–1
       Thur; 9–5 Sat.

Specialise in restoring light fittings and
silverware.

PROVIDE Home Inspections. Free
Estimates. Chargeable
Collection/Delivery Service.
SPEAK TO Paul Manser.
Member of LAPADA and Guild of
Master Craftsmen.
SEE Clocks, Porcelain.

T. R. BAILEY
11 St Andrew's Road, Stogursey,
Bridgwater, **Somerset TA5 1TE**
TEL   0278 732887
OPEN   By Appointment.

Specialise in providing fine quality
fruitwood and hardwood handles and
accessories for silverware.

PROVIDE Free Estimates.
Collection/Delivery Service by
arrangement.
SPEAK TO Tim Bailey.
SEE Furniture.

ROGER & SYLVIA ALLAN
The Old Red Lion, Bedingfield, Eye,
Suffolk IP23 7LQ
TEL   0728 76 491
OPEN   By Appointment.

Specialise in restoring painted snuff-
boxes and ceramics.

PROVIDE Home Inspections. Free
Estimates.
SPEAK TO Roger Allan.

SEE Oil Paintings, Furniture.

BRIAN R. BROOKES
Brookes Forge Flempton, Flempton,
Bury St Edmunds, **Suffolk IP28 6EN**
TEL   0284 728473
OPEN   2.30–6 Mon–Fri.

Specialise in making and restoring
chandeliers together with a wide variety
of decorative ironwork. Brass castings are
produced from clients' patterns; these
can be patinated to match colour and
tone of original. Details of patterns are
accurately copied. Single items can be
undertaken.

PROVIDE Home Inspections. Free
Estimates. Free Collection/Delivery
Service.
SPEAK TO Brian Brookes.

This workshop is included on the register
of conservators maintained by the
Conservation Unit of the Museums and
Galleries Commission.

SUFFOLK BRASS
Thurston, Bury St Edmunds, **Suffolk
IP31 3SN**
TEL   0359 30888 and 0379 898670
OPEN   9–6 Mon–Fri; 9–12 Sat.

Specialise in casting brass by the hot wax
or sand process from original brassware
for furniture fittings. Also make hand-
forged iron fittings.

PROVIDE Free Estimates. Free
Collection/Delivery Service (same day).
SPEAK TO Mark Peters or Thane Meldrum.

SEE Lighting.

CRY FOR THE MOON
31 High Street, Godalming, **Surrey
GU7 1AU**
TEL   0483 426201
FAX   0483 860117
OPEN   9.30–5.30 Mon–Sat.

Specialise in restoring antique and fine
jewellery and silver.

PROVIDE Free Estimates.
SPEAK TO Mr Ackroyd or Mr Hibbert.

NORMAN FLYNN
RESTORATIONS
37 Lind Road, Sutton, **Surrey SM1 4PP**
TEL   081 661 9505
OPEN   7.45–3.30 Mon–Fri.

Specialise in restoring antique and
modern enamel.

PROVIDE Home Inspections. Free
Estimates. Free Collection/Delivery
Service each week to London.
SPEAK TO Norman Flynn.

SEE Porcelain.

S. L. HEZSELTINE AND CO. (SILVERSMITHS)
'Nice Things', Station Road, Gomshall, **Surrey GU5 9NS**
TEL   081 642 6388 or 0831 30 7080
OPEN   By Appointment only.

Specialise in restoring all forms of silver, gold and jewellery. Supply and fit new combs to silver backs, renovate perfume sprays including new puffers, supply inkstands liners, repair broken silver teapot handles and undertake hand engraving. Also supply blue glass liners and new mirrors.

PROVIDE Home Inspections. Free Estimates. Free Collection/Delivery Service.
SPEAK TO S. L. Hezseltine.
Mr Hezseltine is a Master Silversmith.

RICHARD QUINNELL LTD
Rowhurst Forge, Oxshott Road, Leatherhead, **Surrey KT22 OEN**
TEL   0372 375148
FAX   0372 386516
OPEN   9–5 Mon–Fri.

Specialise in restoring metal – wrought iron, cast iron, steel, stainless steel, copper, bronze, brass, aluminium, lead, spelter and occasionally precious metals.

PROVIDE Home Inspections. Free Estimates. Chargeable Collection/Delivery Service.
SPEAK TO Richard Quinnell MBE.

Founder Member British Artist Blacksmiths Association. This workshop is included on the register of conservators maintained by the Conservation Unit of the Museums and Galleries Commission.

R. SAUNDERS
71 Queens Road, Weybridge, **Surrey KT13 9UQ**
TEL   0932 842601
OPEN   9.15–5 Mon–Sat; closed Wed.

Specialise in restoring and cleaning English silver.

PROVIDE Home Inspections. Free Estimates. Free Collection/Delivery Service.
SPEAK TO J. B. Tonkinson.
SEE Furniture, Porcelain, Oil Paintings.

SIMPSON DAY RESTORATION
Studio 13, Acorn House, Cherry Orchard Road, Croydon, **Surrey CR0 6BA**
TEL   081 681 8339
OPEN   9.30–6 Mon–Fri.

Specialise in restoring Canton enamels.

PROVIDE Free Estimates.
SPEAK TO Sarah Simpson or Sarah Day.
SEE Porcelain.

W. BRUFORD & SON LTD
11–13 Cornfield Road, Eastbourne, **East Sussex BN21 3NA**
TEL   0323 25452
OPEN   9–1, 2–5.30 Mon–Fri; 9–1, 2–5 Sat.

Specialise in repairing and restoring Victorian and Edwardian jewellery and silver.

PROVIDE Free Estimates.
SPEAK TO N. Bruford or J. Burgess.
Fellow of the Gemmological Association.
SEE Clocks.

DAVID CRAIG
Toll Cottage, Station Road, Durgates, Wadhurst, **East Sussex TN5 6RS**
TEL   089 288 2188
OPEN   9–5.30 Mon–Fri.

Specialise in restoring enamels.

PROVIDE Chargeable Estimates. Chargeable Collection/Delivery Service.
SPEAK TO David Sutcliffe.
SEE Porcelain.

RECOLLECTIONS
1A Sydney Street, Brighton, **East Sussex BN1 4EN**
TEL   0273 681517
OPEN   10.30–5 Mon–Sat.

Specialise in polishing and repairing metalwork, including brass and copper.

PROVIDE Local Home Inspections. Local Collection/Delivery Service.
SPEAK TO Bruce Bagley or Peter Tooley.

WELLER & E.T.C.
12 North Street, Eastbourne, **East Sussex BN21 3HG**
TEL   0323 410972
OPEN   9.15–5 Mon–Fri; 9.15–1 Sat.

Specialise in restoring silver plating, brass repairs, polishing, lacquering and engraving trophies.

PROVIDE Home Inspections. Free Estimates.
SPEAK TO Mr Rothwell.

YELLOW LANTERN ANTIQUES LTD
34 & 34B Holland Road, Hove, **East Sussex BN3 1JL**
TEL   0273 771572
OPEN   9.30–1, 2.15–5.30 Mon–Fri; 9–1, 2.15–4.30 Sat.

Specialise in cleaning ormolu and bronze.

PROVIDE Home Inspections. Free Estimates. Free Collection/Delivery Service.
SPEAK TO Mr or Mrs B. R. Higgins.
Member of LAPADA.
SEE Furniture.

GARNER & CO.
Stable Cottage, Steyning Road, Wiston, **West Sussex BN44 3DD**
TEL   0903 814565
OPEN   By Appointment (Tel Mon–Fri 9–5.30).

Specialise in repairing lead and brass objects as well as conserving and repairing metal chandeliers.

PROVIDE Home Inspections. Estimates.
SPEAK TO Sid Garner.
SEE Clocks, Furniture, Porcelain.

SUGG LIGHTING LIMITED
Sussex Manor Business Park, Gatwick Road, Crawley, **West Sussex RH10 2GD**
TEL   0293 540111
FAX   0293 540114
OPEN   By Appointment.

Specialise in restoring traditional gas and electric pendant lights.

PROVIDE Free Estimates.
SPEAK TO Sales Office.
SEE Lighting.

WEST DEAN COLLEGE
West Dean, Chichester, **West Sussex PO18 0OZ**
TEL   0243 63 301
FAX   0243 63 342
OPEN   9–5 Mon–Fri.

Specialise in training conservators and restorers in the field of fine metalwork, which they will also restore.

PROVIDE Local Home Inspections. Free Estimates.
SPEAK TO Peter Sarginson.
SEE Books, Clocks, Furniture, Porcelain.

MARTIN PAYNE ANTIQUES
30 Brook Street, Warwick, **Warwickshire CV34 4BL**
TEL   0926 494948
OPEN   10–5.30 Mon–Sat.

Specialise in repairing antique and collectable silver.

PROVIDE Home Inspections. Free

Estimates. Free Collection/Delivery
Service.
SPEAK TO Martin Payne.
Member of LAPADA.

MARK THOMAS STEVENS
70 Saltisford, Warwick, **Warwickshire
CV34 4TT**
TEL   0926 495542
OPEN   9–5.30 Mon–Fri.

Specialise in restoring silver, Old
Sheffield Plate, EPNS. Also make modern
and reproduction silverware.

PROVIDE Free Estimates.
SPEAK TO Mark Stevens.
This workshop is included on the register
of conservators maintained by the
Conservation Unit of the Museums and
Galleries Commission.

HECTOR COLE
IRONWORK
The Mead, Great Somerford,
Chippenham, **Wiltshire SN15 5JB**
TEL   0249 720485
OPEN   By Appointment – best to phone
        in the evenings

Specialise in restoring and renovating
antique ironwork using wrought iron.
Also make reproductions of medieval
ironwork.

PROVIDE Free Estimates.
SPEAK TO Hector Cole.

MAC HUMBLE
ANTIQUES
7–9 Woolley Street, Bradford-on-Avon,
Wiltshire BA15 1AD
TEL   02216 6329
OPEN   9–6 Mon–Sat.

Specialise in restoring metalwork.

PROVIDE Home Inspections. Refundable
Estimates. Free Collection/Delivery
Service.
SPEAK TO Mac Humble.
SEE Furniture, Carpets.

SHENSTONE
RESTORATIONS
23 Lansdown Road, Swindon, **Wiltshire
SN1 3NE**
TEL   0793 644980
OPEN   By Appointment.

Specialise in restoring smaller decorative
items, including marquetry and inlay.
They work in bone, mother-of-pearl,
ebony and ivory and its substitutes as
well as Boulle marquetry.

PROVIDE Local Home Inspections.
Chargeable Estimates. Chargeable
Collection/Delivery Service.
SPEAK TO Blair Shenstone.
SEE Furniture.

RON FIELD
(METALWORK)
Rowhouse House, Wykeham,
Scarborough, **North Yorkshire
YO13 9QC**
TEL   0723 862640
OPEN   9–5.30 Mon–Fri or By
        Appointment.

Specialise in repairing and restoring
antique and vintage metalwork of all
types, including mechanical antiques and
particularly items of interior decor.

PROVIDE Home Inspections.
Free/Refundable Estimates.
Free/Chargeable Collection/Delivery
Service.
SPEAK TO Ron Field.
Member of the Guild of Master
Craftsmen.

DUNCAN GRIMMOND
The Old Granary, Uppercourt Terrace,
Ripon, **North Yorkshire HG4 1PD**
TEL   0765 600982
OPEN   10–4 Thur or By Appointment.

Specialise in restoring jewellery,
silverware, ivory, tortoiseshell, mother-
of-pearl, non-wood inlay and non-
ferrous metalwork.

PROVIDE Home Inspections by arrangement. Chargeable Collection/Delivery Service. SPEAK TO Duncan Grimmond.

DAVID MASON & SON
7–9 Westmoreland Street, Harrogate, **North Yorkshire HG91 5AY**
TEL 0423 567305
OPEN 9–5 Mon–Sat.

Specialise in repairing jewellery.

PROVIDE Home Inspections. Free Estimates. Chargeable Collection/Delivery Service. SPEAK TO John Mason.
Member of NAG, Yorkshire Goldsmiths Association and FGA.
SEE Clocks.

NIDD HOUSE ANTIQUES
Nidd House, Bogs Lane, Harrogate, **North Yorkshire HG1 4DY**
TEL 0423 884739
OPEN 9–5 Mon–Fri or By Appointment.

Specialise in restoring lead castings and pewter work.

PROVIDE Home Inspections. Free Local Estimates. Chargeable Collection/Delivery Service. SPEAK TO Mr D. Preston.
Members of the Guild of Master Craftsmen and UKIC. This workshop is included on the register of conservators maintained by the Conservation Unit of the Museums and Galleries Commission. SEE Porcelain, Furniture, Collectors (Scientific Instruments)

JAMES DENNIS VANCE
Eastgate Antiques, 30 Eastgate, Pickering, **North Yorkshire YO18 7DU**
TEL 0751 72954
OPEN 10–5 Mon–Sat.

Specialise in restoring antique

metalware, including the repairing and polishing of copper, brass, pewter and spelter.

PROVIDE Home Inspections. Free Estimates. Chargeable Collection/Delivery Service. SPEAK TO James Vance.

G. P. S.
3 Woodseats Road, Sheffield, **South Yorkshire S8 0PD**
TEL 0742 581777
FAX 0742 581777
OPEN 9–5 Mon–Fri.

Specialise in restoring silver, silverplate, copper, brass, pewter, old Sheffield plate etc.

PROVIDE Home Inspections. Free Estimates. Free Collection/Delivery Service. SPEAK TO Mr C. Rattigan.
Member of UKIC. Mr Rattigan is Silversmith to the Chatsworth House Estate.

FILLIANS ANTIQUES
2 Market Walk, Huddersfield, **West Yorkshire HD1 2QA**
TEL 0484 531609
FAX 0484 432688
OPEN 9–5.30 Mon–Sat.

Specialise in restoring antique jewellery and silver.

PROVIDE Home Inspections. Free Collection/Delivery Service. SPEAK TO G. Neary.

T. M. TUKE
18 Main Street, Greyabbey, Newtownards, **Co. Down**
TEL 024774 416 or 252
FAX 024774 250
OPEN 11–5 Mon–Sat; closed Thur.

Specialise in repairing silver.

PROVIDE Home Inspections. Free
Estimates. Free Collection/Delivery
Service.
SPEAK TO Tom Tuke.
Member of BHI.
SEE Clocks.

J. BYRNE & SONS
22 South Anne Street, Dublin 2,
Co. Dublin
TEL   01 718709
OPEN   9–5.30 Mon–Sat.

Specialise in restoring, repairing and
reproducing jewellery.

PROVIDE Free Estimates.
SPEAK TO Jim or Richard Byrne.

DENIS CLANCY
31 Forest Hills, Rathcoole, **Co. Dublin**
TEL   01 580439
OPEN   By Appointment.

Specialise in restoring brass chandeliers.

PROVIDE Home Inspections. Free
Estimates. Free Collection/Delivery
Service.
SPEAK TO Derek Clancy.
Member of IPCRA.
SEE Porcelain.

DESMOND TAAFFE
51 Dawson Street, Dublin 2, **Co. Dublin**
TEL   01 719609
OPEN   9–5.30 Mon–Fri.

Specialise in restoring antique and
domestic silver and churchware.

PROVIDE Free Estimates.
SPEAK TO Desmond Taaffe.

OLD ST ANDREWS
GALLERY
9 Albany Place, St Andrews, **Fife
KY16 9HH**
and 10 Golf Place, St Andrews, **Fife
KY16 9JA**
TEL   0334 7840 and 0334 78712
OPEN   10–5 Mon–Fri.

Specialise in repairing silver and
jewellery.

PROVIDE Home Inspections. Free
Estimates. Free Collection/Delivery
Service.
SPEAK TO Mr or Mrs Brown.
SEE Sporting Equipment (Golf).

GALLERY
48A Union Street, Aberdeen, **Grampian
AB2 1HS**
TEL   0224 625909
OPEN   9–5.30 Mon–Sat.

Specialise in repairing and restoring
jewellery. They also make jewellery.

PROVIDE Home Inspections. Free
Estimates.
SPEAK TO Michael Gray.

GILES PEARSON
Brightmony House, Auldern, **Highland
IV12 5HZ**
TEL   0667 55550
OPEN   9–6 Daily.

Specialise in cane handles for silver and
silver-plated tea and coffee pots.

PROVIDE Home Inspections. Free
Estimates. Collection/Delivery Service
by arrangement.
SPEAK TO Giles Pearson.

This workshop is in the Scottish
Conservation Directory.
SEE Furniture.

THURSO ANTIQUES
Drill Hall, 21 Sinclair Street, Thurso,
Highland
TEL   0847 63291
FAX   0847 62824
OPEN   10–5 Mon–Fri and 10–1 Sat.

Specialise in cleaning and redesigning
jewellery.

PROVIDE Free Estimates.
Collection/Delivery Service by
arrangement.

SPEAK TO G. Atkinson.
SEE Oil Paintings.

J. R. DREVER
87A West Bow, Edinburgh, **Lothian EH1 2JP**
TEL   031 225 2514
OPEN   8.30–5 Mon–Fri.

Specialise in restoring all kinds of jewellery.

PROVIDE Free Estimates.
SPEAK TO J. R. Drever.
This workshop is in the Scottish Conservation Directory.

HAMILTON AND INCHES
87 George Street, Edinburgh, **Lothian EH2 3EY**
TEL   031 225 4898
FAX   031 220 6994
OPEN   9–5 Mon–Fri; 9–12.30 Sat.

Specialise in restoring gold and silver antique and modern jewelley and objects.

PROVIDE Home Inspections. Free Estimates. Chargeable Collection/ Delivery Service.
SPEAK TO Densil Skinner.
Member of NAG.
SEE Clocks.

HOUNDWOOD ANTIQUES RESTORATION
7 West Preston Street, Edinburgh, **Lothian EH8 9PX**
TEL   031 667 3253
OPEN   By Appointment.

Specialise in restoring objets d'art, including ormolu, bronze and pewter.

PROVIDE Home Inspections. Free Estimates. Chargeable Collection/Delivery Service.
SPEAK TO Mr A. Gourlay.
SEE Furniture, Porcelain.

CPR ANTIQUES AND SERVICES
96 Main Street, Barrhead, Glasgow, **Strathclyde G78 1SE**
TEL   041 881 5379
OPEN   10–1, 1.30–5 Mon, Wed–Sat; closed Tues.

Specialise in restoring brass, copper, spelter and pewter, chrome stripped, spare parts made for certain items.

PROVIDE Free Estimates.
SPEAK TO Mrs C. Porterfield.

NEIL LIVINGSTONE
3 Old Hawkhill, Dundee, **Tayside DD1 5EU**
TEL   0382 21751
OPEN   9–5 Mon–Fri.

Specialise in repairing jewellery.

PROVIDE Free Estimates. Chargeable Collection/Delivery Service.
SPEAK TO Neil Livingstone.
SEE Arms, Furniture, Oil Paintings, Picture Frames.

CARPETS, TEXTILES
AND COSTUME

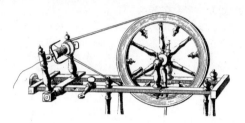

DO

Roll up rather than fold textiles where possible
Store fine lace rolled in acid-free tissue paper
Ask any laundry how much they will charge for cleaning your Victorian damask linen tablecloth –
prices can range from two pounds to twenty-two pounds a cloth!
Remember that while plain household or damask linen is extremely tough and durable, lace-
or crochet-trimmed cloths need more careful handling
Place fine linen inside a large stocking or pair of tights before machine washing
Starch linen when washing it – tablecloths especially will stay cleaner and crisper longer
Wash fine lace, crochet and pina cloths in soap flakes or a very mild liquid soap

DON'T

Hang embroidered silk work, pictures, samplers or indeed any textile in direct sunlight
Despair when buying discoloured antique linen – plain or damask linen is very tough and can
withstand being washed at boiling point, or on the 90°C programme in the washing machine
Be put off using well-known high-street laundries for cleaning plain table and bed linen. They
are often considerably cheaper than the 'specialist' laundries
Forget old-fashioned 'blue' added to linen during a wash will help to achieve the snowy, crisp
look

243

FIONA HUTTON & FRANCES LENNARD

Textile Conservation, Ivy House Farm, Banwell, **Avon BS24 6LB**

TEL　　0934 822449
FAX　　0934 823565
OPEN　9–5 Mon–Fri.

Specialise in restoring all types of textiles damaged by accident, poor storage or bad display conditions, including painted and printed textiles, woven tapestries, embroideries, upholstery and costume.

PROVIDE Home Inspections. Chargeable Estimates. Chargeable Collection/Delivery Service.
SPEAK TO Fiona Hutton or Frances Lennard.
Members of UKIC. This workshop is included on the register of conservators maintained by the Conservation Unit of the Museums and Galleries Commission.

ANGELA BURGIN FURNISHING AND DESIGN LTD

6–8 Gordon Street, Luton, **Bedfordshire LU1 2QP**

TEL　　0582 22563
FAX　　0582 30413
OPEN　8–5 Mon–Thur or By Appointment.

Specialise in offering a highly specialised conservation service on all periods of curtaining.

PROVIDE Home Inspections. Free Estimates. Free Collection/Delivery Service.
SPEAK TO Angela Burgin.
Ms Burgin is a Member of the Association of Master Upholsterers.
SEE Furniture.

THE TEXTILE RESTORATION STUDIO

20 Hargreaves Road, Timperley, Altrincham, **Cheshire WA15 7BB**

TEL　　061 904 9944
FAX　　061 903 9144
OPEN　9.30–5 By Appointment.

Specialise in cleaning, conserving and repairing all types of antique textiles, including samplers, canvas and bead work, tapestry, white work, embroidery, costume and ecclesiastical furnishings and vestments, lace.

PROVIDE Home Inspections. Free Estimates. Collection/Delivery Service by arrangement.
SPEAK TO Jacqueline or Michael Hyman.
SEE Collectors (Dolls), Silver, Lighting.

EVELINE HARTLEY

Orientis, Digby Road, Sherborne, **Dorset DT9 3NR**

TEL　　0935 816479 or 813274
OPEN　10.15–12.45, 2.30–4.30 Tues, Thur, Fri, Sat or By Appointment.

Specialise in restoring Oriental rugs (excluding Chinese), textiles and embroideries.

PROVIDE Home Inspections. Free Estimates. Free Collection/Delivery Service.
SPEAK TO Mrs Hartley.
Member of the Rug Restorers Association.

ALLYSON McDERMOTT (INTERNATIONAL CONSERVATION CONSULTANTS)

Lintz Green Conservation Centre, Lintz Green House, Lintz Green, Rowlands Gill, **Durham NE39 1NL**

TEL　　0207 71547 or 0831 104145 or 0831 257584
FAX　　0207 71547
OPEN　9–5.30 Mon–Fri.

Specialise in conservation of historic hangings, painted textiles and screens.

PROVIDE Home Inspections. Free Estimates. Chargeable Collection/Delivery Service.
SPEAK TO Allyson Mc Dermott or Gillian Lee.

They have a Southern Regional Office at 45 London Road, Cheltenham, **Gloucestershire**.
SEE Art Researchers, Oil Paintings, Lighting, Picture Frames, Specialist Photographers.

ANNABEL WYLIE
Hamilton House, The Green, Great Bentley, Colchester, **Essex CO7 8LY**
TEL   0206 251518
OPEN   By Appointment.

Specialise in conserving furnishing textiles, rugs, embroidered pictures, costumes and accessories.

PROVIDE Home Inspections. Free/Chargeable Estimates. Chargeable Collection/Delivery Service.
SPEAK TO Annabel Wylie.

COCOA
7 Queens Circus, Montpellier, Cheltenham, **Gloucestershire GL50 1RX**
TEL   0242 233588
OPEN   10–5 Mon–Sat.

Specialise in restoring antique lace, wedding gowns, linens, antique veils.
SPEAK TO P. A. O'Sullivan.

THE LADIES' WORK SOCIETY LIMITED
Delabere House, New Road, Moreton-in-Marsh, **Gloucestershire GL56 OAS**
TEL   0608 50447
OPEN   10–1, 2–5 Mon–Fri; 10–1, 2–4 Sat.

Specialise in designing needlework for

period furniture and conserving antique textiles.

PROVIDE Local Home Inspections. Refundable Estimates. Chargeable Collection/Delivery Service.
SPEAK TO Stanley Duller.

ERIC PRIDE ORIENTAL RUGS
44 Suffolk Road, Cheltenham, **Gloucestershire GL50 2AQ**
TEL   0242 580822
OPEN   10–5 Tues–Fri.

Specialise in cleaning and restoring old handwoven rugs, carpets, kilims and tapestries, both European and Oriental.

PROVIDE Free Estimates.
SPEAK TO Eric Pride.

ELIZABETH W. TAYLOR
Cirencester Workshops (Brewery Arts), 9A Brewery Court, Cirencester, **Gloucestershire GL7 1JH**
TEL   0285 641177
OPEN   9–5 Mon–Fri; By Appointment Sat.

Specialise in restoring Oriental rugs and carpets.

PROVIDE Free Estimates.
SPEAK TO Elizabeth Taylor.
Member of the Rug Restorers Association.

WENDY YEOMANS
20 Elvetham Road, Fleet, **Hampshire GU13 8QP**
Workshop: 32 Minley Road, Cove, Farnborough, **Hampshire**
TEL   0252 629756
OPEN   9–5 Mon–Fri or By Appointment.

Specialise in restoring antique textiles, especially antique bed hangings, ornate canopies, embroideries and tapestries.

PROVIDE Home Inspections. Free

Estimates. Chargeable
Collection/Delivery Service.
SPEAK TO Wendy Yeomans.
Member of UKIC.

WENDY TOULSON
Bank Villa, Kingswood, Kington,
Hereford & Worcester HR5 3HG
TEL　　0544 231442
OPEN　By Appointment Only.

Specialise in conserving all fine historic
textiles. They also carry out surveys of
collections, advise on preventative
conservation, storage and exhibition
mounting.

PROVIDE Home Inspections.
Free/Chargeable Estimates.
SPEAK TO Wendy Toulson.

Member of IIC, UKIC and the Museums
Association. This workshop is included
on the register of conservators
maintained by the Conservation Unit of
the Museums and Galleries Commission.

NICOLA WARREN ˙
Willow House, 16 Bridge Street,
Kington, **Hereford & Worcester
HR5 3DL**
TEL　　0544 230251
OPEN　By Appointment.

Specialise in restoring antique and
Oriental rugs, kilims, sumachs,
embroideries etc.

PROVIDE Chargeable Estimates.
SPEAK TO Nicola Warren.
Member of the Rug Restorers
Association.

JO BOOSEY
The Tun House, Whitwell, Hitchin,
Hertfordshire SG4 8AG
TEL　　0438 871563
OPEN　By Appointment.

Specialise in restoring Oriental rugs.

PROVIDE Home Inspections by

arrangement. Free/Chargeable
Estimates. Free/Chargeable
Collection/Delivery Service.
SPEAK TO Jo Boosey.

HERTFORDSHIRE CONSERVATION SERVICE
Seed Warehouse, Maidenhead Yard, The
Wash, Hertford, **Hertfordshire
SG14 1PX**
TEL　　0992 588966
FAX　　0992 588971
OPEN　9–6 Mon–Fri By Appointment.

Specialise in restoring leather, livery and
wall hangings.

PROVIDE Home Inspections.
Free/Chargeable Estimates. Chargeable
Collection/Delivery Service.
SPEAK TO J. M. MacQueen.

This workshop is included on the
register of conservators maintained by
the Conservation Unit of the Museums
and Galleries Commission.

SEE Collectors (Dolls), Lighting,
Furniture, Porcelain, Oil Paintings,
Picture Frames.

JUDITH DORE
Textile & Costume Conservation, Castle
Lodge, 271 Sandown Road, Deal, **Kent
CT14 6QU**
TEL　　0304 373684
OPEN　By Appointment.

Specialise in the conservation,
identification, display and storage of
textile and costume objects.

PROVIDE Home Inspections by
arrangement. Free/Chargeable
Estimates. Chargeable
Collection/Delivery Service.
SPEAK TO Judith Dore.

DESMOND & AMANDA NORTH

The Orchard, Hale Street, East Peckham, **Kent TN12 5JB**

TEL   0622 831353
OPEN   By Appointment.

Specialise in cleaning and undertaking some repairs to old Oriental rugs and carpets.

PROVIDE Chargeable Home Inspections. Free Estimates.
SPEAK TO Desmond or Amanda North.

PERSIAN RUG SHOP

Vines Farm, Matthews Lane, West Peckham, Maidstone, **Kent ME18 5JS**

TEL   0732 850228
OPEN   9–5.30 Daily By Appointment.

Specialise in cleaning and restoring Oriental rugs and carpets.

PROVIDE Home Inspections. Chargeable Estimates. Chargeable Collection/Delivery Service.
SPEAK TO Rod King.

CAROLINE J. BOOTH TEXTILE CONSERVATOR

Fold Farm, Higher Eastwood, Todmorden, **Lancashire OL14 8RP**

TEL   0706 816888
OPEN   10–5 Mon–Fri.

Specialise in a full range of services for historic textiles both woven and embroidered, including samplers, materials for dolls' houses and costumes for dolls and automata. Condition and conservation reports provided and advice given on handling, storage and display. Ms Booth uses traditional conservation techniques so that any work done is reversible.

PROVIDE Home Inspections. Chargeable Estimates. Chargeable Collection/Delivery Service.
SPEAK TO Caroline Booth.
SEE Collectors (Dolls).

PEARCE RUGS & FRINGES

The Cottage, Hamilton Lane, Scraptoft, Leicester, **Leicestershire LE7 9SB**

TEL   0533 414941
OPEN   By Appointment.

Specialise in cleaning, repairing and renovating Oriental rugs. Can also re-weave, clean and repair other types of carpeting.

PROVIDE Home Inspections. Chargeable Estimates. Chargeable Collection/Delivery Service.
SPEAK TO Mr B. W. Pearce.

Also supply a mail order service for carpet fringes.

TATTERSALL'S

14 Orange Street, 2 Bear Yard, Orange Street, Uppingham, **Leicestershire LE15 9SQ**

TEL   0572 821171
OPEN   9.30–5 Tues–Sat; closed Mon & Thur.

Specialise in restoring antique and old Persian rugs.

PROVIDE Home Inspections. Free Estimates. Chargeable Collection/Delivery Service.
SPEAK TO Janice Tattersall.
SEE Furniture.

DUNCAN WATTS ORIENTAL RUGS

64 St Marys Road, Market Harborough, **Leicestershire LE16 7DU**

TEL   0858 432314
OPEN   10–5.30 Mon–Sat; closed Wed.

Specialise in restoring Oriental rugs.

PROVIDE Home Inspections. Free Estimates. Free Collection/Delivery Service.
SPEAK TO Duncan Watts.

WENDY A. CUSHING LTD
410 Greenheath Business Centre, 31
Three Colts Lane, **London E2 6JB**
TEL 071 739 5909
FAX 071 729 5130
OPEN 9–5.30 Mon–Fri.

Specialise in restoring trimmings for
furnishings.

PROVIDE Home Inspections. Free
Estimates.
SPEAK TO Wendy Cushing or Derek Pattle.

POPPY SINGER
213 Brooke Road, **London E5 8AB**
TEL 081 806 3742
OPEN By Appointment.

Specialise in conserving furnishing
textiles, rugs, embroidered pictures,
costumes and accessories.

PROVIDE Home Inspections.
Free/Chargeable Estimates. Chargeable
Collection/Delivery Service.
SPEAK TO Poppy Singer.

BEHAR PROFEX LTD
The Alban Building, St Albans Place,
Upper Street, **London N1 0NX**
TEL 071 226 0144
OPEN 8–6 Mon–Thur; 8–5 Fri.

Specialise in cleaning, conserving and
restoring Oriental and European hand-
made carpets, rugs, textiles and
tapestries.

PROVIDE Home Inspections. Free
Estimates. Collection/Delivery Service.
SPEAK TO Robert Behar.

This family firm has been established for
seventy years and is a member of the
UKIC and the Guild of Master
Craftsmen.

CAMU AND GOLDBERG TEXTILE CONSERVATION
36 Woodland Gardens, **London
N10 3UA**
TEL 081 883 0300
OPEN 9–6 Mon–Fri or By
Appointment.

Specialise in restoring historic and
antique textiles, including tapestries,
furnishing textiles, curtains, rugs and
carpets, embroideries, canvas work,
banners, painted textiles, samplers,
wedding veils, costume. They have
purpose-built facilities for the safe
cleaning of large and small textiles. Most
of the work is based on hand-sewing of
objects on to appropriate support fabrics
after cleaning.

PROVIDE Home Inspections.
Free/Refundable Estimates. Local
Collection/Delivery Service.
SPEAK TO Naomi Goldberg.
This workshop is included on the register
of conservators maintained by the
Conservation Unit of the Museums and
Galleries Commission.
SEE **London W4**

DAVID J. WILKINS ORIENTAL RUGS
27 Princess Road, **London NW1 8JR**
TEL 071 722 7608
OPEN 9.15–5 Mon–Fri.

Specialise in all types of repairs and
cleaning of Oriental rugs.

PROVIDE Home Inspections. Free
Estimates. Chargeable
Collection/Delivery Service.
SPEAK TO David Wilkins or Gill Lowe.

JOSEPH LAVIAN
Block 'F', 53–79 Highgate Road,
London NW5 1TL
TEL 071 482 1234 and 485 7955
FAX 071 267 9222
OPEN 9.30–6 Mon–Fri.

Specialise in restoring antique Oriental

carpets, rugs, kilims, Aubussons, tapestries and textiles.

PROVIDE Home Inspections. Free/Chargeable Estimates. Chargeable Collection/Delivery Service.
SPEAK TO Joseph Lavian.

JANIE LIGHTFOOT
24 Cholmondeley Avenue, **London NW10 5XN**
TEL   081 961 5468 or 963 1532
FAX   089 961 6020
OPEN   9–5 Mon–Fri.

Specialise in restoring tapestry, Oriental rugs and textiles, shoes, embroideries, costume, flags, banners, needlepoint, Aubusson, ecclesiastical and church pieces etc.

PROVIDE Free/Chargeable Estimates. Free/Chargeable Collection/Delivery Service.
SPEAK TO Janie Lightfoot.

MAYORCAS LTD
38 Jermyn Street, **London SW1Y 6DN**
TEL   071 629 4195
OPEN   9.30–5.30 Mon–Fri; 10–1 Sat.

Specialise in cleaning and repairing antique textiles, tapestry, needlework, silks, damasks.

PROVIDE Discretionary Home Inspections. Collection/Delivery Service.
SPEAK TO Andrew Morley Stephens.

Members of BADA.

WATTS & CO
7 Tufton Street, **London SW1P 3QE**
TEL   071 233 0424
FAX   071 233 1130
OPEN   9–5 Mon–Fri.

Specialise in restoring church embroidery and reproducing antique textiles. Special commissions undertaken.

PROVIDE Free Estimates. Chargeable Collection/Delivery Service.
SPEAK TO Shelagh Scott.

N. SONMEZ
Chenil Galleries, 181–183 Kings Road, **London SW3 5EB**
TEL   071 351 6611
OPEN   10–6 Mon–Sat.

Specialise in restoring antique Persian, Russian and Turkish carpets.

PROVIDE Home Inspections. Free/Chargeable Estimates.
SPEAK TO N. Sonmez.

HAROUT BARIN
57A New Kings Road, **London SW6 4SE**
TEL   071 731 0546
FAX   071 384 1620
OPEN   9.30–6 Mon–Sat.

Specialise in cleaning and restoring Oriental carpets, European tapestries, Aubussons and needlepoints.

PROVIDE Home Inspections. Free Estimates. Free Collection/Delivery Service.
SPEAK TO Harout Barin.

MARTIN GEORGE CLARKE
Unit S6, 245A Coldharbour Lane, **London SW9 8RR**
TEL   071 924 0452
OPEN   9–6 Mon–Sat.

Specialise in restoring antique rugs and carpets, including Aubussons and European tapestries. Cleaning and conservation service, including custom spinning and natural dyeing e.g. wool, cotton.

PROVIDE Home Inspections. Free Estimates. Free Local Collection/Delivery Service.
SPEAK TO Martin Clarke.

Member of the Rug Restorers
Association.

LUNN ANTIQUES LTD
86 New Kings Road, **London SW6 4LU**
TEL   071 736 4638
FAX   071 371 7113
OPEN   10–6 Mon–Sat.

Specialise in restoring antique linen and
lace.

PROVIDE Home Inspections. Free
Estimates. Chargeable
Collection/Delivery Service.
SPEAK TO Mr or Mrs Lunn.

THE KILIM WAREHOUSE LTD
28A Pickets Street, **London SW12 8QB**
TEL   081 675 3122
FAX   081 675 8494
OPEN   10–6 Mon–Fri; 10–4 Sat.

Specialise in cleaning and restoring
kilims and flatweaves.

PROVIDE Chargeable Estimates.
SPEAK TO José Luczyc-Wyhowska.

RAYMOND BENARDOUT
18 Grosvenor Street, **LondonW1X 9FD**
TEL   071 355 4531
FAX   071 491 9710
OPEN   9–5.30 Mon–Fri.

Specialise in cleaning and restoring
carpets, rugs, tapestries and needlework,
including Aubussons.

PROVIDE Home Inspections.
Free/Chargeable Estimates. Chargeable
Collection/Delivery Service.
SPEAK TO Raymond Benardout.

ESSIE CARPETS
62 Piccadilly, **London W1V 9HL**
TEL   071 493 7766
FAX   071 495 3456
OPEN   9.30–6.30 Sun–Fri; closed Sat.

Specialise in restoring Persian carpets
and Oriental rugs.

PROVIDE Home Inspections. Chargeable
Collection/Delivery Service.

KENNEDY CARPETS
9A Vigo Street, **London W1X 1AL**
TEL   071 439 8873
FAX   071 437 1201
OPEN   9.30–6 Mon–Sat.

Specialise in restoring decorative
European and Oriental carpets 1850–
1920 and fine 19th century Indian
carpets and rugs.

PROVIDE Free Estimates.
SPEAK TO Mr M. Kennedy.

SHAIKH & SON (ORIENTAL RUGS) LTD
16 Brook Street, **London W1Y 1AA**
TEL   071 629 3430
OPEN   10.30–6.30 Mon–Sat.

Specialise in repairing and cleaning
Oriental rugs.

PROVIDE Home Inspections. Free
Estimates. Free Collection/Delivery
Service.
SPEAK TO Mr A. Shaikh.

FRANSES CONSERVATION
11 Spring Street, **London W2 3RA**
TEL   071 262 1153
FAX   071 930 8451
OPEN   9–5 Mon–Fri.

Specialise in cleaning, conserving and
restoring fine carpets, needlework and
tapestries, including Aubussons and
Savonneries.

PROVIDE Home Inspections by
arrangement. Free Estimates.
Chargeable Collection/Delivery Service.
SPEAK TO Spencer Franses.

CAMU AND GOLDBERG TEXTILE CONSERVATION
37 Alexandra Road, **London W4 1AX**
TEL   081 995 9539
OPEN   9–6 Mon–Fri or By
Appointment.

Specialise in restoring historic and antique textiles, including tapestries, furnishing textiles, curtains, rugs and carpets, embroideries, canvas work, banners, painted textiles, samplers, wedding veils, costume. They have purpose-built facilities for the safe cleaning of large and small textiles. Most of the work is based on hand-sewing of objects on to appropriate support fabrics after cleaning.

PROVIDE Home Inspections. Free/Refundable Estimates. Local Collection/Delivery Service.
SPEAK TO Melanie Camu.

This workshop is included on the register of conservators maintained by the Conservation Unit of the Museums and Galleries Commission.
SEE **London N10**

FRANÇOISE BROUGH
Maida Vale, **London W9**
TEL   071 289 8708
OPEN   10–6 Mon–Fri By Appointment.

Specialise in restoring fine rugs, carpets and kilims.

PROVIDE Home Inspections. Free Estimates. Collection/Delivery Service by arrangement.
SPEAK TO Françoise Brough.
Member of the Guild of Master Craftsmen and the Textile Society.

DAVID BLACK ORIENTAL CARPETS
96 Portland Road, **London W11 4LN**
TEL   071 727 2566
FAX   071 229 4599
OPEN   11–6 Mon–Sat.

Specialise in cleaning and repairing antique and modern Oriental carpets, textiles and English Arts & Crafts carpets.

PROVIDE Free Estimates.
SPEAK TO David Black.
Member of BADA.

JACK FAIRMAN (CARPETS) LTD
218 Westbourne Grove, **London W11 2RH**
TEL   071 229 2262
FAX   071 229 2263
OPEN   10–6 Mon–Fri; 10–1 Sat.

Specialise in cleaning and repairing Oriental carpets, rugs and tapestries.

PROVIDE Home Inspections. Free Verbal Estimates. Free Collection/Delivery Service.
SPEAK TO Serina Page.

KASIA & ELA TEXTILE RESTORATION STUDIO
Unit 11, Kolbe House, 63 Jeddo Road, **London W12 9EE**
TEL   081 740 4977
OPEN   8–5 Mon–Fri.

Specialise in restoring flatweaves, including tapestries, Aubussons, needlework and kilims.

PROVIDE Home Inspections. Free Estimates. Free Collection/Delivery Service within London.
SPEAK TO Kasia Kolendarska or Ela Sosnowska.

THE NATIONAL TRUST TEXTILE CONSERVATION WORKROOM
Blickling Hall, Blickling, Norwich, **Norfolk NR11 6NF**
TEL   0263 733 471
FAX   0263 734 924
OPEN   9–5.30 Mon–Fri.

Specialise in conserving textiles, including costume and large woven tapestries. Will also survey collections.

PROVIDE Home Inspections. Chargeable Estimates.

SPEAK TO Ksynia Marko.

This is the first time their conservation services are being offered to non-Trust clients.

THE LEATHER CONSERVATION CENTRE
34 Guildhall Road, Northampton,
Northamptonshire NN1 1EW
TEL   0604 232723
FAX   0604 602070
OPEN   9–6 Mon–Fri.

Specialise in conservation of all types of leather, including costume.

PROVIDE Home Inspections. Chargeable Estimates. Chargeable Collection/Delivery Service.
SPEAK TO Christopher Calnan.
SEE Lighting, Furniture.

MISS LYNDALL BOND
Textile Conservation Services, 3–4 West Workshops, Tan Gallop, Welbeck, Worksop, **Nottinghamshire S80 3LW**
TEL   0909 481655
OPEN   By Appointment.

Specialise in conserving costume.

PROVIDE Home Inspections. Chargeable Estimates. Chargeable Collection/Delivery Service.
SPEAK TO Lyndall Bond.

CHRISTOPHER LEGGE ORIENTAL CARPETS
25 Oakthorpe Road, Summertown, Oxford, **Oxfordshire OX2 7BD**
TEL   0865 57572
FAX   0865 54877
OPEN   9.30–5 Mon–Sat.

Specialise in cleaning, conserving,

restoring and re-weaving old and antique tribal rugs and carpets.

PROVIDE Home Inspections by arrangement. Free Estimates.
SPEAK TO Christopher or Ann Marie Legge

Also provide courses on rugs and their repair and conservation.

THE ANTIQUE RESTORATION STUDIO
The Old Post Office, Haughton,
Staffordshire ST18 9JH
TEL   0785 780424
FAX   0785 780157
OPEN   9–5 Mon–Fri.

Specialise in restoring antique and modern textiles.

PROVIDES Home Inspections. Free Estimates. Free Collection/Delivery Service.
SPEAK TO D. P. Albright.
SEE Furniture, Porcelain, Oil Paintings.

CLARE GILCHRIST
37 West Street, Dorking, **Surrey RH4 1BU**
TEL   0306 876370 or 0483 35790
FAX   0486 412983
OPEN   10–5 Mon–Sat; closed Wed.

Specialise in restoring antique and semi-antique Oriental carpets and rugs.

PROVIDE Home Inspections. Free Estimates. Free Collection/Delivery Service.
SPEAK TO Adam M. R. Gilchrist or Clare Gilchrist.

THE ROYAL SCHOOL OF NEEDLEWORK
Apartment 12A, Hampton Court Palace, East Molesey, **Surrey KT8 9AU**
TEL   081 943 1432
FAX   081 943 4910
OPEN   9.30–4 Mon–Fri.

Specialise in restoring and conserving antique textiles, including large hand-woven tapestries, needlework rugs, samplers and stump work.

PROVIDE Chargeable Home Inspections. Free Estimates at the School. Chargeable Collection/Delivery Service.
SPEAK TO Mrs Elizabeth Elvin.

TEXTILE CONSERVATION CENTRE
Apartment 22, Hampton Court Palace, East Molesey, **Surrey KT8 9AU**
TEL 081 977 4943
FAX 081 977 9081
OPEN 9–5 Mon–Fri.

Specialise in conserving early, historic and modern textiles. Also train textile conservators.

PROVIDE Chargeable Consultative Visits. Free Estimates at the Centre.
SPEAK TO Nell Hoare, Director.

KAREL WEIJAND
Lion & Lamb Courtyard, Farnham, **Surrey GU9 7LL**
TEL 0252 726215
OPEN 9.30–5.30 Mon–Sat or By Appointment.

Specialise in full restoration, repair and cleaning service for antique Oriental rugs, hand-made carpets and textiles.

PROVIDE Home Inspections. Free Estimates. Chargeable Collection/Delivery Service.
SPEAK TO Karel Weijand.
Member of LAPADA.

DENNIS WOODMAN ORIENTAL CARPETS
105 North Road, Kew, **Surrey TW9 4HJ**
TEL 081 878 8182
OPEN 10–6 Mon–Sat, 10–2 Sun.

Specialise in restoring rugs and flat weaves.

PROVIDE Local Home Inspections. Free Estimates.
SPEAK TO Dennis Woodman.
Member of the Rug Restorers Association.

CLIVE ROGERS ORIENTAL RUGS
22 Brunswick Road, Hove, Brighton, **East Sussex BN3 1DG**
TEL 0273 738257
FAX 0273 738687
OPEN By Appointment.

Specialise in cleaning, conservation and historical analysis of early tribal and village rugs, kilims and some Near Eastern textiles.

PROVIDE Home Inspections. Free Local Estimates. Chargeable Collection/Delivery Service.
SPEAK TO Clive Rogers or Elizabeth Fereday.

MAJID AMINI
Church House, Church Street, Petworth, **West Sussex GU28 0AD**
TEL 0798 43344
FAX 0798 42673
OPEN 9–5 Mon–Sat.

Specialise in cleaning and restoring Oriental rugs and carpets.

PROVIDE Home Inspections. Free Estimates.
SPEAK TO Majid Amini.
Mr Amini lectures on Oriental rug care and restoration at West Dean College and is the author of *Oriental Rugs – Care and Repair*.

KATHARINE BARKER
St John's House Museum, St John's, Warwick, **Warwickshire CV34 4NF**
TEL 0926 412732
OPEN 9–5 Mon–Fri By Appointment.

Specialise in restoring textiles, including

costume, embroideries, tapestries and banners.

PROVIDE Home Inspections. Free/Chargeable Estimates. SPEAK TO Katharine Barker.

Ms Barker is an Associate of the Museums Association and a Member of UKIC. This workshop is included on the register of conservators maintained by the Conservation Unit of the Museums and Galleries Commission.

CARPET CONSERVATION WORKSHOP

Unit 2, Danebury Court, South Portway Business Park, Old Sarum, Salisbury, **Wiltshire SP4 6EB**
TEL　　0722 411854
FAX　　0722 339161
OPEN　8–6 Mon–Fri or By Appointment.

Specialise in washing and repairs to large carpets with facilities for secure storage (up to 20 foot rolls), insect infestation treatments, latex glue removal treatments, reweaving for infills, dyeing, lining and preparing underlays for use.

PROVIDE Home Inspections. Free Estimates. Collection/Delivery Service by arrangement.
SPEAK TO Jonathan or Heather Tetley.

Member of UKIC. This workshop is included on the register of conservators maintained by the Conservation Unit of the Museums and Galleries Commission.

KATHRYN JORDAN

The Barn, Estate Yard, Castle Combe, Nr. Chippenham, **Wiltshire SN14 7HU**
TEL　　0249 782142
FAX　　0249 782233
OPEN　9–4 By Appointment only.

Specialise in restoring Oriental rugs and carpets, kilims and woven textiles. Also cleaning and conserving rugs.

PROVIDE Home Inspections.

Free/Chargeable Estimates. Free Collection/Delivery Service. SPEAK TO Kathryn Jordan.

MAC HUMBLE ANTIQUES

7–9 Woolley Street, Bradford-on-Avon, **Wiltshire BA15 1AD**
TEL　　02216 6329
OPEN　9–6 Mon–Sat.

Specialise in restoring needlework.

PROVIDE Home Inspections. Refundable Estimates. Free Collection/Delivery Service.
SPEAK TO Mac Humble.
SEE Furniture, Silver.

BART BLOK

41 Kirkgate, Knaresborough, **North Yorkshire HG5 8BZ**
TEL　　0423 865414
FAX　　0243 869 614
OPEN　8.30–5.30 Mon–Sat or By Appointment.

Specialise in the care, repair and restoration of rugs, kilims and woven artefacts from Europe and the Orient using where necessary hand-spun wool and natural dyes.

PROVIDE Home Inspections. Free Estimates. Collection/Delivery Service.
SPEAK TO Bart Blok.
Member of UKIC and Rug Restorers Association.

LONDON HOUSE ORIENTAL RUGS AND CARPETS

9 Montpellier Parade, Harrogate, **North Yorkshire HG1 2TJ**
TEL　　0423 567167
OPEN　10–5.30 Tues–Sat.

Specialise in restoring and repairing Oriental rugs and carpets.

PROVIDE Free Estimates.
SPEAK TO Christian Ries.
SEE **West Yorkshire.**

GORDON REECE GALLERY
Finkle Street, Knaresborough, **North Yorkshire HG5 8AA**
TEL 0423 866219
FAX 0423 868044
OPEN 10.30–5 Mon–Sat, closed Thur; 2–5 Sun.

Specialise in restoring knotted Oriental rugs and kilims.

PROVIDE Free Estimates. Free Collection/Delivery Service.
SPEAK TO Gordon Reece or Jane Munro.

THE DAVIE GALLERY
8 Castlegate, Tickhill, Doncaster, **South Yorkshire DN11 9QU**
TEL 0302 751199
OPEN 9.30–5 Mon–Sat; closed Wed.

Specialise in conserving and restoring textiles.

PROVIDE Home Inspections. Free Estimates. Free Collection/Delivery Service.
SPEAK TO Ian Davie.
Mr Davie is a member of the FATG.
SEE Picture Frames, Oil Paintings.

W. E. FRANKLIN (SHEFFIELD) LTD
116–120 Onslow Road, Sheffield, **South Yorkshire S11 7AH**
TEL 0742 686161
FAX 0742 687324
OPEN 8.30–5.30 Mon–Fri or By Appointment.

Specialise in restoring carpets and rugs, including Orientals.

PROVIDE Free Estimates. Chargeable Collection/Delivery Service.
SPEAK TO William E. Franklin.

They have had fifty years' experience. Members of the Association of Cleaning and Restoration (USA), the National Carpet Cleaners Association and the Fabric Care Research Association. This workshop is included on the register of conservators maintained by the Conservation Unit of the Museums and Galleries Commission.

LONDON HOUSE ORIENTAL RUGS AND CARPETS
238–240 High Street, Boston Spa, By Wetherby, **West Yorkshire LS23 6AD**
TEL 0937 845123
OPEN 10–5.30 Tues–Sun.

Specialise in restoring and repairing Oriental carpets and rugs.

PROVIDE Free Estimates.
SPEAK TO Martin or Inger Ries.
SEE **North Yorkshire.**

CATHY McCLINTOCK TEXTILE CONSERVATION
Unit 18, 204 Kilroot Park, Larne Road, Carrickfergus, **Co. Antrim**
TEL 096 03 51429
OPEN By Appointment.

Specialise in restoring antique textiles, including tapestries, costume, linen, needlework and lace.

PROVIDE Home Inspections. Free/Chargeable Estimates.
SPEAK TO Cathy McClintock.
Member of IPCRA, UKIC, IIC and SSCR. This workshop is included on the register of conservators maintained by the Conservation Unit of the Museums and Galleries Commission.

JENNY SLEVIN
China Restoration Studio, Monkstown, **Co. Dublin**
TEL 01 280 3429
OPEN By Appointment.

Specialise in restoring embroidery and fans.

PROVIDE Home Inspections.

Free/Chargeable Estimates.
Collection/Delivery Service by
arrangement.
SPEAK TO Jenny Slevin.
Member of IPCRA.
SEE Porcelain, Furniture, Picture Frames,
Collectors (Wax).

CHISHOLME ANTIQUES
5 Orrock Place, Hawick, **Borders
TD9 0HQ**
TEL   0450 76928
OPEN   9–6 Mon–Fri.

Specialise in repairing and restoring
antique tapestry and beadwork chair
covers.

PROVIDE Home Inspections. Free
Estimates. Chargeable
Collection/Delivery Service.
SPEAK TO Mr Roberts.
SEE Furniture.

JAMES ANDERSON RITCHIE
Art Restoration Service, 6 Woodhill
Place, Aberdeen, **Grampian AB2 4LF**
TEL   0224 310491
OPEN   9–5.30 or By Appointment.

Specialise in restoring samplers and
cleaning tapestries.

PROVIDE Local Home Inspections. Free
Estimates. Chargeable
Collection/Delivery Service.
SPEAK TO J. Anderson Ritchie.
This workshop is in the Scottish
Conservation Directory.
SEE Oil Paintings, Picture Frames.

JOHN MACLEAN
112 Thirlstane Street, Edinburgh,
Lothian EH9 1AS
TEL   031 447 4225
OPEN   By Appointment.

Specialise in repairing and restoring
Oriental rugs and carpets.

PROVIDE Home Inspections. Free
Estimates. Free Collection/Delivery
Service.
SPEAK TO John Maclean.
Member of Rug Restorers Association
and SSCR.

WHYTOCK & REID
Sunbury House, Belford Mews,
Edinburgh, **Lothian EH4 3DN**
TEL   031 226 4911
FAX   031 226 4595
OPEN   9–5.30 Mon–Fri; 9–12.30 Sat.

Specialise in restoring antique and 20th
century rugs and carpets.

PROVIDE Home Inspections. Free
Estimates. Free/Chargeable
Collection/Delivery Service.
SPEAK TO David Reid.
SEE Furniture.

DAVID AND SARA BAMFORD
The Workhouse, Industrial Estate,
Presteigne, **Powys LD8 2UF**
TEL   0544 267849
FAX   0544 267849
OPEN   10–5.30 Mon–Sat By
       Appointment Only.

Specialise in restoring conserving and
cleaning Oriental rugs and textiles. They
also remake hand-knotted rugs and
carpets at their workshops in Turkey.

PROVIDE Home Inspections. Free
Estimates. Free Local
Collection/Delivery Service.
SPEAK TO David or Sara Bamford.

BOOKS, MANUSCRIPTS, MAPS AND GLOBES

DO

Keep books in a room with a constant, preferably controlled, temperature – the cooler the better

Be careful with central heating, which tends to dry out books. Vellum and cloth-bound books tend to warp; leather bindings tend to weaken and crack at the joints

Keep leather bindings clean and supple with occasional applications of a leather dressing such as hide food

Ascertain the commercial value of a book before having it repaired. Although professional repairs are comparatively inexpensive, they may not be worthwhile unless a book is of sentimental importance

DON'T

Store books in a sunny room. If this is unavoidable, keep them in a shaded area, away from direct sunlight. Coloured leather fades in the sun and spines are particularly affected. Framed maps and manuscripts should also be protected from direct sunlight

Open leather-bound volumes carelessly – some hinges and joints will crack if a book is opened unnecessarily widely

Pack books too tightly on a shelf

Remove books from a shelf by hooking a forefinger over the head of the spine.

Remove or obscure early bookplates or erase signatures. Evidence of previous ownership (provenance) can add importance and value

Use adhesive tape to repair a book. The glue it contains is corrosive and leaves a stain which it is almost impossible to remove

GEORGE BAYNTUN

Manvers Street, Bath, **Avon BA1 1JW**
TEL   0225 466000
FAX   0225 482122
OPEN   9–1, 2–5.30 Mon–Fri; Sat By
        Appointment only (9.30–1).

Specialise in restoring rare books and
fine bindings.

PROVIDE Home Inspections. Free
Estimates. Postal Service.
SPEAK TO George Bayntun.

BRISTOL-BOUND BOOKBINDING

2nd Floor, 14 Waterloo Street, Clifton,
Bristol, **Avon BS8 4BT**
TEL   0272 238279
OPEN   10–6 Tues–Sat.

Specialise in restoring leather and cloth
bindings, fine bindings and leather
repairs.

PROVIDE Free Estimates. Chargeable
Collection/Delivery Service.
SPEAK TO Mrs R. M. James.

CEDRIC CHIVERS

9 A/B Aldermoor Way, Longwell Green,
Bristol, **Avon BS15 7DA**
TEL   0272 352617
FAX   0272 618446
OPEN   8–4.30 Mon–Fri.

Specialise in refurbishment, repair and
rebinding of books and the repair and
conservation of paper.

PROVIDE Free Estimates. Chargeable
Collection/Delivery Service.
Established for 113 years.

AMANDA SLOPE BOOKBINDER

17 Church Street, Great Missenden,
Buckinghamshire HP16 0JX
TEL   0494 891319
OPEN   By Appointment.

Specialise in restoring bookbindings and

will make embroidered book covers.

PROVIDE Home Inspections. Free
Estimates. Chargeable
Collection/Delivery Service.
SPEAK TO Amanda Slope.
Member of Society of Bookbinders and
Society of Designer Bookbinders.

BRIGNELL BOOKBINDERS

2 Cobble Yard, Napier Street,
Cambridge, **Cambridgeshire
CB1 1HP**
TEL   0223 321280
OPEN   8.30–5 Mon–Fri, 8.30–12.30
        Sat.

Specialise in restoring all types of books
from old to new.

PROVIDE Home Inspections. Free
Estimates. Collection/Delivery Service.
SPEAK TO Barry Brignell.

DAVID ENGLISH

225 Carter Street, Fordham, Ely,
Cambridgeshire CB7 SJU
TEL   0638 720216
OPEN   8–5 Mon–Sat.

Specialise in repairing and restoring
antiquarian books, new bindings in
cloth, vellum, leather and paper.

PROVIDE Free Estimates.
SPEAK TO David English.

STOAKLEY BOOKBINDERS

67A Bridge Street, Cambridge,
Cambridgeshire CB2 1VR
TEL   0223 355941
OPEN   8.30–6 Mon–Fri, 9–1 Sat.

Specialise in fine bindings – all forms of
restoration, leather and cloth, journals,
theses, map mounting, desk-top leathers,
inlays, box making, traditional hand
binders.

PROVIDE Home Inspections. Free

Estimates. Chargeable
Collection/Delivery Service.
SPEAK TO Mr C. Elbden or Mr M.
Lawrence.

Established 1884.

ART WORKS
54B Church Street, Falmouth, **Cornwall
TR11 3DS**
TEL   0326 211238
OPEN   By Appointment.

Specialise in restoring antiquarian
books.

PROVIDE Home Inspections. Free
Estimates. Chargeable
Collection/Delivery Service.
SPEAK TO Suzanne Nunn.

BOOKBUILD
The Gatehouse, West Charleton, Nr.
Kingsbridge, **Devon TQ7 2AL**
TEL   0548 531294
OPEN   9–5.30 Mon–Sat and By
          Appointment.

Specialise in restoring antiquarian
books, book housings, manuscript
housings and all associated items,
including albums, drop-back boxes etc.
They pay particular attention to period
detail and execute all work to National
Trust specifications. They also offer a
specialist design binding service for
unusual housing of letters and
documents. The primary emphasis of
their work is to retain as much as possible
of original structure, material and style.

PROVIDE Home Inspections.
Collection/Delivery Service.
SPEAK TO Colin Roberts or Judith Lamb.

Bookbuild is associated with both the
Society of Bookbinders and Book
Restorers and Designer Bookbinders.

FRANCIS BROWN CRAFT BOOKBINDER
24 Camden Way, Dorchester, **Dorset
DT1 2RA**
TEL   0305 266039
OPEN   9–12.30 and 2–5.30 Mon–Fri.

Specialise in all types of bookbinding
and restoration, gold blocking, edge
gilding, box-making design.
SPEAK TO Francis Brown.

RITA BUTLER
Stour Gallery, 28 East Street, Blandford,
Dorset DT11 7DR
TEL   0258 456293
OPEN   10–1, 2–4 Tues, Thur–Sat; 10–1
          Wed.

Specialise in cleaning and restoring
maps.

PROVIDE Home Inspections. Free
Estimates. Chargeable
Collection/Delivery Service.
SPEAK TO Rita Butler.
SEE Oil Paintings.

STEPHEN AND PAMELA ALLEN
3 West Terrace, Western Hill, Durham,
Durham DH1 4RN
TEL   091 386 4601
OPEN   8.30–6 Mon–Fri or By
          Appointment.

Specialise in restoring maps, parchment
and archival material.

PROVIDE Home Inspections. Free
Estimates. Chargeable
Collection/Delivery Service.
SPEAK TO Stephen Allen or Pamela Allen.
Member of IPC.
SEE Oil Paintings.

ACORN PRESS BOOKBINDING SERVICES
103 London Road, Stanway, Colchester,
Essex CO3 5AW
TEL   0206 46101
FAX   0206 571201
OPEN   9–5 Mon–Fri.

Specialise in the restoration and repair of books and bindings.

PROVIDE Home Inspections. Free Estimates. Chargeable Collection/Delivery Service.
SPEAK TO Brian Strudwick.
Member of the Guild of Master Craftsmen.

BEELEIGH ABBEY BOOKS
Beeleigh Abbey, Maldon, **Essex CM3 4AD**
TEL   0621 856308
FAX   0621 850064
OPEN   9–6 Mon–Thur; Fri By Appointment.

Specialise in fine bindings.

PROVIDE Home Inspections. Free Estimates. Free Collection/Delivery Service.
SPEAK TO Alan Liddell.
Member of the ABA.

DAVID BANNISTER
26 Kings Road, Cheltenham,
Gloucestershire GL52 6BG
TEL   0242 514287
FAX   0242 513890
OPEN   By Appointment.

Specialise in restoring, colouring and cataloguing maps.

PROVIDE Free Estimates. Chargeable Collection/Delivery Service.
SPEAK TO David Bannister.
SEE Oil Paintings.

THE BOOKBINDERY
St Michael's Abbey, Farnborough,
Hampshire GU14 7NQ
TEL   0252 547573
OPEN   8.30–12, 1.30–5 Mon–Fri.

Specialise in hand-crafted bookbinding; all types of bookbinding undertaken.

PROVIDE Free Estimates. Free Collection/Delivery Service on large consignments only.
SPEAK TO Mr L. Prior.
Benedictine monastery, holding craft certificates for the restoration of old books.

JAMES FLAVELL BOOKBINDER AND RESTORER
26 Foreland Road, Bembridge, Isle of Wight, **Hampshire PO35 5XW**
TEL   0983 872856
OPEN   9–5.30 Mon–Fri, 9–12.30 Sat.

Specialise in restoring antiquarian books, documents and manuscripts, maps. Gold tooling, designer and presentation binding, paper de-acidification, general binding.

PROVIDE Home Inspections. Free Estimates. Free Collection/Delivery Service.
SPEAK TO James Flavell.
Mr Flavell is City and Guilds qualified, Member of the Society of Bookbinders, Associate Member of Designer Bookbinders. This workshop is included on the register of conservators maintained by the Conservation Unit of the Museums and Galleries Commission.
SEE Oil Paintings, Furniture.

R. & L. LANCEFIELD
'Toad Hall', Burnetts Lane, Horton Heath, Eastleigh, **Hampshire SO5 7DJ**
TEL   0703 692032
OPEN   9–5.30 Mon–Fri or By Appointment.

Specialise in restoring books and manuscripts – all types of conservation undertaken on these items, either single pieces or collections.

PROVIDE Home Inspections. Free Estimates. Free/Chargeable Collection/Delivery Service.
SPEAK TO Rex Lancefield.

Member of IPC. This workshop is included on the register of conservators maintained by the Conservation Unit of the Museums and Galleries Commission.
SEE Oil Paintings.

THE PETERSFIELD BOOKSHOP
16a Chapel Street, Petersfield, **Hampshire GU32 3DS**
TEL   0730 63438
FAX   0730 63438
OPEN   9–5.30 Mon–Sat.

Specialise in book-binding repair.

PROVIDE Home Inspections by arrangement. Free Estimates. Collection/Delivery Service by arrangement.
SPEAK TO Frank Westwood.
SEE Oil Paintings, Picture Frames.

LEONORA WEAVER
6 Aylestone Drive, Hereford, **Hereford & Worcester HR1 1HT**
TEL   0432 267816
OPEN   By Appointment.

Specialise in restoring and hand-colouring maps.

PROVIDE Free Estimates. Collection/Delivery Service sometimes available.
SPEAK TO Leonora Weaver.
SEE Oil Paintings.

CASTLE FINE ART STUDIO
26 Castle Street, Dover, **Kent CT16 1PW**
TEL   0304 206360
OPEN   10–1, 2–5.30 Mon–Fri; 10–1 Sat.

Specialise in restoring archival material, ephemera and maps.

PROVIDE Home Inspections. Free Estimates. Free Local Collection/Delivery Service.
SPEAK TO Ms Deborah Colam.

Member of IPC. This workshop is included on the register of conservators maintained by the Conservation Unit of the Museums and Galleries Commission.
SEE Oil Paintings, Picture Frames.

G. & D. I. MARRIN & SONS
149 Sandgate Road, Folkestone, **Kent CT20 2DA**
TEL   0303 253016
FAX   0303 850956
OPEN   9.30–5.30 Mon–Sat.

Specialise in restoring antiquarian books and maps.

PROVIDE Home Inspections. Chargeable Estimates. Chargeable Collection/Delivery Service.
SPEAK TO John or Patrick Marrin.
They are ABA and PBFA members.
SEE Oil Paintings.

RICHARD ZAHLER
Lane House, Fowgill, Bentham, Lancaster, **Lancashire LA2 7AH**
TEL   05242 61988
OPEN   9–6 Mon–Fri or By Appointment.

Specialise in restoring maps.
SPEAK TO Richard Zahler.

Member of UKIC and the Guild of Master Craftsmen. This workshop is

included on the register maintained by the Conservation Unit of the Museums and Galleries Commission.
SEE Oil Paintings, Picture Frames.

THE OLD HOUSE GALLERY
13–15 Market Place, Oakham, **Leicestershire LE15 6DT**
TEL   0572 755538
OPEN   10–5 Mon–Fri; 10–4 Sat; closed Thur p.m.

Specialise in restoring antiquarian maps.

PROVIDE Home Inspections. Free Local Collection/Delivery Service.
SPEAK TO Richard Clarke.
SEE Oil Paintings.

SUE RAWLINGS
17 Nithsdale Crescent, Market Harborough, **Leicestershire LE16 9HA**
TEL   0858 464605
OPEN   9–5.30 Mon–Fri.

Specialise in restoring books and archives.

PROVIDE Home Inspections. Free Estimates. Free Local Collection/Delivery Service.
SPEAK TO Sue Rawlings.
Member of IPC. This workshop is included on the register of conservators maintained by the Conservation Unit of the Museums and Galleries Commission.
SEE Oil Paintings.

RILEY, DUNN & WILSON LTD
Pegasus House, 116–120 Golden Lane, **London EC1Y 0UD**
TEL   071 251 2551
FAX   071 490 2338
OPEN   9–5 Mon–Fri.

Specialise in restoring antiquarian books and paper conservation, including manuscripts, prints, drawings and maps.

Also rebind and repair bindings.

PROVIDE Home Inspections. Free Estimates. Free Collection/Delivery Service.
SPEAK TO the Office Manager.
SEE **West Yorkshire, Central.**

COLLEGE OF ARMS
Queen Victoria Street, **London EC4V 4BT**
TEL   071 248 2762
OPEN   10–4 Mon–Fri.

Specialise in fine binding and paper conservation, undertaken by the College of Arms Conservation Department.
SPEAK TO the Head of Conservation.
SEE Heraldry.

DON BAKER
3 Canonbury Park South, **London N1 2JR**
TEL   071 226 2314
OPEN   By Appointment.

Specialise in repairing Islamic manuscripts and parchment.

PROVIDE Free Estimates.
SPEAK TO Don Baker.
SEE Silver.

GRAHAM BIGNELL PAPER CONSERVATION
27–29 New North Road, **London N1 6JB**
TEL   071 251 2791
OPEN   9–6 Mon–Sat By Appointment.

Specialise in restoring books, maps and archives. Also do collection surveys.

PROVIDE Home Inspections. Free Estimates. Chargeable Collection/Delivery Service.
SPEAK TO Graham Bignell.

Member of AIC, UKIC and IPC. This workshop is included on the register of conservators maintained by the

Conservation Unit of the Museums and Galleries Commission.
SEE Oil Paintings.

CELIA J. ALBERMAN AND DANIEL SWAYNE

58B Burma Road, **London N16 9BJ**
TEL   071 267 9909
OPEN   By Appointment.

Specialise in restoring books, boxes and fine bindings.

PROVIDE Home Inspections.
Free/Chargeable Estimates.
Collection/Delivery Service by arrangement.
SPEAK TO Celia Alberman or Daniel Swayne.

Member of IPC, Society of Bookbinders and Designer Bookbinders.

CATHERINE RICKMAN ART CONSERVATION

11 Berkley Road, **London NW1 8XX**
TEL   071 586 0384
OPEN   9–6 Mon–Fri By Appointment.

Specialise in restoring manuscripts and philatelic materials.

PROVIDE Home Inspections. Free Verbal Estimates.
SPEAK TO Catherine Rickman.
Member of IPC, UKIC, IIC and AIC.
This workshop is included on the register of conservators maintained by the Conservation Unit of the Museums and Galleries Commission.
SEE Oil Paintings.

JANE ZAGEL

31 Pandora Road, **London NW6 1TS**
TEL   071 794 1663
OPEN   9–6 Mon–Fri.

Specialise in restoring books.

PROVIDE Home Inspections. Refundable Estimates. Chargeable Collection/Delivery Service.
SPEAK TO Jane Zagel.

This workshop is included on the register of conservators maintained by the Conservation Unit of the Museums and Galleries Commission.
SEE Oil Paintings, Specialist Photographers.

SANGORSKI & SUTCLIFFE/ZAEHNSDORF LTD

175R Bermondsey Street, **London SE1 3UW**
TEL   071 407 1244
FAX   071 357 7466
OPEN   9–4.30 Mon–Fri.

Specialise in restoring and repairing bookbinding.

PROVIDE Home Inspections. Free Estimates. Free Collection/Delivery Service.
SPEAK TO Janet Blake.
Make visitors' books, game books, cellar books and stationery items to individual specification.
SEE **London W1.**

KIM ELIZABETH LEYSHON PICTURE RESTORER

2 Walerand Road, **London SE13 7PG**
TEL   081 318 1277
OPEN   By Appointment.

Specialise in restoring terrestrial and celestial globes.

PROVIDE Home Inspections. Free Estimates. Free Collection/Delivery Service.
SPEAK TO Kim Leyshon.
Member of IPC, IIC and UKIC.
SEE Oil Paintings.

CATHERINE HODGSON

265 Croxted Road, **London SE21 8NN**
TEL   081 761 2567
OPEN   By Appointment.

Specialise in repairing both cloth and

leather books. Will also design and bind presentation books.

PROVIDE Home Inspections. Free Estimates. Chargeable Collection/ Delivery Service.
SPEAK TO Catherine Hodgson.

CLARE REYNOLDS
20 Gubyon Avenue, **London SE24 0DX**
TEL   071 326 0458
OPEN   9–5 Mon–Fri.

Specialise in restoring archives, manuscripts and parchment.

PROVIDE Home Inspections. Free Estimates. Chargeable Collection/ Delivery Service.
SPEAK TO Clare Reynolds.
SEE Oil Paintings.

SHEPHERDS BOOKBINDERS LTD
76B Rochester Row, **London SW1P 1JU**
TEL   071 630 1184
FAX   071 931 0541
OPEN   9–5.30 Mon–Fri, 10–1 Sat.

Specialise in bookbinding restoration and archive conservation.

PROVIDE Free Estimates.
SPEAK TO Rob Shepherd.
SEE Oil Paintings.

BERNARD C. MIDDLETON
3 Gauden Road, **London SW4 6LR**
TEL   071 622 5388
FAX   071 622 5388
OPEN   9–6 Mon–Fri.

Specialise in the restoration of antiquarian books and rebinding in period styles.

PROVIDE Free Estimates.
SPEAK TO Bernard Middleton.

CAROLINE BENDIX
14 Blake Gardens, **London SW6 4QB**
TEL   071 384 2407
OPEN   8.30–6.30 Mon–Fri.

Specialise in library conservation, advising on the treatment and housing of collections of books, training of volunteers in refurbishment.

PROVIDE Home Inspections.
SPEAK TO Caroline Bendix.

BRIGID RICHARDSON
91 Langthorne Street, **London SW6 6JS**
TEL   071 381 0198
OPEN   Mon–Sat By Appointment.
Specialise in conservation of documents.

PROVIDE Home Inspections. Free/Chargeable Estimates. Chargeable Collection/Delivery Service.
SPEAK TO Brigid Richardson.
Member of IPC. This workshop is included on the register of conservators maintained by the Conservation Unit of the Museums and Galleries Commission.
SEE Oil Paintings.

SYLVIA SUMIRA CONSERVATION OF GLOBES
158 Old South Lambeth Road, **London SW8 1XX**
TEL   071 587 1593
FAX   071 587 1593
OPEN   10–6 Mon–Fri By Appointment Only.

Specialise in restoring globes.

PROVIDE Home Inspections. Chargeable Estimates.
SPEAK TO Sylvia Sumira.
Member of IPC, IIC, UKIC and SIS.

BATES AND BASKCOMB

191 St John's Hill, **London SW11 1TH**
TEL   071 223 1629
OPEN   9.30–5.30 Mon–Fri and By
        Appointment.

Specialise in restoring works of art on paper, including maps.

PROVIDE Local Home Inspections. Free/Chargeable Collection/Delivery Service.
SPEAK TO Debbie Bates or Camilla Baskcomb.
SEE Oil Paintings.

KEITH HOLMES

27 Dalebury Road, **London SW17 7HQ**
TEL   081 672 4606
OPEN   8–8 Daily.

Specialise in restoring archival and any paper or related material e.g. vellum.

PROVIDE Home Inspections. Free Estimates. Chargeable Local Collection/Delivery Service.
SPEAK TO Keith Holmes.
Member of IIC. This workshop is included on the register of conservators maintained by the Conservation Unit of the Museums and Galleries Commission.
SEE Oil Paintings.

PH7 PAPER CONSERVATORS

Unit 210, The Business Village, 3–9 Broomhill Road, **London SW18 4JQ**
TEL   081 871 5075
FAX   081 877 1940
OPEN   9–5.30 Mon–Fri or By
        Appointment.

Specialise in restoring works of art on paper, including posters, letters, documents and ephemera.

PROVIDE Home Inspections. Free Estimates. Free Collection/Delivery Service.
SPEAK TO Victoria Pease.

Member of IPC, UKIC and IIC. This workshop is included on the register of conservators maintained by the Conservation Unit of the Museums and Galleries Commission.
SEE Oil Paintings.

SANGORSKI & SUTCLIFFE/ZAEHNSDORF LTD

4th floor, 23 Albemarle Street, **London W1**
TEL   071 499 8579 (Tel 071 407
        1244 to make appointment).
FAX   071 357 7466
OPEN   9–4.30 Mon–Fri By
        Appointment Only.

Specialise in bookbinding restoration and repair.

PROVIDE Home Inspections. Free Estimates. Free Collection/Delivery Service.
SPEAK TO Janet Blake.
SEE **London SE1.**

LYVER & BOYDELL GALLERIES

15 Castle Street, Liverpool, **Merseyside L2 4SX**
TEL   051 236 3256
OPEN   10.30–5.30 Mon–Fri; Sat By
        Appointment.

Specialise in restoring and framing maps.

PROVIDE Home Inspections. Free Estimates.
SPEAK TO Paul or Gill Breen.
SEE Picture Frames.

ANNE HORNE PAPER CONSERVATOR

36 Lebanon Park, Twickenham, **Middlesex TW1 3DG**
TEL   081 892 0688
FAX   081 744 2177
OPEN   By Appointment Only.

Specialise in restoring documents.

PROVIDE Local Home Inspections. Free
Estimates. Free Local
Collection/Delivery Service.
SPEAK TO Anne Horne.
SEE Oil Paintings.

R. & S. LANE BOOKBINDING
Heath House, 2 Smiths Lane, Fakenham,
Norfolk NR21 8LG
TEL   0328 862151
OPEN   By Appointment.

Specialise in all types of bookbinding,
journals and theses, presentation copies
and full restoration.

PROVIDE Home Inspections. Free
Estimates. Free Collection/Delivery
Service.
SPEAK TO Richard or Susan Lane.

ARTHUR AND ANN RODGERS
7 Church Street, Ruddington,
Nottingham, **Nottinghamshire
NG11 6HA**
TEL   0602 216214
OPEN   9–5 Tues, Wed; 9–1 Thur, Fri;
           9–5 Sat.

Specialise in hand-colouring, cleaning,
restoring and repairing of maps.

PROVIDE Home Inspections. Chargeable
Estimates. Free Collection/Delivery
Service.
SPEAK TO Arthur Rodgers.
SEE Oil Paintings.

CHRIS HICKS
64 Merewood Avenue, Sandhills,
Oxford, **Oxfordshire OX13 8EF**
TEL   0865 69346
OPEN   By Appointment.

Specialise in restoring and conserving
printed books and bindings of all
periods.

PROVIDE Home Inspections.
Free/Chargeable Estimates. Free/
Collection/Delivery Service by
arrangement.
SPEAK TO Chris Hicks.
Member of IPC.

PETER HANKS
149 Manor Rise, Walton Stone,
Staffordshire ST15 0HY
TEL   0785 815730
OPEN   By Appointment.

Specialise in restoring books, maps and
archives.

PROVIDE Home Inspections. Free
Estimates. Chargeable
Collection/Delivery Service.
SPEAK TO Peter Hanks.
Member of IPC and Society of
Bookbinders. This workshop is included
on the register of conservators
maintained by the Conservation Unit of
the Museums and Galleries Commission.

MICHAEL BRIAN BECKHAM
Chilton Mount, Newton Road, Sudbury,
Suffolk CO10 6RN
TEL   0787 73683 or 73610
OPEN   By Appointment.

Specialise in restoration and
conservation of books and archives,
seals, leather, parchment.

PROVIDE Home Inspections.
Free/Chargeable Estimates. Chargeable
Collection/Delivery Service.
SPEAK TO Michael Beckham.
Member of IPC, SSCR and UKIC.
SEE Oil Paintings.

PHILIPPA ELLISON
Fords Farm, Winston, Nr. Stowmarket,
Suffolk IP14 6BD
TEL   0728 860572
OPEN   9–5 Mon–Fri.

Specialise in restoring works of art on

paper, particularly plate books, repair work and facsimile. Advice on general care available.

PROVIDE Home Inspections. Free Estimates. Collection/Delivery Service.
SPEAK TO Philippa Ellison.

Member of IPC. This workshop is included on the register of conservators maintained by the Conservation Unit of the Museums and Galleries Commission.
SEE Oil Paintings, Picture Frames.

CHARLES W. P. KEYES
6 Moores Close, Debenham, Stowmarket, **Suffolk IP14 6RU**
TEL   0728 860624
OPEN   By Appointment.

Specialise in paper conservation.

PROVIDE Home Inspections. Free Estimates. Chargeable Collection/Delivery Service.
SPEAK TO Charles Keyes.
Member of IPC.
SEE Oil Paintings.

KING'S COURT GALLERIES
54 West Street, Dorking, **Surrey RH4 1BS**
TEL   0306 881757
FAX   0306 875305
OPEN   9.30–5.30 Mon–Sat.

Specialise in paper conservation and restoration, including antique maps.

PROVIDE Home Inspections. Free Estimates.
SPEAK TO Mrs J. Joel.
SEE Oil Paintings.

MUCH BINDING
Lower Hammonds Farm, Ripley Lane, West Horsley, **Surrey KT24 6JP**
TEL   04865 3175
OPEN   By Appointment.

Specialise in hand bookbinding and the

restoration and repair of all types of leather and cloth bindings, albums etc.

PROVIDE Home Inspections. Free Estimates.
SPEAK TO Gina Isaac.

Member of the Surrey Guild of Craftsmen. Mrs Isaac is Hon. Sec. of the Society of Bookbinders.

THE CONSERVATION WORKSHOP
6 Green Man Yard, Boreham Street, Nr. Herstmonceaux, **East Sussex BN27 4SF**
TEL   0323 833842
OPEN   9.30–6 Mon–Fri or By Appointment.

Specialise in conserving books and manuscripts.

PROVIDE Home Inspections. Free Estimates. Free Local Collection/Delivery Service.
SPEAK TO Ian Maver or Corinne Hillman.

Members of IPC, UKIC, Royal Photographic Society, Society of Archivists and Wallpaper History Society. This workshop is included on the register of conservators maintained by the Conservation Unit of the Museums and Galleries Commission.
SEE Oil Paintings.

ANNA HORNSTEIN
Dower House Farm Workshops, Blackboys, Uckfield, **East Sussex TN22 5HJ**
TEL   0435 866149 or 0424 433260
OPEN   9–5.30 Mon–Fri or By Appointment.

Specialise in conservation of books and archives, protective boxes and portfolios made to specification.

PROVIDE Home Inspections. Free Estimates. Free Local Collection/Delivery Service.
SPEAK TO Anna Hornstein.
Member of IPC. This workshop is

included on the register of conservators maintained by the Conservation Unit of the Museums and Galleries Commission.

SUSSEX CONSERVATION STUDIO
'Hill Bank', Broad Street, Cuckfield, **West Sussex RH17 5DX**
TEL   0444 451964
OPEN   8.30–5.30 Mon–Fri or By Appointment.

Specialise in restoring maps and documents. Cleaning, repair work and retouching are all carried out to conservation standards using up-to-date techniques.

PROVIDE Free Estimates. Home Inspections by arrangement. Free Local Collection/Delivery Service.
SPEAK TO Reginald or Bernadette Selous.
Members of the IPC. This workshop is included on the register of conservators maintained by the Conservation Unit of the Museums and Galleries Commission.
SEE Oil Paintings.

WEST DEAN COLLEGE
West Dean, Chichester, **West Sussex PO18 0OZ**
TEL   0243 63 301
FAX   0243 63 342
OPEN   9–5 Mon–Fri.

Specialise in training conservators and restorers in the field of early manuscripts and rare books and will also undertake restoration.

PROVIDE Local Home Inspections. Free Estimates.
SPEAK TO Peter Sarginson.
SEE Clocks, Furniture, Porcelain, Silver.

D. M. BEACH
52 High Street, Salisbury, **Wiltshire SP1 2PG**
TEL   0722 333801
OPEN   9–5.30 Mon–Sat.

Specialise in restoring maps and repairing bookbindings.

PROVIDE Home Inspections. Free Estimates. Free Local Collection Service.
SEE Oil Paintings.

BOOTH'S ANTIQUE MAPS AND PRINTS
30 Edenvale Road, Westbury, **Wiltshire BA13 3NY**
TEL   0373 823271
FAX   0373 858185
OPEN   By Appointment.

Specialise in restoring antique maps.

PROVIDE Home Inspections. Chargeable Collection/Delivery Service.
SPEAK TO John Booth.
Mr Booth is a FRSA.
SEE Oil Paintings.

ANDREW FANE
Thistle Cottage, Great Bedwyn, Nr. Marlborough, **Wiltshire SN8 3LH**
TEL   0672 870549
OPEN   8.30–5.30 Mon–Fri or By Appointment.

Specialise in restoring documents.

PROVIDE Home Inspections. Free Estimates. Free/Chargeable Collection/Delivery Service.
SPEAK TO Andrew Fane.
Member of IPC.
SEE Oil Paintings.

JOHN SMART BOOKBINDERS AND RESTORERS EST'D 1935
The Old Wagon and Horses, Brinkworth, Chippenham, **Wiltshire SN15 5AD**
TEL   0666 510517
OPEN   8–8 Mon–Sat.

Specialise in restoring books and documents, washing, paper restoration.

PROVIDE Home Inspections. Free

Estimates. Chargeable Collection/Delivery Service.
SPEAK TO John or Richard Smart.
Member of IPC, Society of Bookbinders, Society of Designer Bookbinders. This workshop is included on the register of conservators maintained by the Conservation Unit of the Museums and Galleries Commission.

WINSTANLEY SALISBURY BOOKBINDERS
213 Devizes Road, Salisbury, **Wiltshire SP2 9LT**
TEL   0722 334998
OPEN   8.30–5.30 Mon–Fri.

Specialise in book restoration and paper conservation.

PROVIDE Free Estimates. Chargeable Collection/Delivery Service
SPEAK TO Alan Winstanley.
Mr Winstanley also makes fine new bindings to individual requirements.
SEE Oil Paintings.

ARTHUR HENRY FAIRHURST
23A Raincliffe Avenue, Scarborough, **North Yorkshire YO12 5BU**
TEL   0723 372780
OPEN   10–5 Mon–Fri.

Specialise in bookbinding and restoring and repairing books.

PROVIDE Home Inspections. Free Estimates. Local Collection/Delivery Service.
SPEAK TO Arthur Fairhurst.

CHARTERHOUSE BOOKBINDING
62 Granville Road, Shipley, **West Yorkshire BD18 2DN**
TEL   0274 480693
OPEN   10–6 Mon–Fri.

Specialise in the restoration and

conservation of 19th century cloth-bound books as well as all types of printed and manuscript items on paper i.e. books, pamphlets, posters and handbills. They can restore or rebind almost any style of bookbinding.

PROVIDE Home Inspections. Free Estimates. Free Collection/Delivery Service.
SPEAK TO Eamonn Fitzmaurice.
This workshop is included on the register of conservators maintained by the Conservation Unit of the Museums and Galleries Commission.

RILEY, DUNN & WILSON LTD
Red Doles Lane, Leeds Road, Huddersfield, **West Yorkshire HD2 1YE**
TEL   0484 534323
FAX   0484 435048
OPEN   8.15–3.45 Mon–Fri.

Specialise in the restoring, repairing and rebinding of antiquarian books, including paper conservation. Also supply book boxes.

PROVIDE Home Inspections. Free Estimates. Free Collection/Delivery Service.
SPEAK TO Geoff Crosland.
Member of the Society of Bookbinders and the IPC.
SEE **London EC1, Stirling**.

SUSAN CORR
Paper Conservation Studio, 48 Woodley Park, Dundrum, Dublin 14, **Co. Dublin**
TEL   01 2987661
OPEN   By Appointment.

Specialise in conservation of archive documents.

PROVIDE Home Inspections. Free Estimates. Collection/Delivery Service by arrangement.

SPEAK TO Susan Corr.
Member of IPCRA and IPC.
SEE Oil Paintings.

PATRICK McBRIDE
Paper Conservation Studio, IDA Tower
Complex, Pearse Street, Dublin 2,
Co. Dublin
TEL   01 775656
FAX   01 775487
OPEN   By Appointment.

Specialise in restoring archival materials,
letters, manuscripts, papier mâché
objects.

PROVIDE Home Inspections. Chargeable
Estimates. Free Collection/Delivery
Service.
SPEAK TO Patrick McBride.
Member of IPCRA, IPC and ICOM.
SEE Oil Paintings.

KAREN REIHILL
Conservation Dept., National Gallery of
Ireland, Merrion Square West, Dublin 2,
Co. Dublin
TEL   01 615133
OPEN   By Appointment.

Specialise in restoring and conserving
works of art on paper, including maps
and letters.

PROVIDE Free/Chargeable Estimates.
SPEAK TO Karen Reihill.
Member of IPCRA.
SEE Oil Paintings.

CELBRIDGE PAPER CONSERVATION STUDIO
The Mill, Celbridge, **Co. Kildare**
TEL   01 6271 037
OPEN   By Appointment.

Specialise in conserving works of art on
paper – large maps, posters, screens,
wallpaper, archival material.

PROVIDE Home Inspections. Chargeable

Estimates. Free Collection/Delivery
Service.
SPEAK TO David Skinner or Rosalind
Smith.
Member of IPCRA.

MRS ELIZABETH LUMSDEN
Craft Bookbinder and Restorer, The
Glack, Dunkeld, Perthshire, **Borders
PH8 0ER**
TEL   035072 8849
FAX   035072 8849
OPEN   8–8 Daily.

Specialise in restoring all leather and
cloth bindings, paper and archive
restoration.

PROVIDE Home Inspections. Free
Estimates. Chargeable
Collection/Delivery Service.
SPEAK TO Mrs E. Lumsden.
This workshop is in the Scottish
Conservation Directory.

RILEY, DUNN & WILSON LTD
Bellevue Bindery, Glasgow Road,
Camelon, Falkirk, **Central FK1 4HP**
TEL   0324 21591
FAX   0324 611508
OPEN   8.30–5 Mon–Fri.

Specialise in restoring antiquarian
books, repairing bindings and rebinding.
Paper conservation including
manuscripts, prints, drawings and maps.

PROVIDE Home Inspections. Free
Estimates. Free Collection/Delivery
Service.
SPEAK TO John Penman.
SEE **London EC1, West Yorkshire**.

TOM VALENTINE
Caronvale Bindery, 18 The Main Street, Larbert, Falkirk, **Central FK5 3AN**
TEL 0324 552247
OPEN By Appointment.

Specialise in archival work, restoring books and manuscripts, bookbinding, paper conservation.

PROVIDE Home Inspections. Free Collection/Delivery Service.
SPEAK TO Tom Valentine.
Mr Valentine is a member of the Society of Bookbinders.

A. W. LUMSDEN CRAFT BOOKBINDING
Edgefield Road Industrial Estate, Loanhead, **Lothian EH20 9TB**
TEL 031 440 0726
FAX 031 440 2628
OPEN 8–5 Mon–Fri.

Specialise in restoring books, spray de-acidification, tissue and silk repairs, all styles of bookbinding.

PROVIDE Local Home Inspections. Free Estimates. Free Collection/Delivery Service.
SPEAK TO A. W. Lumsden or F. A. Lumsden.
This workshop is in the Scottish Conservation Directory.

FIONA ANDERSON
Rhugarbh Church, Barcaldine, Oban, Argyll, **Strathclyde PA37 1SE**
TEL 0631 72504
OPEN 9–5 By Appointment.

Specialise in restoring antiquarian books and good second-hand books. If necessary paper can be de-acidified and re-sized, leather bindings restored and re-backed. Cloth bindings also repaired.

PROVIDE Home Inspections. Free Estimates. Free Local Collection/Delivery Service.
SPEAK TO Fiona Anderson.
This workshop is in the Scottish Conservation Directory.

CARL UTTERIDGE
Capel Bethel, Dinas Mawddwy, Machynlleth, **Powys SY20 9JA**
TEL 0650 531432
OPEN 9–6 Mon–Sat.

Specialise in restoring maps.

PROVIDE Home Inspections. Free Estimates. Free Local Collection/Delivery Service.
SPEAK TO Carl Utteridge or Jennifer A'Brook.
Member of UKIC. This workshop is included on the register of conservators maintained by the Conservation Unit of the Museums and Galleries Commission.
SEE Oil Paintings.

COLLECTORS' ITEMS

CAMERAS

LES FRANKHAM FRPS
166 Westcote Drive, Leicester,
Leicestershire LE3 0SP
TEL   0533 550825
OPEN   9–4 Mon–Fri.

Specialise in restoring classic cameras,
Zeiss-Ikon, Voigtlander, Rollei and all
cameras post-1890.
SPEAK TO Les Frankham.

T. A. CUBITT
240 Torbay Road, Harrow, **Middlesex
HA2 9QE**
TEL   081 866 9289
OPEN   8.30–5.30 Mon–Fri.

Specialise in restoring vintage cameras.

PROVIDE Free Estimates.
SPEAK TO Mr Cubitt.

DOLLS AND DOLLS' HOUSES

A. F. DUDLEY trading as 'THE FURNITURE CLINIC'
Vine House, Reach, **Cambridgeshire
CB5 0JD**
TEL   0638 741989
FAX   0638 743239
OPEN   By Appointment.

Specialise in restoring dolls.

PROVIDE Home Inspections. Free
Estimates. Free Collection/Delivery
Service.
SPEAK TO Mr A. Dudley.

Member of the Guild of Master
Craftsmen and the Association of Master
Upholsterers.
SEE Clocks, Furniture, Collectors
(Mechanical Music, Toys).

THE TEXTILE RESTORATION STUDIO
20 Hargreaves Road, Timperley,
Altrincham, **Cheshire WA15 7BB**
TEL 061 904 9944
FAX 061 903 9144
OPEN 9.30–5 Mon–Fri.

Specialise in cleaning, conserving and repairing antique dolls.

PROVIDE Home Inspections. Free Estimates. Collection/Delivery Service by arrangement.
SPEAK TO Jacqueline Hyman.

SEE Carpets, Lighting, Silver.

D. C. BLAIR
12 Columbia Street, Cheltenham,
Gloucestershire GL52 2JR
TEL 0242 511378
OPEN By Appointment Only.

Specialise in restoring period dolls, dolls' houses and toy castles.

PROVIDE Home Inspections. Chargeable Collection/Delivery Service.
SPEAK TO D. C. Blair.

LILIAN MIDDLETON'S ANTIQUE DOLL SHOP
Days Stable, Sheep Street, Stow-on-the-Wold, **Gloucestershire GL54 1AA**
TEL 0451 30381
OPEN 9–5 Mon–Sat; 11–5 Sun.

Specialise in providing a comprehensive dolls' hospital service. Make bisque dolls' heads on the premises (180 different types).

PROVIDE Home Inspections. Free Estimates. Free Collection/Delivery Service.
SPEAK TO Lilian Middleton.
SEE **Wiltshire.**

HERTFORDSHIRE CONSERVATION SERVICE
Seed Warehouse, Maidenhead Yard, The Wash, Hertford, **Hertfordshire SG14 1PX**
TEL 0992 588966
FAX 0992 588971
OPEN 9–6 Mon–Fri By Appointment.

Specialise in restoring china dolls.

PROVIDE Home Inspections. Free/Chargeable Estimates. Chargeable Collection/Delivery Service.
SPEAK TO J. M. MacQueen.

This workshop is included on the register of conservators maintained by the Conservation Unit of the Museums and Galleries Commission.
SEE Carpets, Porcelain, Lighting, Furniture, Oil Paintings, Picture Frames.

THE LILLIPUT MUSEUM OF ANTIQUE DOLLS AND TOYS
High Street, Brading, **Isle of Wight PO36 0DJ**
TEL 0983 407231
OPEN Daily 1–5 winter, 9.30–9.30 summer; Closed mid-Jan to mid-March

Specialise in restoring all types of dolls and teddy bears.

PROVIDE Free Estimates.
SPEAK TO G. K. Munday.
Member of the Guild of Master Craftsmen.

CAROLINE J. BOOTH TEXTILE CONSERVATOR
Fold Farm, Higher Eastwood,
Todmorden, **Lancashire OL14 8RP**
TEL 0706 816888
OPEN 10–5 Mon–Fri.

Specialise in a full range of services for historic textiles both woven and embroidered, including materials for dolls' houses and costumes for dolls and automata. Condition and conservation reports provided and advice given on handling, storage and display. Ms Booth uses traditional conservation techniques so that any work done is reversible.

PROVIDE Home Inspections. Chargeable Estimates. Chargeable Collection/Delivery Service.
SPEAK TO Caroline Booth.
SEE Carpets.

MARCELLA FLETCHER
24–26 Leyland Road, Penwortham, Preston, **Lancashire PR1 9XS**
TEL   0772 744970
OPEN   By Appointment.

Specialise in dolls' hospital service for Victorian and Edwardian dolls.

PROVIDE Home Inspections. Free Estimates. Chargeable Collection/Delivery Service.
SPEAK TO Marcella Fletcher.

CHELSEA LION
Chenil Galleries, 181–183 Kings Road, **London SW3 5EB**
TEL   071 351 9338
OPEN   11–5 Mon–Sat.

Specialise in restoring dolls.

PROVIDE Free Estimates.
SPEAK TO Steve Clark.
SEE Collectors (Toys).

THE DOLLS' HOSPITAL
16 Dawes Road, **London SW6 7EN**
TEL   071 385 2081
OPEN   9.30–5 Mon, Tues, Fri; 10–4 Sat.

Specialise in repairing and restoring antique dolls.

PROVIDE Free Estimates.
SPEAK TO Mr J. Smith

FAITH S. EATON
16 Clifton Gardens, **London W9 1DT**
TEL   071 289 2359

Specialise in wax restoration and conservation of dolls and dolls' houses. Ms Eaton also advises on security and display.

PROVIDE Home Inspections if expenses paid. Refundable Estimates. Chargeable Collection/Delivery Service.
SPEAK TO Faith Eaton.

Author of *Care and Repair of Antique and Modern Dolls*, Founder Member of Doll Club of Great Britain, Dollmakers Circle, Washington DC Doll Club. This workshop is included on the register of conservators maintained by the Conservation Unit of the Museums and Galleries Commission.

MARGARET GLOVER
42 Hartham Road, Isleworth, **Middlesex TW7 5ES**
TEL   081 568 4662
OPEN   By Appointment.

Specialise in restoring wax dolls of every kind.

PROVIDE Free Estimates.
SPEAK TO Margaret Glover.
SEE Collectors (Mechanical Music, Wax)

SARAH BROMILOW
180 Reading Road, Henley-on-Thames, **Oxfordshire RG9 1EA**
TEL   0491 577001
FAX   0491 410735
OPEN   9–5 Mon–Fri.

Specialise in repairing and restoring dolls' houses.

PROVIDE Verbal Estimates over the telephone. Chargeable Collection/Delivery Service
SPEAK TO Sarah Bromilow.
SEE Collectors (Toys).

PETER STRANGE
'The Willows', Sutton, Oxford,
Oxfordshire OX8 1RU
TEL   0865 882020
OPEN   By Appointment Only.

Specialise in china doll restoration, especially the invisible repairing of broken and damaged bisque dolls' heads and bisque figurines, as well as sleeping eyes and lashes.

PROVIDE Home Inspections. Free Estimates. Chargeable Collection/Delivery Service.
SPEAK TO Peter Strange.

RECOLLECT STUDIOS (C. JACKMAN)
The Old School, London Road, Sayers Common, **West Sussex BN6 9HX**
TEL   0273 833314
OPEN   10–5 Tues–Sat.

Specialise in restoring antique and modern collectors' dolls, wax doll making, porcelain heads, composition parts, bodies. (Antique dolls not accepted by post.)

PROVIDE Free Estimates.
SPEAK TO Mrs Carol Jackman or Mr Paul Jago.
Member of the Doll Artisan Guild and the UKIC. Also teach doll restoration.

LILIAN MIDDLETON'S DOLL SHOP
5 Brown Street, Salisbury, **Wiltshire SP1 10N**
TEL   0722 333303
OPEN   9–5 Mon–Sat.

Specialise in a dolls' hospital service.

PROVIDE Home Inspections. Free Estimates. Free Collection/Delivery Service.
SPEAK TO Joyce Heard.
SEE **Gloucestershire.**

SECOND CHILDHOOD
20 Byram Arcade, Westgate, Huddersfield, **West Yorkshire HD1 1ND**
TEL   0484 530117 or 603854
OPEN   10.30–3.30 Tues–Sat

Specialise in restoring antique dolls and related items, dolls' hospital.

PROVIDE Free Estimates. Free Local Collection/Delivery Service.
SPEAK TO Michael or Elizabeth Hoy.
SEE Collectors (Toys).

DAPHNE FRASER
Glenbarry, 58 Victoria Road, Lenzie, Glasgow, **Strathclyde G66 5AP**
TEL   041 776 1281
OPEN   By Appointment.

Specialise in restoring dolls and dolls' houses.

PROVIDE Free Estimates.
SPEAK TO Daphne Fraser.
This workshop is in the Scottish Conservation Directory.

SEE Collectors (Toys), Oil Paintings, Furniture, Picture Frames.

HAIR

CHARLES CLEMENTS
4–5 Burlington Arcade, Piccadilly, **London W1V 9A13**
TEL   071 493 3923
OPEN   9–5.30 Mon–Fri; 9–4.30 Sat.
Specialise in rebristling hairbrushes, replacing mirrors and combs.

PROVIDE Free Estimates.
SPEAK TO Charles Clements.

MECHANICAL MUSIC

VINTAGE WIRELESS CO. LTD
Tudor House, Cossham Street, Mangotsfield, Bristol, **Avon BS17 3EN**
TEL   0272 565472
FAX   0272 575442
OPEN   9.30–1.30 Sat; Mon–Fri mail order only.

Specialise in components and service information on Vintage Valve hi-fi radios.
SPEAK TO T. G. Rees.
They do not offer a restoration service at present.

D. N. CARD
1A Chester Street, Caversham, Reading, **Berkshire RG4 8JH**
TEL   0734 470777
OPEN   9–12.30, 2–5 Mon–Fri or By Appointment.

Specialise in restoring music boxes.

PROVIDE Home Inspections. Free Estimates. Chargeable Collection/Delivery Service.
SPEAK TO David Card.
Mr. Card is CMBHI. This workshop is included on the register of conservators maintained by the Conservation Unit of the Museums and Galleries Commission.
SEE Clocks.

S. J. BIRT & SON
21 Windmill Street, Brill, Aylesbury, **Buckinghamshire HP18 9TG**
TEL   0844 237440
OPEN   By Appointment.
Specialise in restoring musical boxes.

PROVIDE Home Inspections. Free Estimates. Free Collection/Delivery Service.

SPEAK TO Mr S. J. Birt.
SEE Clocks.

A. F. DUDLEY trading as 'THE FURNITURE CLINIC'
Vine House, Reach, **Cambridgeshire CB5 0JD**
TEL   0638 741989
FAX   0638 743239
OPEN   By Appointment.

Specialise in restoring automata.

PROVIDE Home Inspections. Free Estimates. Free Collection/Delivery Service.
SPEAK TO Mr A. Dudley.
Members of the Guild of Master Craftsmen and the Association of Master Upholsterers.
SEE Clocks, Furniture, Dolls, Toys.

J. V. PIANOS & CAMBRIDGE PIANOLA CO.
The Limes, Landbeach, Cambridge, **Cambridgeshire CB4 4DR**
TEL   0223 861408 or 861348 or 861507
FAX   0223 441276
OPEN   By Appointment.

Specialise in complete rebuilding of player-pianos, pianolas and nickelodeons.

PROVIDE Home Inspections. Chargeable Estimates. Chargeable Collection/Delivery Service.
SPEAK TO F. T. Poole.
SEE Musical Instruments.

MILL FARM ANTIQUES
50 Market Street, Disley, Stockport, **Cheshire SK12 2DT**
TEL   0663 764045
OPEN   9–6 Mon–Sat.

Specialise in restoring cylinder- and disc-playing musical boxes.

PROVIDE Home Inspections. Free Estimates. Free Collection/Delivery Service.
SPEAK TO F. E. Berry.
SEE Clocks.

MAURICE YARHAM
Holly Cottage, Birdsmoorgate, Paynes Downe, Nr. Bridport, **Dorset DT6 5PL**
TEL   02977 377
OPEN   7–7 Mon–Fri.

Specialise in repairing, restoring and conserving antique musical boxes.

PROVIDE Home Inspections. Free Estimates. Chargeable Collection/Delivery Service.
SPEAK TO Maurice Yarham.
SEE Clocks.

KEITH HARDING'S WORLD OF MECHANICAL MUSIC
Oak House, High Street, Northleach, **Gloucestershire GL54 3EU**
TEL   0451 60181
FAX   0451 61133
OPEN   10–6 Sun–Sat.

Specialise in restoring musical boxes and automata.

PROVIDE Home Inspections. Free Estimates. Free Local Collection/Delivery Service.
SPEAK TO Keith Harding.
SEE Clocks.

GEORGE WORSWICK
108–110 Station Road, Bardney, **Lincolnshire LN3 5UF**
TEL   0526 398352
OPEN   By Appointment.

Specialise in restoring and repairing mechanisms of antique musical boxes of the cylinder type and music combs of disc-playing music boxes.

PROVIDE Free Estimates.
SPEAK TO George Worswick.
Mr Worswick is FBHI.

DAVID NEWELL
55 Shelton Street, **London WC2H 9HE**
TEL   071 836 1000
OPEN   10–6 Mon–Fri By Appointment.

Specialise in restoring musical boxes and automata.

PROVIDE Free Estimates in shop.
SPEAK TO David Newell.
Mr Newell is FBHI.
SEE Clocks.

MARGARET GLOVER
42 Hartham Road, Isleworth, **Middlesex TW7 5ES**
TEL   081 568 4662
OPEN   By Appointment.

Specialise in re-dressing automata in exact reproduction of original dress using antique materials.

PROVIDE Free Estimates.
SPEAK TO Margaret Glover.
SEE Collectors (Dolls, Wax).

WICKENDEN CLOCKS
53 Gorse Road, Thorpe St Andrew, Norwich, **Norfolk NR7 OAY**
TEL   0603 32179
OPEN   9–5 Sun–Sat.

Specialise in restoring music boxes.

PROVIDE Home Inspections. Free Estimates. Free Local Collection/Delivery Service.
SPEAK TO Eric Wickenden.
SEE Clocks.

RICHARD HIGGINS
The Old School, Longnor, Nr.
Shrewsbury, **Shropshire SY5 7PP**
TEL   074373 8162
OPEN   8–6 Mon–Fri.

Specialise in restoring music boxes.

PROVIDE Home Inspections.
Free/Chargeable Estimates.
Collection/Delivery Service by
arrangement.
SPEAK TO Richard Higgins.

Member of BAFRA and UKIC. This
workshop is included on the register of
conservators maintained by the
Conservation Unit of the Museums and
Galleries Commission.
SEE Furniture, Clocks.

JOHN COWDEROY ANTIQUES
42 South Street, Eastbourne, **East
Sussex BN21 4XB**
TEL   0323 20058
FAX   0323 410163
OPEN   9.30–1, 2.30–5 Mon–Fri; 9.30–
1 Wed, Sat.

Specialise in restoring musical boxes.

PROVIDE Home Inspections. Free
Estimates. Chargeable
Collection/Delivery Service.
SPEAK TO Ruth Cowderoy.

Member of LAPADA.
SEE Clocks, Furniture.

T. P. BROOKS
Sycamores, School Lane, Lodsworth,
Petworth, **West Sussex GU28 9DH**
TEL   07985 248

Specialise in restoring musical boxes and
automata.

PROVIDE Home Inspections. Free
Estimates. Free Collection/Delivery
Service.
SPEAK TO Mr T. P. Brooks.

Member of UKIC. This workshop is
included on the register of conservators
maintained by the Conservation Unit of
the Museums and Galleries Commission.
SEE Clocks.

TIME RESTORED & CO.
18–20 High Street, Pewsey, **Wiltshire
SN9 5AQ**
TEL   0672 63544
FAX   0672 63544
OPEN   By Appointment.

Specialise in restoring musical boxes and
automata.

PROVIDE Home Inspections. Free
Estimates. Free Collection/Delivery
Service.
SPEAK TO J. H. Bowler-Reed.
SEE Clocks.

DAVID BARKER
Antique Clock Restoration, Inglenook,
Ferncliffe Drive, Utley, Keighley, **West
Yorkshire BD20 6HN**
TEL   0535 606306
OPEN   Mon–Sat By Appointment.

Specialise in restoring automata and
small antique mechanisms.

PROVIDE Home Inspections. Free
Estimates. Free/Chargeable
Collection/Delivery Service.
SPEAK TO David Barker.

This workshop is included on the register
of conservators maintained by the
Conservation Unit of the Museums and
Galleries Commission.
SEE Clocks.

GRANT LEES
98 Gala Park, Galashiels, Selkirkshire,
Borders TD1 1EZ
TEL   0896 3721
OPEN   9–6 Mon–Sat, closed Wed and
Sat a.m.

Specialise in musical boxes.

PROVIDE Home Inspections. Free
Estimates. Chargeable
Collection/Delivery Service.
SPEAK TO Grant Lees.
This workshop is in the Scottish
Conservation Directory.
SEE Clocks, Furniture.

J. TUBBECKE
Antique Clocks, 11 Island Street,
Galashiels, **Borders TD1 1NZ**
TEL   0896 58958
OPEN   10–5 Mon, Tues, Thur, Fri; 10–
        1.30 Sat.

Specialise in restoring music boxes.

PROVIDE Home Inspections. Free
Estimates. Free Collection/Delivery
Service.
SPEAK TO J. Tubbecke or T. Treeby.
This workshop is in the Scottish
Conservation Directory.
SEE Clocks.

JIM WEIR
Woodbank, Charleston, Glamis, by
Forfar, Angus, **Highland DD8 1UF**
TEL   030 784 473
FAX   030 784 473
OPEN   By Appointment.

Specialise in restoring antique musical
boxes.

PROVIDE Home Inspections.
Free/Chargeable Estimates. Chargeable
Collection/Delivery Service.
SPEAK TO Jim Weir.
This workshop is in the Scottish
Conservation Directory.

DAVID GAY
23 Taypark, 30 Dundee Road, West
Ferry, Dundee, **Tayside DD5 1LX**
TEL   0382 739845
OPEN   By Appointment.

Specialise in restoring barrel organs and
automata.

PROVIDE Free Estimates.
SPEAK TO David Gay.

PAPER

JANE McNAMARA CONSERVATOR
14 Chelsfield Gardens, **London
SE26 4DJ**
TEL   081 699 7173
OPEN   9–5 Mon–Fri By Appointment.

Specialise in conservation of three-
dimensional paper artefacts, fans and
paper-covered boxes.

PROVIDE Home Inspections. Free
Estimates. Free Local
Collection/Delivery Service.
SPEAK TO Jane McNamara.
Member of IPC. This workshop is
included on the register of conservators
maintained by the Conservation Unit of
the Museums and Galleries Commission.
SEE Oil Paintings.

D. A. ROGERS CORDELL ANTIQUES
13 St Peter's Street, Ipswich, **Suffolk
IP1 1FX**
TEL   0473 219508 and 230685
FAX   0473 230685 (Att. Rogers)
OPEN   10–4 Mon–Fri.

Specialise in restoring paper objects,
quill work, box lining, Victorian scraps.

PROVIDE Local Home Inspections. Free
Estimates. Local Chargeable
Collection/Delivery Service.
SPEAK TO D. A. Rogers.

PENS

CLASSIC PENS LIMITED
Bassett Business Units, Hurricane Way,
North Weald, Epping, **Essex CM16 6AA**
TEL   0992 524444
OPEN   8.30–5 Mon–Fri.

Specialise in restoring pens; Parker,
Sheaffer, Waterman, Montblanc, Mabie
Todd (Swan), Conway Stewart, etc.

PROVIDE Free Estimates.
SPEAK TO Andy Lambrou.

JASMIN CAMERON
Antiquarius J6, 131–141 Kings Road,
London SW3 5ST
TEL   071 351 4154
OPEN   10.15–5.30 Tues–Sat.

Specialise in restoring vintage and
collectors' fountain pens.

PROVIDE Free Estimates.
SPEAK TO Jasmin Cameron.

PENFRIEND (LONDON) LTD
Bush House Arcade, Bush House,
Strand, **London WC2B 4PH**
TEL   071 836 9809
OPEN   9.30–5.30 Mon–Fri.

Specialise in restoring fountain pens and
pencils.

PROVIDE Free Estimates.
SPEAK TO Mr P. Woolf.

SCIENTIFIC INSTRUMENTS

THE BAROMETER SHOP
2 Lower Park Row, Bristol, **Avon BS1 5BJ**
TEL   0272 272565
OPEN   9–5.30 Mon, Wed, Fri 9–1 Sat.

Specialise in restoring scientific
instruments.

PROVIDE Home Inspections. Free
Estimates. Free Collection/Delivery
Service.
SPEAK TO Mrs Honey.
SEE Clocks, Furniture.
SEE **Hereford & Worcester**

PETER D. BOSSON
10B Swan Street, Wilmslow, **Cheshire
SK9 1HE**
TEL   0625 525250 and 527857
OPEN   10–12.45, 2.15–5 Tues–Sat.

Specialise in restoring scientific
instruments.

PROVIDE Home Inspections. Free
Estimates. Free Collection/Delivery
Service within fifty miles.
SPEAK TO Peter Bosson.
SEE Clocks.

THE CHETTLE GUILD
The Stables, Chettle House, Chettle,
Blandford, **Dorset DT11 8DB**
TEL   0258 89576
OPEN   9–6 Mon–Sat.

Specialise in restoring scientific
instruments.

PROVIDE Home Inspections. Free
Estimates. Free Local
Collection/Delivery Service.
SPEAK TO Alastair or Andrew Arnold.
SEE Arms, Clocks, Furniture.

THE BAROMETER SHOP
4 New Street, Leominster, **Hereford &
Worcester HR6 8BT**
TEL   0568 613652
OPEN   9–5.30 Mon–Sat, closed Wed.

Specialise in restoring scientific
instruments.

PROVIDE Home Inspections. Free

Estimates. Free Collection/Delivery
Service.
SPEAK TO Richard Cookson.

Mr Cookson is CMBHI.
SEE Furniture, Clocks.
SEE **Avon.**

OLD ROPERY ANTIQUES
East Street, Kilham, Nr. Driffield, **North
Humberside YO25 0ST**
TEL   026282 233
OPEN   9.30–5 Mon–Sat.

Specialise in restoring scientific
instruments.

PROVIDE Home Inspections. Chargeable
Estimates. Chargeable
Collection/Delivery Service.
SPEAK TO John Butterfield.
SEE Clocks, Furniture.

ELLIOTT NIXON
5 Alexandra Road, Stoneygate, Leicester,
Leicestershire LE2 2BB
TEL   0533 705713
OPEN   9–6 Mon–Sat.

Specialise in a full restoration and
conservation service for scientific
instruments.

PROVIDE Home Inspections. Free
Estimates. Free Local
Collection/Delivery Service.
SPEAK TO Elliott Nixon.

Mr Nixon is FBHI. This workshop is
included on the register of conservators
maintained by the Conservation Unit of
the Museums and Galleries Commission.
SEE Clocks.

HENNELL SILVER LTD
12 New Bond Street, **London
W1Y 0H6**
TEL   071 629 6888
FAX   071 493 8158
OPEN   9.30–5.30 Tues–Sat.

Specialise in restoring antique medical
instruments.

PROVIDE Home Inspections. Free
Estimates. Free Collection/Delivery
Service.
SPEAK TO A. C. Kaufmann.
SEE Silver.

RELCY ANTIQUES
9 Nelson Road, **London SE10 9JB**
TEL   081 858 2812
FAX   081 293 4135
OPEN   10–6 Mon–Sat.

Specialise in restoring scientific and
nautical instruments.

PROVIDE Home Inspections.
Free/Chargeable Estimates.
Collection/Delivery Service by
arrangement.
SPEAK TO Robin Challis.

SEE Furniture, Oil Paintings, Silver.

HUMBLEYARD FINE ART
3 Fish Hill, Holt, **Norfolk NR25 6BD**
TEL   0263 713362
OPEN   10–5 Mon–Sat; closed Fri.

Specialise in repairing and restoring
scientific, medical and nautical
instruments.

PROVIDE Home Inspections. Free
Estimates. Chargeable Collection/
Delivery Service.
SPEAK TO James Layte.
SEE Clocks.

PETER WIGGINS
Raffles, Southcombe, Chipping Norton,
Oxfordshire OX7 5QH
TEL   0608 642652
OPEN   9–6 Mon–Fri.

Specialise in restoring scientific
instruments.

PROVIDE Home Inspections. Free

Estimates. Chargeable
Collection/Delivery Service.
SPEAK TO Peter Wiggins.
SEE Clocks.

NIDD HOUSE ANTIQUES

Nidd House, Bogs Lane, Harrogate,
North Yorkshire HG1 4DY
TEL　0423 884739
OPEN　9–5 Mon–Fri or By
　　　Appointment.

Specialise in restoring scientific
instruments.

PROVIDE Home Inspections. Free Local
Estimates. Chargeable
Collection/Delivery Service.
SPEAK TO Mr D. Preston.
Member of the Guild of Master
Craftsmen, UKIC. This workshop is
included on the register of conservators
maintained by the Conservation Unit of
the Museums and Galleries Commission.
SEE Furniture, Porcelain, Silver.

NOLF & MANN

29 Breadalbane Terrace, Wick,
Highland KW1 5AT
TEL　0955 4284
OPEN　By Appointment.

Specialise in restoring scientific
instruments.

PROVIDE Home Inspections.
Free/Chargeable Estimates. Chargeable
Collection/Delivery Service.
SPEAK TO T. Nolf.
SEE Arms.

SHIP MODELS

SCALE MODELS INTERNATIONAL

Museum Building, Church Road,
Waterloo, Liverpool, **Merseyside
L22 5NB**
TEL　051 924 4998
OPEN　9–5.30 Mon–Fri or By
　　　Appointment.

Specialise in restoring ship models and
ship model display cases and maritime
artefacts.

PROVIDE Home Inspections. Free
Estimates. Chargeable
Collection/Delivery Service.
SPEAK TO T. L. Nelson-Ewen.
Member of UKIC. This workshop is
included on the register of conservators
maintained by the Conservation Unit of
the Museums and Galleries Commission.

KELVIN THATCHER

22 Croxton Hamlet, Nr. Fulmodeston,
Fakenham, **Norfolk NR21 0NP**
TEL　0328 878051
OPEN　10–7 Mon–Sat.

Specialise in cleaning and restoring ship
models, providing new showcases and
movement and transportation of fragile
models.

PROVIDE Home Inspections. Free Local
Estimates. Chargeable
Collection/Delivery Service.
SPEAK TO Kelvin Thatcher.
Member of UKIC. This workshop is
included on the register of conservators
maintained by the Conservation Unit of
the Museums and Galleries Commission.

DONALD SMITH MODELMAKERS

Bridge Road, Kintore, Aberdeenshire,
Highland AB51 0UL
TEL　0467 32493 or 0836 365021
FAX　0467 32493
OPEN　8.30–5.30 Mon–Fri.

Specialise in restoring ship models of all types ranging from Board of Admiralty models to builders' full and half-models.

PROVIDE Free Estimates. Chargeable Collection/Delivery Service.
SPEAK TO Donald Smith.
Member of the Guild of Master Craftsmen. This workshop is in the Scottish Conservation Directory.

TAXIDERMY

ANN & JOHN BURTON
Natural Craft Taxidermy, 21 Main Street, Ebrington, Nr. Chipping Camden, **Gloucestershire GL55 6NL**
TEL   038678 231
OPEN   By Appointment.

Specialise in taxidermy commissions and restoration work.

PROVIDE Home Inspections. Chargeable Estimates. Chargeable Collection/Delivery Service.
SPEAK TO Ann or John Burton.

MALCOLM PAUL HARMAN
North Lodge, Quex Park, Birchington, **Kent CT7 0BG**
TEL   0843 42042
OPEN   By Appointment.

Specialise in all types of taxidermy mounts and casework, including rugs, fish, birds, African and Asian big game and large-scale dioramas for museums. They also mount fresh material and will provide a maintenance service. They do not sell or buy material.

PROVIDE Home Inspections. Free Estimates. Chargeable Collection/Delivery Service.
SPEAK TO Mr Malcolm Harman.
This workshop is included on the register of conservators maintained by the

Conservation Unit of the Museums and Galleries Commission.

GET STUFFED
105 Essex Road, **London N1 2SL**
TEL   071 226 1364
OPEN   10.30–4 Mon–Wed, Fri; 10.30–1 Thur; 11–4 Sat.

Specialise in all aspects of taxidermy and also supply glass domes.

PROVIDE Free Estimates. Chargeable Collection/Delivery Service.
SPEAK TO Robert Sinclair.

HEADS 'N' TAILS
Bourne House, Church Street, Wiveliscombe, **Somerset TA4 2LT**
TEL   0984 23097
OPEN   By Appointment.

Specialise in fine taxidermy, including restoration, particularly cased fish.

PROVIDE Home Inspections. Free Estimates. Chargeable Collection/Delivery Service.
SPEAK TO D. McKinley.

MARK WINSTON-SMITH
5 Pigeon Street, Snitterfield, Stratford-Upon-Avon, **Warwickshire CV37 0LP**
TEL   0789 731485
OPEN   10–10 Daily By Appointment.

Specialise in all taxidermy, producing mounted natural history specimens of anatomical accuracy and lifelike, artistic appearance.

PROVIDE Home Inspections. Free Estimates. Chargeable Collection/Delivery Service.
SPEAK TO Sally Winston-Smith.
Member of the Guild of Taxidermists.

BORDER TAXIDERMY STUDIOS
5 East Stewart Place, Hawick, Roxburgh, **Borders TD9 8BQ**
TEL   0450 76092
OPEN   8.30–5 Mon–Fri or By
       Appointment.
Specialise in providing taxidermy services for birds, fish, mammals and groundwork. Will do surveys of collections.

PROVIDE Local Home Inspections. Free Estimates. Local Collection/Delivery Service.
SPEAK TO Colin Scott.
Member of the Guild of Taxidermists. This workshop is in the Scottish Conservation Directory.

GEORGE C. JAMIESON
'Cramond Tower', Kirk Cramond, Edinburgh, **Lothian EH4 6NS**
TEL   031 336 1916
FAX   031 336 1916
OPEN   8.30–5.30 Mon–Fri or By
       Appointment.

Specialise in all aspects of taxidermy, fish casts repaired, game hemo restorations, museum work and case work.
PROVIDE Chargeable Home Inspections. Free Local Estimates. Chargeable Collection/Delivery Service.
SPEAK TO George Jamieson.
Professional Member of the Guild of Taxidermists in birds, mammals and fish. This workshop is in the Scottish Conservation Directory.

CHRIS CAMPBELL
Unit 4, Foundry Road, Bonnybridge, **Stirlingshire FK4 2BD**
TEL   0324 813410
FAX   0324 813410
OPEN   9–5.30 Mon–Fri or By
       Appointment.
Specialise in restoring damaged

taxidermy items, including cleaning, fumigation, repairs to casework, renovation.

PROVIDE Home Inspections. Free Estimates. Chargeable Collection/Delivery Service.
SPEAK TO Chris Campbell.
This workshop is in the Scottish Conservation Directory.

TOYS AND ROCKING HORSES

JOHN MARRIOTT ROCKING HORSES
86 Village Road, Bromham, **Bedfordshire MK43 8HU**
TEL   02302 3173
OPEN   8–8 Daily.
Specialise in manufacturing and restoring traditionally styled rocking and carousel horses.

PROVIDE Free/Chargeable Home Inspections. Free/Chargeable Estimates. Free Local Collection/Delivery Service.
SPEAK TO John Marriott.

A. F. DUDLEY trading as 'THE FURNITURE CLINIC'
Vine House, Reach, **Cambridgeshire CB5 0JD**
TEL   0638 741989
FAX   0638 743239
OPEN   By Appointment.

Specialise in restoring rocking horses.

PROVIDE Home Inspections. Free Estimates. Free Collection/Delivery Service.

SPEAK TO Mr A. Dudley.
Members of the Guild of Master
Craftsmen and the Association of Master
Upholsterers.
SEE Clocks, Furniture, Collectors (Dolls,
Mechanical Music).

MICHAEL BARRINGTON
The Old Rectory, Warmwell, Dorchester,
Dorset DT2 8HQ
TEL   0305 852104
OPEN   8.30–5.30 or By Appointment.

Specialise in restoring model steam
engines.

PROVIDE Free Local Estimates.
Free/Chargeable Collection/Delivery
Service.
SPEAK TO Michael Barrington.
SEE Clocks, Furniture.

J. & D. WOODS
180 Chorley Road, Westhoughton,
Bolton, **Lancashire BL5 3PN**
TEL   0942 816246
OPEN   By Appointment.

Specialise in constructing and restoring
all types of rocking horses. They also
supply accessories and are one of the few
companies able to restore and make skin-
covered horses.

PROVIDE Home Inspections. Free
Estimates. Chargeable
Collection/Delivery Service.
SPEAK TO John Woods.

ANTHONY JACKSON
20 Westry Corner, Barrowby, Grantham,
Lincolnshire NG32 1DF
TEL   0476 67477
OPEN   8–5 Mon–Fri or By
          Appointment.

Specialise in restoring rocking horses.

PROVIDE Home Inspections. Free
Estimates. Free Local
Collection/Delivery Service.
SPEAK TO Anthony or Amanda Jackson.

CHELSEA LION
Chenil Galleries, 181–183 Kings Road,
London SW3 5EB
TEL   071 351 9338
OPEN   11–5 Mon–Sat.

Specialise in restoring teddy bears and
rocking horses.

PROVIDE Free Estimates.
SPEAK TO Steve Clark.
SEE Collectors (Dolls).

PHIL HILL (ROCKING HORSES)
188 Alcester Road South, Kings Heath,
Birmingham, **West Midlands B14 6DE**
TEL   021 444 0102
OPEN   9.30–6 Mon–Fri or By
          Appointment.

Specialise in restoring wooden rocking
horses and carousel animals.

PROVIDE Home Inspections. Free
Estimates. Free Collection/Delivery
Service.
SPEAK TO Phil Hill.
SEE Furniture.

PETER WATTS ROCKING HORSES
10 Cremorne Road, Four Oaks, Sutton
Coldfield, **West Midlands B75 5AH**
TEL   021 308 1477
OPEN   Mon–Sat By Appointment.

Specialise in restoring any wooden
rocking horses, also metal and plastic
horses where possible. No stuffed horses
considered.

PROVIDE Home Inspections. Free
Estimates. Chargeable
Collection/Delivery Service.
SPEAK TO Peter Watts.

Member of the Guild of West Midlands Artists and Craftsmen Ltd. This workshop is included on the register of conservators maintained by the Conservation Unit of the Museums and Galleries Commission.

SARAH BROMILOW
180 Reading Road, Henley-on-Thames, **Oxfordshire RG9 1EA**
TEL   0491 577001
FAX   0491 410735
OPEN   9–5 Mon–Fri.

Specialise in repairing and restoring rocking horses and other wooden toys.

PROVIDE Verbal Estimates over the telephone. Chargeable Collection/Delivery Service
SPEAK TO Sarah Bromilow.

SEE Collectors (Dolls).

HADDON ROCKING HORSES LTD
Station Road, Wallingford, **Oxfordshire OX10 0HX**
TEL   0491 36165
OPEN   9–4.30 Mon–Fri.

Specialise in restoring rocking horses.

PROVIDE Free Estimates. Chargeable Collection/Delivery Service.
SPEAK TO Andrea Roberts.

THE ROCKING HORSE WORKSHOP
Ashfield House, The Foxholes, Wem, **Shropshire SY4 5UJ**
TEL   0939 232335
OPEN   9–6 Daily.

Specialise in restoring all types of rocking horses 17th century to present day. Also manufacture new horses and supply parts for do-it-yourself rocking horses.

PROVIDE Home Inspections. Free

Estimates. Chargeable Collection/Delivery Service.
SPEAK TO Mr David James Kiss or Mrs Noreen Kiss.

CLIVE GREEN
The Lychgate, 20 Broadmark Lane, Rustington, **West Sussex BN16 2HJ**
TEL   0903 786639
OPEN   By Appointment.

Specialise in restoring carved wooden rocking horses.

PROVIDE Local Home Inspections.
SPEAK TO Clive Green.

Mr Green is co-author with Anthony Dew of *Restoring Rocking Horses*, a Member of UKIC and Chairman of the British Toymakers Guild 1991, 1992. This workshop is included on the register of conservators maintained by the Conservation Unit of the Museums and Galleries Commission.

ROBERT MULLIS ROCKING HORSE MAKER
55 Berkley Road, Wroughton, Nr. Swindon, **Wiltshire SN4 9BN**
TEL   0793 813583
OPEN   By Appointment Only.

Specialise in restoring rocking horses on bow rockers or safety stands using traditional methods. New horses made to order according to individual requirements.

PROVIDE Home Inspections. Free Estimates. Chargeable Collection/Delivery Service.
SPEAK TO Robert Mullis.

BEARWOOD MODELS
20 Westminster Road, Malvern Wells, **Worcestershire WR14 4EF**
TEL   0684 568977
OPEN   By Appointment.

Specialise in repairing and restoring old toys, particularly clockwork repairs to model railway locomotives.

PROVIDE Free Estimates.
SPEAK TO R. W. Chester-Lamb.
SEE Clocks.

ANTHONY DEW
The Rocking Horse Shop, Old Road, Holme upon Spalding Moor, York, **North Yorkshire YO4 4AB**
TEL   0430 860563
FAX   0430 860563
OPEN   9–5 Mon–Sat By Appointment

Specialise in restoring and making rocking horses. Mr Dew will supply all parts and accessories and makes tailor-made-to-measure kits for restorers.

PROVIDE Home Inspections. Free Estimates. Collection/Delivery Service by arrangement.
SPEAK TO Pat Dew.

Anthony Dew will also take commissions for other carving work.

SECOND CHILDHOOD
20 Byram Arcade, Westgate, Huddersfield, **West Yorkshire HD1 1ND**
TEL   0484 530117 or 603854
OPEN   10.30–3.30 Tues–Sat.

Specialise in teddy bear repairs.

PROVIDE Free Estimates. Local Free Collection/Delivery Service.
SPEAK TO Michael or Elizabeth Hoy.
SEE Collectors (Dolls).

DAPHNE FRASER
Glenbarry, 58 Victoria Road, Lenzie, Glasgow, **Strathclyde G66 5AP**
TEL   041 776 1281
OPEN   By Appointment.

Specialise in restoring rocking horses.

PROVIDE Free Estimates.

SPEAK TO Daphne Fraser.
This workshop is in the Scottish Conservation Directory.
SEE Collectors (Dolls), Oil Paintings, Picture Frames, Furniture.

ALAN LEES
38 Patna Road, Kirkmichael, Maybole, Ayrshire, **Strathclyde KA19 7PJ**
TEL   06555 386
OPEN   By Appointment.

Specialise in restoring and conserving rocking horses and equestrian toys of any age and condition using traditional methods and materials. They can also make replica horses to commission using traditional methods and materials.

PROVIDE Local Home Inspections. Free Estimates. Free Local Collection/Delivery Service.
SPEAK TO Mr Alan Lees.

This workshop is in the Scottish Conservation Directory.

A. P. E. S. ROCKING HORSES
Ty Isaf, Pont Y Gwyddel, Llanfair T.H., Abergele, **Clwyd LL22 9RA**
TEL   0745 79365
OPEN   By Appointment.

Specialise in restoring rocking horses, tricycles (horses), horses and carts, pull-along horses etc. All horses are sympathetically restored and photographs of previous work are available on request.

PROVIDE Home Inspections. Free Estimates. Chargeable Collection/Delivery Service.
SPEAK TO Mr J. Stuart MacPherson or Mrs P. MacPherson.

Member of UKIC. This workshop is listed on the register of conservators maintained by the Conservation Unit of the Museums and Galleries Commission.

WAX

MARGARET GLOVER
42 Hartham Road, Isleworth,
Middlesex TW7 5ES
TEL   081 568 4662
OPEN   By Appointment.

Specialise in restoring all types of wax
artefacts, including wax portraits and
small sculptures.

PROVIDE Free Estimates.
SPEAK TO Margaret Glover.
SEE Collectors (Dolls, Mechanical
Music).

JENNY SLEVIN
China Restoration Studio, Monkstown,
Co. Dublin
TEL   01 280 3429
OPEN   By Appointment.

Specialise in restoring wax figures.

PROVIDE Home Inspections.
Free/Chargeable Estimates.
Collection/Delivery Service by
arrangement.
SPEAK TO Jenny Slevin.
Member of IPCRA.
SEE Carpets, Furniture, Picture Frames,
Porcelain.

MUSICAL
INSTRUMENTS

ROBERT SHAFTOE
58 High Street, Pavenham, Bedford,
Bedfordshire MK43 7PE
Workshop: The Chapel, Park Road,
Stevington, Bedford, **Bedfordshire
MK43 7QG**
TEL   02302 3609 (evenings).
OPEN   8–6.30 Mon–Sat or By
       Appointment.

Specialise in restoring pipe organs and
early keyboard instruments.

PROVIDE Home Inspections.
Free/Chargeable Estimates.
Collection/Delivery Service.
SPEAK TO Robert Shaftoe.

Established 1964. This workshop is
included on the register of conservators
maintained by the Conservation Unit of
the Museums and Galleries Commission.

J.V. PIANOS &
CAMBRIDGE PIANOLA
CO.
The Limes, Landbeach, Cambridge,
Cambridgeshire CB4 4DR
TEL   0223 861408 or 861348 or
       861507
FAX   0223 441276
OPEN   By Appointment.

Specialise in complete rebuilding of
pianos.

PROVIDE Home Inspections. Chargeable
Estimates. Chargeable Collection/
Delivery Service.
SPEAK TO F. T. Poole.

SEE Collectors (Mechanical Music).

MICHAEL JOHNSON
Upper Sunnyside, Lowther Street,
Penrith, **Cumbria CA11 7UW**
TEL   0768 64424
OPEN   By Appointment.

Specialise in all aspects of restoration to
violins, violas, cellos, basses and bows.
New instruments are finely made in the
Italian tradition, specialising in copies of
fine instruments.

PROVIDE Home Inspections. Free
Estimates. Chargeable
Collection/Delivery Service.
SPEAK TO Michael Johnson.

JOHN DIKE
The Manse, Gold Street, Stalbridge,
Dorset DT10 2LX
TEL   0963 62285
OPEN   9–5 Mon–Fri; 9–12.30 Sat.

Specialise in restoring instruments and
bows of the violin family.

PROVIDE Home Inspections. Free
Estimates. Collection/Delivery Service
by arrangement.
SPEAK TO John Dike.

PAXMAN (CASES) LTD
3 Tudor Court, Harold Court Road,
Romford, **Essex RM3 0AE**
TEL   04023 45415
OPEN   10–6 Mon–Fri.

Specialise in restoring musical
instrument cases and brass, string and
woodwind instruments.

PROVIDE Free Estimates.
SPEAK TO Peter Robinson.
SEE **London WC2**

MICHAEL COLE
Little Tatchley, 334 Prestbury Road,
Cheltenham, **Gloucestershire
GL52 3DD**
TEL   0242 517192
OPEN   8.30–5.30 Mon–Sat By
        Appointment.

Specialise in restoring early pianos, pre-
1820, and harpsichords. All aspects of
musical instrument restoration,
including furniture work and musical
function, tuning and concert hire. Parts
and materials supplied, including new
strings.

PROVIDE Home Inspections. Free
Estimates. Chargeable
Collection/Delivery Service.
SPEAK TO Michael Cole.
Member of UKIC and FOMRHI. This
workshop is included on the register of
conservators maintained by the

Conservation Unit of the Museums and
Galleries Commission.

SAXON ALDRED ORGAN BUILDER
28 Crouch Hall Lane, Redbourn,
Hertfordshire AL3 7EU
TEL   0582 793408 or 792871
FAX   0582 793402
OPEN   8.30–6 Mon–Fri.

Specialise in restoration and
maintenance of pipe organs. Will also
build new organs.

PROVIDE Free Local Home Inspections.
Free Local Estimates. Free Local
Collection/Delivery Service.
SPEAK TO J. S. Aldred.
Associate of the Incorporated Society of
Organ Builders and Member of the
Federation of Organ Builders. This
workshop is included on the register of
conservators maintained by the
Conservation Unit of the Museums and
Galleries Commission.

PERIOD PIANO COMPANY
Park Farm Oast, Hareplain Road,
Biddenden, Nr. Ashford, **Kent
TN27 8LJ**
TEL   0580 291393
FAX   0580 712583
OPEN   By Appointment.

Specialise in restoring early pianos from
1870 to 1900, also harpsichords and
spinets. Recently restored Beethoven's
1817 grand piano in the Hungarian
National Museum and the 1848 grand
piano used by Chopin for his last English
tour. They will do commissioned
reproductions.

PROVIDE Home Inspections.
Free/Chargeable Estimates. Chargeable
Collection/Delivery Service.
SPEAK TO David Winston.
Member of UKIC. This workshop is
included on the register of conservators

maintained by the Conservation Unit of the Museums and Galleries Commission.

JEFFREY CLAMP
Lime Cottage, Oasby, Nr. Grantham, **Lincolnshire NG32 3NB**
TEL   05295 466
OPEN   8.30–6 Daily or By
       Appointment.

Specialise in restoring keyboard musical instruments, Viennese and English forte pianos, square pianos, harpsichords etc. They also have a nationwide tuning and maintenance service.

PROVIDE Home Inspections. Free Estimates. Free Collection/Delivery Service.
SPEAK TO Jeffrey Clamp.

Member of UKIC. This workshop is included on the register of conservators maintained by the Conservation Unit of the Museums and Galleries Commission.

N. P. MANDER LTD
St Peter's Close, Warner Place, Hackney Road, **London E2 7AF**
TEL   071 739 4747
FAX   071 729 4718
OPEN   By Appointment.

Specialise in construction and repair of pipe organs.

PROVIDE Home Inspections. Refundable Estimates (normally £100). Free Collection/Delivery Service.
SPEAK TO Mr J. P. Mander.

JOSEPH MALACHI O'KELLY
Luthier, 2 Middleton Road, **London E8 4BL**
TEL   071 254 7074
OPEN   By Appointment.

Specialise in restoring plucked-string musical instruments, lutes, guitars and ouds. Mr O'Kelly works with wood, ivory

and tortoiseshell on both Western and Islamic instruments.

PROVIDE Free Verbal Estimates. Chargeable Home Inspections. Chargeable Collection/Delivery Service.
SPEAK TO Joseph O'Kelly.

Also give estimates on restoration for instruments in auction. This workshop is included on the register of conservators maintained by the Conservation Unit of the Museums and Galleries Commission.

JOHN PAGE
Unit B66, Clerkenwell Workshops, 29–31 Clerkenwell Close, **London EC1R 0AT**
TEL   071 222 3298
OPEN   By Appointment.

Specialise in restoring harps, including casework and gilding.

PROVIDE Home Inspections. Free Estimates. Collection/Delivery Service.
SPEAK TO John Page.

MICHAEL PARFETT
Unit 407, Clerkenwell Workshops, 31 Clerkenwell Close, **London EC1R 0AT**
TEL   071 490 8768
OPEN   By Appointment.

Specialise in all aspects of restoration to harpsichords, harps, square pianos and other keyboard instruments. Decoration of harpsichord cases undertaken.

PROVIDE Home Inspections. Free Estimates. Local Free Collection/Delivery Service.
SPEAK TO Michael Parfett.

Licenciate of the City and Guilds of London, Member of UKIC. This workshop is included on the register of conservators maintained by the Conservation Unit of the Museums and Galleries Commission.
SEE Furniture, Picture Frames.

BRIDGEWOOD & NEITZERT
Ilex Works, 10 Northwold Road, **London N16 7HR**
TEL   071 249 9398
FAX   071 249 9398
OPEN   9–6 Mon–Sat.

Specialise in repairing and restoring violins, violas, cellos, double basses and bows, particularly of the baroque and classical periods.

PROVIDE Home Inspections. Free Estimates. Chargeable Collection/ Delivery Service.
SPEAK TO Gary Bridgewood or Tom Neitzert.

This workshop is included on the register of conservators maintained by the Conservation Unit of the Museums and Galleries Commission.

ROBERT MORLEY & CO. LTD
34 Engate Street, **London SE13 7HA**
TEL   081 318 5838
FAX   081 297 0720
OPEN   9–5 Mon–Sat.

Specialise in repairing and restoring pianos, harpsichords, celestes, spinets, virginals and clavichords, both antique and modern.

PROVIDE Home Inspections. Free Local Estimates. Free Local Collection/Delivery Service.
SPEAK TO John Morley.

J. & A. BEARE LTD
7 Broadwick Street, **London W1V 1FJ**
TEL   071 437 1449
FAX   071 439 4520
OPEN   9–12.15, 1.30–5 Mon–Fri.

Specialise in restoring violins, violas, cellos and bows.

PROVIDE Free Estimates.

J. R. GUIVIER & CO. LTD
99 Mortimer Street, **London W1N 7TA**
TEL   071 580 2560
FAX   071 436 1461
OPEN   9–5 Mon–Fri.

Specialise in restoring and repairing violins, violas, cellos.

PROVIDE Free Estimates.
SPEAK TO Mr Wilks.

PHIL PARKER LTD
106A Crawford Street, **London W1H 1AL**
TEL   071 486 8206
OPEN   10–5.30 Mon–Wed, Fri; 10–4 Thur; 10–3 Sat.

Specialise in restoring brass instruments.

PROVIDE Free Estimates.
SPEAK TO Dave Woodhead.

THE HARPSICHORD WORKSHOP
130 Westbourne Terrace Mews, **London W2 6QG**
TEL   071 723 9650
OPEN   By Appointment.

Specialise in repairing and restoring harpsichords, spinets and virginals.
SPEAK TO Mark Ransom.

PAXMAN (CASES) LTD
116 Long Acre, **London WC2**
TEL   071 240 3642
OPEN   9–5 Mon–Fri; 10–5 Sat.

Specialise in restoring musical instrument cases and brass, string and woodwind instruments.

PROVIDE Free Estimates.
SPEAK TO Bob Paxman.
SEE **Essex.**

291

J. G. TREVOR-OWEN
181–193 Oldham Rd, Rochdale,
Greater Manchester OL16 5QZ
TEL   0706 48138
OPEN   1.30–7 Mon–Fri or By
       Appointment.
Specialise in restoring violins.

PROVIDE Home Inspections. Refundable
Estimates.
SPEAK TO J. G. Trevor-Owen.
SEE Clocks, Furniture, Oil Paintings.

MARTIN BLOCK INSTRUMENT REPAIRS
12 Elm Park, Stanmore, **Middlesex HA7 4BJ**
TEL   081 954 4347
OPEN   9–6 Mon–Fri (24-hour
       answering service).

Specialise in repairing and restoring
saxophones and clarinets.

PROVIDE Free Estimates.
SPEAK TO Martin Block.
Mr Block is a Member of the Institute of
Musical Instrument Technology.

COLLINGHAM PIANOS
11 High Street, Collingham, Newark,
Nottinghamshire NG23 7LA
TEL   0636 892553
OPEN   By Appointment.

Specialise in restoring pianos, player-
pianos (pianolas) and reed organs
(harmoniums).

PROVIDE Home Inspections. Free
Estimates. Chargeable
Collection/Delivery Service.
SPEAK TO Nicholas Wynne.

Member of the Guild of Master
Craftsmen.

GOETZE AND GWYNN
The Tan Gallop, Welbeck, Worksop,
Nottinghamshire S80 3LW
TEL   0909 485635
OPEN   8–6 Mon–Fri.

Specialise in restoring organs, mainly
pre-Victorian.

PROVIDE Home Inspections. Free
Estimates. Collection/Delivery Service.
SPEAK TO Martin Goetze or Dominic
Gwynn.
Member of IIC, UKIC, International
Society of Organbuilders, British
Institute of Organ Studies. This
workshop is included on the register of
conservators maintained by the
Conservation Unit of the Museums and
Galleries Commission.

EARLY KEYBOARD AGENCY
43 Kennet Road, Headington, Oxford,
Oxfordshire OX3 7BH
TEL   0865 65989
OPEN   8–6 Mon–Fri.

Specialise in restoring second-hand or
new harpsichords, clavichords, spinets
and virginals etc.

PROVIDE Home Inspections. Free
Estimates. Chargeable
Collection/Delivery Service.
SPEAK TO Martin J. Robertson.

ALISTAIR FRAYLING-CORK
2 Mill Lane, Wallingford, **Oxfordshire OX10 0DH**
TEL   0491 26221
OPEN   10–6 Mon–Fri; Sat By
       Appointment.

Specialise in restoring stringed
instruments.

PROVIDE Home Inspections. Free
Estimates. Chargeable
Collection/Delivery Service.
SPEAK TO Alistair Frayling-Cork.

Member of BAFRA.
SEE Furniture, Clocks.

DAVID LEIGH c/o LAURIE LEIGH ANTIQUES
36 High Street, Oxford, **Oxfordshire OX1 4AN**
TEL   0865 244197 or 0608 810607
OPEN   By Appointment.

Specialise in restoring early keyboard instruments, including spinets, harpsichords, pre-1820 square pianos and pre-1825 grand pianos.
SPEAK TO David Leigh.

Mr Leigh is a professional classical soloist.

PAUL NEVILLE, HARPSICHORDS AND FORTEPIANOS
C.K.S. Workshop, 74 The Street, Blundeston, Lowestoft, **Suffolk NR32 5AB**
TEL   0502 730356
OPEN   By Appointment after 6 p.m.

Specialise in structural, musical and decorative restoration of harpsichords and fortepianos. Also supply specialist materials.

PROVIDE Home Inspections. Refundable Estimates. Chargeable Collection/Delivery Service.
SPEAK TO Paul Neville.

This workshop is included on the register of conservators maintained by the Conservation Unit of the Museums and Galleries Commission.

JOHN ROBINSON PIANOS
Red Lion Cottage, Barnardiston, Haverhill, **Suffolk CB9 7TT**
TEL   044086 613
OPEN   By Appointment.

Specialise in restoring grand and upright

pianos. Action re-conditioning, re-stringing, regulating and tuning, soundboard repairs, casework repairs and French polishing.

PROVIDE Home Inspections. Free Estimates. Chargeable Collection/Delivery Service.
SPEAK TO John Robinson.
Established 1978. Member of the Guild of Master Craftsmen and affiliate of the Piano Tuners Association.

ANDREW LANCASTER
Music Room Antiques, 143 West Street, Dorking, **Surrey RH4 1BL**
TEL   0306 741724
OPEN   9.30–5.30 Fri & Sat.

Specialise in restoring square and grand pianofortes to fine playing order using authentic materials throughout.

PROVIDE Home Inspections. Free Estimates. Chargeable Collection/Delivery Service.
SPEAK TO Andrew Lancaster.
SEE **West Sussex.**

SHARON McCALLUM
Workshop, 27 Lesbourne Road, Reigate, **Surrey RH2 7BU**
TEL   0737 223481
OPEN   By Appointment.

Specialise in repairing and restoring brass instruments, especially trombones.

PROVIDE Free Estimates.
SPEAK TO Sharon McCallum.

ANDREW LANCASTER
School House, Bucks Green, Nr. Horsham, **West Sussex RH12 3JP**
TEL   0403 822189
FAX   0403 823089
OPEN   By Appointment.

Specialise in restoring square and grand fortepianos to fine playing order using authentic materials throughout.

PROVIDE Home Inspections. Free
Estimates. Chargeable
Collection/Delivery Service.
SPEAK TO Andrew Lancaster.
SEE **Surrey.**

DAVID J. LAW
Ash House, East Street, Long Compton,
Shipston-On-Stour, **Warwickshire**
CV36 5JJ
TEL   0608 84493
OPEN   By Appointment.

Specialise in restoring harpsichords,
virginals, spinets, clavichords and square
and fortepianos to 1830. Full
photographic report and drawing service
available.

PROVIDE Home Inspections. Free
Estimates. Chargeable
Collection/Delivery Service.
SPEAK TO David Law.

Mr Law is co-author of *A Handbook of
Historical Stringing Practice for
Keyboard Instruments 1671–1856.* This
workshop is included on the register of
conservators maintained by the
Conservation Unit of the Museums and
Galleries Commission.

PETER CONACHER AND COMPANY LTD
Springwood Organ Works, Water Street,
Huddersfield, **West Yorkshire**
HD1 4BB
TEL   0484 530053
OPEN   9–5 Mon–Fri.

Specialise in restoring pipe organs of all
types, including barrel organs,
fairground organs, harmoniums and reed
organs. They also carry out tuning and
small repairs.

PROVIDE Home Inspections. Chargeable
Estimates. Chargeable
Collection/Delivery Service.
SPEAK TO John Sinclair Willis.

Established 1854. Fellow of the Institute
of Musical Instrument Technology,
Fellow of the Incorporated Society of
Organ Builders and Fellow of the RSA.
This workshop is included on the register
of conservators maintained by the
Conservation Unit of the Museums and
Galleries Commission.

WILLIAM D. PATTERSON
Mellifonts Town, Bartlemy, **Co. Cork.**
TEL   025 36549
OPEN   By Appointment.

Specialise in restoring stringed
instruments and bows.

PROVIDE Home Inspections. Free
Estimates. Collection/Delivery Service
by arrangement.
SPEAK TO William Patterson.

Member of IPCRA.

WILLIAM HOFFMAN
Unit 1A, Greystones Shopping Centre,
Mill Road, Greystones, **Co. Wicklow**
TEL   281 9614
FAX   287 3299
OPEN   10.30–1.30 Tues–Sat.

Specialise in restoring violins, violas,
cellos and their bows.

PROVIDE Free/Chargeable Estimates.
SPEAK TO William Hoffman.
Member of IPCRA and ILA.

GRANT O'BRIEN
St Cecilia's Hall, Niddry Street,
Edinburgh, **Lothian EH1 1LJ**
TEL   031 556 8075 and 650 2805
OPEN   By Appointment.

Specialise in restoring early keyboard
instruments.

PROVIDE Home Inspections.
Free/Chargeable Estimates.
Collection/Delivery Service by
arrangement.
SPEAK TO Grant O'Brien.

BRIAN RATTRAY
34 Spylaw Street, Colinton, Edinburgh,
Lothian EH13 0JT
TEL   031 441 1098
OPEN   9–5.30 Mon–Fri.

Specialise in restoring stringed
instruments of the violin family.

PROVIDE Free Estimates.
SPEAK TO Brian Rattray.
This workshop is in the Scottish
Conservation Directory.

SAN DOMENICO STRINGED INSTRUMENTS
175 Kings Road, Cardiff, **South
Glamorgan CF1 9DF**
TEL   0222 235881
FAX   0222 344510
OPEN   10–4.30 Mon–Fri; 10–1 Sat.

Specialise in restoring violins, violas,
cellos and bows.

PROVIDE Home Inspections. Free
Estimates. Free Collection/Delivery
Service.
SPEAK TO Howard Morgan.

ARMS AND ARMOUR AND SPORTING EQUIPMENT

DO

As little restoration as possible – originality is important to antiques
Always store in a dry environment at room temperature
Keep metal parts lightly oiled or greased
Clean barrels after use
Always ensure that fine quality guns are overhauled and repaired by gun specialists –
more guns are ruined by bad workmanship than anything else
Avoid denting the barrels as the process of raising the dents causes overall wear

DON'T

Polish, as this produces wear
Operate the firing mechanism when you are not intending to fire the weapon, as
this can cause damage
Attempt to take your gun to pieces
Store in a baize-lined case for long periods – any dampness in the baize can cause
serious corrosion
Re-blue barrels unless absolutely necessary, as this will cause wear

ARMS AND ARMOUR

JASON ABBOT GUNMAKERS LTD
1–3 Bell Street, Princes Risborough, **Buckinghamshire HP17 0AD**
TEL   08444 6677
FAX   0844 274155
OPEN   By Appointment.

Specialise in restoring fine quality English guns.

PROVIDE Free Estimates. Free/Chargeable Collection/Delivery Service.
SPEAK TO Jason Abbot.

JOCK HOPSON CONSERVATION SERVICE
Holes Lane, Olney, **Buckinghamshire MK46 4BX**
TEL   0234 712306
FAX   0234 712306
OPEN   By Appointment.

Specialise in restoring Japanese armour.

PROVIDE Home Inspections. Free/Chargeable Estimates. Chargeable Collection/Delivery Service.
SPEAK TO Jock Hopson.

Member of UKIC. This workshop is included on the register of conservators maintained by the Conservation Unit of the Museums and Galleries Commission.
SEE Furniture, Picture Frames.

TERENCE PORTER ANTIQUE ARMS
The Old Forge, High Street, North Marston, **Buckinghamshire MK18 3PD**
TEL   029667 422 or 029673 8255
FAX   029667 448
OPEN   9.30–5 Mon–Fri.

Specialise in restoration work on all American and European arms and armour.

PROVIDE Home Inspections. Free Estimates. Chargeable Collection/Delivery Service.
SPEAK TO Sandra Garner or Terry Porter.

THE CHETTLE GUILD
The Stables, Chettle House, Chettle, Blandford, **Dorset DT11 8DB**
TEL   0258 89576
OPEN   9–6 Mon–Sat.

Specialise in restoring arms and armour.

PROVIDE Home Inspections. Free Estimates. Free Local Collection/Delivery Service.
SPEAK TO Alastair or Andrew Arnold.
SEE Clocks, Furniture, Collectors (Scientific Instruments).

H. S. GREENFIELD AND SON
4–5 Upper Bridge Street, Canterbury, **Kent CT1 2NB**
TEL   0227 456959
FAX   0227 765030
OPEN   8.30–5.30 Mon–Sat.

Specialise in repairing vintage shotguns and fishing tackle.

PROVIDE Home Inspections. Chargeable Estimates. Chargeable Collection/Delivery Service.
SPEAK TO T. S. Greenfield.

LINCOLN CONSERVATION STUDIO
c/o Museum of Lincolnshire Life, Burton Road, Lincoln, **Lincolnshire LN1 3LY**
TEL   0522 533207
OPEN   9–5 Mon–Fri.

Specialise in restoring arms and armour
to museum conservation standards.

PROVIDE Home Inspections.
Free/Chargeable Estimates. Chargeable
Collection/Delivery Service.
SPEAK TO John Hurd, Stephanie Margrett
or David Fisher.
Members of UKIC. This workshop is
included on the register of conservators
maintained by the Conservation Unit of
the Museums and Galleries Commission.
SEE Porcelain, Furniture, Lighting.

ST PANCRAS ANTIQUES
150 St Pancras, Chichester, **West Sussex
PO19 1SH**
TEL   0243 787645
OPEN   9.30–5 Mon–Sat; 9.30–1 Thur.

Specialise in restoring European arms
and armour.

PROVIDE Home Inspections. Free
Estimates.
SPEAK TO Ralph Willatt.

D. W. DYSON (ANTIQUE WEAPONS)
Wood Lea, Shepley, Huddersfield, **West
Yorkshire HD8 8ES**
TEL   0484 607331
FAX   0484 607331
OPEN   By Appointment.

Specialise in restoration of all types of
arms including pistols, guns and swords.

PROVIDE Home Inspections. Free
Estimates. Collection/Delivery Service
by arrangement.
SPEAK TO David Dyson.
Also manufacture miniature arms and
presentation pieces to customers'
specifications. Experienced in working
with precious metals.

TONY PTOLOMEY
Comlongon Castle, Clarencefield,
Dumfries & Galloway DG1 4NA
TEL   038 787 283
OPEN   By Appointment.

Specialise in restoring European and
Oriental armour.

PROVIDE Free Estimates.
SPEAK TO Tony Ptolomey.

THE BARON OF EARLSHALL
Earlshall Castle, Leuchars, by St
Andrews, **Fife KY16 0DP**
TEL   0334 839205
OPEN   By Appointment.

Specialise in restoring antique arms and
armour. The Baron is a specialist in
Scottish weapons.

PROVIDE Home Inspections. Free
Estimates. Free Collection/Delivery
Service.
SPEAK TO The Baron of Earlshall.

NOLF & MANN
29 Breadalbane Terrace, Wick,
Highland KW1 5AT
TEL   0955 4284
OPEN   By Appointment.

Specialise in restoring firearms.

PROVIDE Home Inspections.
Free/Chargeable Estimates. Chargeable
Collection/Delivery Service.
SPEAK TO T. Nolf.
SEE Collectors (Scientific Instruments).

THE HIGHLAND SHOP
Blair Atholl, **Tayside PH18 5SG**
TEL   079 681 303
OPEN   9–5 Daily (Summer); 9–5 Tue–
       Sat (Winter).

Specialise in restoring antique weapons,
individual and collections, edged and
firearm.

PROVIDE Home Inspections. Free
Estimates. Chargeable
Collection/Delivery Service.
SPEAK TO Edward H. Slaytor.

Mr Slaytor is an indentured gunsmith (London).

NEIL LIVINGSTONE
3 Old Hawkhill, Dundee, **Tayside DD1 5EU**
TEL 0382 21751
OPEN 9–5 Mon–Fri.
Specialise in restoring firearms.

PROVIDE Free Estimates. Chargeable Collection/Delivery Service.
SPEAK TO Neil Livingstone.
SEE Furniture, Oil Paintings, Picture Frames, Silver.

HERMITAGE ANTIQUITIES
10 West Street, Fishguard, **Dyfed SA65 9AE**
TEL 0348 873037 and 872322
OPEN 9.30–5.30 Mon–Sat; 9.30–1 Wed and Sat.

Specialise in antique arms restoration, especially 16th and 17th century.

PROVIDE Home Inspections. Free Estimates. Chargeable Collection/Delivery Service.
SPEAK TO J. B. Thomas.

SPORTING EQUIPMENT

BILLIARDS

WILLIAM BENTLEY BILLIARDS
(Antique Billiards Specialist), Standen Manor Farm, Hungerford, **Berkshire RG17 0RB**
TEL 0488 681711
FAX 0488 685197
OPEN 9–5 Mon–Fri or By Appointment.

Specialise in restoring billiard tables, cabinets and billiard dining tables including French polishing.

PROVIDE Home Inspections. Free/Chargeable Estimates. Free/Chargeable Collection/Delivery Service.
SPEAK TO Travers Nettleton.

HAMILTON AND TUCKER BILLIARD CO. LTD
Park Lane, Knebworth, **Hertfordshire SG3 6PJ**
TEL 0438 811995
FAX 0438 814939
OPEN 9–5 Mon–Fri.

Specialise in restoring period billiard tables and associated accessories.

PROVIDE Home Inspections. Free Estimates. Chargeable Collection/Delivery Service.
SPEAK TO Hugh Hamilton.

MALLARD RESTORATIONS
Unit 6, The Dove Centre, 109 Bartholomew Road, **London NW5 2BJ**
TEL 071 267 7547
OPEN 9–6 Mon–Fri.

Specialise in restoring billiard and snooker tables.

PROVIDE Home Inspections. Free Estimates. Chargeable Collection/Delivery Service.
SPEAK TO Jeff Walkden.

A. & D. BILLIARDS & POOL SERVICE LTD
1419 Pershore Road, Stirchley, Birmingham, **West Midlands B30 2JL**
TEL 021 458 4369
FAX 021 451 3261
OPEN 8–4.30 Mon–Fri; 9–4.30 Sat.

Specialise in restoring all types of billiard and pool tables, bar billiard tables repaired and recovered.

PROVIDE Home Inspections. Free Estimates, Collection/Delivery Service. SPEAK TO Andy Williams or Dave Thomason.

GOLF

HICKORY STICKS GOLF CO. (ST ANDREWS) LTD
Church Square, St Andrews, **Fife KY16 9NN**
and 6 Abbey Street, St Andrews, **Fife KY16 9LA**
TEL   0334 77203 and 77299
FAX   0334 77203 and 77099
OPEN   8.30–5 Mon–Fri.

Specialise in restoring golf clubs and associated equipment of any age, especially pre-1900 clubs.

PROVIDE Home Inspections. Free Estimates. Chargeable Collection/Delivery Service. SPEAK TO Barry Kerr.

Mr Kerr has had thirty-two years' experience as a clubmaker and a golf professional. He is a member of British Golf Collectors Society, American Golf Collectors Society and Professional Clubmakers Society. This workshop is in the Scottish Conservation Directory.

OLD ST ANDREWS GALLERY
9 Albany Place, St Andrews, **Fife KY16 9HH**
and 10 Golf Place, St Andrews, **Fife KY16 9JA**
TEL   0334 7840 and 78712
OPEN   10–5 Mon–Sat.

Specialise in advice on care of antique golf clubs.

PROVIDE Home Inspections. Free Estimates. Free Collection/Delivery Service. SPEAK TO Mr or Mrs Brown. SEE Silver.

RIDING

TRENT SADDLERS WORKSHOP
Unit 10, Chaucer Court Workshops, Chaucer Street, Nottingham, **Nottinghamshire NG1 5LP**
TEL   0602 473832
OPEN   9.30–6 Mon, Tues, Thur; 10–4 first Saturday of each month.

Specialise in repairs to leather goods such as hand and shoulder bags, executive cases and luggage. This includes the renovation and repair of reptile leather. Also servicing, repair and refurbishment of saddlery and bridlework and associated equine equipment.

PROVIDE Chargeable Home Inspections. Free Verbal Estimates. Chargeable Collection/Delivery Service. SPEAK TO Christopher or Clare Beswick.

ART RESEARCHERS AND HERALDRY

ART RESEARCHERS

TIMOTHY P. SAXON
229 New Bedford Road, Luton,
Bedfordshire LU3 1LN
TEL   0582 27790
OPEN   By Appointment.

Specialise in freelance fine art and
picture research, especially biographical
information on lesser known Modern
British documented artists and searching
for their paintings using genealogical
methods. History, literary and family
history research also undertaken.

SPEAK TO Timothy P. Saxon.

Member of Association of Genealogists
and Record Agents (AGRA).

DAVID JOHN HAWKE
3 Clewerfields, Alma Road, Windsor,
Berkshire SL4 5BW
TEL   0753 855541
OPEN   By Appointment.

Specialise in research into Renaissance
and 17th century history of art and
heraldic research.

PROVIDE Home Inspections.
SPEAK TO David John Hawke.

Member of the Association of Art
Historians.

INDEPENDENT ART
RESEARCH LTD
P.O. Box 391, Cambridge,
Cambridgeshire CB5 8XE
TEL   0223 67232
FAX   0223 67250
OPEN   By Appointment.

Specialise in researching the materials
and technology of ancient and historical
precious metals, specialist and scientific
authenticity research for museums and
collectors worldwide.

301

PROVIDE Home Inspections. Chargeable Estimates. Chargeable Collection/Delivery Service.
SPEAK TO Dr Jack Ogden.
Dr Ogden is a director of the Cambridge Centre for Precious Metal Research.

DR A. THOMAS
Italian Dept., Faculty of Modern Languages, Cambridge University, Cambridge, **Cambridgeshire**
TEL   0223 337733
OPEN   By Appointment.

Specialise in research into 15th century Italian Art, Florentine Artists' Workshop Organisation, Neri Di Bicci. Connection between narrative and text in Western European painting.

PROVIDE Home Inspections.
SPEAK TO Dr A. Thomas.
Member of the Association of Art Historians, the Society of Renaissance Studies.

PAMELA ALLEN
3 West Terrace, Western Hill, Durham, **Durham DH1 4RN**
TEL   091 386 4601
OPEN   8.30–6 Mon–Fri or By Appointment.

Specialise in researching 19th and 20th century paintings and prints.

PROVIDE Home Inspections. Free Estimates. Chargeable Collection/Delivery Service.
SPEAK TO Pamela Allen.
Member of IPC.
SEE Oil Paintings, Books.

ALLYSON McDERMOTT (INTERNATIONAL CONSERVATION CONSULTANTS)
Lintz Green Conservation Centre, Lintz Green House, Lintz Green, Rowlands Gill, **Durham NE39 1NL**
TEL   0207 71547 or 0831 104145 or 0831 257584
FAX   0207 71547
OPEN   9–5.30 Mon–Fri.

Specialise in historical research and authentication.

PROVIDE Home Inspections. Free Estimates. Chargeable Collection/Delivery Service.
SPEAK TO Allyson McDermott or Gillian Lee.
They have a Southern Regional Office at 45 London Road, Cheltenham, **Gloucestershire**.
SEE Carpets, Lighting, Oil Paintings, Picture Frames, Specialist Photographers.

ANNE HILDER
7 The Shrubbery, Upminster, **Essex RM14 3AH**
TEL   0708 221453
OPEN   By Appointment.

Specialise in research into Medieval Art, 18th and 19th century English and French paintings and German Romanticism.
SPEAK TO Anne Hilder.
Member of the Association of Art Historians.

JUNE MACFARLANE-COHEN
Tilbury-juxta-Clare, Halstead, **Essex CO9 4JJ**
TEL   0787 237526
OPEN   By Appointment.

Specialise in research into the Norwich School, East Anglian School, Bingham

Pottery, Omega Workshops, post-revolutionary Russian Art, Christopher Dresser, Bauhaus, Victorian studies.

SPEAK TO June Macfarlane-Cohen.
Member of the Association of Art Historians.

VERONICA WILLIAMS
Head of Religious Studies & Philosophy, King Alfred's College, Sparkford Road, Winchester, **Hampshire SO22 6EZ**
TEL   0962 841515
OPEN   By Appointment.

Specialise in research into religion and art from 1100–1500 A.D. including some Oriental traditions.
SPEAK TO Veronica Williams.

Member of the Association of Art Historians.

JOHN K. D. COOPER
39 Arnos Grove, **London N14 7AE**
TEL   081 886 2695
OPEN   By Appointment.

Specialise in research into antique silver and fine arts, medals and coins.

PROVIDE Home Inspections.
SPEAK TO John Cooper.

Member of the Association of Art Historians. Mr Cooper is an Honorary Advisor to the National Trust.

JESSICA HARNESS
Garden Flat, 13 Belsize Park Gardens, **London NW3 4JG**
TEL   071 722 0807
OPEN   By Appointment.

Specialise in research into 16th century Italian paintings and sculpture and 19th century British and French Art.
SPEAK TO Jessica Harness.

Member of the Association of Art Historians and Society of Renaissance Studies.

WARREN HEARNDEN
Flat 4, 98 Greencroft Gardens, **London NW6 3PH**
TEL   071 624 8075
OPEN   By Appointment.

Specialise in research into Renaissance Art, 18th century French paintings, Rembrandt and 19th century European Art.

PROVIDE Home Inspections.
SPEAK TO Warren Hearnden.

Member of the Association of Art Historians.

MARINA WALLACE
18 Dundonald Road, **London NW10 3HR**
TEL   081 960 5278
OPEN   By Appointment.

Specialise in research into 15th and 16th century Venetian, Renaissance, Italian and Ottoman Art. Also researches Modern Italian Art.

PROVIDE Home Inspections.
SPEAK TO Marina Wallace.

Member of the Association of Art Historians.

DR BRIGITTE CORLEY
51 Middleway, **London NW11 6SH**
TEL   081 455 4783
OPEN   By Appointment.

Specialise in research into Northern European Art 1350–1500, particularly German paintings.
SPEAK TO Dr Brigitte Corley.

Member of the Association of Art Historians, FRSA, Turner Society, Renaissance Society.

CHRISTINE POULSON
63 Choumert Road, **London**
SE15 4AR
TEL   071 732 5700
OPEN   By Appointment.

Specialise in research into 19th and 20th century fine and applied arts.
SPEAK TO Christine Poulson.
Member of the Association of Art Historians, Architectural Historians and the Victorian Society.

CAROLINE KNIGHT
49 Benbow Road, **London W6 0AU**
TEL   081 748 0981
OPEN   By Appointment.

Specialise in research into British interior decoration of the 16th to 18th centuries.
SPEAK TO Caroline Knight.
Member of the Association of Art Historians.

JULIA KING
5 Alexa Court, 73 Lexham Gardens,
London W8 6JL
TEL   071 373 9971
OPEN   By Appointment.

Specialise in researching 17th, 18th and 19th century decorative arts from the Renaissance onwards, Art Nouveau graphics, 17th century paintings and sculpture and American Art.
PROVIDE Home Inspections.
SPEAK TO Julia King.
Member of the Association of Art Historians and the Walpole Society.

JAMES NALL-CAIN
Flat 2, 14 Gloucester Square, **London**
W8 2TB
TEL   071 402 4989
OPEN   By Appointment.

Specialise in research into fine and decorative arts.
SPEAK TO James Nall-Cain.

THE FINE ART & ANTIQUE RESEARCH CONSULTANCY
34 Crane Road, Twickenham,
Middlesex TW2 6RY
TEL   081 894 2513
FAX   071 244 8532
OPEN   By Appointment.

Specialise in researching paintings, sculpture and decorative arts of all periods.

PROVIDE Home Inspections.
SPEAK TO Sara Peterson or Catherine Milburn.

MICHAEL ORR PATERSON
24 Adamsrill Close, Enfield, **Middlesex**
EN1 2BP
TEL   081 360 8898
OPEN   By Appointment.

Specialise in research into 18th century English and Victorian paintings , modern figurative art and Wedgwood pottery.

PROVIDE Home Inspections.
SPEAK TO Michael Orr Paterson.

Member of the Association of Art Historians. This workshop is included on the register of conservators maintained by the Conservation Unit of the Museums and Galleries Commission.

BRIAN DAVIS
Little Drift, Necton, Swaffham, **Norfolk**
PE37 8HZ
TEL   0760 440 420
OPEN   By Appointment.

Specialise in research into British Art 1750–1850, British Romanticism, 19th century British architecture and 19th century French Art.

PROVIDE Home Inspections.
SPEAK TO Brian Davis.

Member of the Association of Art Historians.

MIKLOS RAJNAI
Dilham Grange, North Walsham, **Norfolk NR28 9PZ**
TEL   0692 60860
OPEN   By Appointment.

Specialise in research into English Art 1750–1850, Norwich School and still life c.1700.

PROVIDE Home Inspections.
SPEAK TO Miklos Rajnai.

Member of the Association of Art Historians.

DR NICHOLAS EASTAUGH
The Studio, Newmans Lane, St James' Road, Surbiton, **Surrey KT6 4QQ**
TEL   081 390 6420 or 943 9137
FAX   081 390 6420
OPEN   By Appointment Only.

Specialise in research into methods and materials of paintings, including infra-red reflectography and x-radiography to study artists' techniqes, underdrawing, alterations and condition, macro-photography, ultra-violet and surface examination, pigment, layer structure and media analysis for dating purposes, comparative studies of paintings in their historical context with critical literature reviews.

PROVIDE Free Estimates.
SPEAK TO Dr Nicholas Eastaugh Ph.D; Dip. Cons.; B.Sc.

This workshop is included on the register of conservators maintained by the Conservation Unit of the Museums and Galleries Commission.

DR JOHN M. MITCHELL CBE
The Cottage, Pains Hill Corner, Limpsfield, **Surrey RH8 0RB**
TEL   0883 723354
OPEN   By Appointment.

Specialise in research into 19th and 20th century European Art.
SPEAK TO Dr John Mitchell.

Member of the Association of Art Historians.

IAN PICKFORD
Tolverne, Station Road, Chobham, Nr. Woking, **Surrey GU24 8AL**
TEL   0276 858494
OPEN   By Appointment.

Specialise in research into English silver and Old Sheffield Plate.

PROVIDE Home Inspections.
SPEAK TO Ian Pickford.

Member of the Association of Art Historians and Freeman of the Goldsmiths' Company.

DR ANTHONY F. HOBSON
Pear Tree Cottage, Ilmington, Shipston-on-Stour, **Warwickshire CV36 4LG**
TEL   060 882 423
OPEN   By Appointment.

Specialise in research into 19th century English, Italian and American Art. Also research into heraldry.

PROVIDE Home Inspections.
SPEAK TO Dr Anthony Hobson.

Member of the Association of Art Historians and Hon. FHS.

DR CHRISTA GARDNER VON TEUFFEL
108 Kenilworth Road, Coventry, **Warwickshire CV4 7AH**
TEL   0203 418261
OPEN   By Appointment.

Specialise in research into 14th and 15th century Italian Art, the Renaissance, 14th, 15th and 16th century German painting.

PROVIDE Home Inspections.
SPEAK TO Dr Christa Gardner von Teuffel.

Member of the Association of Art Historians.

LESLIE KNIGHTSBRIDGE-KNIGHT

Broadwell Leigh, White Street, Market Lavington, **Wiltshire SN10 4DP**
TEL　　0380 812750
OPEN　　By Appointment.

Specialise in research into Franco-Flemish manuscripts of the 15th century, Renaissance Art in Northern Europe and Modern European Art.

PROVIDE Home Inspections.
SPEAK TO Leslie Knightsbridge-Knight.

Member of the Association of Art Historians.

NICOLA GORDON BOWE

Parsley Cottage, 11 Ashfield Avenue, Ranelagh, Dublin 6, **Co. Dublin**
TEL　　01 97 5822
OPEN　　By Appointment.

Specialise in researching 19th and 20th century art design, especially the Arts and Crafts Movement.

PROVIDE Chargeable Home Inspections.
SPEAK TO Nicola Gordon Bowe.

Member of the Association of Art Historians, the Design History Society, the Decorative Arts Society and the American Decorative Arts Society.

DR SYLVIA AULD

Fine Art Department, University of Edinburgh, 19 George Street, Edinburgh, **Lothian EH8 9LD**
TEL　　031 650 3975
OPEN　　By Appointment.

Specialise in research into 15th and early 16th century Islamic Art.

PROVIDE Home Inspections.
SPEAK TO Dr Sylvia Auld.

Member of the Association of Art Historians, Fellow of the Society of Scottish Antiquaries.

CERI THOMAS

Villa Seran, 23 Park Road, Barry, **South Glamorgan CF6 8NW**
TEL　　0446 735616
OPEN　　By Appointment.

Specialise in researching Renaissance and post-war British painting.

PROVIDE Home Inspections.
SPEAK TO Ceri Thomas.

Member of the Association of Art Historians.

HERALDRY

COLLEGE OF ARMS
Queen Victoria Street, **London EC4V 4BT**
TEL   071 248 2762
OPEN   10–4 Mon–Fri.

Specialise in searches in the Official Heraldic and Genealogical Records of the College of Arms, undertaken on a professional basis.
SPEAK TO the Officer-in-Waiting.
SEE Books.

PETER BEAUCLERK DEWAR
45 Airedale Avenue, **London W4 2NW**
TEL   081 995 6770
FAX   081 747 8459
OPEN   By Correspondence or Arrangement.

Specialise in heraldic, genealogical and historical research. Also provide an armorial identification service.

PROVIDE Home Inspections by arrangement. Free Estimates.
SPEAK TO Peter Beauclerk Dewar.

JOHN ALLEN
Applecroft, Binfield Heath, Henley-on-Thames, **Oxfordshire RG9 4LT**
TEL   0734 478712
OPEN   By Appointment.

Specialise in researching armorials found on paintings, antiques etc. Also provide an armorial identification service.

Documentary support of all identifications is provided as a matter of routine.

PROVIDE Home Inspections by arrangement. Free Estimates. Postal service on photocopies, polaroids or sketches submitted by post.
SPEAK TO John Allen.

OFFICE OF THE CHIEF HERALD OF IRELAND
2 Kildare Street, Dublin 2, **Co. Dublin**
TEL   01 611626
OPEN   10–12, 2–4.30 Mon–Fri.

Specialise in granting coats-of-arms and will do arms searches if given relevant information.
SPEAK TO Fergus Gillespie.

COURT OF THE LORD LYON
HM New Register House, Edinburgh, **Lothian EH1 3YT**
TEL   031 556 7255
FAX   031 557 2148
OPEN   10–12, 2–4 Mon–Fri.

Specialise in researching heraldry.
SPEAK TO Mrs C. V. G. Roads, MVO, Lyon Clerk and Keeper of the Records.

INSURANCE
AND SECURITY

TOWRY LAW (GENERAL INSURANCE) LIMITED
Godolphin Court, Stoke Poges Lane, Slough, **Buckinghamshire SL1 3PB**
TEL 0753 821241
FAX 0753 70881
OPEN 9–5 Mon–Fri.

Specialise in household insurance for collectors of fine art and antiques.

PROVIDE Home Inspections. Free Estimates.
SPEAK TO Roger Parkinson.

FRIZZELL COUNTRYSIDE INSURANCE
Bolton House, 56–58 Parkstone Road, Poole, **Dorset BH15 2PH**
TEL 0202 765050
FAX 0202 679348
OPEN 9–5 Mon–Fri.

Specialise in providing insurance tailored for the needs of clients in respect of their homes, fine art and valuables.

PROVIDE Home Inspections. Free Estimates.
SPEAK TO Derek Geldart.

ARTSCOPE INTERNATIONAL INSURANCE SERVICES LIMITED
2 Victoria Road, Farnborough, **Hampshire GU14 7NS**
TEL 0252 544000
FAX 0252 543152
OPEN 9–5 Mon–Fri.

Specialise in providing specialist insurance and advice for private collectors and galleries.
SPEAK TO Richard King or Richard Evans.

MINET LIMITED
Fine Arts and Jewellery Division, Minet House, 66 Prescot Street, **London E1 8BU**
TEL 071 481 0707
FAX 071 488 9786
OPEN 9–5.30 Mon–Fri.

Specialise in arranging insurance in the field of jewellery and fine arts.
SPEAK TO James M. A. Mark, Managing Director.

SNEATH KENT & STUART LTD
Stuart House, 53–55 Scrutton Street, **London EC2A 4QQ**
TEL   071 739 5646
FAX   071 739 6467 or 739 2656
OPEN   9–5.30 Mon–Fri.

Specialise in insurance for dealers, auctioneers and collectors.
SPEAK TO Stephen Brown, David Ezzard or Geoffrey Sneath.

They are official brokers to LAPADA and the FATG.

CAMERON RICHARD AND SMITH INSURANCE SERVICES LTD
Boundary House, 7–17 Jewry Street, **London EC3N 2HP**
TEL   071 488 4554
FAX   071 481 1406
OPEN   9.30–5.30 Mon–Fri.

Specialise in fine art insurance, including furniture, jewellery, objets d'art and classic cars.

PROVIDE Home Inspections by arrangement.
SPEAK TO Charles Williams.

CROWLEY COLOSSO LIMITED
Ibex House, Minories, **London EC3N 1JJ**
TEL   071 782 9782
FAX   071 782 9783
OPEN   9–6.30 Mon–Fri.

Specialise in fine arts and antiques insurance for private collectors, museums, galleries, shippers/packers, auction houses and restorers/conservators.

PROVIDE Free Estimates.
SPEAK TO Dominic Hepworth.

R. K. HARRISON INSURANCE BROKERS LTD
3–4 Royal Exchange Buildings, **London EC3V 3NL**
TEL   071 626 0184
FAX   071 626 0115
OPEN   9–5 Mon–Fri.

Specialise in the placing of insurance for fine art collections and historic homes, also insurances for the farmer and landowner and commercial and industrial insurances.

PROVIDE Home Consultations. Free Quotations.
SPEAK TO Derek J. Woodward.

MILLER ART INSURANCE and MILLER PRIVATE CLIENTS
Dawson House, 5 Jewry Street, **London EC3N 2EX**
TEL   071 488 2345
FAX   071 481 3651
OPEN   9.30–5.30 Mon–Fri.

Specialise in arranging insurances for collectors, museums, dealers and all those involved in the art and antiques trades.

PROVIDE Home Inspections. Free Estimates.
SPEAK TO David Needham or Andrew Jobson.

RICHARDS LONGSTAFF (INSURANCE) LTD
Battlebridge House, 97 Tooley Street, **London SE1 2RF**
TEL   071 407 4466
FAX   071 403 3610
OPEN   9.30–5.30 Mon–Fri.

Specialise in fine art insurance.

PROVIDE Home Inspections.
SPEAK TO Ian Hill-Wood.

more realistic premiums but who also value tailor-made arrangements with professional service and advice.

HANOVER INSURANCE BROKERS
13 Relton Mews, Knightsbridge, **London SW7 1ET**
TEL   071 581 1477
FAX   071 225 1411
OPEN   9–5 Mon–Fri.

Specialise in insurance, particularly for collectors of fine art, jewellery and antiques. They can tailor-make policies for individual clients.

PROVIDE Home Inspections. Free Estimates.
SPEAK TO Barbara Hollis.

BELLEVUE INSURANCE (HOME DIVISION)
66 Silver Street, Enfield, **Middlesex EN1 3EP**
TEL   081 836 7447, 363 4966 and 367 0878
FAX   081 367 5780
OPEN   9.30–5.30 Mon–Fri.

Specialise in offering a specialised service for insurance of home contents and buildings, only placed with leading insurance companies.

PROVIDE Home Inspections by arrangement. Free Estimates.
SPEAK TO Jeremy Pringle – 081 367 2252/0878.

STERLING SECURITY SYSTEMS
Sterling House, 305–307 Chiswick High Road, **London W4 4HH**
TEL   081 747 0072
FAX   081 994 4394
OPEN   8.30–6 Mon–Fri.

Specialise in intruder alarms, access control systems and c.c.t.v. systems.

PROVIDE Home Inspections. Free Estimates.
SPEAK TO M. A. Hill.

PENROSE FORBES LTD
29–30 Horsefair, Banbury, **Oxfordshire OX16 0AE**
TEL   0295 259892
FAX   0295 269968
OPEN   9–5.30 Mon–Fri.

Specialise in fine art insurance.
SPEAK TO Michael Forbes.

S. G. D. SECURITY/ELECTRICAL
26–28 Dalcross Street, Roath, Cardiff, **South Glamorgan CF2 4UB**
TEL   0222 464120
OPEN   By Appointment.

Specialise in security systems, including alarms, door access, video and closed circuit television.

PROVIDE Home Inspections. Free Estimates.
SPEAK TO G. S. Whitty.

TOLSON MESSENGER LTD
Insurance Brokers, 148 King Street, **London W6 0QU**
TEL   081 741 8361
FAX   081 741 9395
OPEN   9–6 Mon–Fri.
Specialise in personal service for security-conscious householders seeking

LIGHTING, DISPLAY
AND SUPPLIERS

THE TEXTILE RESTORATION STUDIO
20 Hargreaves Road, Timperley, Altrincham, **Cheshire WA15 7BB**
TEL   061 904 9944
FAX   061 903 9144
OPEN   9.30–5 Mon–Fri.

Specialise in supply of completely acid-free storage boxes and acid-free tissue paper for the safe storage of treasured textile items. Will supply from one box upwards.

PROVIDE Home Inspections. Free Estimates. Collection/Delivery Service by arrangement.
SPEAK TO Jacqueline Hyman.
SEE Carpets, Silver, Collectors (Dolls).

ALLYSON McDERMOTT (INTERNATIONAL CONSERVATION CONSULTANTS)
Lintz Green Conservation Centre, Lintz Green House, Lintz Green, Rowlands Gill, **Durham NE39 1NL**
TEL   0207 71547 or 0831 104145 or
       0831 257584
FAX   0207 71547
OPEN   9–5.30 Mon–Fri.

Specialise in providing chemical and microscopic analysis, environmental control and collection management, storage and exhibition.

PROVIDE Home Inspections. Free Estimates. Chargeable Collection/Delivery Service.
SPEAK TO Allyson McDermott or Gillian Lee.
SEE Art Researchers, Carpets, Oil Paintings, Picture Frames, Specialist Photographers.

HERTFORDSHIRE CONSERVATION SERVICE
Seed Warehouse, Maidenhead Yard, The Wash, Hertford, **Hertfordshire SG14 1PX**
TEL   0992 588966
FAX   0992 588971
OPEN   9–6 Mon–Fri By Appointment.

Specialise in carrying out collection surveys and offer advice on storage, aftercare and environmental monitoring.

PROVIDE Home Inspections. Free/Chargeable Estimates. Chargeable Collection/Delivery Service.

SPEAK TO J. M. MacQueen.

This workshop is included on the register of conservators maintained by the Conservation Unit of the Museums and Galleries Commission.

SEE Collectors (Dolls), Furniture, Carpets, Porcelain, Oil Paintings, Picture Frames.

UTILITARIAN FOLDING BOOKCASES
4 Wrenwood, Welwyn Garden City, **Hertfordshire AL7 1QG**
TEL   0707 332965
OPEN   By Appointment.

Specialise in supplying folding bookcases and display stands.

PROVIDE Home Inspections. Free Estimates. Chargeable Delivery Service.
SPEAK TO Nicky Tutt.

ANTIQUE RESTORATIONS
The Old Wheelwright's Shop, Brasted Forge, Brasted, Westerham, **Kent TN16 1JL**
TEL   0959 563863
FAX   0959 561262
OPEN   9–5 Mon–Fri; 10–1 Sat.

Specialise in brass castings, including handles and mounts. Anything not in their catalogue can be cast by special order.

PROVIDE Refundable Estimates. 28-Day Postal Service.
SPEAK TO Raymond Konyn.
Members of BAFRA.
SEE Clocks, Furniture, Lighting.

C. & A. J. BARMBY
140 Lavender Hill, Tonbridge, **Kent TN9 2NJ**
TEL   0732 771590
OPEN   9.30–5 Mon–Sat or Mail Order.

Specialise in supplying display stands,

ultra-violet lamps, magnifiers, metal-testers, digital scales, swing balances, Chelsea filters.

PROVIDE Home Inspections. Chargeable Collection/Delivery Service.
SPEAK TO Chris Barmby.
SEE Specialist Booksellers.

J. L. BOLLOM & CO. LTD
P. O. Box 78, Croydon Road, Beckenham, **Kent BR3 4BL.**
TEL   081 658 2299
FAX   081 658 8671
OPEN   9–5.30 Mon–Fri.

Specialise in providing a complete range of wood finishes and restoration products.

PROVIDE Delivery Service.
SPEAK TO Tony Wickenden.

ST JOHN A. BURCH
Myrtle House, Headcorn Road, Grafty Green, **Kent ME17 2AR**
TEL   0622 850381
FAX   0622 850381
OPEN   By Appointment.

Specialise in conservation lighting for organic materials, including watercolours, oils and manuscripts.

PROVIDE Home Inspections. Chargeable Estimates.
SPEAK TO St John Burch.
Mr Burch is a chartered designer, FRSA.

LIBERON WAXES LTD
Mountfield Industrial Estate, Learoyd Road, New Romney, **Kent TN28 8XU**
TEL   0679 67555
FAX   0679 67555
OPEN   9–5.30 Mon–Fri.

Specialise in antique restoration and care products for staining, and dyeing.

PROVIDE Chargeable Collection/Delivery Service.
SPEAK TO Isabelle Haumont.

LINCOLN CONSERVATION STUDIO
c/o Museum of Lincolnshire Life, Burton Road, Lincoln, **Lincolnshire LN1 3LY**
TEL   0522 533207
OPEN   9–5 Mon–Fri.

Specialise in advising on display, storage, packaging, security and environmental control.

PROVIDE Home Inspections. Free/Chargeable Estimates. Chargeable Collection/Delivery Service.
SPEAK TO John Hurd, Stephanie Margrett or David Fisher.
Members of UKIC. This workshop is included on the register of conservators maintained by the Conservation Unit of the Museums and Galleries Commission.
SEE Arms, Furniture, Porcelain.

RANKINS (GLASS) COMPANY LIMITED
The London Glass Centre, 24–34 Pearson Street, **London E2 8JD**
TEL   071 729 4200
FAX   071 729 7135
OPEN   8–5.50 Mon–Fri.

Specialise in non-reflective safety glass for paintings, custom-made display cabinets and anti-bandit and bullet-resistant glass.

PROVIDE Chargeable Estimates. Free/Chargeable Collection/Delivery Service.
SPEAK TO Mr K. Hussein or Mr C. Clifford.

CHATSWORTH COMMERCIAL LIGHTING
6 Highbury Corner, **London N5 1RD**
TEL   071 609 9829
FAX   071 700 4804
OPEN   9–6 Mon–Fri (24-hour answering service).

Specialise in picture and gallery lighting from domestic and professional gallery sector to museums.

PROVIDE Home Inspections. Free Estimates.
SPEAK TO John Khan.

W. S. JENKINS & CO. LTD
Jeco Works, Tariff Road, **London N17 0EN**
TEL   081 808 2336
FAX   081 365 1534
OPEN   9–5 Mon–Fri.

Specialise in providing a complete range of wood finishings and restoration material for antique furniture and listed buildings.

PROVIDE Free Catalogue and Price List. Free Delivery Service.
SPEAK TO Paul Humphrey.
Their technical department will be pleased to help anyone with any problems on restoration of antiques.

PICREATOR ENTERPRISES LTD
44 Park View Gardens, **London NW4 2PN**
TEL   081 202 8972
OPEN   By Appointment.

Specialise in supply of materials for professional restoration and conservation of fine art objects. Manufacture 'Renaissance' wax polish and other own-brand restoration products. Mail order.
SPEAK TO John Lawson.

ACRYLIC DESIGN
697 Harrow Road, **London NW10 5NY**
TEL   081 969 0478 and 960 7215
FAX   081 960 8149
OPEN   8–4.30 Mon–Thur, 8–4 Fri.

Specialise in supplying display stands for all types of antiques, point-of-sale display aids, notice holders, made-to-measure stands.

PROVIDE Home Inspections. Free Estimates. Chargeable Collection/Delivery Service.
SPEAK TO Mr R. Jennings.
Catalogue available if you send two first class stamps.

LIGHT PROJECTS LTD
23 Jacob Street, **London SE1 2BG**
TEL   071 231 8282
FAX   071 237 4342
OPEN   9.30–5.30 Mon–Fri.

Specialise in supplying fine art lighting for galleries, historic houses and private residences including lighting design, project management, installation.

PROVIDE Home Inspections. Free Estimates. Chargeable Collection/Delivery Service.
SPEAK TO Richard Aldridge.

AIR IMPROVEMENT CENTRE
23 Denbigh Street, **London SW1V 2HF**
TEL   071 834 2834
FAX   071 821 8485
OPEN   9.30–5.30 Mon–Fri; 10–1 Sat.

Specialise in humidity control. Advise on and supply humidifiers, dehumidifiers and hygrometers.

PROVIDE Local Home Inspections. Free Estimates. Free Delivery Service.
SPEAK TO Valerie Taplin.

GREEN AND STONE
259 Kings Road, **London SW3 5EL**
TEL   071 352 6521
FAX   071 351 1098
OPEN   9–5.30 Mon–Fri; 9.30–6 Sat.

Specialise in supplying all fine art materials for painting, restoration and decorative trades.

PROVIDE Local Home Inspections. Free

Estimates. Free Local Collection/Delivery Service.
SPEAK TO Mrs Hiscott or Miss Moore.
SEE Oil Paintings, Picture Frames.

ABSOLUTE ACTION LIMITED
Mantle House, Broomhill Road, Wandsworth, **London SW18 4JQ**
TEL   081 871 5005
FAX   081 877 9498
OPEN   8.30–6 Mon–Fri.

Specialise in fibre optic lighting systems for display and conservation.

PROVIDE Home Inspections. Free Estimates. Chargeable Collection/Delivery Service.
SPEAK TO Phillip Reddiough.

CONNOLLY LEATHER LTD
Wandle Bank, **London SW19 1DW**
TEL   081 542 5251 and 543 4611
FAX   081 543 7455
OPEN   9–12.45, 1.30–4 Mon–Fri.

Specialise in supplying leather table tops, wall panels and screens.

PROVIDE Home Inspections. Free Estimates. Free Collection/Delivery Service.
SPEAK TO Mr C. Carron.
SEE Furniture.

PICTURE PLAQUES
142 Lambton Road, **London SW20 0TJ**
TEL   081 879 7841
OPEN   By Appointment.

Specialise in hand-finished wooden picture plaques in gold leaf or white gold leaf.

PROVIDE Free Estimates.
SPEAK TO Kate Sim.

314

COSTERWISE LTD
16 Rabbit Row, **London W8 4DX**
TEL   071 221 0666
FAX   071 229 7000
OPEN   9–5 Mon–Fri.

Specialise in supplying protective packaging materials, bubble pack etc.

PROVIDE Free Estimates. Collection/Delivery Service.
SPEAK TO Helen Clegg.

DAUPHIN DISPLAY CABINET CO.
118A Holland Park Avenue, **London W11 4PA**
TEL   071 727 0715
FAX   071 221 8371
OPEN   9–5.30 Mon–Fri; 9.30–1 Sat.

Specialise in display stands and cabinets for the antique and collectors' market.

PROVIDE Home Inspections. Free Estimates. Chargeable Collection/Delivery Service.
SPEAK TO John Harrison-Banfield.

JUSTIN F. SKREBOWSKI
82E Portobello Road, **London W11 2QD**
TEL   071 792 9742
OPEN   1–6.30 Tues–Fri; 7 a.m.–6 p.m. Sat.

Specialise in supplying stands, easels, browsers, folio stands.

PROVIDE Chargeable Estimates. Chargeable Collection/Delivery Service.
SPEAK TO Justin Skrebowski.

PAPERSAFE
146 Chapel Road, Oldham, **Greater Manchester OL8 4QJ**
TEL   061 682 9652
OPEN   By Appointment.

Specialise in supplying book and paper repair materials.

PROVIDE Home Inspections. Free Estimates. Chargeable Collection/Delivery Service.
SPEAK TO Graham Moss.

Member of IPC and Society of Bookbinders.
SEE Books.

PROTEC
62 Windermere Avenue, Wembley, **Middlesex HA9 8RY**
TEL   081 908 4601
OPEN   By Appointment or Mail Order.

Specialise in supplying bubble wrap, tissue, film-fronted bags, adhesive tapes plus Protec clearview dustwrapper film.

PROVIDE packaging supplies list on request.
SPEAK TO Lawrence Tierney.

TURNROSS & CO.
130 Pinner Road, Harrow, **Middlesex HA1 4JE**
TEL   081 863 5036
OPEN   9–5 Thur–Sat.

Specialise in upholstery supplies, brass castors and fittings.

PROVIDE Free Estimates.
SPEAK TO A. R. Rosman.

THE LEATHER CONSERVATION CENTRE
34 Guildhall Road, Northampton, **Northamptonshire NN1 1EW**
TEL   0604 232723
FAX   0604 602070
OPEN   9–6 Mon–Fri.

Specialise in giving advice on sources of appropriate specialist leather and conservation materials.

PROVIDE Home Inspections. Chargeable Estimates. Chargeable Collection/Delivery Service.
SPEAK TO Christopher Calnan.
SEE Carpets, Furniture.

MIDLAND SCHOOL OF FRENCH POLISHING

18A Mansfield Road, Eastwood, **Nottinghamshire NG16 3AQ**
TEL   0773 531157 or 715911
OPEN   9–4.30 Mon–Thur.

Specialise in courses throughout the year (maximum of four students per course) in French polishing, wax and ornamental finishes.
SPEAK TO Alfred Fry.

BERKELEY STUDIO

The Old Vicarage, Castle Cary, **Somerset BA7 7EJ**
TEL   0963 50748
FAX   0963 51107
OPEN   9–5 Mon–Fri By Appointment Only.

Specialise in making picture plaques and display cabinets.

PROVIDE Home Inspections. Free Estimates. Free Collection/Delivery Service.
SPEAK TO John Harries.

SUFFOLK BRASS

Thurston, Bury St Edmunds, **Suffolk IP31 3SN**
TEL   0359 30888 and 0379 898670
OPEN   9–6 Mon–Fri; 9–12 Sat.

Specialise in casting brass by the hot wax or sand process from original brassware for furniture fittings. Also make hand-forged iron fittings.

PROVIDE Free Estimates. Free Collection/Delivery Service (same day).
SPEAK TO Mark Peters or Thane Meldrum.
SEE Silver.

DRYMASTER INTERNATIONAL LTD

Navigation House, 5 High Street, Hampton Wick, Kingston-upon-Thames, **Surrey KT1 4DA**
TEL   081 977 2350
FAX   081 977 2350
OPEN   9.30–5.30 Mon–Fri.

Specialise in supplying dehumidifiers, humidifiers, air cleaning units and air conditioners.

PROVIDE Free Estimates.
SPEAK TO Mr J. Oades.

COLEBROOKE CONSULTING LTD – BOB HAYES

Diamonds, Bells Yew Green, **East Sussex TN3 9AX**
TEL   0892 750307
FAX   0892 750222
OPEN   9–5.30 Mon–Fri.

Specialise in environmental control and the care, maintenance and management of historic buildings with their contents.
SPEAK TO Bob Hayes.

Mr Hayes is Technical Advisor to the National Trust's Historic Buildings Department.

ALBERT PLUMB

31 Whyke Lane, Chichester, **West Sussex PO19 2JS**
TEL   0243 788468
OPEN   9.30–5 Mon–Sat.

Specialise in supplying waxes and other items for restoration. Brass fittings, handles, upholstery fittings.

PROVIDE Home Inspections. Free Estimates. Chargeable Collection/Delivery Service.
SPEAK TO Albert Plumb.
SEE Furniture.

SUGG LIGHTING LIMITED

Sussex Manor Business Park, Gatwick Road, Crawley, **West Sussex RH10 2GD**

TEL　　0293 540111
FAX　　0293 540114
OPEN　By Appointment.

Specialise in supplying traditional gas and electric pendant lights.

PROVIDE Free Estimates.
SPEAK TO Sales Office.
SEE Silver.

SUN–X (U.K.) LIMITED

2 Madeira Parade, Madeira Avenue, Bognor Regis, **West Sussex PO22 8DX**

TEL　　0243 826441
FAX　　0243 829691
OPEN　8.30–12.30, 1.30–5 Mon–Fri.

Specialise in supplying and fitting ultra-violet filters to all types of glass and artificial lighting, neutral density light-reducing filters and traditional and modern blinds.

PROVIDE Home Inspections. Free Estimates. Chargeable Collection/Delivery Service.
SPEAK TO David French.

ALAN MORRIS (WHOLESALE)

10 Coughton Lane, Alcester, **Warwickshire B49 5HN**

TEL　　0789 762800
OPEN　By Appointment or Mail Order.

Specialise in supplying display stands for ceramics, dolls and pictures as well as wire and disc plate-hangers. Also provide peelable price labels and strung tickets and polishing and cleaning cloths.

SPEAK TO Alan Leadbeater.

ROD NAYLOR

208 Devizes Road, Hilperton, Trowbridge, **Wiltshire BA14 7QP**

TEL　　0225 754497
OPEN　By Appointment.

Specialise in supplying hard-to-find items for restorers such as three-dimensional copying machines, embossed lining paper.

PROVIDE Home Inspections. Free Local Estimates. Free Local Collection/Delivery Service.
SPEAK TO Rod Naylor.
SEE Furniture, Porcelain.

SPECIALIST PHOTOGRAPHERS AND BOOKSELLERS

SPECIALIST PHOTOGRAPHERS

ALLYSON McDERMOTT (INTERNATIONAL CONSERVATION CONSULTANTS)

Lintz Green Conservation Centre, Lintz Green House, Lintz Green, Rowlands Gill, **Durham NE39 1NL**

TEL   0207 71547 or 0831 104145 or 0831 257584
FAX   0207 71547
OPEN   9–5.30 Mon–Fri.

Specialise in photography for insurance and catalogues.

PROVIDE Home Inspections. Free Estimates. Chargeable Collection/Delivery Service.
They have a Southern Regional Office at 45 London Road, Cheltenham, **Gloucestershire**.
SPEAK TO Allyson McDermott or Gillian Lee.

SEE Art Researchers, Carpets, Lighting, Oil Paintings, Picture Frames.

SHELAGH COLLINGWOOD

18 Clarence Road, Harpenden, **Hertfordshire AL5 4AH**

TEL   0582 761191
OPEN   8.30–7 Mon–Sat or By Appointment.

Specialise in high quality photographs of furniture, pictures, jewellery, silver, porcelain etc. as an insurance record against loss, theft or damage. Objects are photographed in situ with studio lights. Special assignments undertaken.

PROVIDE Free Estimates.
SPEAK TO Shelagh Collingwood.

Ms Collingwood is registered with Hertfordshire Crime Prevention.

318

JOHN JONES FRAMES LTD
Unit 4, Finsbury Park Trading Estate, Morris Place, **London N4 3JG**
TEL   071 281 5439
FAX   071 281 5956
OPEN   8–6 Mon–Fri, 9–2 Sat, 12–4 Sun.

Specialise in providing a fully equipped fine art photographic service.

PROVIDE Free Estimates. Chargeable Collection/Delivery Service.
SPEAK TO John Jones, John Dawson or Nick Hawker.
SEE Oil Paintings, Picture Frames.

ALEX SAUNDERSON PHOTOGRAPHY
103 Riversdale Road, **London N5 2SU**
TEL   071 359 1605
OPEN   9–6 Mon–Sat.

Specialise in photographing furniture and fine art. They provide quality transparencies and black and white prints of furniture, sculpture, paintings, interiors, exteriors and portraits.

PROVIDE Home Inspections. Free Estimates. Chargeable Collection/Delivery Service.
SPEAK TO Alex Saunderson.

IMAGETREND
12 Chesterford Gardens, **London NW3 7DE**
TEL   071 435 7383
FAX   071 431 0960
OPEN   By Appointment.

Specialise in photographing paintings and sculpture and any two- or three-dimensional art work. They provide a comprehensive service for artists and galleries both in their studio or on location.

PROVIDE Home Inspections. Free Estimates. Free Local Collection/Delivery Service.
SPEAK TO Ken Grundy.

JANE AND PAUL ZAGEL
31 Pandora Road, **London NW6 1TS**
TEL   071 794 1663
OPEN   9–6 Mon–Fri.

Specialise in fine art photography as part of restoration record and for publication.
SPEAK TO Jane Zagel.
SEE Books, Oil Paintings.

CUBITT AND FANE LTD SECURITY PHOTOGRAPHERS
7 Tedworth Gardens, **London SW3 4DN**
TEL   071 376 8197
OPEN   By Appointment.

Specialise in photographing art and antiques for security and insurance purposes. The photographs are taken on site on colour transparency film (no negatives) all of which are returned to the client. They keep only minimal records of past and present communications with clients and these are in code and at a separate address. All enquiries are dealt with in complete confidence and references are available on request. They are recognised by the Art and Antique Squad at Scotland Yard.

PROVIDE Home Inspections. Free Estimates.
SPEAK TO Amanda Cubitt or Caroline Fane.

A. C. COOPER LTD
10 Pollen Street, **London W1R 9PH**
TEL   071 629 7585
FAX   071 409 3449
OPEN   8.30–5.30 Mon–Fri.

Specialise in fine art colour or black and white photography either in studio or on location. In-house printing and processing.

PROVIDE Home Inspections. Free Estimates.

319

SPEAK TO Trevor Chriss.
Established seventy-five years.

PRUDENCE CUMING ASSOCIATES LTD
28–29 Dover Street, **London W1X 3PA**
TEL 071 629 6430
FAX 071 495 2458
OPEN 8.30–5.30 Mon–Fri.

Specialise in photographing works of art including paintings, drawings, sculptures, jewellery, furniture, silver, ceramics.

PROVIDE Studio and location shooting.
SPEAK TO Prudence Cuming.
Established since 1967.

P. J. GATES (PHOTOGRAPHY) LTD
94 New Bond Street, **London W1Y 9LA**
TEL 071 629 4962
OPEN 9.15–5.30 Mon–Fri.

Specialise in photographing works of art worldwide with a particular aim for top quality results at all times. Large-format colour transparencies as well as life-size reproductions available.

PROVIDE Home Inspections. Free Estimates.
SPEAK TO P. J. Gates.

RODNEY TODD-WHITE AND SON
3 Clifford Street, **London W1X 1RA**
TEL 071 734 9070
FAX 071 287 9727
OPEN 9–5.30 Mon–Fri.

Specialise in photographing fine art objects.

PROVIDE Home Inspections. Free Estimates. Chargeable Collection/Delivery Service.
SPEAK TO Michael Todd-White.

KEN SMITH PHOTOGRAPHY
6 Lussielaw Road, Edinburgh, **Lothian EH9 3BX**
TEL 031 667 6159 or 657 4327
OPEN By Appointment.

Specialise in photography of fine and decorative arts and architecture including jewellery, silverware, ceramics, glass, paintings, furniture, militaria.

PROVIDE Home Inspections. Free Estimates. Chargeable Colection/Delivery Service.
SPEAK TO Leslie Paul-Florence.
Member of the Association of Historical and Fine Art Photographers.

SPECIALIST BOOKSELLERS

REFERENCE WORKS
12 Commercial Road, Swanage, **Dorset BH19 1DF**
TEL 0929 424423
FAX 0929 422597
OPEN By Appointment; Telephone Orders 9–5.30 Mon–Sat.

Specialise in books on ceramics of all countries.

PROVIDE Mail Order Service.
SPEAK TO Barry Lamb.

PHILLIPS OF HITCHIN
The Manor House, Hitchin, **Hertfordshire SG5 1JW**
TEL 0462 432067
OPEN 9–5.30 Mon–Sat.

Specialise in reference books on antiques, particularly furniture.
SPEAK TO Jerome Phillips.

SEE Furniture.

C. & A. J. BARMBY
140 Lavender Hill, Tonbridge, **Kent**
TN9 2AY
TEL   0732 771590
OPEN   9.30–5 Mon–Sat or Mail Order.

Specialise in antique reference books.

PROVIDE Chargeable
Collection/Delivery Service.
SPEAK TO Chris Barmby.
SEE Lighting.

THOMAS HENEAGE
42 Duke Street, **London SW1Y 6DJ**
TEL   071 930 9223
FAX   071 839 9223
OPEN   10–6 Mon–Fri.

Specialise in books on the fine and decorative arts.

ST GEORGE'S GALLERY BOOKS LTD
8 Duke Street, **London SW1Y 6BN**
TEL   071 930 0935
FAX   071 976 1832
OPEN   10–6 Mon–Fri.

Specialise in books and exhibition catalogues on all aspects of the fine and decorative arts.

SIMS REED LTD
58 Jermyn Street, **London SW1Y 6LX**
TEL   071 493 5660
FAX   071 493 8468
OPEN   10–6 Mon–Fri.

Specialise in monographs, art reference and modern illustrated books.

PROVIDE Home Inspections.
Free/Chargeable Estimates. Chargeable
Collection/Delivery Service.
SPEAK TO Nina Lyndsay.

DON KELLY
Antiquarius MB, 135 Kings Road,
London SW3 4PW
TEL   071 352 4690
FAX   071 352 5350
OPEN   10–5.30 Mon–Sat.

Specialise in selling new and out-of-print reference books on the fine and applied arts. Searches undertaken. Mail order available.

SPEAK TO Don Kelly.

THE ART BOOK REVIEW
1 Stewarts Court, 220 Stewarts Road,
London SW8 4UD
TEL   071 720 1503
FAX   071 720 3158
OPEN   By Appointment or Mail Order.

Specialise in selling in-print reference works on all aspects of the fine and applied arts, architecture, design and photography.

PROVIDE Chargeable
Collection/Delivery Service.
SPEAK TO Kate Sayner, Editor.

Four issues published per year featuring over 200 new titles from publishers worldwide.

MARLBOROUGH RARE BOOKS LTD
144 New Bond Street, **London**
W1Y 9FD
TEL   071 493 6993
FAX   071 499 2479
OPEN   9.30–6 Mon–Fri.

Specialise in selling all fields of antiquarian books.

PROVIDE Home Inspections. Chargeable
Estimates. Chargeable
Collection/Delivery Service.
SPEAK TO Alex Fotheringham.

CAROL MANHEIM
31 Ennismore Avenue, **London**
W4 1SE
TEL   081 994 9740
FAX   081 995 5396
OPEN   Mail Order Service.

Specialise in 19th and 20th century British and Continental out-of-print art reference books and catalogues, including sculpture, fashion and photography.
PROVIDE Free Book Search Service.
SPEAK TO Carol Manheim.

NOTTING HILL BOOKS
132 Palace Gardens Terrace, **London**
W8 4RT
TEL   071 727 5988
OPEN   10.30–6 Mon–Sat; 10.30–1
        Thur.

Specialise in buying and selling books on fine art and antiques.
SPEAK TO Sheila Ramage.

ZWEMMER ART BOOKS
24 Litchfield Street, **London**
WC2H 9NJ
TEL   071 379 7886
FAX   071 497 3290
OPEN   9.30–6 Mon–Wed, Fri; 10–6
        Thur & Sat.

Specialise in books on the fine and decorative arts including out-of-print and foreign language books.
SPEAK TO Simon Ellison.
Established in 1921.

JOHN IVES BOOKSELLER
5 Normanhurst Drive, Twickenham,
Middlesex TW1 1NA
TEL   081 892 6265
OPEN   By Appointment.

Specialise in scarce and out-of-print books on antiques and collecting, costume and needlework and architecture.
PROVIDE Mail Order Service.
SPEAK TO John Ives.

NICHOLAS MERCHANT
3 Promenade Court, Promenade Square,
Harrogate, **North Yorkshire HG1 2PJ**
TEL   0423 505370
FAX   0423 506183
OPEN   By Appointment.

Specialise in reference books on all aspects of the decorative arts, including antiques, fine art, architecture and interior design.
PROVIDE Mail Order Service.
SPEAK TO Nicholas Merchant.

POTTERTON BOOKS
The Old Rectory, Sessay, Thirsk, **North Yorkshire YO7 3LZ**
TEL   0845 401218
FAX   0845 401439
OPEN   9.30–4.30 Mon–Fri or By
        Appointment.

Specialise in books on the fine and decorative arts, including interior design and decoration. Also supply library accessories.
SPEAK TO Clare Jameson.

TRANSPORT
AND PACKING

ALL WRAPPED UP PACKAGING SUPPLIES
45 St John's Road, Moggerhanger,
Bedfordshire MK44 3RJ
TEL   0767 40777
OPEN   By Appointment.

Specialise in wrapping and labels of all kinds in 'small user' quantities.

PROVIDE Postal Service.
SPEAK TO Mr J. Harvey.

ALAN FRANKLIN TRANSPORT
Unit 8, 27 Blackmoor Road, Ebblake
Industrial Estate, Verwood, **Dorset**
BH31 6BE
TEL   0202 826539
FAX   0202 827337
OPEN   8.30–6 Mon–Fri; 8–2 Sat.

Specialise in transporting antiques and works of art throughout Europe, air freight and containerised shipments worldwide. Storage facilities in United Kingdom and France.

SPEAK TO Alan Franklin or James Scollen.

GEO. COPSEY & CO. LTD
Danes Road, Romford, **Essex**
RM7 0HL
TEL   081 592 1003
FAX   0708 727305
OPEN   8–5 Mon–Fri.

Specialise in packing and removal of fine art and antiques.

PROVIDE Home Inspections. Free Estimates.
SPEAK TO Barry Tebbutt.

ALBAN SHIPPING LTD
43 Hatfield Road, St Albans,
Hertfordshire AL1 4JE
TEL   0727 41402
FAX   0727 46370
OPEN   8–5.30 Mon–Fri.

Specialise in the collection, packaging and export or delivery of antiques and collectors' items.

PROVIDE Home Inspections. Free Estimates.
SPEAK TO Andrew Jackman.

323

01 FINE ART SERVICES LTD
London Fields, 282 Richmond Road, **London E8 3QS**
TEL   081 533 6124
FAX   081 533 2718
OPEN   9–6 Mon–Fri.

Specialise in the transportation of paintings and sculpture within the South East of England from one painting to entire exhibitions. They can also offer an installation and storage service.

PROVIDE Home Inspections. Free Estimates. Chargeable Collection/Delivery Service.
SPEAK TO Elizabeth Cooper.

MOMART PLC.
199–205 Richmond Road, **London E8 3NJ**
TEL   081 986 3624
FAX   081 533 0122
OPEN   Daily By Appointment.

Specialise in fine art handling, including 'state of the art' storage, transportation both national and international, case making/packing and exhibition installation.
SPEAK TO Richard Chapman, Transport Director; Kevin Richardson, Shipping Director.

LOCKSON SERVICES LTD
29 Broomfield Street, Poplar, **London E14 6BX**
TEL   071 515 8600
FAX   071 515 4043
OPEN   9–6 Mon–Fri.

Specialise in fine art, antique and general packing and shipping and transportation within the UK.

PROVIDE Free Estimates.
SPEAK TO David Armitage Snr.

L. J. ROBERTON LTD
Marlborough House, Cooks Road, **London E15 2PW**
TEL   081 519 2020
FAX   081 519 8571
OPEN   9–5 Mon–Fri.

Specialise in export packing and shipping of antiques and fine art, including a countrywide collection service.
SPEAK TO Mr J. Tebbutt.
Member of LAPADA.

WINGATE AND JOHNSTON LTD
78 Broadway, **London E15 1NG**
TEL   081 555 8123
FAX   081 519 8115
OPEN   9–5.30 Mon–Fri.

Specialise in packing and shipping of antiques and fine art.

PROVIDE Home Inspections. Free Estimates.
SPEAK TO Paul Brecht.

STEPHEN MORRIS SHIPPING LTD
Barpart House, Kings Cross Freight Depot, York Way, **London N1 0UZ**
TEL   071 354 1212
FAX   081 802 4110
OPEN   8–6 Mon–Fri.

Specialise in packing and shipping fine art and antiques.

PROVIDE Home Inspections. Free Estimates.
SPEAK TO Stephen Morris or John Holser.

PITT & SCOTT LTD
20–24 Edengrove, **London N7 8ED**
TEL   071 607 7321
FAX   071 607 0566
OPEN   8–5 Mon–Fri.

Specialise in international packing and

shipping of fine art, domestic moving and storing.

PROVIDE Home Inspections. Free Estimates.
SPEAK TO Anthony Roberts.

KUWAHARA LIMITED
Unit 5, Bittacy Business Centre, Bittacy Hill, **London NW7 1BA**
TEL   081 346 7744
FAX   081 349 2916
OPEN   9–5.30 Mon–Fri.

Specialise in packing and shipping and are international removers.

PROVIDE Home Inspections.
SPEAK TO S. Kuwahara or K. Blair.

ANGLO-PACIFIC (FINE ART) LIMITED
Unit 2, Bush Industrial Estate, Standard Road, North Acton, **London NW10 6DF**
TEL   081 965 0667
FAX   081 965 4954
OPEN   8–6 Mon–Fri.

Specialise in security storage, packing and shipping of fine art and antiques, packing for hand-carrying, insurance.

PROVIDE Free Estimates.
SPEAK TO Phyllis Kearns.

HEDLEYS HUMPERS LTD
Units 3 & 4, 97 Victoria Road, North Acton, **London NW10 6ND**
TEL   081 965 8733
FAX   081 965 0249
OPEN   7–7 Mon–Fri.

Specialise in worldwide packing and shipping.

PROVIDE Home Inspections. Free Estimates.
SPEAK TO Bob Archer.

TRANS EURO WORLDWIDE
Fine Art Division, Drury Way, Brent Park, **London NW10 0JN**
TEL   081 784 0100
FAX   081 451 6419
OPEN   9–5.30 Mon–Fri; 10–4 Sat.

Specialise in export packing and worldwide freighting by road, sea and air, full door-to-door service. Insurance arranged from single pieces to complete container loads.

PROVIDE Home Inspections. Free Estimates.
SPEAK TO Gerry Ward or Richard Edwards.

TRANSNIC LTD
Arch 434, Gordon Grove, **London SE5 9DU**
TEL   071 738 7555
FAX   071 738 5190
OPEN   9–6 Mon–Fri or By Appointment Sat.

Specialise in fine art transportation and storage. Also picture hanging.

PROVIDE Chargeable Collection/Delivery and Storage Service.
SPEAK TO Nicholas Tetley.

C. R. FENTON & COMPANY
7 Munton Road, **London SE17 1PR**
TEL 071 277 1539
FAX   071 277 1540
OPEN   9–5.30 Mon–Fri.

Specialise in fine art packing, shipping and storage.

PROVIDE Home Inspections. Free Estimates.
SPEAK TO Brian Bath.

Member of the British International Freight Association.

EUROPE EXPRESS
125 Sydenham Road, **London**
SE26 5HB
TEL   081 776 7556 and mobile 0860 239660
FAX   081 776 7606
OPEN   9–6 Mon–Fri.

Specialise in road transport removals to Europe, including Sardinia and Sicily.
SPEAK TO Tony Morgan.

FEATHERSTON SHIPPING LTD
24 Hampton House, 15/17 Ingate Place, **London SW8 3NS**
TEL   071 720 0422
FAX   071 720 6330
OPEN   8–6 Mon–Fri.

Specialise in packing and shipping fine art and antiques.

PROVIDE Home Inspections. Free Estimates.
SPEAK TO Caedmon Featherston.

THE PACKING SHOP LTD
Units K & L, London Stone Business Estate, Broughton Street, **London**
SW8 3QR
TEL   071 627 5605
FAX   071 622 7740
OPEN   9–6 Mon–Fri.

Specialise in same-day shipment of small consignments, as well as air freight, sea freight and packing.

PROVIDE Home Inspections. Free Estimates.
SPEAK TO Karen Bagot.
SEE **London SW10.**

T. ROGERS & CO. (PACKERS) LTD
PO Box 8, 1A Broughton Street, **London SW8 3QL**
TEL   071 622 9151
FAX   071 627 3318
OPEN   8–5 Mon–Fri.

Specialise in transporting, packing, warehousing and shipping of fine art and antiques as well as security storage and picture hanging.

PROVIDE Home Inspections. Free Estimates.
SPEAK TO Michael Evans.

THE PACKING SHOP LTD
535 Kings Road, **London SW10 OSZ**
TEL   071 352 2021
FAX   071 351 7576
OPEN   9–6 Mon–Fri; 10–1 Sat.

Specialise in fine art and antique packing and shipping with emphasis on same-day collection and two to three day delivery worldwide.

PROVIDE Home Inspections. Free Estimates.
SPEAK TO Eileen Abbas.
SEE **London SW8.**

PANTECHNICON GROUP LTD
Unit 3, The Gate Centre, Syon Gate Way, Great West Road, Brentford, **Middlesex**
TW8 9DD
TEL   081 568 6195
FAX   081 847 3126
OPEN   8.30–5 Mon–Fri.

Specialise in UK, European and international removals of furniture, effects and antiques. They have regular services to France, Belgium and Spain. Storage facilities are available.

PROVIDE Home Inspections. Free Estimates.
SPEAK TO John Stopforth.

VULCAN INTERNATIONAL SERVICES
Unit 8, Ascot Road, Clockhouse Lane, Feltham, **Middlesex TW14 8QF**
TEL   0784 244152
FAX   0784 248183
OPEN   8.30–6 Mon–Fri.

Specialise in transporting fine art and antiques. They also provide specialised export and import packing and international shipping services as well as a domestic removal service. Full insurance cover available.

PROVIDE Home Inspections. Free Estimates. Chargeable Collection/Delivery Service.
SPEAK TO Mr Dennis Jarvis, General Manager.

GANDER & WHITE SHIPPING LTD
New Pound, Wisborough Green, Nr. Billingshurst, **West Sussex RH14 0AY**
TEL   0403 700044
FAX   0403 700814
OPEN   9–6 Mon–Fri.

Specialise in packing, moving and shipping fine art, antiques and household removals.

PROVIDE Home Inspections. Free Estimates.
SPEAK TO Maureen De'Ath.

A SELECTION OF FULL-TIME COURSES FOR TRAINING IN CONSERVATION

Basford Hall College
Department of Construction
Stockhill Lane
Nottingham
NG6 0NB
TEL 0602 704541
Course Furniture Reproduction and
Restoration.

Brunel College of Technology Bristol
Department of Printing and Graphic
Communication
Ashley Down
Bristol BS7 9BU
TEL 0272 241241
FAX 0272 249134
Course Bookbinding, Restoration and
Paper and Document Conservation.

Buckinghamshire College
Queen Alexandra Road
High Wycombe
Buckinghamshire HP11 2JZ
TEL 0494 522141
FAX 0494 524392
Course [a] Furniture Design and
    Craftsmanship.
    [b] Furniture Restoration and
    Craftsmanship.

Camberwell School of Arts and Crafts
The London Institute
Department of Art History and
Conservation
Peckham Road
London SE5 8UF
TEL 071 703 0987 or 703 2923

FAX 071 703 3689
Course Paper Conservation.

**Carmarthenshire College of
Technology and Art**
Faculty of Art and Design
Job's Well Road
Carmarthen
Dyfed SA31 3HY
TEL 0267 235855
Course [a] Sculpture/Restoration
    Sculpture.
    [b] Design Crafts
    (Sculpture/Restoration
    Sculpture).

Central Manchester College
The John Unsworth Building
Lower Hardman Street
Manchester M3 3ER
TEL 061 953 5995
Course Advanced Furniture Crafts
(Restoration).

City & Guilds of London Art School
124 Kennington Park Road
London SE11 4DJ
TEL 071 582 7049
Course Restoration and Conservation
Studies.

Courtauld Institute of Art
Somerset House
Strand
London WC2R 0RN
TEL 071 873 2777
Course [a] Conservation of Paintings.

328

[b] Conservation of Wall
Paintings.

Guildford College of Technology
Stoke Park
Guildford
Surrey GU1 1EZ
TEL 0482 31251
Course Fine Bookbinding and
Conservation.

Hamilton Kerr Institute
University of Cambridge
Mill Lane
Whittlesford
Cambridgeshire CB2 4NE
TEL 0223 832040
Course Conservation of Easel Paintings.

Herefordshire Technical College
Engineering Department
Folly Lane
Hereford
HR1 1LS
TEL 0432 352235
Course Restoration (Metalwork).

**Lincolnshire College of Art and
Design**
Lindum Road
Lincoln
LN2 1NP
TEL 0522 512912
Course Conservation and Restoration
Studies.

London College of Furniture
41 Commercial Road
London E1 1LA
TEL 071 320 1000
Course Furniture (Restoration).

London College of Printing
Department of Print Finishing Processes
Elephant and Castle
London SE1 6SB
TEL 071 735 9100
Course [a] Creative Printing Crafts.
[b] Design (Bookbinding).

Bruce Luckhurst
The Little Surrenden Workshops

Ashford Road
Bethersden
Kent TN26 3BG
TEL 023382 0589
Course Conservation and Restoration of
Antique Furniture.

Newcastle-upon-Tyne Polytechnic
School of Conservation
Durham Road
Gateshead
Tyne & Wear NE9 5BN
TEL 091 477 0524
Course [a]Conservation of Fine Art
(Easel Paintings).
[b] Conservation of Fine Art
(Works of Art on Paper).

Royal College of Art
Kensington Gore
London SW7 2EU
TEL 071 584 5020
Course Conservation.

Rycotewood College
Department of Fine Craftsmanship and
Design
Priest End
Thame
Oxfordshire OX9 2AF
TEL 084421 2501
Course Design (Crafts) Furniture
Restoration.

Textile Conservation Centre
Apartment 22
Hampton Court Palace
East Molesey
Surrey KT8 9AU
TEL 081 977 4943
Course Textile Conservation.

West Dean College
West Dean
Chichester
West Sussex PO18 0QZ
TEL 024 363 301
Course [a] Antique Furniture
Restoration.
[b] Porcelain and Ceramic
Conservation.
[c] Bookbinding and the Care

of Books.
[d] Antique Clock Restoration.
[e] Metal Restoration.
[f] Tapestry Weaving.
[g] Musical Instrument
Making.

York College of Art and Technology
School of Technology
Carpentry and Joinery Section
Dringhouses
York
YO2 1UA
TEL 0904 704141
Course Antique Furniture Restoration.

GLOSSARY AND USEFUL ADDRESSES

ABA
Antiquarian Booksellers Association
Suite 2
26 Charing Cross Road
London WC2
TEL 071 379 3041

Association of Art Historians
Register of Freelance Art and Design
Historians
10 Davisville Road
London W12 9SJ
TEL 081 743 4697

ABPR
Association of British Picture Restorers
Station Avenue
Kew
Surrey TW9 3QA
TEL 081 948 5644

Association of Master Upholsterers
Unit One
Clyde Road Works
Clyde Road
Wallington
Surrey SM6 8PZ
TEL 081 773 8069
FAX 081 773 8103

BADA
British Antique Dealers' Association
20 Rutland Gate
London SW7 1BD
TEL 071 589 4128

BAFRA
British Antique Furniture Restorers
Association
(Executive Administrator)
37 Upper Addison Gardens
Holland Park

London W14 8AJ
TEL 071 603 5643

BHI
CMBHI
MBHI
British Horological Institute
Upton Hall
Upton, Newark
Notts.
TEL 0636 813795

BWCMG
British Watch and Clockmakers Guild
West Wick
Marsh Road
Burnham-on-Crouch
Essex CM0 8NE
TEL 0621 783104

City and Guilds of London Institute
46 Britannia Street
London WC1Y 9RG
TEL 071 278 2468
FAX 071 278 9460

The Conservation Unit of the Museums
and Galleries Commission
16 Queen Anne's Gate
London W1H 9AA
TEL 071 233 3683
FAX 071 233 3686

FATG
The Fine Art Trade Guild
16–18 Empress Place
London SW6 1TT
TEL 071 381 6616
FAX 071 381 2596

GA
Gemmological Association of Great
Britain
27 Greville Street
London EC1N 8SU
TEL 071 404 3334

GADR
Guild of Antique Dealers and Restorers
23 Belle Vue Road
Shrewsbury
Shropshire SY3 7LN
TEL 0743 271 852

Historic Houses Association
2 Chester Street
London SW1X 7BB
TEL 071 259 5688
FAX 071 259 5590

IPC
The Institute of Paper Conservation
Leigh Lodge
Leigh
Worcester
WR6 5LB
TEL 0886 832323

IIC
International Institute for Conservation
of Historic and Artistic Works
6 Buckingham Street
London WC2N 6BA
TEL 071 839 5975
FAX 071 976 1564

IGS
Irish Georgian Society
Lexlip Castle
Co. Kildare
TEL 01 767053
FAX 01 6620290

IPCRA
Irish Professional Conservators' and
Restorers' Association
Mr Grellan D. Rourke (Chairman)
c/o The Office of Public Works
51 St Stephens Green
Dublin 2
TEL 01 613111 ext. 2375

or Ms Anne Hyland (Hon. Secretary)
Beechmount
Roscrea
Co. Tipperary
TEL 0505 22310

LAPADA
London and Provincial Antique Dealers'
Association
535 Kings Road
Chelsea
London SW10 0SZ
TEL 071 823 3511

RSA
Royal Society of Arts
8 John Adam Street
London WC2N 6EZ
TEL 071 930 5115

Royal Society of Miniature Painters
(Membership Secretary, Mrs S Burton)
15 Union Street
Wells
Somerset BA5 2PU
TEL 0749 674472

Rug Restorers' Association
c/o Dennis Woodman
Oriental Carpets
105 North Road
Kew
Surrey TW9 4HJ
TEL 081 878 8182

(Formerly)
CoSIRA
Rural Development Commission
(Headquarters)
141 Castle Street
Salisbury
Wiltshire
SP1 3TP
TEL 0722 336 255

Scottish Conservation Bureau
Historic Scotland
3 Stenhouse Mill Lane
Edinburgh EH11 3LR
TEL 031 443 1666

SSCR
Scottish Society for Conservation and
Restoration
(The Membership Secretary, Fiona
Butterfield)
Overhall
Kirkfield Bank
Lanark ML11 9TZ
TEL 0555 66291

Society of Bookbinders
c/o Mrs J A Isaac
Lower Hammonds Farm
Ripley Lane
West Horsley
Surrey KT24 6JP
TEL 04865 3175

United Kingdom Institute for
Conservation
37 Upper Addison Gardens
London W14 8AJ
TEL 071 603 5643

Worshipful Company of Clockmakers
St Dunstans House
Carey Lane
London EC2V 8AA
TEL 071 606 7010

Worshipful Company of Goldsmiths
Goldsmiths' Hall
Foster Lane
London EC2U 6BN
TEL 071 606 8971

BY APPOINTMENT TO
H.M. QUEEN ELIZABETH II
ANTIQUE FURNITURE RESTORERS
CHARLES PERRY RESTORATIONS LTD. ST. ALBANS

A comprehensive restoration and conservation service to all types of antique furniture and objects carried out by highly skilled craftsmen in our own workshop.

CHARLES PERRY RESTORATIONS LTD.
PRAEWOOD FARM, HEMEL HEMPSTEAD ROAD, ST. ALBANS, HERTS AL3 6AA
TELEPHONE: (0727) 53487 · FAX: (0727) 46668

(REGULAR TRANSPORT IN ALL PARTS OF THE COUNTRY)